BUDDHIST ART AND THOUGHT

BUDDHIST ART AND THOUGHT

SHASHIBALA

AKSHAYA PRAKASHAN
NEW DELHI

First Published : 2007
Reprint : 2025

ISBN 10 : 81-88643-06-8
ISBN 13 : 978-81-88643-06-6

Published by Harish Chandra
for Akshaya Prakashan
208, M.G. House, 2 Community Centre
Wazirpur Industrial Area, Delhi-110 052
E-mail: harish@akshayaprakashan.com
Phone: 011-41610957, Mobile : 9818452269

Printed in India.

CONTENTS

PREFACE

The teachings of Śākyamuni Buddha, disseminating the message of beauty and bliss, of wisdom and compassion, sparkling on the horizons of Asia, are lofty like mountains and pure like moon light. Crossing the vast deserts and oceans, they made a home in the hearts of the Asians. They affected the aroma of humanity, gave a vision of creation through experience and realization. Universal implications of Buddhism were so vast that they embraced every form of human activity, encompassing political and social life. Thus Buddhism has been a mighty impulsive force to ideas, and a profound movement, leading to peace eternal.

Supremely alive divine art forms were created by the Asians, fascinated by the serene but strong personality of Lord Śākyamuni. Grand monastic complexes were constructed in the Northwestern frontiers of ancient India on a large scale of the area which emerged as a cradle of Buddhism where cultural elements of various lands fused into it. These concretized trends traveled to China, Korea and Japan via Central Asia. For example the cult of mystical medicine seems to be a proliferation of the Northwest frontiers. The idea of worshipping Four Divine Kings as a group, comes from the Parthian and the Kuṣāṇa concept of division of state. It traveled to China from the Northwest and then to Korea and Japan. It gained popularity to such an extent that almost in every monastery in Japan, one can find the group standing on the corners of platforms in the halls of worship. Light symbolism was also brought to Japan from the Northwest through China. The solar deities—Amitabha, Vairocana and Maitreya occupied a prime position in the Japanese Buddhist pantheon. Japan produced a number of colossal images. The idea of colossi was also derived from the famous Bamiyan Buddhas. Thus Buddhist art forms were transmitted from the Northwest to the Far East, incorporating various characteristics on their way.

'Amitābha: The Buddha of Immeasurable Light in Japanese Art' throws light on the form and function of Amitābha in Japan. The cult of Amitābha represents transcendental tendencies in Buddhism. His paradise Sukhāvatī is the land of bliss, known in Japan as Jōdō. Devotion to Jōdō in Japan is traced back to the Asuka period (AD 552-645). The first maṇḍala visualizing the Pure Land, was produced after the death of Prince Shōtoku Taishi. Eighth century saw further increase in its large scale production. It was seen as a place of happiness for the living and peace for the dead. Amitābha is one of the four Buddhas, expounded in Suvarṇaprabhāsa-sūtra for protection of state. Amitābha sitting in Sukhāvatī was painted as an aid to meditate to eliminate mental suffering or for longevity. Such paintings were called *henso* in Japan. Amitābha is painted as one of the five Buddhas in the twin maṇḍalas—Mahākaruṇāgarbha-And Vajradhatu-maṇḍalas. His name was recited for salvation. Special services were organized for *nembutsu* and mediatation called *Jogyo sammai*. For such occasions huge images of Amitābha were enshrined in specially built halls. He sits in the posture of meditation. During the Heian period, some members of royal families built monasteries to create Sukhāvatī on the earth to enjoy its bliss. Special halls were built to house nine kinds of images of Amitābha as expounded by Sukhāvatīvyūha-sūtra. Nine forms of Amitābha symbolize protection of nine grades of beings, migrated to Sukhāvatī. In Raigō paintings Amitābha comes as a saviour to receive the soul of the deceased. In return Raigōs he can be seen carrying back the soul to Sukhāvatī.

Sukhāvatīvyūha- , Amitāyurdhyāna- , and Amitābha-sūtras expound veneration to Amitābha. Amitāyurdhyāna is one of the favourite sūtras, painted in the Dun-hunag caves in China. It visualizes the paradise of Amitābha. When devotion to Amitābha reached Japan, a number of paintings were produced in a variety of forms over the centuries. They served as an aid to meditate to eliminate the sufferings. One such type of painting is known as Taima maṇḍala. It represents thirteen stages of meditation, five levels of *dhāraṇā,* the story of imprisonment of King Bimbisāra by his son Ajātaśatru. The chapter on 'Yoga: the Basis of Taima maṇḍala' presents a detail analysis of the graphic divisions and symbolism of all the constituents — dancing figures and musicians, musical instruments floating in air, jem trees and sun disc, palaces and pavillions, birds and peacocks, the souls residing in the paradise, and Buddhas and Bodhisattvas flying down from heaven, and finally the souls of the king and the queen merging with the Ultimate—Amitābha.

Yoga a means for transcendence lifts from the lowermost levels to the highest spheres of thought, where sufferings eliminate. Its philosophy, contained in the sūtras, was visualized through paintings. Inner walls of caves in China were chosen for such illuminations following the Indian patterns, because they were seen as the best places for meditation, situated far from the din of the world of the common man. A large number of such abodes of silence were carved at Bamiyan, Kizil, Dun-huang, Yun-kang, Maichishan and Lung-men etc.

Buddhism carried the philosophy of Avataṁsaka-sūtra, its grand view of totality inspired colossal images all over East Asia. The first colossi was carved out of rocks at Bamiyan, alongwith thousands of caves, monastic cells and sanctuaries. The two Buddhas, 175 feet and 210 feet in height were carved in 5th-7th century. When Hsüan-tsang reached there in AD 632, he witnessed their glory. The idea of creation of colossal images reached Japan. The chapter on Buddhist colossi in Japan presents an overview of colossal images sculpted there from sixth century onwards.

When essence of *dharma* cannot be expressed in words, it has to be manifested through illustrations for a *yogi.* Maṇḍalas are drawn as symbolic and schematic representations to visualize the double process of disintegration and reintegration of the consciousness. It is also a symbolic representation of intuition that is produced in the process of meditation. Buddhas, Bodhisattvas and other divine beings sit in different enclosures. A *sādhaka* begins to meditate from the lowermost level that is drawn as the outermost enclosure. That enclosure is called outer *vajrakula.* Deities sitting in the *vajrakula* of Mahākaruṇāgarbha-maṇḍala constitute the lowermost sphere of concentration. Beyond that, is the world of Buddhas and Bodhisattvas.

The chapter 'Maṇḍala and Meditation' gives details of the three realms of existence—Kāmadhātu, Rūpadhātu and Arūpadhātu. They represent upward layers of universe and the process of creation.

Vairocana at the center, is the *Dharmakāya*. For realization of Vairocana's transcendental form, an adherent has to reach the highest level of meditation. He crosses all the levels in between the lowest and the highest.

'India and East Asia: A Cultural Symbiosis' opens with a note on cultural connections with a special reference to the contributions of Shingon sect in Japan. Buddhism had reached Japan officially in AD 552 but with the advent of ninth century, Japanese life had been transformed by assimilation of a new system that was rich in metaphysics and symbolism, magnificent in rites and ritual and impressive in form and subtle mystery. The chapter gives details of ceremonies performed in Shingon monasteries, specially, *homa*. Indian Brāhmaṇas were placed highly in the Japanese society. A number of Indian sages were assimilated in the Japanese Buddhist pantheon as divine beings. Deities of time and space—astral divinities, planets, constellations, zodiacal signs and Hindu deities form a part of the pantheon. By that time commonest of the people had begun to participate in the highest realms of thought.

'Bodhisattvas in Buddhist Art and Thought' poses more questions than putting forth answers. The subject needs an intensive and extensive research. Bodhisattvas are innumerable because there are different Bodhisattvas in different traditions. All the sūtras supply their own lists of Bodhisattvas. Their number and characteristics can be different in various chapters of a sūtra. They are to be classified as Bodhisattvas, Mahāsattva Bodhisattvas, Jñānasattvas, Vajrasattvas, Dhyānī Bodhisattvas, and Śrī Bodhisattavs etc.

The chapter also deals with the problem of generalization of the term 'Bodhisattva'. It suggests some of the deities who should not be identified as Bodhisattvas. Some of the Bodhisattvas among thirty-three manifestations of Avalokiteśvara are worshipped for specific professions. They should not be taken as Avalokiteśvaras but as Lokeśavaras because they were created from local beliefs. The two chapters on 'Bodhisattvas in Buddhist Art and Thought' and 'Bodhisattvas of Defence' are the first step towards classification of a large number of Bodhisattvas in Buddhist art and thought.

Characteristic features of Bodhisattvas place them into various categories. Some of them represent power and personality of the Buddha while others constitute the third jewel—*saṅgha*, grouped around him. Some of them are meditation-centered while others perform various types of philanthropic functions. Bodhisattvas of Pure Land tradition are different from those of Healing cult or Gaṇḍavyūha. Texts like Saddharmapuṇḍarīka-sūtra contain long lists of names of Bodhisattvas in their chapters.

Some of the Bodhisattvas are identified as symbols of debate and defense. They symbolize a combination of meditation and martial arts. Wisdom paired with skillful means has made Budhdism as the most successful religion of the world. People are tempted into the *dharma* by vanquishing the heretics and asserting the self. Its foundation was laid by Amoghavajra when he lived in a military camp. He performed a ritual at the Imperial Palace in China in AD 760. The Emperor's immediate advisors took on the role of tutelary deities and his bodyguards took places assigned to the Vajra Bodhisattvas.

Cave paintings in India were a great source of inspiration all over Asia. Thus art of Ajanta spread as Ajantaism. Its impact can be traced in the north, east and southeast. It was known for its technique, style, color and theme. But the murals at the Hōryūji monastery took the style and technique, from Ajanta and painted the interiors of its major hall of worship, visualizing the scenes of the paradises of the four Buddhas—Amitābha, Maitreya, Bhaiṣajyaguru and Śākyamuni. The chapter gives details of the murals, their compositions and iconographic details.

The philosophy of dhyāna transmitted by Bodhidharma still lives in China, Korea and Japan. It has influenced the minds of the intellectuals, poets and politicians. Its philosophy is reflected in their ways of living and thinking. The chapter relates the history of its transmission and propagation, fundamental principles, literary basis of its philosophy, training given by the Zen monasteries, influence of Zen on the art of painting, Japanese architecture and on planning of gardens. Japanese aestheticism is closely associated to the cult of tea and martial arts. Zen has entered into almost every sphere of cultural life.

The thoughts intertwined, new forms in iconography emerged with a new world of imagery created by the creative mind. There are Four Guardian Kings known as Shitennō in Japan. They attained a divine personality in the Sino-Japanese tradition. Possibly the concept had developed from the Parthian and the Kuṣāṇa traditions of division of a state into four parts. They evolve in the seventh chapter of Suvarṇaprabhāsa-sūtra and promise to protect the kings and kingdoms alongwith royal families, if one recites, listens preserves or makes offerings of the sūtra. It was elevated to a prestigious position in Japan in the early seventh century and in China specially by the T'ein T'ai priests. A large number of images of the group were housed in monasteries over the past centuries, for an all round protection of the state. The chapter on 'Four Divine Guardian Kings' gives the history of their evolution, iconography and function.

India ceased to possess any Sanskrit manuscripts earlier than the tenth century but Japan has preserved a rich heritage of Sanskrit manuscripts from early seventh century. Palm-leaf manuscripts have been kept at the Hōryūji monastery in Japan since AD 609. One of them is Prajñāpāramitāhṛdaya-sūtra. It is primarily valuable for its palaeographic antiquity using the same material as was used in India. Technical contrivances used by the writer and the style of letters resemble the Indian style.

Sanskrit is a common linguistic inheritance of India and Japan. The Japanese emperors in search of transcendental values embraced the tradition of sūtras written in Sanskrit as a core for national unity and integrity. Today a rich literary treasure of Sanskrit literature consisting of dhāraṇīs, tantras, sūtras and other texts has been kept in Japan for nearly 1400 years. Entry of Sanskrit Buddhist scriptures into Japan was their identification with the central axis of human advance. Manuscripts in Sharada script on palm leaf are discovered from monasteries and museums.

Siddham, a variety of Brāhmī, and an elder sister of Nāgarī, owed its popularity in China and Japan especially to the rise of the Mantrayana Buddhism. It was used for writing dhāraṇīs, mantras and seed syllables, *bijākṣaras*. It became a living script of such intrinsic value as to deserve a place in the realm of fine arts and is indeed considered on par with painting. A number of Chinese and

Japanese monks devoted themselves to study the script. A large number of Sanskrit hymns were taken to Japan from China for recitation on special occasions. Special musical notations were written to chant the mantras. This special genre of music is termed Bombai or Shomyo. To this day there are special colleges of Buddhist music at Kyoto and Koyasan. The Japanese alphabets Katakana and Hiragana are based on the Sanskrit sound sequence: a, i, u, e, o, ka, ki, ku, ke, ko and soon. The alphabets were devised by the great monk Kōbō Daishi who began to democratize education by founding a school for the children of the common people.

Japan shared the depths of its cultural sphere with India for past fourteen hundred years. The Japanese scholars in past and present have been working for enhancing the ties of the *dharma*. Prof. Raghu Vira, an explorer-pilgrim went to the distant lands in Asia. He was moved by the cultural ambience, including existence of Sanskrit manuscripts in Japan. He began an indepth study of its culture and ethos to open up new avenues of scholarly interaction by inviting Indologists from Japan and inspiring them to work on various fields of Buddhism. He initiated a new tradition of academic exchange and to recapture the culture of work. The chapter on 'Academic Relations Between India and Japan during the Twentieth Century' throws light on the contributions of Late Prof. Raghu Vira to bring the two countries closer.

Maṇḍalas were produced on the basis of sūtras as an aid to the devotee, a *sādhaka*, who was on the way to enlightenment. Two famous maṇḍalas in Shingon tradition in Japan are Vajradhātu- and Mahākaruṇāgarbha-maṇḍalas. They represent the profound truth, levels of meditation and emergence of the world from the Great source. They depict a movement from the multiple facticity of existence at the lowermost level to a focused concentration at the highest point. Graphic representation of the Vajradhātu-maṇḍala is based on Tattva-saṅgraha. The chapter on graphic representation of Vajradhātu-maṇḍala deals with the problem of its division.

French, German, Indo-British, Japanese and Russian expeditions to the ancient kingdoms of Central Asia have explored an unknown history of Asian civilization and culture. Thousands of fragments of manuscripts, paintings, sculptures, and other artifacts were brought back after excavating the sand buried monasteries. An era of splendour in all the spheres of life was unearthed. The chapter on India and Central Asia introduces the long lost history of cultural relations of India with the ancient kingdoms lying on the Silk Route which played an important role in propagation, preservation and advancement of Buddhism, until the Islamic invasions. It relates the story of explorations and the important sites situated on the northern and the southern Silk Routes. Works of art and architecture created by the people of these areas, their language and literature, scripts used by them, calligraphic works, performing arts and rituals and ceremonies, added color to the life of the people. There was a continuous flow of teachers and monks traveling from India to China and vice a versa. Chinese pilgrims have left glowing accounts of Central Asian kingdoms.

A large number of monasteries were built on the Silk Route where scholars worked to disseminate the Buddhist wisdom. But nothing survives after Islamic invasions. Descriptions of these monasteries are given in literary sources. Tibetan literary sources provide enough material on the history of monasteries in Khotan, which was an oasis kingdom, situated to the south of

Taklamakan desert. It was equally a famous center for trade of jade. The kingdom flourished for more than a thousand years. The chapter on 'Monasteries of Khotan in Tibetan Literary Sources' throws light on Khotan as an important center both for religious activities and trade, Indo-Khotanese relations and offers details of the monasteries given in Tibetan sources.

Deification of rulers was a solemn act of legislation. Religion and kingship are united in beneficence because religion cannot endure without a king nor kingship can stand without religion. Its origin can be traced back to the 3rd century BC. Kings devoted to Buddhism were apotheosized as the Buddha. Examples can be quoted from Mathura and Surkh-kotal or from Rāmāyaṇa. In Indonesia apart from ancestor worship, kings resorted to derive sanctity and power to sustain and rule as sovereigns. The chapter on 'Apotheosis of an Indonesian King of the Singasari Dynasty' identifies the image of Bhairava from Singasari as King Kṛtanagara who strived to gain victory against Kublai Khan, through spiritual power derived from a dedication ceremony. Three more images are taken for identification—Mahiṣāsuramardinī, Gaṇapati, sitting on a seat of skulls and a guardian from Singasari. The chapter also talks about Bhairava dedication by the Kāpālikas.

Cultural heritage of Indonesia was rich. The scale of their temples was so grand that it could never be touched in India. Some of the temples were built for performing special ceremonies on special occasions. The chapter on 'Fire Altar for Aśvamedha Ceremony in Indonesia' identifies the huge bird as a fire altar built for a Vedic sacrifice known as Aśvamedha. Performance of the sacred ritual was meant to renew divine mandate and empowerment to rule. It gives references from Sanskrit literature to support the hypothesis. According to the Indian tradition *Aśvamedha* was performed on hilltops. At Chandi Cheto a Śiva Liṅgga was also consecrated to pray for sovereignty and national defense. An *aśvamedha* ceremony would have been performed to save the declining kingdom of Majapahit during the fourteenth century.

Sanskrit was a harmonizing factor in the countries of Southeast Asia. The earliest lithic record discovered from Vietnam is dated 2nd-3rd century. In Indonesia the first dated Sanskrit inscription belongs to the reign of Jayavarman II (AD 475-512). The chapter on 'Sanskrit Inscriptions from Indonesia' gives an overview of the Sanskrit inscriptions dating from fifth to ninth century. They are written in different meters of poetics. Amaramālā and Chandaḥkiraṇa are suggested to be the major sources to assist the writers.

Buddha's words reached the people in various countries in their own languages through translation of thousands of texts, done in several parts of the world. A Srilankan King was the first to appoint scribes to record the ageless teachings which were passed on to the following generations through recitations. This way the Buddhist Tripiṭaka came into existence. Beyond the Northwest limits of India they were translated painstakingly and accurately for last two thousand years, into Chinese, Tibetan, Mongolian and Manchu. The chapter on 'Sanskrit Texts in Chinese and Tibetan Translations' offers an overview of Sanskrit literature transmitted to these countries and translated into their languages. Officially, Buddhism reached China in AD 67, when two Indian scholars reached there with horses laden with scriptures. But translation of Indian scriptures began in the second-third century. Mahayana sūtras in Sanskrit are the best-known examples of Sanskrit texts found in China. Today Chinese Tripiṭaka is a valuable source for a comprehensive study of the lost

Sanskrit texts. Tibetans have also preserved a rich heritage of Sanskrit literature translated into Tibetan from 7th-17th century. The two collections Kañjur and Tañjur contain 1108 and 3458 texts. They include works on logic, grammar, poetics, lexicography, medicine, *śilpaśāstra*, chemistry and a number of other fields of knowledge. Historically and academically these are very important because in most of the cases original Sanskrit texts are lost.

Indological studies in 18th-19th Century attracted a number of scholars in Europe to visit India. One of them was George Nicholai Roerich, who made India his home. He carried in his heart the fire of 1life. He joined his father Nicholas Roerich who was a philosopher, a painter, a thinker, explorer and an archeologist, at an early stage. The authoress writes about the life and works of George Roerich with a special reference to his works as an indologist. He researched and wrote on the search for Shambhala, a symbol of aspirations for a bright future. A number of texts describe the location of Shambhala. Buddhists in various countries have been trying to locate it, visit there, but nobody so far has reached any concrete conclusion. Shambhala may be a visionary land. Nicholas Roerich looked at Shambhala as an imaginary kingdom, untouched by man, situated in the secret recesses of the Himalayas which are seen by him as abodes of light. During his expedition he was fascinated by the stories told by lamas about Shambhala.

Hevajra is a Tantric deity of royal cults, looking wrathful, mysterious, awe inspiring and esoteric. He holds attributes of war. He was worshipped for divine empowerment through rituals and dedication ceremonies. Kublai Khan performed Hevajra ceremony to conquer Southeast Asia. He was initiated into his maṇḍala. In India, Bengal was an important centre for the teachings of Hevajra. From there the tradition traveled to Nepal and Tibet and then to Mongolia. His images are found from various sites in Southeast Asia also. He holds attributes of war suggesting his power to defeat enemy. The Tibetan tradition clearly identifies eight forms of Hevajra falling into two categories—Śastra-dhara and Kapāla-dhara. On the basis of the paper the hypothesis may be accepted that as Śastra-dhara Hevajra was worshipped before going to battlefield and as Kapāla-dhara on returning victorious.

1

BUDDHIST ART FROM THE NORTHWEST TO THE FAR EAST

Natural phenomena and deified spirits played an important ceremonial and symbolic role in the lives of the Japanese, who expressed their gratitude to them directly, without any projection in terms of anthropomorphic forms. The Japanese religion was shaped by the changing weathers, beauty and mystery of nature and vagaries of climate. Nature was seen both as mighty as well as divine. A river or a waterfall has a power to flow; Moon has a power to shine; and wind can blow. The attitude of the Japanese towards life was a result of their innate sensitivity and harmony with nature, unity between man and environment, and gratitude for multiple aspects of nature: thunder, rain, clouds, cherry blossoms and full Moon.

The descendants of the Sun Goddess Amaterasu no Omikami, in the land of the Rising Sun, Japan, overwhelmed by the beauty of nature, abundance of vegetation, flowing rivers and green mountains, received Buddhism, accepted its philosophy, studied art and architecture, created paintings and sculptures and performed rituals and ceremonies on special occasions. Buddhism was consummated. It gave vitality, refined their religious and aesthetic sentiments, opened up new horizons for an all round development, and paved a way for political unification and consolidation. Buddhism was firmly rooted in Japan soon after its transmission through Central Asia, China and Korea.

It is difficult to give an exact date of the introduction of Buddhism to Japan initially, but officially it was brought in AD 552, when the Korean king of Paekche dynasty sent Buddhist images to the Japanese Emperor Kimmei. On his recommendations, Buddhism received an easy acceptance by the followers of Shinto: the way to God, a religion, polytheistic in nature. Although in the early years Buddhism was accepted hesitatingly out of a fear of havoc that could be caused by their local Kamis, but soon it was given the prestigious position of a state religion by the rulers. A variety of divinities, Buddhas and Bodhisattvas, awe inspiring guardians, compassionate Avalokiteśvara, goddesses of learning and richness: Sarasvatī and Lakśmī, Buddha of Healing and above all, the abstract philosophical concepts were found suitable to the needs of an advancing civilization.

Most of the art forms were carried to Japan from the Northwest frontiers of ancient India through Central Asia, China and Korea. Because of geographical proximity, Kuṣāṇa Empire was the source for the earliest Buddha images in China. Another source for them was the art of Gupta school, that attained ascendance as the Gupta Empire in Central India moved towards its apogee. The art of the Yun-kang caves in China reflects a combination of the Kuṣāṇa and the Gupta styles and in Japan, it can be seen in the art forms produced during the Hakuho period. The Buddhas are massive and dignified, they display an expression of nobility and simplicity. Their bodies are covered by translucent garments.

Early Classical Age

In the early years of the classical age, AD 552-645, when the Korean King sent a statue of the Buddha along with scriptures, canopies, banners, priests, architects, sculptors, painters etc., for a cultural, social, political and spiritual advancement, a continuous flow of Koreans to Japan resulted in construction of a large number of temples housing hundreds of images, embroideries, paintings etc. Torii Busshi is the most renowned Korean sculptor among those who settled in Japan and trained the Japanese in techniques of image making and other art forms. According to Honzon Reiho Catalogue, clay for making images was brought by Torii Busshi from China. Clay statues preserved in an amazingly good condition indicate the level of techniques employed by them. But as soon as Japan established its contacts with the main land China. Direct connections resulted in direct influence and transmission.

Buddhist art and thought had made its way into China from India in AD 67, when two Indian monks Kāśyapa Mātaṅga and Dharmarakṣa had carried Buddhist texts and relics on the Imperial order, to China. According to legends Indian missionaries reached the Chinese capital as early as 217 BC under the Ts'in dynasty and quasi-historical records state that a golden statue of Lord Buddha was taken to China by the Chinese general, in 12 BC from Central Asia.

Japanese artists tried new styles for making sculptures under the guidance of Torii Busshi, displaying a new ideology. The grandson of a Chinese Buddhist, Chiba Tatto, came to Japan as an envoy from the court of the Liang dynasty, his son Tokusai became a monk and his daughter Zenshin became a nun. During that phase a number of Koreans, experts in divination, calendar making, astronomy and medicine etc, went to Japan. Moreover, a host of Korean artists skilled in architecture, sculpture, painting, weaving and other crafts kept on journeying to Japan because Paekche was followed by the Kingdom of Silla to work for the propagation of Buddhism.

The Japanese learnt the Chinese and Korean formulae for bronze casting and techniques for lacquering. New cultural dimensions were opened up and a political system was set up with the coming of Buddhism. Prince Shōtoku Taishi framed and promulgated the first Constitution of Japan, called 'Seventeen Article Constitution' based on the Buddhist philosophy of *Pañcaśīla*. The devoted Prince was a man of administrative skills combined with rare talent and great ability. He wrote commentaries in Chinese on Saddharma-puṇḍarīka-sūtra, Vimalakīrti-nirdeśa-sūtra and Śrīmālā-siṁhanāda-sūtra. These are the first books written by a Japanese. He founded the Hōryūji monastery, which served as a university, as an institute of music and arts, a free hospital, both a *puṇya-kṣetra* and an *arcanā-kṣetra,* a place for merit making and praying, and also for training priests. The Prince sent missions to China along with students and priests for an in-depth knowledge of Buddhism.

Images of Bhaiṣajyaguru and Śākyamuni at the Hōryūji monastery bear influence of the Gandhara school of art that evolved around second century AD, on the upper reaches of Indus, during the reign of King Kaniṣka of the Kuṣāṇas. Buddhist images produced during the 2nd-3rd century AD have Greek looks and wear a heavy drapery, realistically portrayed. The drapery worn by Śākyamuni and Bhaiṣajyaguru in the Golden Hall of the Hōryūji monastery is the thickest ever produced in Japan. Their hands and facial features look stiff because model images for them were rock cut images of China. Japan began to produce in bronze, as it does not have rocky surface fit for chiselling. The boat shape halos are influenced by the style found at the Chinese cave temples and Korean bronzes from Koguryo and Paekche dynasty (6^{th}century). Style of Lung-men caves, full of classical grace had already reached the Korean peninsula. China remained the major source of knowledge for the Japanese. Hsüan tsang after coming back from India, received disciples from various countries including Dōshō and thirteen other priests from Japan. In AD 653 Dōshō received instructions into the philosophy of the Dhyāna school. Hsüan-tsang presented him the sūtra of Vijñapti-mātratā-siddhi and other texts, when he left for Japan and there he propagated them untill his death.

Although Chinese culture was hesitatingly adopted in the beginning, but a flood of influence began to pour in, in the early eighth century with the setting up of diplomatic relations. It brought in a rich material civilization. Apart from the art of sculpture, painting, architecture and crafts, Chinese literature, Confucius and Taoist thoughts were also eagerly accepted.

Thus Nara period became the golden age in Japanese history of art. It produced the most remarkable sculptures and paintings. The best quality lacquer sculptures based on Chinese techniques are still preserved at the monasteries of Nara. Lacquer craft became so important that all the households were ordered to plant 30-70 trees and bring pints of lacquer juice when required by the temples for production of images, furniture and a variety wares. Gradually Japan proved to be the most favourable soil for dissemination of Buddhist culture. Evidently a number of artifacts, that are lost in China, can be found in Japan. Buddhism had touched its heights in terms of aestheticism, quality of production and techniques under the T'ang dynasty when Chinese empire had reached the height of its power and their art had become richly diversified.

Buddhism on its way to Japan through Central Asia was influenced by local art forms and culture. For example ornaments worn by Bodhisattvas in Japan, especially in the murals on the walls of the Golden Hall of the Hōryūji monastery are a blend of Indian and Central Asian styles. Magnificence, lavish ornaments, beauty and dignity of the Bodhisattvas, painted on the walls of Hōryūji, reflect the material splendour of the age. Plastic and sensuous treatment of forms in Japanese sculpture reflect Indian ideals of beauty. No conflict is seen between the spiritual and physical world, ideally portrayed. Sensuousness of Nara period images can be traced back to the Gupta art. Tribhaṅga posture of the Sun and Moon Bodhisattvas flanking Bhaiṣajyaguru at the Yakushiji monastery are the finest examples.

Rise of Healing Cults

Hōryūji, the oldest extant monastery houses an image of the Healing Buddha, Bhaiṣajyaguru, Yakushi Nyorai in its Golden Hall, sculpted by Torii Busshi. The statue was commissioned for a fast recovery of Emperor Yomei from illness. This marks the beginning of the

Healing cult in Japan. A number of images of Bhaiṣajyaguru are found in Japan, China and Central Asia in different forms. The cult of Bhaiṣajyaguru in Japan is based on the philosophy of Bhaiṣajyarāja-sūtra, Yakushi-kyō brought to Japan from China, translated into Chinese during the Eastern Ch'in dynasty (AD 317-420) by Śrīmitra. Later translations were done by Dharmagupta (AD 615), Hsüan-tsang (AD 650) and I-ching (AD 707). Not much is known regarding the origin of Bhaiṣajyaguru in India, as he did not gain much popularity here. It is quite likely that the idea of the Healing Buddha was derived from the concept of the Historical Buddha as a spiritual healer or physician. The paradise of Bhaiajyaguru, Adhirati was accepted as a Deva Heaven and not as a realm of final liberation. This cult of mythical medicine seems to be an important proliferation of the Northwestern ideas and perceptions in the mainland India. Our tradition speaks of bhājakas who were healers and saviours both.

Protection of the State

Four Divine Guardian Kings called Shitennō stand on the platform on four corners in the Golden Hall of the Hōryūji monastery. This is the beginning of the faith in 'protection of the nation' by them. Suvarṇaprabhāsa-sūtra ascribes the worship of Four Divine Guardian Kings called Shitennō, who often stand inside the halls of worship in Japanese monasteries. They wear Northwestern style armours and shoes, carry their respective attributes and stand still in frontal postures. Often their heads are encircled by haloes indicating their divine personalities. The earliest extent set of their images is found from the Hōryūji monastery. Though the concept is frequently found in Purāṇic literature; names and iconographical details are also available but the idea of housing their images developed from the Parthian and Kusāṇa concept of state. The Parthians and the Sassanians used to divide their state into four parts. When Demetrius took possession of Gandhara, Punjab and the Indus Valley, he entrusted the responsibility of administration of the state to four viceroys.

The Four Divine Guardians are said to be present to listen to the sermon delivered by Śākyamuni at Vaiśāli, they pledged in the presence of the Buddha to protect the nation from all sorts of calamities, sorrows and pestilence. Their images, often along with Brahmā and Indra as maintainers of law and protectors of the state, complete with symbolic characteristic features and colors etc. are associated with four cardinal points of the compass and placed in the four directions. In the Suvarṇaprabhāsa-sūtra they are called great kings: *Viṣravaṇo mahārājo Dhṛtarāṣṭro mahārājo Virūḍhako mahārajo Virūpākṣa mahāraja* ...(Suvarṇaprabhāsa-sūtra p. 36)

In Tibet, they are known as guardians of the universe or protectors of the world (Tib.: Rgyal-chen mahārājas, great kings) and in Chinese: T'ien Wang. Dhṛtarāṣṭra is said to be the lord of Gandharvas, Virūḍhaka of Kumbhāṇḍas, Virūpākṣa of Nāgas and Vaiṣravaṇa of Yakṣas. In Tibetan Lamaist style, they are portrayed as giants wearing an elaborate antique armour with their faces displaying awe inspiring expression. Their identity as kings is portrayed by five lobed crowns bearing five Dhyāni Buddhas or their seed syllables and their martial personality is marked by helmets.

Prince Shōtoku Taishi constructed Shitennōji as a fulfilment of his vow when he came back victorious. Although the original temple was destroyed by fire, its foundations remained intact and the temple has been reconstructed on them. According to Kao-sang-chw'en (Kosoden AD 519) Kāśyapa Mātaṅga (Shomoto) who arrived in China in AD 67, expounded the sūtra in a small country (?) attached to India. Following are the Chinese translations of the Suvarṇa-prabhāsa-sūtra:

Dharmarakṣa II, AD 414-423 (Nanjio 127)

Pao-kwei, AD 597 (Nanjio 130)

Jñānagupta, AD 600 (Nanjio 130)

Paramārtha, AD 548-557 (Nanjio 130)

Yaśogupta, AD 561-578 (Nanjio 130)

I-tsing, AD 700-712 (Nanjio 126)

Japanese translations: There are three or four renderings into Japanese by Jinamitra, Śīlendrabodhi and others. In AD 702 when Emperor Mommu was ill; 100 men became monks and expounded the sūtra in the four provinces. In AD 703, it was read by an imperial order to pray for rain in four great temples of Nara: Yakushiji, Gangoji, Kōfukuji and Daianji. The Emperor ordered to read it in AD 705 to save the people from drought and for peace in the state. It was again ordered to be read in AD 728.

Light Symbolism

Transcendental Buddha, Amitābha, the Buddha of eternal light is enumerated as one of the five Dhyāni Buddhas : Vairocana, Akṣobhya, Amitābha, Amoghasiddhi and Ratnasambhava. He is popular in Japan as Amida, a shortened form of Amitābha and Amitāyus ṭ Buddhas of eternal light and eternal life respectively. The light symbolism was brought to Japan from the Northwest through China. Larger Sukhāvatīvyūha-sūtra, shorter Sukhāvatīvyūha-sūtra and Amitābha-sutra, the three major texts related to Amitābha worship, were brought from China. Sukhāvatīvyūha-sūtra, one of the fundamental texts was first received at the Japanese court in AD 640. Tenjukoku-mandara is the earliest maṇḍala of Amitābha, made for peaceful repose of the soul of Prince Shōtoku Taishi in the paradise of Amitābha, Sukhāvatī.

The first Japanese image of Amitābha can seen in the Lady Tachibana portable shrine, kept at the Hōryūji monastery. Amitābha is sitting on a huge lotus seat flanked by two attending figures standing on lotus flowers. A screen like canopy is fixed at their back visualizing a scene of his heaven with seven Buddhas of past and divine souls residing there.

Saidaiji monastery built by the daughter of Emperor Shomu, houses an image of Amitābha as one of the four Buddhas: Śākyamuni, Amitābha, Ratnasambhava and Akṣobhya. Possible date ascribed to the group is AD 770-780. Saidaiji, the Great West Temple was commissioned when she resolved to emulate her father by constructing a huge temple in the western part of the city.

The Imperial family in Japan began to produce Amida maṇḍalas, known as Henso paintings, as early as Nara period. The earliest example is the frescos on the west wall of the Golden Hall of the Hōryūji monastery painted in the 8th century. Others are from the Yakushiji and Kōfukuji monasteries. The paradise of Amitābha is mentioned in Mahāprajñā-pāramitā-sūtra translated by Hsüan tsang (T 220) also. The concept of Amida Jodo hen, a maṇḍala representing the Pure Land of Amitābha was known in China in the 7th century. During the reign of the Sung dynasty (AD 960-1279), it gained popularity among the people of both lay and religious societies. Approximately during the same period, it flourished in Japan in the Late Heian Period. As the Lord of Sukhāvatī, Amitābha was painted in Raigō scenes flying down with his retinue to receive the soul of the deceased and also going back carrying the soul to Sukhāvatī. Such painting are known as return Raigō.

Transmission of the Philosophy of Dhyāna

The philosophy of Dhyāna was transmitted by the Indian teacher Bodhidharma, the third son of the King of Kāñchi in India to China in AD 520 or 527. Laṅkāvatāra-sūtra, one of the fundamental texts of Zen Buddhism was translated into Chinese in AD 443, prior to the coming of Bodhidharma. Zen known as Ch'an in China was taken to Japan both by the Chinese and the Japanese monks. Monk Dōshō, a disciple of Hsüan tsang had brought the meditative practices to Japan. Chinese priest Tao-hsüan went to Japan in the eighth century followed by his disciple Gyōhō. Emperor Soga's wife invited I-kung from China in the second quarter of the 9th century to propagate the philosophy of Zen. But it was effectively planted in Japan by monk Eisai (1141-1215) and Dōgen (1200-1353). Today it has become a warm reality of the Japanese culture.

Saddharma-puṇḍarīka-sūtra

Saddharma-puṇḍarīka-sūtra, a profound religious classic is one of the earliest texts brought to Japan from China. Its first translation was done by Kumārajīva popularly known as Kumāraju in Japan. Prince Shōtoku Taishi (574-622) wrote a commetary on the Lotus-sūtra. Belief in it was widespread during his time. It has remained a rich source of inspiration for the Japanese artists since 6th century. Priests, nuns and lay believers believe in the sūtra's promise of spiritual reward for those who pay homage to it. The plaque at Hase-dera monastery, the main object of worship is a marvellous exposition of the teachings of Saddharmapuṇḍarīka-sūtra. It contains the ageless teachings of compassionate Buddha Śākyamuni. The sūtra became popular as the central scripture in Japan, in the 13th century, when it was preached by the monk Nichiren Daishonin.

From Ajanta to Hōryūji

All over the Buddhist world mural paintings were done on the inside walls of monasteries and temples to instruct the monks and to provide them surroundings that were fit for meditation. Hundreds of caves with painted interiors are their best examples in Asia. Jātaka stories were the major the source of inspiration in Burma, Srilanka and Thailand etc., the Theravada countries, lying to the Southeast of India. But in Central Asia, China and Japan, the themes are derived from Mahayanic scriptures. Mural paintings on the walls of the Golden Hall of the Hōryūji monastery are the oldest and the most magnificent ever done in Japan. At Ajanta the themes are taken from the Jātaka stories while at Hōryūji there are four paradise scenes of the four Buddhas: Amitābha, Śākyamuni, Bhaiṣajyaguru and Maitreya.

The paintings at Hōryūji look close to Ajanta in style, technique, use of colours and physical details. But their execution at Hōryūji is grand in composition, figures are full of noble grace and their faces have a spiritual and compassionate depth. Every small detail is brilliantly decorated. Sitting and standing postures, transparent clothes and heavy jewels visualize an impact of Indian art while wire like line is essentially a Chinese mode of drawing. Whatever has survived the fire of 1949, is a wonder for the world of art historians. Buddhas and Bodhisattvas reflect the minds of the artists who had drawn inspiration from Buddhist scriptures and whose hearts were full of faith and devotion. The north wall bears the paradises of Maitreya on the left and Bhaiṣajya on the right. Amitābha occupies the west wall of the hall and Śākyamuni is painted on the east wall. Eight Bodhisattvas fill the eight sides in the four corners. The idea of worshipping the four Buddhas in a group is based on the philosophy of Hosso sect, Vijñānavāda doctrine.

Transmission of Vajrayāna

According to Shingon or Vajrayāna tradition in Japan the eight patriarchs who transmitted the doctrine, rites and visual forms are: Mahāvairocana, Vajrasattva, Nāgārjuna, Nāgabodhi, Vajrabodhi, Amoghavajra, Hui-kuo and Śubhakarasiṁha. Among the eight patriarchs, Vajrabodhi from Kāñchī is given the credit for its transmission to East Asia. At the age of 31, he travelled to South India and began his studies under Nāgabodhi, a disciple of Nāgārjuna. He studied the Vajraśekharayoga-sūtra. Nāgārjuna was an eminent authority in tantras. Vajrabodhi was followed by his disciple Amoghavajra in China in AD 719-741 and AD 746-774. From China the philosophy of esoterism was carried to Japan by the two great monks: Kōbō Daishi and Dengyō Daishi. They left for China in AD 804, went to Ch'ang-an; Dengyō Daishi proceeded to mount T'ien T'ai and studied the philosophy of T'ien T'ai sect and practiced meditation. He met Śubhakarasiṁha a disciple of an Indian teacher from Nalanda university. He initiated Dengyō Daishi in esoterism which resulted in a drastic change in the future direction of Japanese Tendai art and thought. Monk Kōbō Daishi returned from China in AD 805 and propagated the philosophy of Shingon sect, that became the most dominant and revolutionary sect in Japanese spheres of religion and art.

Colossal Images

The idea of making colossal images came from Bamiyan and Chinese rock cut cave temples of Lung-men to Japan. The best-known colossus in Japan is Daibutsu at Tōdaiji monastery in Nara. The concept derived inspiration from the philosophy of the basic scripture of the Kegon sect, Buddhāvataṁsaka-mahā-vaipulya-sūtra, Daihoko-butsu Kegonkyō, popularly known as Kegonkyō. It is a product of contributions of Indian authors over several generations that made extensive cultural and philosophical contribution to the Japanese history. Not only the philosophers but also artists and devotees were inspired by its grand view of totality, exerting considerable influence on the development of Japanese Buddhist art. At Tōdaiji, Vairocana sits on a lotus seat of thousand petals as the supreme Buddha who controls all the phenomena and dwells in the land of eternally tranquil light.

Buddhism in the Northwest of ancient India incorporated a variety of cultural elements from various lands lying to its west and east. These syncretized trends that travelled to Japan through Central Asia and China, and finally got firmly rooted there. Japan sought a civilizing force through the sūtras of a variety of cults including the light cults propagated through Suvarṇaprabhāsa, Avataṁsaka- and Gaṇḍavyūha-sūtras. They are the combinations of light and beauty, purity and royalty. Buddhism thus became the core of Japanese civilization, which was transmitted from the Northwest frontiers of ancient India via Central Asia and China.

2

AMITĀBHA : THE BUDDHA OF IMMEASURABLE LIGHT IN JAPANESE ART

When man transcends the material world and ascends the spiritual, he aspires to accomplish the ultimate goal of life. Higher aspirations lead him to the higher levels of thought and action. To be happy he dedicates prayers for a long life, free from sickness. He prays for happiness in this world and for a blissful world beyond, that is paradise: *sahasrayājī vā imān lokān prāpnoti* (Tāṇḍya 16.8.9), paradise is attained by a person who performs a thousand sacrifices. As he gets the right vision and the right perspective, he becomes a devotee of the Benefactor, and draws a magnanimous image of his saviour in his mind. Amitābha is seen as a saviour and his paradise, Sukhāvatī in the west, is an ideal abode. He is the Transcendent Sun, a source of light. His images were produced in various forms and attitudes to fulfill a variety of aspirations of the state, the aristrocracy and the masses.

Sukhāvatī-vyūha-sūtra says, "The light of the Buddha shines with immeasurable brilliance in the countries of the ten directions and in no place is it obstructed". He presides over the western quarter. Devotion to the Buddha of immeasurable light is based on Larger Sukhāvatī-vyūha-, Shorter Sukhāvatī-, Amitābha- and Amitāyuradhyāna-sūtras. Parthian Prince, An-shih-kao introduced the tradition into China and from there it was carried to Japan. Amitāyurdhyāna-sūtra was translated by Kālayaśas (K191) in AD 383-442/424-442. In AD 613-681 a commentary was written by Shan-tao AD 613-781, who systematized the Pure Land thought in China. His writings were even known in Japan during the Nara period.

Our knowledge is scanty on the belief in Amitābha or his paradise in early India. The earliest forms of Larger Sukhāvatī- and Amitābha-sūtras appeared approximately during the 1st century AD in the NW of ancient India. Chinese pilgrims have referred in their memoirs to the devotion to Amitābha in India. They have mentioned about shrines dedicated to him. Authors like Nāgārjuna and Vasubandhu also have spoken about him.

In Japan Amitābha is known as Amida Nyorai. Nowhere in Sanskrit documents do we find a name reduced to Amita, which could correspond to this epithet. The Larger-Sukhāvatī-vyūha-sūtra mentions him as Amitābha except once as Amitāyur. The Japanese abbreviation Amida is used for both: Amitābha and Amitāyus. Amitāyus is the Buddha of Immeasurable Life and Amitābha, the Buddha of Immeasurable Light. The life of Amitāyus and of his people lasts for immeasurable and unlimited period, *asankhya kalpas*, and therefore he is called Amitāyus, Immeasurable Life. The term Tathāgata Amitāyus is translated as Muryōju Nyorai, meaning immeasurable life and

Tathāgata Amitābha as Muryōkō Nyorai, meaning immeasurable light. In later period the two Sanskrit names were transliterated as Amidayu and Amidaba. Then '*yu*' and '*ba*' were omitted, and thus both of them were known as 'Amida'.

Generally speaking Amitābha was worshipped in two aspects: as an ideal Buddha (Ributsu) and as a living personality preaching in the Western paradise. Daido Engi, the legends recorded in the Daido era, kept at Shitennōji temple says that an Amida triad was brought from T'ang China by the Japanese monk Eko (Okazaki 1977:9). The sects that developed around Amitābha in Japan are: Jōdō-shū and Jōdō-shin-shū. Jōdō is based on the philosophy of Sukhāvatī-vyūha-sūtra, Amitāyur-buddhānu-smṛti-sūtra and Sukhāvatī-(amṛta)-vyūha-sūtra translated by Kumārajīva. Pure Land sūtras formed a popular subject of study. Priests used to study the sūtras, comment on them and deliver lectures. Different sūtras were recognized as authorities by different sects, e.g. Eon, a priest of Sanron sect went to Japan from China in AD 640 and delivered lectures on Larger-Sukhāvatī-vyūha-sūtra and related works at a vegetarian repast held at Kudaradaiji. Another monk of the same sect shared the devotion and he is known to have created a Jōdo mandara.

Heavenly Abode of Amitābha

Devotion to Jōdo or Pure Land was present in Japan as early as the Asuka period (AD 552-645). Sukhāvatī-vyūha-sūtra was first recited at the court in Japan in AD 640. The first known reference to Larger-Sukhāvatī-sūtra (Daimuryōjukyō) appears in the writings of Prince Shōtoku Taishi who had a firm belief in the paradise of Amitābha. Tenjukoku mandara created in the memory of the Prince is the earliest example of the visualization of Pure Land. After the demise of Prince Shotoku Taishi, his consort ordered a pair of large embroideries representing the paradise to which the dead Prince's soul was presumed to have migrated. Only fragments of these embroideries remain today in the Chuguji nunnery, adjoining Hōryūji. The Tenjukoku mandara bears inscriptions containing the wish of the Prince Shōtoku for a happy rebirth in the Tenjukoku. This suggests existence of the concept of Sukhāvatī but it seems to be rather vague.

Later, the Japanese were inspired by the rise of Jōdo concept in T'ang China to worship Amitābha exclusively. Philosophical and religious substance of the sūtras pertaining to Amitābha played an important role. More influential among them was Sukhāvatī-vyūha-sūtra that describes Amitābha's forty-eight vows, that he would not enter into his final *nirvāṇa* unless all the sentient beings shared it.

Nara period saw further increase in the devotion. Empress Kōmyō (710-760) was a believer in the Pure Land faith, seven days after her death an edict was issued throughout the country to make copies of Pure Land maṇḍalas and to copy the related sūtras in all the provinces. In AD 761 a temple in the Kōfukuji confines was built in her memory. A tapestry was hung on its wall to visualize Sukhāvatī.

Happiness for the Living and Peace for the Dead

Devotion to Amitābha was primarily designed for prosperity in the present life during the Hakuho period, i.e. an inscription found on the Amida triad of the Yamato Shirinji temple, dated

AD 649 requests happiness for the living and peace for the dead. Lady Tachibana shrine is a masterwork from the Hakuho period. The shrine, generally dated AD 710, presents a view of the paradise. It is a Jōdōhen, representing Amida's Pure Land in sculptural medium. Amitābha sits on a lotus emerging out of a pond attended by two Bodhisattvas. His right hand is in *semui* or reassurance mudrā while the left is in *yogan* or wish granting posture. The two Bodhisattvas stand on lotuses. Behind them on the screen are the seven Buddhas and souls of the departed and reborn in Sukhāvatī, sitting on lotus buds or flowers. Their faces are full of a joyous spirituality. Their draperies swirl upwards with the lotus stems. Souls in Sukhāvatī are also painted on the pedestal of the shrine.

State Function of Amida Worship

Suvarṇa-prabhāsa-sūtra (Konkōmyō-kyō), expounds devotion to the Four Buddhas: Śākyamuni, Bhaiṣajyaguru, Amitābha, and Maitreya. The Hosso sect in Japan also prescribed veneration for the same group. The Buddhas sitting in their paradises painted on the walls in Hōryūji are the earliest examples where they are venerated in a group. The paradise of Amitābha painted on the western wall presents almost a similar view as portrayed in the Lady Tachibana Shrine with Amitabha sitting on a huge lotus emerging out of a pond. The two Bodhisattvas: Avalokiteśvara and Mahāsthāmaprāpta flank him.

The same group of the Buddhas was sculpted for the Saidaiji monastery in Nara during the eighth century. They are said to be originally housed in the pagoda that has vanished now. They are often dated as AD 770-780. A number of images of Amitābha with his attending Bodhisattvas were sculpted during the Nara period, e.g. Amida triad, treasure gallery, Hōryūji and Amida triad, National Museum, Tokyo. A group of Four Buddhas in sculptural form in the pagoda of Kofukuji was executed in AD 730. There, Amitābha is attended by two Bodhisattvas, eight chanting Bodhisattvas and eight Bodhisattvas holding lotus seats (Fukuyama 1976 : 11).

Meditation on Sukhāvatī for Longevity

Amitāyurdhyāna-sūtra (Kammuryōjukyō) was the basic sūtra for visualisation of the paradise of Amida in the form of a henso representation called Taima-maṇḍala in Japan. It is a visual transformation of the doctrinal theme of the sūtra. It was preached by Śākyamuni to Queen Vaidehī in Rājagṛha when she was leading a painful life after being imprisoned by her son who wanted to starve his father to death. She meditated on Sukhāvatī for longevity in this world and attaining Pure Land after death.

The sūtra was translated into Chinese by Kālayaśas and a commentary was written on it by Shan-tao. More than thirty commentaries exist but the most important is by Shan-tao. Hōnen Shonin also relied primarily on it for developing his own thought and himself wrote a commentary, Kammuryōjukyō-shaku. No Tibetan or Sanskrit versions of the sūtra are found. According to some scholars it was composed outside India.

The concept of Amida Jōdo-hen representing the Pure Land of Amitābha originated in China. There existed a strong faith in him among people of all the classes. The maṇḍala was painted in Dun-huang caves in China, a number of times. It became popular under the Sung dynasty (AD 960-1279) among the people of both lay and religious societies.

In Japan, the age when this maṇḍala prospered is 7th-12th century. During the Nara period they were made by emperors' families a number of times. Hōryūji murals are the earliest example. Yakushiji temple also preserves a maṇḍala that was made in the sixth year of Empress Jito's reign. Kōfukuji has another maṇḍala that was made in AD 730. Besides these there are many, e.g. a twenty deity maṇḍala of Amitābha was painted by Shinkakau (1170-80, TZ 86.19) in Besson Zakki. Amitābha with eight great Bodhisattvas was also painted by him (TZ 87.22). Taimadera monastery produced a painting following the Chinese style of depiction of Pure Land, based on Amitāyurdhyāna-sūtra (Kammuryōjukyō) with the commentary by Shan-tao. But by that time, belief in Amitābha was not widespread, so the chanting of his name was not practised.

Amitābha, the focal point of Taima maṇḍala is sitting cross legged on a huge lotus seat, the King and the Queen are praying in front, below them is the representation of the ninth degree of birth in his Paradise. They are painted as having a vision of themselves, as reborn there, sitting on lotus seats. Five gem trees, *ratna vṛkṣas* are painted on the right and the left at the back of the throne of Amitābha. A number of buildings are painted at different levels forming a towerlike structure on the both the sides of the paradise. The towers are topped by jewels encircled by halos or flames.

Probably gems appear from the *brahmarandhra* of Amitābha. Beyond that is Amitābha in a more subtle form attended by the King and the Queen sitting with the two Bodhisattvas inside his palace flanked by two on both the sides. Beyond that is the final stage. Above this scene are Buddhas and Bodhisattvas flying down from the heaven from all the directions. In between are birds and musical instruments floating in air in the sky. Some flying goddesses are also painted along with.

Amitābha: One of the Five Buddhas in the Twin-maṇḍalas

Amitābha is one of the five central Buddhas in the Mahākaruṇā-garbha-maṇḍala brought by Kōbō Daishi. Mahāvairocana sits at the center of an eight petalled lotus in the central mansion. On the eight petals of the lotus sit four Buddhas and four Bodhisattvas. The four buddhas are: Ratnaketu (Hōdōbutsu), Sankusumitarāja (Kaifuke-ō-butsu), Amitābha (Muryō-butsu) and Divya-dundubhi-megha-nirghoṣa (Tenkuraion butsu). Amitābha occupies the western petal of the central mansion.

In the Vajradhātu-maṇḍala the central figure of the six, out of nine sections, is Vairocana. In the four sections: Mahā-, Sūkṣma-, Dharma- and Karma-maṇḍalas he is surrounded by four Buddhas: Akṣobhya, Ratnaketu, Amitābha and Amoghasiddhi.

Amitābha wears monk's garments, has short curls and sits on a lotus. His face is golden, the colour of autumn, which corresponds to the west, gold also symbolizes plentitude and indestructibility. He accomplishes the mudrā of concentration.

Nembutsu, Recitation of the Name of Amitābha, for Salvation

Pure Land faith came to play an increasingly important role during the Heian period in the Tendai sect. Recitation of the name of Amitābha became a key to paradise. Monk

Ennin propagated that Jōgyō sammai or perpetual chanting meditation was as effective as lotus meditation. Further it was popularized by another Tendai priest Ensai who held special nembutsu services on the 15th day of every month. Soon aristocracy began to patronize. Some of the members of the Imperial family embraced the devotion. Elder sister of Emperor Kazan died peacefully while engaged in Jōgyō sammai and Nembutsu services were subsequently performed on her memorial days. Later a group of Chinese scholars and monks began to organize biannual meetings. Jōgyō sammai became a dominant form of meditation on mount Hiei and the Abbot Ryōgen himself wrote commentaries on Pure Land sūtras for the aristocrats. But later he began to preach to the common people raising the devotion to its pinnacle.

An image of Amitābha was placed for the beginners to meditate, attempting to visualize the Pure Land mentally. At an advanced stage the devotee was directed to meditate on the formless Amitābha. Monk Genshin was one of the first Tendai monks who declared that his goal was birth in Pure Land. He expressed his views in his treatise Ōjōyōshū that became popular among the aristocratic class and in fact has been the best seller in Japanese history up to modern times throughout Japan.

Amitābha Figures for Meditation

The Japanese monk Saichō brought a new way of meditation called Shi-kan. 'Shi' means *śamatha*, tranquility or concentration and 'kan' is vipassana, right knowledge or insight. Shi-kan was divided into four forms of meditation based upon the physical posture of the devotee. According to the first manner a devotee was to sit and meditate facing the image of Bodhisattva Mañjuśrī. In the second method he was to circumambulate the image of Amitābha chanting the Nembutsu for ninety days. The devotee has to focus his mind upon the Pure Land or thirty-two marks of the Buddha. This led to construction of special halls of meditation in the Tendai temples known as Jōgyōdō or Hokkedō. Jōgyōsammaidō, meditation hall, built by monk Ennin in AD 848 beacame the major place of inspiration for the evolution of Japanese Pure Land Buddhism (Matsunaga 1978 : 1.158). During the Heian period Amida-Jōdo-hen was mainly painted as fresco in the main hall. This led to enshrining large size images of Amitābha in meditation halls, sitting in dhyāna mudrā.

Amitābha in Meditation

Amitābha sits in dhyāna mudrā known as Amida-jō-in. Both of his hands rest on his lap with palms up, placed one upon the other. The last two phalanges of his index fingers are verticle and touching back to back. The thumbs come together with the tips touching index fingers. It is the mudrā of meditation. The two hands represent two worlds. The left being the world of beings, the Matrix world and the right the world of the Buddhas, the Diamond world. The right hand supports the left, showing that the world of Buddhas sustains the world of phenomena. The circle formed by the thumbs and the index fingers represent the perfection of Dharma in the two worlds, since the circle is the symbol of perfection. The same mudrā was made by Śākyamuni, when he was meditating under the Bodhi tree. One of the best-known examples among the images of Amitābha is in Kamakura, sitting majestically in open but was originally enshrined in the Kotoku-in monastery.

Sukhāvatī: An Ideal Abode on this Earth

Sukhāvatī was seen as an ideal abode by the aristocrats. They wished to create the paradise on this very earth and aspired to reside therein. Several replicas of Pure Land were built. In 1019 when Michinaga was in ill health, he decided to construct a temple on the eastern side of his private mansion in Kyoto to house nine images of Amitābha. The temple was named Hōjōji. Michinaga's son, Yorimichi built another at Byōdōin. Inside the hall a huge image of Amitābha is sitting in meditation while his paradise is painted on the walls and Bodhisattavas are placed in side niches.

Late Heian period was an age of dazzling descriptions of Pure Land. Because of these attractive descriptions, salvation through faith became an attitude of mind. The Fujiwaras erected over 30 halls to enshrine images of Amitābha. Amitābha at the Hōkaiji monastery is another example of a large size image. It is an Amida hall not far from Uji in northeast Kyoto. Konjikidō hall of Chusonji monastery is another example of one such hall. It is the visualization of the concept of heaven on earth as described in the Upaniṣads: *iyam (pṛthivī) vai svargasya lokasya pratiṣṭhā; ya evam veda saśarīra eva svargam lokameti* (Taittariya-saṁhitā 3.11.7.3), those who realize that paradise is there on this earth, they go there with this physical body.

Amitābha as a Saviour of the Nine Classes

Sukhāvatī-vyūha-sūtra expounded the nine grades of rebirth in the Pure Land. A Tendai monk Ryōgen preached the philosophy of rebirth of nine classes of believers in Amitābha's paradise. In the 10th century he worte Gokuraku Jōdo Kuhon Ōjō-gi, commentary on the nine categories of rebirth in the Pure Land. Several halls with images of nine forms of Amitābha as saviours of the nine levels of people, were constructed but only one of them remains today, that is Joruriji in south Kyoto built in early 12th century. These forms are also painted in the lower court of the Taima maṇḍala and Amitābha is envisioned as saving the nine classes of mankind. The top degree of people is that of saints, the second of virtuous men and the third of sinners.

Amitābha as a Saviour in Raigō Paintings

Heavens are said to be somewhere up in the sky: *uparīvā svargo lokaḥ* (Taittariya-saṁhitā 3.2.1.5, 3.2.2.9, 3.2.3.12). They are beyond this world: *paro vā* asmānllokāt *svargo lokaḥ* (Aitareya 9.20). Buddhists were much concerned with the ill state of mind at the approach of death. So the sūtras frequently depict the Buddha preaching to sick or seriously ill to calm their minds. It was believed that if a man lives an evil life for hundred years but thinks of Buddha at the moment of death, he is led towards paradise for rebirth. Fear of death is capable to inspire to be converted to a religious life. It is said that heaven was created by gods by performing *yajñas*, penance, working hard and offerings: *deva vai yajñena śrameṇa tapasāhūtibhiḥ svargam lokamajayan* (*Aitareya* 2.13).

Jōdo faith was fostered by the Tendai sect. Monk Genshin (942-1017) also known as Eshin, active in mid Heian period wrote the Ōjō Yōshū (Essentials of Rebirth in the Pure Land). He explained the philosophic basis and practical means of Jōdō faith. The most influential was his statement about Amitābha's descent (Raigō). The Buddha descends from the heaven and receives the soul of the dying faithful into his Pure Land as explained in Sukhāvatī-vyūha- and Amitāyur-dhyāna-sūtras. Larger Sukhāvatī-sūtra says that Amitābha took a vow to stand before the sentient beings at the moment of death if he had been invoked with a sincere mind (Matsunaga 1978: 1.237). Going to paradise is not easy: *svargo vai loko dūrohaṇam* (Aitareya 4.20, 21).

Similar notions are found in Avalokiteśvara-, Lotus- and Bhaiṣajyaguru-sūtras. They describe that Buddhas and Bodhisattvas appear to those who are about to die. Raigō, born out of Jōdo maṇḍalas, became a frequent subject of Jōdo faith. The concept gave rise to a variety of Raigō paintings. They were undoubtedly executed with the knowledge of approaching death in mind.

Descent of Amitābha accompanied by twenty-five Bodhisattvas was one of the most popular themes in painting and sculpture. The Bodhisattvas of the joyous group play on musical instruments, hold banners, bring materials for worship and Avalokiteśvara brings an empty lotus seat for the soul of the deceased. Amida Raigō in the Pheonix hall of Byōdō-in temple at Uji near Kyoto and a painting kept at the Kongōbuji monastery are among the best-preserved examples.

Phoenix hall represents the Shin sect, a branch of Jōdo sect. Phoenix is the symbol of immortality. Amitābha sits in dhyāna mudrā. The image faces east. Behind him is the paradise painted and twenty-five Bodhisttvas sculpted. A view of Pure Land, Raigō and also a return Raigō are painted on the walls and doors of the hall. In backward Raigō Amitābha is shown in profile and the celestial beings leading the supplicants to the Pure Land (Fukuyama 1976: 1.31). Gradually it was recognized as a means of individual salvation.

Amitābha as a Buddha of the Solar Cult

In the two versions of the Taima maṇḍala preserved at Amida-dera, Nara and Chokoji, Kyoto, a red Sun at the top dominates. It recalls the glory and effulgence (*bharga*) that the rising Sun sheds in the heart of a *sādhaka*. As the Gāyatrī mantra says: *om bhūr bhuvaḥ svaḥ tatsavitur vareṇyam bhargo devasya dhīmahī dhiyo yo naḥ prachodayāt* meaning we contemplate on the effulgence of the divine Sun, so that He may inspire our mediations. The Japanese maṇḍalas show the glowing red Sun, which initiates, impels and inspires the sixteen mediations. He is not the physical Sun but the transcendental Sun, Amitābha (Lokesh Chandra 1999: 1.235). The Sun, the supreme light is described as paradise itself: *svargo vai lokaḥ sūryyo jyojiruttamam* (Yajurveda 20.21, Śatapatha. 12.9.2.8). This Sun is the paradise: *eṣa ādityaḥ svargo lokaḥ* (Taittarīya-saṁhitā 3.8.10.3, 3.9.17.2, 3.8.20.2).

A mystic formula is inscribed in ink, on a solar disc made of wood (diameter of disc 30.7cm.) placed on a lotus, inside the image of Buddha Amitābha in the Phoenix Hall of the Byōdōin monastery at Uji in Kyoto. The mantra reads as follows: *Namo ratna trayāya namah āry Āmitābhāya samyak sambuddhāya tadyathā om amṛte amṛtodhave amṛta-sambhave amṛta-garbhe amṛta-siddhe amṛta-teje amṛta vi-te amṛta-vikrānta-gāmine amṛta-gagana-kīrttikare amṛta-dundubhi-svare sarvārtha-sādhane sarva-karma-kleśa-kṣayaṁkare svāhā//*

Amitābha in Jōdo Sect

Teachings of Pure Land were propagated by the monks Kūya and Genshin followed by the idea of repetitive images that became one of the religious practices. Sculptures of Amitābha produced, reflect both the idea of mercy and gentleness. Monk Hōnen chose the practice of Nembutsu while Dogen advocated the practice of just sitting in front of an Amitābha image. Shinran taught the attainment of an absolute realm in the midst of empirical reality through the Nembutsu. Different monks preached differently but the ultimate goal remained happiness in this world and the world beyond through devotion to Amitābha.

Inspite of a wide spread popularity of devotion to Amitābha and a large scape creation of halls for this worship, image enshrined therein and maṇḍalas painted on walls and silk, the question of its origin remains abscure.

Appendix

Important dates

Later Han/mid 4th century	Muryō shōjō byōdō kakukyō tr. by Chih Lou-chia-ch'an
Wu dynasty	Dai Amidakyō translated by Chih-ch'ien
Kumārajīva	Amidakyō (oldest translation of Amitābha-sūtra)
252	Sukhāvatī-sūtra translated by Saṅghavarman
7th-8th century	Chikō-maṇḍala
753-781	Maṇḍala made by the Princess Chūjō Hime
763	Taima maṇḍala at the Taima-dera
9th-10th century	Paintings of Taima maṇḍala at Dun-huang Caves
1046-1053	Shōkai/Seikai-maṇḍala preserved at Chūshōji, Gokurakuji
1048-1116	Commentary on Amitāyurdhyāna-sūtra by Yüan-tao Ta-chi
1167-8	Taima maṇḍala brought from China by Jugen
13th century	Painting based on Yuan-tao Ta-chi's commentary on Amitāyurdhyāna-sūtra Amida-dera
13th century	Same as above, Chōkōji
1501-3	Replica of Taima maṇḍala, Taima-dera

(Fukuyama 1976:140)

LITERATURE CITED

Aiteraya

Aitereya-Brāhmaṇa.

Fukuyama 1976

Teshio Fukuyama, *Heian Temples: Byōdō-in and Chūsonji,* Heibonsha, Tokyo, 1976.

Hansraj, 1926

Hansraj, *Vaidic Koṣa*, Dayānanda Mahāvidyālaya Sanskrit Granthamālā, Lahore, 1926.

Korean Tripiṭaka, Lewis R. Lancaster, *The Korean Buddhist Canon* : a Descriptive Catalogue, Berkley 1979 (University of California Press).

Lokesh Chandra, 1999.

Lokesh Chandra, *Dictionary of Buddhist Iconography,* International Academy of Indian Culture & Aditya Prakashan, Delhi, 1999.

Matsunaga, 1978

Daigan and Alicia Matsunaga, *Foundation of Japanese Buddhism,* Buddhist Books International, Los Angeles and Tokyo, 1978.

Okazaki, 1977

Joji Okazaki, *Pure Land Buddhist Painting,* Kodansha International Ltd. and Shibundo, Tokyo 1977

Śatapatha-brāhmaṇa.

TZ

Taishō-shinshu Daizokyō, Picture Section, ed., J. Takakusu and Ono, The Taishō Shinshu Daizokyō Kankōkai, Tokyo, 1934.

Tattarīya

Tattiriya-saṁhitā

Taitt. Upa.

Tattirīa Upaniṣad,

Tamura, 2000

Tamura Yoshio, *Japanese Buddhism:* A Cultural History, Kosei Publishing Company, Tokyo, 2000.

Tāṇḍya

Tāṇḍya-Brāhmaṇa

Yajurveda

3

YOGA: THE BASIS OF THE TAIMA MAṆḌALA

Pure Land sect devoted to the worship of Amitābha preached happiness in Sukhāvatī, the Paradise of Amitābha, to the faithful believers, after death. It spread to the East Asia, and for centuries the Chinese and the Japanese philosophers resorted to the philosophy of Amitāyurdhyāna-sūtra (Ch. *Kuan wu-liang-shou ching*) for a graphic representation of Sukhāvatī in the form of Taima-maṇḍala. It deals with the story of Ajātaśatru imprisoning his parents, the King Bimbisāra and the Queen Vaidehī; mental suffering of the Queen and Lord Budha's preaching to recover her from the mental suffering, *duḥkha*. She listens to the teachings of Lord Buddha and begins to concentrate. She practices five *dhāraṇās* that make her fit to practice samādhi. Finally she goes into trance and realises the bliss in Sukhāvatī. The version of Taima Maṇḍala referred to in this text is from Taima-dera monastery (Halen 1987).

Yoga is the basis of the Taima-maṇḍala which was painted several times over the past centuries to be used by the followers of the Jōdo sect as a projection for meditation in order to save the people from mental suffering, to raise them to the level of samādhi. In the maṇḍala the story of sufferings leads to concentration followed by dhāraṇā and samādhi. The story of imprisonment of the King and the Queen by their son, fills the outer left court, sixteen meditations are in the outer right and bottom courts and vision of Sukhāvatī by the Queen is in the Central Sanctum. The Central Sanctum is filled with five *dhāraṇās*, all the architectonic elements of Sukhāvatī, realization of the bliss and the paradise with Buddhas and Bodhisattvas, envisioned by the Queen at various levels of dhyāna, that was practiced in Japan from the year 760 onwards, though traces are also found as early as 6th-7th century.

Taima-maṇḍala as a Projection for Samādhi

Dhyāna sūtras are of a very special category in China and Japan. Dhyāna is an act of attention directed to some particular object. When it is prolonged or intensified, it gives rise to samādhi, its result is the cessation of all mental processes, and that is the aim of Vaidehī. Patañjali defines dhyāna (III.2) as: *tatra pratyayaikatānatā dhyānam*. Dhyāna is the concentrated attention to a single content of consciousness on that place (Fernando 1987: 145). Dhyāna is the seventh of the *Yogāṅgas*, it is the state of continuance, i.e. the unchanging flow of mental efforts to understand the object of meditation. All the dhyānas are bestowers of samādhi (Mantra-yoga-saṁhita 77, Rai 1975:121).

Samādhi : The Final Stage in Yoga

Yoga is eight limbed, *aṣṭāṅga*. The first five: yama, niyama, āsana, prāṇāyāma and pratyāhāra are said to be outer members, *bahiraṅga* while the other three: dhāraṇā, dhyāna and samādhi are inner members, *antaraṅga* (Richard 1999:70). Dhyāna yoga is the knowledge, devoid of duality, pleasant and pure in its stillness, stable and without obstructions. Samādhi yoga is the knowledge without ulterior in motives, without concepts, without desires, without any aim to accomplish things, pure beyond existence and without disturbance. The conscious is without content. It stops being aware of the body.

Six types of yoga are like weapons of a *yogīśvara,* to attain the divine absolute (San Hyang Kamahāyānikan fl. 43ab, Lokesh Chandra 1997: V.78). On realizing the mental suffering of the Queen, Śākyamuni preached her the practice of concentration, which precedes meditation. It is fundamental to the yogic process of introversion. It represents gathering of one's psychic energy, which is accompanied by a high degree of sensory inhibition, *pratyāhāra* and a slowing down of thought. Yogic concentration can have a variety of mental objects, *artha*, ranging from internalised image of the deity to internalised sound, *nāda*, to a locus, *deśa,* within the body. Deepening of concentration leads to meditation (Feurstein 1997: 85). When she enters samādhi then she visualizes Sukhāvatī and realizes that after death she would be taken to a blissful abode.

Followed by sixteen levels of meditation, Vaidehī practices dhāraṇā on the five elements: earth and sky, water and tejas, and vāyu. In the maṇḍala, mental objects are architectonic elements of Sukhāvatī, Amitābha is the deity to be internalized, sound is produced by various musical objects and the locus is visualization of Sukhāvatī. Queen Vaidehī practices *antardhāraṇā* through concentration of mind upon subtle-most objects of the inner-most world (Rai 1975: 120). *Dhāraṇā* is one of the eight parts of yoga. It means concentration, sometimes called collectedness, *samādhāna*. The Yoga-sūtra (3.1) defines it as the binding of consciousness (*citta*) to a single locus (*deśa*). It is thus the practice of continuous attention which is the essence of one pointedness *ekāgratā*.

Visualization of Sukhāvatī has a long history. The earliest painting of the Pure Land at Dunhuang caves in China dates from the first half of the seventh century. In cave 146 a wall painting depicts Amitābha and fifty Bodhisattvas. In cave 139a there is a *hensō* respresentation based on Amitāyurdhyāna-sūtra. In Japan the earliest example of *hensō* painting appears on the back of the Tamamushi shrine at Hōryūji monastery, though scholars give different interpretations, according to some it is Śākyamuni on Vulture peak while others believe it to be the paradise of Amitābha. Another example of representation of the paradise of Amitābha can be traced back to the seventh century when Tenjukoku mandara was embroidered in AD 622. After the death of Prince Shōtoku-Taishi his widow Princess Suiko had ordered it. Tenjukoku means the land of heavenly long life. The Korean priest Eji was the teacher of Shōtoku Taishi and he had predicted of his death and going to the paradise of Amitābha. Frequent references and illustrations of the Pure Land are also found in the documents from the seventh century onwards.

The first painting visualizing Taima-maṇḍala on an almost four meter square tapestry belongs to the Taima-dera monastery in Nara prefecture. Taima-dera was originally known as Zenrinji, a Maitreya temple. The original tapestry is called Konpon (original) Taima and was woven of silk threads (Kidder 1964:189). Actually this is called a *hensō*, an apparitional vision on transformed configuration of the Pure Land. It began to be called a maṇḍala on account of its analogy with the maṇḍalas of the mystic doctrine. Its name in China is "Phases of Amida's Pure Land" or Jōdo Hensō (Lokesh Chandra 1999:1.233).

Purpose

The legend concerning the origin of Taima-maṇḍala is given in the narrative scroll painting, Taima-mandara-engi at Kōmyōji in Kanagawa prefecture. The daughter of a nobleman during the reign of Emperor Junnin (AD 758-64) lost interest in the mundane world and began to yearn for the Western Paradise of Amitābha. On the fifteenth day of the sixth month of AD 763 she cut off her hair to become a nun; she prayed for seven days; on the twentieth day a nun appeared and ordered the former Princess to gather a hundred horseloads of lotus stems. She dug a well and dyed them. On the twenty-third day another nun appeared and completed the weaving of the maṇḍala (Okazaki 1977:42).

According to another tradition the painting is attributed to the Princess Chūjō Hime (AD 753-781), the daughter of Fujiwara no Toyonari, who had made a thousand copies of Shōson-jōdo-kyō (Nj. 199) and presented them to Zenrinji (temple of the wood of meditation). She became a nun, took up her residence at the Zenrinji, kept on praying for seven days to see a manifestation of Amitābha. He appeared after six days in the form of a lady and ordered her to collect a thousand lotus stems. He made a pure well, washed the stems, changed them into five coloured threads. Then Avalokiteśvara appeared on the 23rd day and made the Taima-maṇḍala. At present, fragments of the silk painting are preserved in the treasury of the Taima-dera (a clan temple of the Taima clan) and its replica made in the Bunki era (AD 1501-1503) is placed in the Mandara-dō for the worshippers. It is made in imitation of the pictures of Shan-tao. The Kwangyo-mandara of Chion-in, Kyoto, is said to have been brought from China at Hōnen Shōnin's request by his pupil, the Japanese Jōdo priest Jūgen who had gone to China in AD 1167-8 and had died in 1195 (Lokesh Chandra 1999:1.233).

Basic Sūtra

Visualization of the paradise of Amitābha in the Taima-maṇḍala is based on Amitāyurdhyāna-sūtra (Kammuryōjukyō) preached by Śākyamuni to Queen Vaidehī in Rājagṛha translated into Chinese by Kālayaśas into Chinese or rather on the commentary on it by Shan-tao (Waley 1931: xx-xxii). It is a visual transformation of the doctrinal theme of the sūtra (Ch. Kuan wu-liang-shou-ching). More than thirty commentaries exist but the most important is by Shan-tao. Hōnen Shōnin also relied primarily on it for developing his own thought and himself wrote a commentary, Kammuryōjukyō-shaku. No Tibetan or Sanskrit versions are found. According to some scholars it was composed outside India (Senchakushū 1998: 21). A twenty deity maṇḍala of Amitābha was painted by Shinkaku (1170-80, TZ 86.19) in Besson Zakki.

Structure of the Maṇḍala

A number of variations can be seen in the details of the structure of the Taima-maṇḍala, copied over the centuries, but its basic structure follows the teachings of Amitāyurdhyāna-sūtra and visualization of Sukhāvatī is based on the details given by other sūtras of the Jōdo sect, i.e. Amitābha-sūtra and Sukhāvatīvyūha-sūtra. Amitābha is the Transcendental Sun, *Amita-ābha*. Red sun at the top dominates the maṇḍala and recalls the radiance and splendor in the two hanging scrolls kept at the Amida-dera and at Chōkōji, Kyoto.

Outer Courts

Court of the prefatory legend, jōbungi (left):

Episodes of the life of Ajātaśatru and Vaidehī are painted on the outer left court. During the lifetime of Śākyamuni, Prince Ajātaśatru plotted with the Buddha's cousin and nemesis Devadatta in the capital of the kingdom of Magadha, to kill his own father King Bimbisāra. The story of his imprisonment, starving him, Queen Vaidehī foiling his plan, and finally Śākyamuni coming miraculously to preach, is visualised in the following sequence:

i. Ajātaśatru imprisons his father in the castle and tries to starve him to death;

ii. Queen Vaidehī secretly smuggles food to her husband by anointing her body with honey and ghee mixed with corn flour and by concealing the juice of grapes in her garlands;

iii. Śākyamuni observing the drama from the Vulture's peak sends his disciples Maudgalyāyayana and Pūrṇa to Bimbisāra to preach the law to the imprisoned king;

iv. Ajātaśatru visits the prison and inquires whether or not his father has died;

v. On hearing his mother's intervention, he is about to kill her when his ministers persuade him not to commit a second crime;

vi. Instead, he imprisons his mother as well, who listens to Maudgalyāyana and the other disciple, Ānanda sent by Śākyamuni, preaching the law;

vii. Vaidehī's prison is miraculously changed into a paradise and the queen worships Śākyamuni, enthroned before her;

viii. Vaidehī begs for salvation in a realm of peace and Śākyamuni shows her many pacific, radiant heavens among which she chooses the western paradise and asks how one may be born there. In reply Śākyamuni outlines the ideals of a moral life sustained by a series of sixteen contemplations, and the ray of light emanating from Buddha's head in which Amitābha's paradise is visible, extends to King Bimbisāra;

ix. Śākyamuni remarks to Ānanda that the Amutāyurdhyāna-sūtra will erase the burdensome accumulation of evil deeds and cause birth in paradise, even if virtuous men and women only hear the names of Amitābha, Avalokiteśvara and Mahāsthāmaprāpta, this may take away their sins of innumerable ages or *kalpas*;

x. The eleventh and final subsection of the court foretells the contents of the outer right hand court and the lower horizontal court.

Court of the specific meditation, Jōzengi (right)

Thirteen meditations are painted on the outer right court of the maṇḍala:

i. Nissōkan: Queen Vaidehī, meditating, looking to the west on the setting Sun, suspended in space like a drum; even if one's eyes are closed a full perception of the Sun will remain.

ii. Suisōkan: Clear water with moon reflected in it. Moon is paired with Sun and likened to the *āmbhasī dhāraṇā*, the concentration on water. Then focus on the perception of ice and think of lapis lazuli without diverting one's attention.

iii. Hojikan: Contemplate on the earth that supports seven jeweled banner. This is the magnificent jewelled realm of the Western Paradise.

iv. Hojukan: Contemplation on trees of paradise.

v. Hochikan: Contemplation on fifty billion multi storied jewelled towers with heavenly musicians.

vi. Horokan: Contemplation on lakes full of lotus flowers.

vii. Kezakan: Contemplation on jewelled lotus throne of Amitābha.

viii. Gyozokan: Contemplation on Amitābha trinity.

ix. Shinshinkan: Contemplation on Amitābha in *sambhoga-kāya*, corporeal body of Amitabha.

x. Kannonkan: Contemplation on Avalokiteśvara.

xi. Seishikan: Contemplation on Mahāsthāmaprāpta.

xii. Fukan: Contemplation on imagine oneself as born in the paradise'.

xiii. Jassokan: Intermingling of great and the small body.

xiv. Vision of the highest birth.

xv. Vision of the middle birth.

xvi. Vision of the lower birth.

Court of the general meditation, sanzengi

The lower horizontal court deals with the remaining three contemplations divided into nine stages that correspond to the nine possible degrees of birth in the Paradise. The fortunate beings are guided to the Pure Land after death by a welcoming procession, Raigō (Okazaki 1977: 46-50). In Amitāyurdhyāna-sūtra those who attain birth in the Pure Land are classified into nine levels according to their innate capacities. Eight of them are painted in the lower part of the lake, symbolizing *āmbhasī dhāraṇā*, while the ninth is painted at the centre in front of Amitābha.

Central Sanctum: Court of the central doctrine, gengibun

Central Sanctum is the vision of Queen Vaidehī, when she is in trance. For an analytical and graphic description of the Central Sanctum, a visual representation of Sukhāvatī with the Queen and the King in right and left axis can be divided into the following constituents:

- five types of *dhāraṇā*
- seven levels of palaces of Amitābha on right and left with both the sides as reflexes of the same
- Amitābha with Avalokiteśvara and Mahāsthāmaprāpta, each accompanied by sixteen other Bodhisattvas
- Upper space filled by musical instruments, birds, flying goddesses and Buddhas

Sukhāvatī, The Paradise of Amitābha

Sukhāvatī (Ch. Chi-le, Jap. Gokuraku) is the Land of Perfect Bliss. Amitābha-sūtra (A-mi-t'o ching) describes it to be in the west, ten trillion Buddha lands away from the earth. There is no suffering in Sukhāvatī. Amitāyurdhyāna-sūtra calls it a land of peace and rest (*an-yang*) and the land of "peace and comfort" (*an-le*). Its details are given in all the sūtras of Jōdo sect. According to Fujita Kotatsu all the versions of Sukhāvatīvyūha-sūtra agree with the following descriptions:

1. Pure Land is in the west;
2. The three paths of evil do not exist there;
3. Although there are no sun, moon and stars, there is no darkness there;
4. There is no mountain at the centre of the universe and no sea;
5. There are numerous water sources such as rivers, lakes and ponds;
6. Seven kinds of precious stones and metals hang from trees;
7. A gentle wind produces a pleasant sound;
8. The wind bears wonderful fragrance of flowers;
9. There is no difference between humans and gods of the highest heavens;
10. Everything that one wishes is immediately present;
11. Precious stones and metals adorn the highest of heavens;
12. There are no seasons, no heat and no cold;
13. There are many places of retreat and study;
14. There are no women there, since all women become men upon entering the Pure Land;
15. Human beings in the Pure Land receive nourishment immediately upon feeling a desire of it;
16. There is no word which implies wrong there;
17. There are rows of Tara trees, nets of god and large lotuses;
18. There is one central Bodhi tree;
19. A river is flowing with perfumed waters, decorated with many lotus flowers, streaming over a series of waterfalls, whose sound carries the teachings of the Buddha;

20. There is no need to gather any food;
21. There are many kinds of perfumes, hair ornaments, clothing, umbrellas, decorative flags, musical instruments and decorative objects;
22. Pure Land is full of wealth, many gods and human beings;
23. There are no forests, gardens and ponds, the voices of the birds carry the teachings of the Buddha and people there can move through air;
24. A heavenly rain containing flowers and jewels falls, bearing with it the sounds of heavenly instruments (Senchakushū 1998:205-6).

Contemplation on the Five Elements in the Central Sanctum

Vaidehī concentrates on the five elements in the Central Sanctum. According to Patañjali, once the mind has been fixed on some point by means of Dhāraṇā, the *yogī* must strive until only a single content is held in his mind: *deśabandhaścittasya dhāraṇā*. This can be either a single representation or idea or a single experience, while he rejects any intruding alien idea or experience or moreover brings to a focus, this single and only content on the point selected in the *dhāraṇā* (Fernando 1987: 145). The five *dhāraṇās* lead to bodily firmness and in addition, each *dhāraṇā* is said to yield certain paranormal powers, *siddhi* (Feurstein 1997:210). Five kinds of *dhāraṇā* are in ascending order like the five *mahābhūtas* of which the material world is composed.

1. Pārthivī-dhāraṇā is meant to be invulnerable. Earth, the lowermost level of the world, is said to be made up of lapis lazuli, which is of blue color; blue is the colour of meditation. Enjoyments on earth are represented by a scene of music and dance. Eight young boys are playing musical instruments at the center, eight goddesses of music are sitting on both the sides of the dance enclosure, four on one side and two dancers are performing a dance. A pair of birds is bringing the words of Lord Buddha to the land of amusement. Two peacocks in the foreground are on the both sides of the dance enclosure, represented as ride of Amitābha, as mentioned in Niṣpannayogāvalī (19.16, p.45): *paścimāyām mayūropari viśvasarojasya varaṭake 'mitābho vajraparyankī raktaḥ,* red colour Amitābha sits in the vajra posture on the seed of the *viśva* lotus, upon a peacock in the west.

   According to Sādhanamālā (p.45, n. 28) also he rides a peacock: *paścimakoṣṭhasya-madhye mayūropari Amitābha ekamukha Vairocanāvatāra rakta-varṇa bhujābhyām hṛdaye dharma-cakra-mudrām.* Single faced Amitābha, a manifestation of Vairocana, of red colour, sits upon a peacock at the centre of the western enclosure and performs the gesture of turning the wheel of the law, by both his hands at the heart level.

2. Āmbhasī-dhāraṇā is for setting a foot on water without sinking. Above the Pārthivī dhāraṇā is Āmbhasī-dhāraṇā represented by a scene of a lake or a lotus pond. Eight degrees of people, reborn in the Western Paradise are sitting on lotus seats; newly born in the paradise look like infants on half blown lotuses. On both the sides are two dragon boats carrying Amitābha triad. Behind them are seven boys on each side, swimming and playing in water

or sitting on lotuses. A pair of birds is flying, bringing the teachings of the Buddha to the sphere of water. In this sphere also the King and the Queen are sitting with folded hands.

3. Āgneyī/Taijasī-dhāraṇā is practiced to be devoid of suffering from the heat of the Sun and fire. It is represented by Sun at the top of the maṇḍala. In the present context it is the final *dhāraṇā* as Sun is the gateway to Sukhāvatī. When Vaidehī reaches this level she gets a vision of the paradise, encompassing all its architectonic elements like trees, towers, palaces and lakes etc. or it can be taken as the first *dhāraṇā* as Amitābha emanates from a solar cult; as the Transcendental Sun.

4. Vāyavī-dhāraṇā leads to listening to the words of wisdom. According to the description of Sukhāvatī given in Amitābha and Sukhāvatī-vyūha-sūtras, words of wisdom are brought by birds. Two pairs of birds are painted above the palaces of Sukhāvatī and the King and the Queen are themselves visualised as birds flying towards the topmost palace of Amitābha. Birds are important in the Zen paintings, often coming as pairs. Maudgalyāyana and Shāriputra are also painted as birds.

5. Ākāśī-dhāraṇā is practiced to acquire power to see what is distant, to hear the distant and to Āmbhasī-dhāraṇā, be teleactive (San-hyang Kamahāyānikan 12b, 13a,b, 14a, Lokesh Chandra 1997:V.29-30). Musical instruments are floating in sky producing *anāhata nāda* representing ākāśī dhāraṇā. So long as the sounds continue, there is the idea of *Ākāśa: tāvadākāśa saṅkalpo yāvacchabdaḥ pravartate* (Haṭhayoga-pradīpikā 100). Whatever is heard in the form of nada, is power. *Nāda* is the final stage of the tattvas, that which is formless is parameśvara:

   Yatkiñcinnādarūpeṇa śrūyate śaktireva sa ।
   Yattattvanto nirākāraḥ sa eva parameśvaraḥ ।।101।।

Nāda is the inner sound (*śabda* or *dhvani*) that becomes audible when the network of psychoenergetic currents (*nāḍī*) has been duly purified. According to the Yogaśikha-upaniṣad (3.3) it is the second level of manifestation of the absolute as sound, *śabda brahman* (Feurstein 1997:192). Vaidehī listens to the *anāhata nāda* produced by the divine musical instruments floating in air, in the sky. It also helps her to concentrate her mind. When one perceives the sound of *anāhata nāda*, the unbeaten sound the knowable, (Amitābha) interpenetrates the sound which is heard, and the mind interpenetrates the knowable. The mind becomes absorbed there, which is the seat of the all pervading, Almighty Lord:

Anāhatasya nādasya dhvanirya upalabhyate ।
Dhvanerantargatam jñeyam jñeyayantargatam manaḥ ।।
Manas tatra layam yāti tadviṣṇoḥ paramam padam ।। *Haṭhayoga-pradīpikā 99*।।

According to Haṭha-yoga-pradīpikā the mind is like a serpent, forgetting all its unsteadiness by hearing the *nāda*, it does not run away anywhere:

Nāda-śravaṇataḥ kṣipramantaraṅga bhujaṅgamaḥ ।
Vismṛtya sarvamekāgraḥ kutracinna dhāvati ।।96।।

Antaḥkaraṇa, mind/heart, like a deer, becomes absorbed and motionless on hearing the sound of bells etc. and then it is very easy for an expert archer to kill it:

Sadyaḥ pratyaya-sandhāyī jāyate nādajo layaḥ || 79||

The *laya* produced by *nāda*, sound, at once gives experience of spiritual powers. The musical instruments floating in the sky can be divided in to three on the basis of sounds produced by them as described in Yogaśikha-upaniṣad:

Ādau jaladhi jīmūta bheri-jharjhara-sambhavaḥ |
Madhye mardala-śaṅkhottha ghaṇṭākāhalajāstathā ||84||

At the first stage the sounds are surging and thundering like the beating of kettle drums and jingling ones. At the intermediate stage they are like those produced by conch, *mṛdaṅga* and bells etc.

Ante tu kinkiṇī vaṅśa-vīṇā-bhramara-niḥsvanaḥ ||85||

At the last stage the sounds resemble those produced from the tinklets, flute, *vīṇā*, bee etc.

Unbeaten sound (*Anāhata nāda*)

Sound is produced by the contact of two objects, or say the hand and the drum in case of an unlettered sound. Instruments floating in air in the maṇḍala are producing *anāhata nāda,* as they are not beaten.

Representation of *Rūpa-dharma* and *Citta-dharma* in the Central Sanctum

In the mystic school, the doctrine of six elements: earth, water, fire, air, ether and clear consciousness, is an important tenet. The first five elements are *rūpa-dharma* and the sixth is *citta-dharma*. They blend together producing Buddhas and all the living beings and there is no difference between them. From the highest point of view, form and mind are one and the same, this is the doctrine of Byōdō. According to Byōdō the five elements are identical with the five kinds of wisdom represented by *vijñāna* (Visser 1931: 15). After listening to the teachings of the Buddha, crossing sixteen levels of meditation and looking at Amitābha in the outer right and lower courts, Queen Vaidehī fixes her mind on a point for going into fourfold trance: *dhyāna*, *nāda*, *rasānanda* and *laya* as described in Gheraṇḍa-saṁhitā (7): *bindu brhmamayam dṛṣṭvā manastatra niyojayet*. Nothing obstructs when one realises *ātman* as full of space, *kha*, a man enters a state of perpetual bliss and then he reaches the level of samādhi:

Ātmānam khamayam dṛṣṭvā na kiñcidapi budhyate|
Sadānandamayo bhūtva samadhistho bhavennaraḥ||8||

In the Central Sanctum of the Taima-maṇḍala on crossing the five levels of concentration on the five elements, Vaidehī reaches the state of samādhi and visualises herself and her husband to be present at various levels of palaces in Sukhāvatī. There, they are represented as Bodhisattvas, as enumerated in some versions of the Taima-maṇḍala.

Dhyāna-yoga is followed by *ṇāda-yoga* and *rasānanda-yoga-samādhi* as described by the text. When he performs *rasānanda-yoga-samādhi* a buzzing sound like that of a beetle rises: *bhṛṅga-nādam tato bhavet* ||10|| Then *manas*, mind is carried and placed at the center of this sound and he will have the knowledge of *so'ham*, He is me or I am He:

> *Antastham bhramarī nādam śrūtvā tatra mano nayet* |
> *Samādhirjāyate tatra cānandaḥ so'hamityataḥ* ||

Vaidehī visuslises herself in the Paradise. Now she is fit to imagine that she is the *śakti: svayam śaktimayo bhavet* ||12|| Being full of bliss there is the stage of becoming on with Brahma, she thinks that she is herself the Almighty, (Amitābha) she attains the samādhi, as said in the Gheraṇḍa-saṁhitā:

> *Ānandamayaḥ sambhūtva aikyam brahmaṇi sambhavet* |
> *Aham brahmeti cādvaitasamādhistena jāyate* ||13||

Vaidehī transcends from the *rūpadhatu* to the *arūpadhatu*, from the world of beings to the world of imagination and realization, which is the final goal.

Seven Levels of Architectonic Elements

1. Eight Great Bodhisattvas with Amitābha on both the sides of the court of dancers and musicians should be Vajrapāṇi, Avalokiteśvara, Ākāśagarbha, Samantabhadra, Maitreya, Mañjuśrī, Sarvanīvaraṇa-viśkambhī and Kṣitigarbha, as painted in a scroll kept at Kanchi-in, Tōji monastery (TZ 106.1-8). All the Bodhisattvas are doing various mudrās. Amitābha is standing on a huge lotus revered by the King and the Queen kneeling in front of him. Two tiny figures in the left corner are devotees, bringing offerings. Another figure walking to the court of Amitābha is also the king with a plate, full of gems. The same arrangement is seen on the right side of the panel.
2. Above the first court is the second court, here Amitābha is sitting with six figures, five of them are doing various mudrās but one is kneeling with folded hands. This should be the King while on the opposite side, there is the Queen, bringing offerings.
3. Above the second is the third court, represented by a double story building. The King is walking up the stairs and then he sits in front of Amitābha with folded hands inside the hall, where Amitābha is sitting with six Bodhisattvas. Two musicians are playing music on the upper story. The same court is painted on the opposite side but there the Queen is bringing offerings.
4. Above the third is another court, again with Amitābha and six Bodhisattvas and the King on the left and the Queen on the right side. This also looks like a double story structure, three Bodhisattvas are standing in front of it on both the sides, while Amitābha is on the upper storey.
5. Another double storey structure can be seen above the fourth, therein monks are represented with shaven heads and without halos. A flying angel is painted coming down. Amitābha with the King and the Queen are there on both the sides.

6. The sixth building is painted to the inner side symbolizing a higher stage of meditation. Therein Amitābha stands with four Bodhisattvas.
7. The lower floor of the sixth structure leads to a corridor in which figures are shown walking towards the center. Finally at the center is Amitābha, attended by Avalokiteśvara to the right and Mahāsthāmaprāpta to the left. Both of them are attended by sixteen Bodhisattvas each. Two structures emerge out of the *brahmarandhras,* crevices of Avalokiteśvara and Mahāsthāmaprāpta, painted beyond the lower levels.

Amitābha, the focal point of the maṇḍala is sitting cross-legged on a huge lotus seat, the King and the Queen are praying in front, below them is the representation of the ninth degree of birth in his Paradise. They are standing, having a vision of themselves as reborn there, sitting on lotus seats. Five gem trees, *ratna vṛkṣas* are painted on the right and the left at the back of the throne of Amitābha. A large number of buildings are painted at different levels forming a tower-like structure on the both the sides of the Paradise; they are topped by jewels like *cintāmani* encircled by halos or flames.

Most Probably they are gems that appear from the *brahmarandhra,* crevice of Amitābha, beyond that is Amitābha in a more subtle form, attended by the King and the Queen sitting with the two Bodhisattvas inside his palace flanked by two more on both the sides. Beyond that is the final stage. The King and the Queen are flying up disguised as birds. The figures remind of *pakṣi hi bhūtvati divaḥ sameti* (AV 4.34.4d) and *dvā suparṇā sayujā sakhāyā* (RV 1.164.20c, AV 9.9.20a, Mund. U.3.1.1a, N 14.30a). Poet Kabir in one of his hymns compares *prāṇa* or soul with a bird and body with a cage: *prāṇa pakheru uḍa gaye.....*

Beyond this scene are Buddhas and Bodhisattvas flying down from the heaven from all the directions. In between are birds and musical instruments floating in air in the sky. Some flying goddesses are also painted. In all they should have been twenty-five as painted in Raigō scenes.

Flying deities as 25 Bodhisattvas in the Raigō

1.	BS Avalokiteśvara	lotus throne	bears to paradise
2.	BS Mahāsthāmaprāpta	prayer	non duality of wisdom and mental concentration
3.	BS Samantabhadra	banner	points out the path to perpetually obedient humanity
4.	BS Yakuō	banner	waves the massage of agelessness and deathlessness
5.	BS Yakujō	jade flag	indicates the ranks of rebirth in distant land
6.	BS Hōjizai	flower garland	expresses the meritorious power of Amitābha's infallible salvation
7.	BS Shishiku	boisterous cavorting	taps out edification, reaching downward for unenlightened folk
8.	BS Darani	swaying sleeves	exhorts to seek upward for spiritual awakening

9.	BS Ākāśagarbha	hip drum	sounds aloud the power to fulfill merit and wisdom
10.	BS Tokuzō	reed pipe	reverberates with eighteen excellences of Budhas
11.	BS Hōzō	flute	blows cool breeze of the three gates to enlightenment
12.	BS Konzō	lyre	manifests thirty seven deities
13.	Kongōzō	lyre	resounds with the oneness of the ten worlds
14.	BS Kōmyōō	lute	lightens perplexity of oppressive knowledge
15.	BS Sankai-e	harp	teaches principal of quiescence and absolute reality
16.	BS Kegon-ō	instrument	fills up the whole universe as object of mind
17.	BS Shuhō-ō	gong	extols the one Buddha vehicle
18.	BS Gakkō-ō	swaying drum	causes the world of ten quarters to reverberate
19.	BS Nisshō-ō	hand drum	extols the four realms embraced in eternally tranquil light
20.	BS Sammami-ō	scattering flowers	dispersed in the realms of empty space and sea
21.	BS Jōjizai-ō	large drum	sounds like a great assembly of non discrimination
22.	BS Daijizai-ō	flower banner	soars up towards absolute non-duality
23.	BS Hakuzō-ō	jeweled flag	flutters in the heaven of Ultimate Truth
24.	Daitoku-ō	jewel	imbued with the teachings free of any taint of illusion
25.	BS Muhenshin	incense	offers to Amitābha

(Okazaki 1977:114-5)

The twenty-five Bodhisattvas mentioned above can be categorised as follows :

No. 1, 2	-	Two Mahasattva Bodhisattvas
No. 3, 4, 5, 22, 23	-	Five pennant bearers
No. 9-19, 21	-	Twelve deities of music
No. 6, 8, 20, 24, 25	-	Five deities of worship
No. 7	-	?

Buddhas in the Upper Portion

Many Buddhas flying down from various directions appear before the practitioner on attaining the state of samādhi, therefore seeing a Buddha came to be regarded as a sign of attaining samādhi, according to the Samādhi-sūtra (Ch. Pan-chou san-mei ching). Shan-tao wrote in his commentary that he could visualize Amitābha and his Paradise according to the method expounded in the Amitāyurdhyāna-sūtra (Senchakushū 1998:199). In the Taima-maṇḍala, the Queen finally had a vision of the Buddhas and Bodhisattvas flying down from all the directions and that is the final stage of meditation. Souls of the King and the Queen are received by the myriads of Buddhas and they become one with them. This is the aim of practicing yoga and entering samādhi which eliminates mental suffering. It gave way to creation of magnificent maṇḍalas representing the paradise of Amitābha, in East and Far Far Asia.

Appendix

Some important dates in the history of Pure Land tradition

383-442/424-442	Amitāyurdhyāna-sūtra translated by Kālayaśas (K191)
613-681	Commentary by Shan-tao (Fu shou kwan-wu-liang-shou-fo ching su)
7th-8th century	Chikō-maṇḍala
753-781	Maṇḍala made by the Princess Chūjō Hime
763	Taima-maṇḍala at the Taima-dera
9th-10th century	Paintings of Taima-maṇḍala at Tun-huang
1046-1053	Shōkai/Seikai-maṇḍala preserved at Chushōji, Gokurakuji
1048-1116	Commentary on Amitāyurdhyāna-sūtra by Yüan-tao Ta-chi
1167-8	Taima-maṇḍala brought from China by Jūgen
13th century	Painting based on Yuan-tao Ta-chi's commentary on Amitāyurdhyāna-sūtra, Amida-dera
13th century	Same as above, Chokoji
1501-3	Replica of Taima-maṇḍala, Taima-dera (Fukuyama 1976: 140)

LITERATURE CITED

Fernando 1978

Fernando Tola, Carmen Dragonetti, translated by K.D.Prithipaul, *The Yoga Sūtra of Patañjali,* New Delhi 1978

Feurstein 1976

Feurstein George, *The Shambhala Encyclopaedia of Yoga,* New Delhi, 1997

Fukuyama 1987

Fukuyama, Toshio, *Heian Temples: Byōdōin and Chusonji,* Weatherhill and Heibonsha, 1976

Sris Chandra Vasu, *Gheraṇḍa-saṁhitā,* Adyar, 1933

Pancham Sinh, *Haṭhayoga-pradīpikā,* Pāṇini Office, Allahbad 1932

Halen 1987

Harry Halen, *Mirrors of the Void, Buddhist Art in the National Museum of Finland,* Museovirasato, Helsinki 1987

Lokesh Chandra 1998

Lokesh Chandra, *Cultural Horizons of India,* Vol. 7, Aditya Prakashan, New Delhi, 1998

Lokesh Chandra 1999

Dictionary of Buddhist Art, Vol. 1, Aditya Prakashan, New Delhi, 1989

Kidder 1964

Kidder, J. Edward, *Japanese Temples,* London, 1964

Yoshiaki 1969

Kudo Yoshiaki and Nishikawa Shinji, *Amitabha Halls and Fujiwara Sculptures,* Genshoku Nippon no Bijutsu No. 6, Tokyo, 1969

MaxMüller 1964

MaxMüller, F, *Sacred Books of the East,* Buddhist Mahayana Texts, No. 49, Delhi, 1964

Tachikawa 1989

Musashi Tachikawa, *bSod names rgya mtsho: The Ṅgor Maṇḍalas of Tibet,* The Center for East Asian Cultural Studies, Tokyo, 1989

Niṣpannayogāvalī, ed. Benoytosh Bhattacharya, Baroda, 1949

Okazaki 1977

Okazaki Jōji, *Pure Land Buddhist Painting,* Tokyo, 1977

Ram Kumar 1975

Rai, Ram Kumar, *Encyclopaedia of Yoga,* Varanasi, 1975

Richard 1967

Richard King, *Indian Philosophy, An Introduction to Hindu and Buddhist Thought,* New Delhi, 1999

Rosenfield 1967

San hyann Kamahāyānikan

San hyann Kamahāyānikan, Lokesh Chandra, *Cultural Horizons of India,* vol. V, Aditya Prakashan, New Delhi, 1997.

Senchakushu 1998

Senchakushu Honen's, *Passages on the Selection of Nembutsu in the Original Vow,* Kuroda Institute, Tokyo 1998

Takakusu 1956

Takakusu Junjiro, *The Essentials of Buddhist Philosophy,* Asia Publishing House, New Delhi, 1956

Visser 1931

Visser, M.W.De, *The Bodhisattva Akasagarbha (Kokuzo) in China and Japan,* Verhandelingam der koninklijke academic van Wetenschappen te Amsterdam Afdeeling Letterkunde, Neeuwe Reeks, Deel XXX No. 1, 1931

Waley 1931

Waley Arthur, *A Catalogue of Paintings Recovered from Dun-huang by Sir Aurel Stein,* London, 1931

4

BODHISATTVAS OF DEBATE AND DEFENCE

Defeating opponents in religio-philosophical debate was a fashion in ancient India. According to the Indian custom when a new scholar was installed, debate was held among the scholars of various schools of philosophical systems. The Buddha's teachings lie in the harmonious combination of the intellect and emotion, of theory and practice, of head and heart. In Buddhist literature, it is expressed in the Śrīmālāsiṁhanāda-sūtra. The martial aspects of Mithra became 'vanquishing the opponents through debate'. He was the protector of the empire and bore the title of *Sol invictus*. 'Invincible Mithra' became Ajita or *invictus* aspect of Maitreya. Debate was a powerful weapon to humble and humiliate, destruct and defeat heretics to win them over to Buddhism. Asaṅga gives the rules of debate in Śrāvaka-bhūmi chapter of the Yogāchāra-bhūmi. A section is devoted to *hetu-vidyā* or the science of reasoning which gives rules of debate (Lokesh Chandra 1997:11).

Skillful means or *upāya-kauśalya*, paired with wisdom or *prajñā* made Buddhism one of the world's most successful religion. This also included vanquishing of heretics through *upāya-kauśalya* and self assertion to tempt people into the true Dharma. Vanquishing the heretics is symbolized by the miracle at Śrāvastī that became a cornerstone of the propagation of Buddhism. It was one of the two poles of Buddhist praxis-*prajñā* or wisdom and *upāya/upāyakauśalya* or skillful means. *Upāyakauśalya* has been a fundamental principle in Mahayana. It is self-assertion and a form of teaching set up to tempt people into the true Dharma. In Bodhicaryāvatāra (7.55) Śāntideva says:

Mayā hi sarvam jetavyam	All is to be conquered by me,
Aham jeyo na kena chit।	I am not to be conquered by anyone.
Mayaiṣa māno voḍhavyo	This is the honor which I shall bear,
Jina-siṁha suto hyahaṁ॥	For I am a son of Conqueror-Lion.

Such passages in Buddhist literature represent aspirations of a sovereign, and expansion of Buddhism that began with emperor Aśoka, a conqueror turned devout, a hero of war turned a messenger of peace. He was on an aggressive path to spread the teachings of Lord Buddha when he built 84,000 *dharmarājika stūpas* in a single day. He summoned the Yakṣas, sent them back with 84,000 holy relics and silk roles. 84,000 *stūpas* were erected in an instant, as told by Aśokāvadāna (p.55) *ṣekasmin divase ekemuhūrtte caturaṣīti dharmarājika-sahasam pratisṭhāpitam*. In other words by the Imperial order of Aśoka all the stūpas dedicated to Yakṣa worship were henceforth Buddhist caityas. Thus Buddhism was on a path of wide acclamation.

When Naropa (1016-1100) went to Nālandā, an announcement was made that a debate will be held in a fortnight. In the middle of the court of the University of Nālandā, a throne was erected for the king, to preside over. Hindu and Buddhist scholars were seated to his right and left. A debate went on with Buddhists for half a month and then with the Hindus for a fortnight. Finally, he had a complete victory over all the opponents. Aggressiveness is evident from the episode. Naropa defeated the heretics in a public place, before assuming the charge of Nālandā. He expressed his feelings in the verses that he composed in the following manner, through:

(i) Iron hook of grammar, logic and spiritual precepts → scattered opponents
(ii) Axe of grammar, logic and spiritual precepts → felled opponents' tree
(iii) Lamp of certainty of logic and precepts → burnt darkncss of ignorance of foes
(iv) Razor of Buddha's doctrine → felled trembling trees of heretics
(v) Raised the banner of Buddha's doctrine

At that time a hundred learned Hindu teachers shaved their heads, converted to Buddhism, and were soon followed by another six hundred. The inmates of the Nālandā University hoisted the great banner, beat the big drum, blew the conch of the Dharma and were full of joy and happiness. The King Digvarman bowed many times and said, ṢI am happy to be your patron¿ (Lokesh Chandra, 1997:122-3).

Worship of Bodhisattvas became fashionable which required their iconographical representations. The need has been more than fulfilled by the creation of a large variety of Bodhisattva images specially in those countries that accepted Buddhism in its Mahayana form. Buddhist art became richer through these artistic creations. In the subsequent phases of the Bodhisattva cult the deified personages were given many forms in order to symbolize their multifarious functions. Sometimes they were given many heads and many arms. The practice has sometimes led to the creation of such complex figures as exemplified by the Thousand-armed Avalokiteśvara in Japan.

Bodhisattvas of Polemics (*śāstrārtha, upāyakauśalya*, debate) in the Vajradhātu-maṇḍala

Sixteen Bodhisattvas of the Vajradhātu-maṇḍala are:

S.No.	Bodhisattvas	Attributes	Manifestations	Essence
1.	Samantabhadra	vajra	Vajrasattva	Stg.Samantabhadra
2.	Amogharāja	aṅkuśa	Vajrarāja	Amogharāja
3.	Māra	śara	Vajrarāga	Māra
4.	Pramodyanāyaka	tuṣṭi	Vajrasādhu	Prāmodyarāja
5.	Khagarbha	ratna	Vajraratna	Ākāśagarbha
6.	Sumahāteja	sūrya	Vajrateja	Mahāteja

7.	Ratnaketu	dhvaja	Vajraketu	Ratnaketu
8.	Mahāsmita	smita	Vajrahāsa	Nityaprītipramuditendriya
9.	Avalokitamaheśa	padma	Vajradharma	Avalokiteśvara
10.	Mañjuśrī	koṣa	Vajratīkṣṇa	Mañjuśrī
11.	Sarvamaṇḍala	sucakra	Vajrahetu	Sahacittotpādasaddharma
12.	Avāca	vāk	Vajrabhāṣa	Avāca
13.	Viśvakarmā	karma	Vajrakarma	Stg.Viśvakarmā
14.	Vīrya	varma	Vajrarakṣa	Duryodhanavīrya
15.	Caṇḍa	khaya	Vajrayakṣa	Sarvamārapramardī
16.	Dṛḍhagraha	graha	Vajrasandhi	Stg.Muṣṭi

In the Vajradhātumaṇḍala, 16 Great Bodhisattvas attend the four Buddhas in the central section. They embody sixteen stages of development that a Bodhisattva passes through after he attains awakening. The sixteen stages are equated with ten *bhūmis*. These are the stages in an ascent to the perfected Buddhahood of Vairocana, but they are also in the descent of Vairocana to aid and benefit all beings.

The Bodhisattvas embody the stages in progress from the *bodhicitta* through practice of awakening and entry into *nirvāṇa*. The stages begin with the four bodhisattvas who attend Akṣ obhya, who is *bodhicitta*. They are:

1. Vajrasattva

The first stage at which the *sādhaka* aquires the excellent knowledge that perceives that self and others are not distinct but merge in identity. This is the base for the development of the virtue of 'benefit for others', the aim and the culmination of the sixteen stages. The five-pronged vajra in his right hand symbolizes his possession of the five Buddha knowledges and the vajra bell the sound of the Dharma, the cause of the first quickening of the *bodhicitta*.

2. Vajrarāja

Vajrarāja symbolises the realization of *bodhicitta*, the attainment of kingship over the passions. Vajrarāja is the method of *bodhicitta* that acts to embrace and draws in beings. He holds both his hands as diamond fists crossing over the chest. The diamond fist signifies the diamond thunderbolt, which strikes and destroys hindrances to awakening.

3. Vajrarāga

Vajrarāga personifies love for all beings, characterized by selflessness, impartiality and renunciation. Vajrarāga is the third stage in which spiritual love functions to liberate and nurture all beings, the beginning of actions of benefit for others (*rita*). Vajrarāga holds an arrow of Great Compassion that pierces the passions in the hearts of beings.

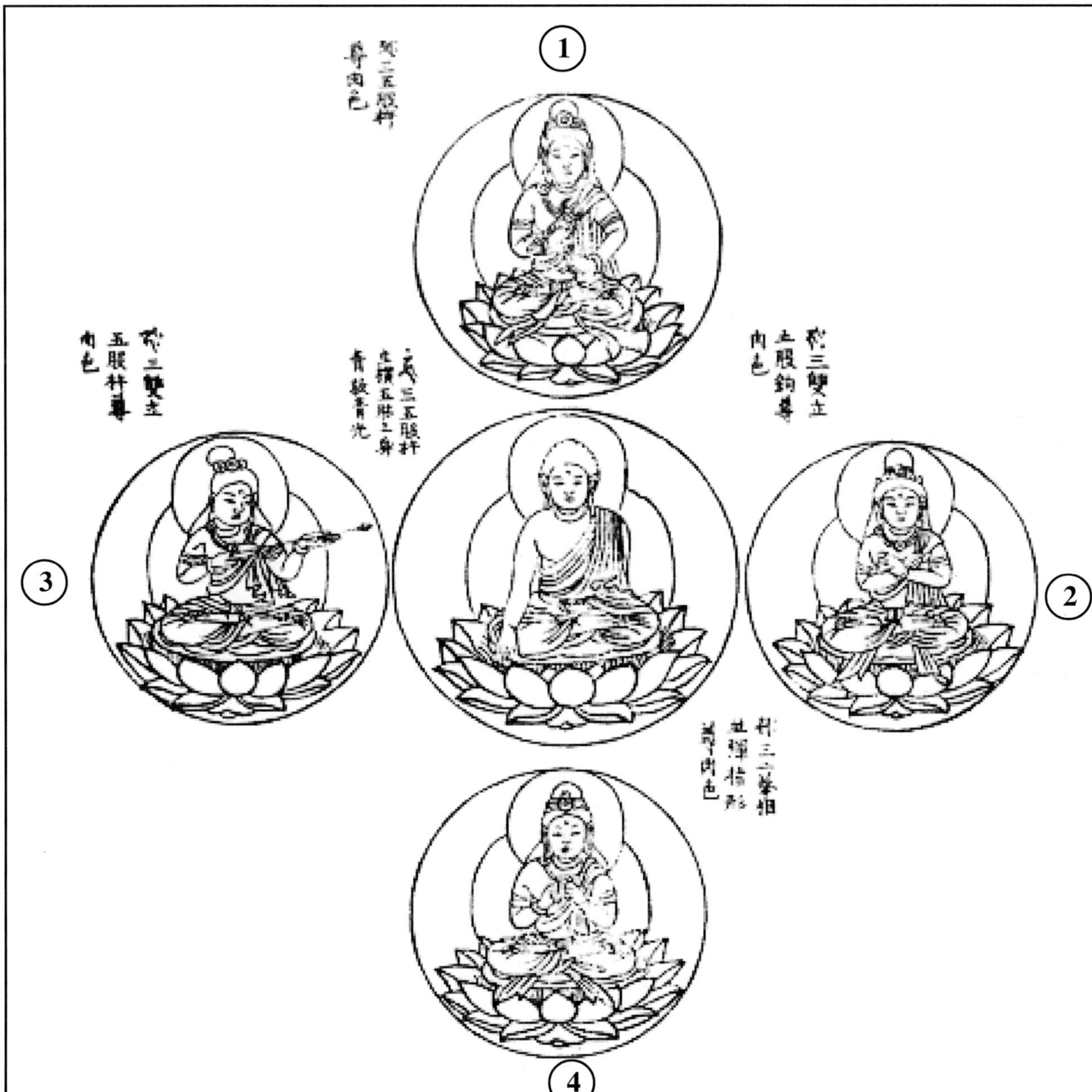
1
2
3
4

4. Vajrasādhu

Vajrasādhu is the joy that arises from the *bodhicitta*. It is the joy that is produced by love at the third stage and is bestowed on all beings by the Bodhisattva. He holds his fists in the gesture of snapping the fingers, which rouses the Bodhisattva from meditation and surprises the *sādhaka* into awakening.

Around Ratnasambhava

Ratnasambhava is the anthropomorphic equivalent of the wish-granting jewel that gives birth to all felicities. The four Bodhisattvas surrounding Ratnasambhava are the four aspects of his virtues of practice and felicity, required as a result of perfecting the Pāramitā of Giving, Dāna-pāramitā. They are:

5. Vajraratna

He personifies wish-granting jewel, *cintāmaṇi*. He is the jewel of initiation, the virtue of Mahāvairocana that initiates innumerable beings into the way, leading to perfected Buddhahood. His virtue cannot be destroyed or damaged, it is infinite and everywhere and at all times the same. He is making the gesture of holding the jewel.

6. Vajratejas

He represents the 'great and awesome light' that shines in all the worlds of sentient beings, illuminating the darkness of ignorance and removing all fear. The light is emitted by the virtue of felicity. Since he is the source of the light of fearlessness he is called 'Diamond Light' or 'Diamond Sun' in Sino-Japanese tradition. He holds a sun disk in his right hand brought in front of his chest.

7. Vajraketu

At this stage Dāna-pāramitā is perfected. The merits of felicity and fearlessness acquired for oneself in the previous stages are now given to others. The name is an abbreviation of Vajraketuratna because a jewel tops the pennant held in his right hand. The jewel satisfies all desires and aspirations, both mundane and supra-mundane.

8. Vajrahāsa

He personifies the laugh of joy that rises when the Pāramitā of Giving is perfected and all the *dharmas* are seen to be aspects of the bliss of the Tathāgatas. Vajrahāsa holds his two fists at his ears. It could mean that he is listening to the laughter of others.

Around Amitābha

Amitābha embodies the virtue of awakening. He possesses the knowledge of subtle perception which perceives the spiritual capacities of beings so that the *dharma* may be preached to them in modes appropriate to their understanding. The four attending Bodhisattvas are aspects of awakening, which is the attainment of Right Knowledge, *samyakjñāna* and the Pāramitā of wisdom, Jñāna-pāramitā. They are:

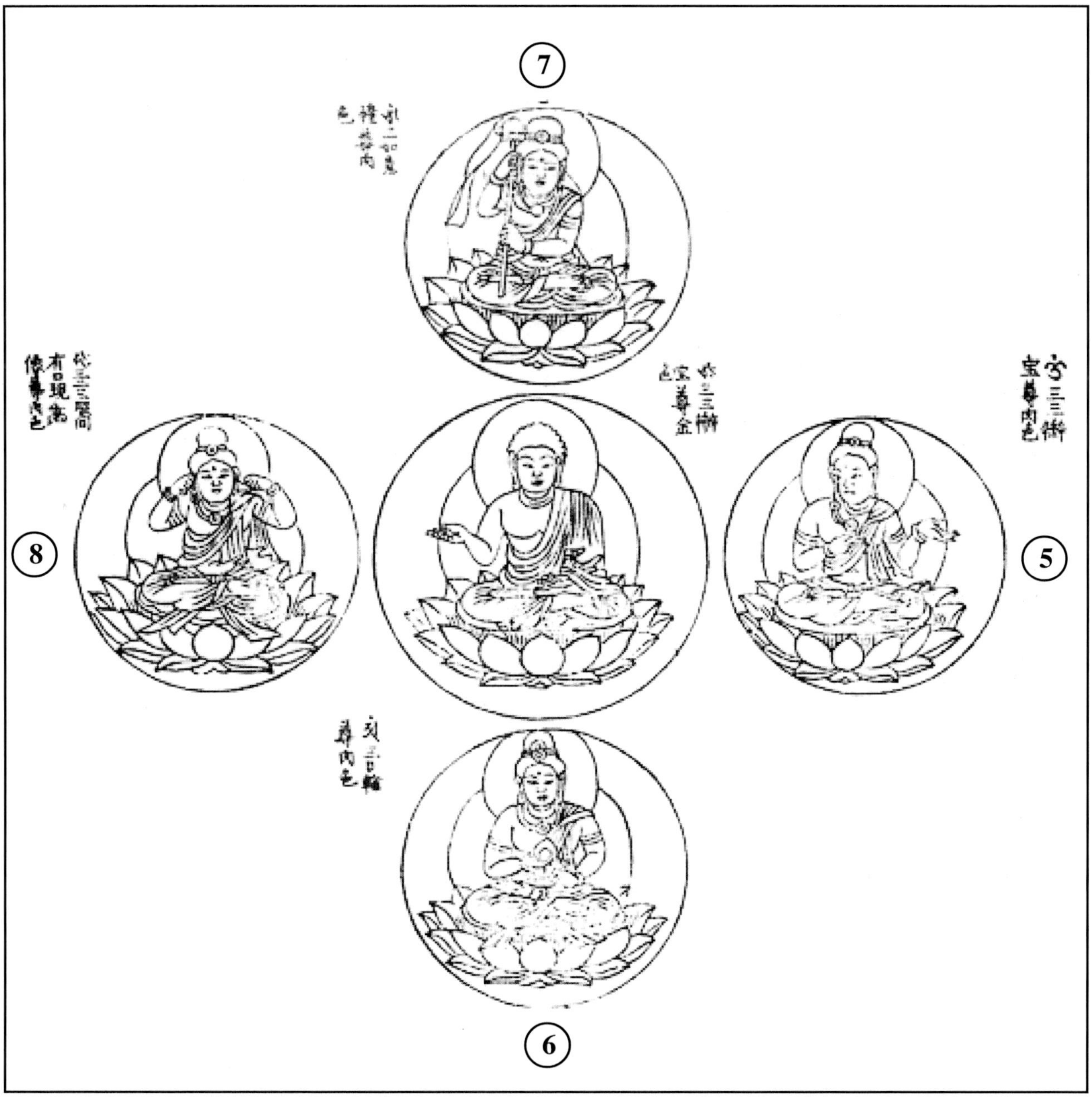
7
8
5
6

9. Vajradharma

He is the causal stage of awakening embodied in Amitābha. He personifies the attainment of wisdom, *prajñā*, that realizes the adamantine *dharma* arising from the adamantine wisdom, which sees the purity of all the *dharmas*. He holds a partially opened lotus in his righ hand and with the left he makes a gesture of opening the lotus which represents the functioning of wisdom to awaken the beings by opening the lotus-mind.

10. Vajratīkṣṇa

He embodies the wisdom that cuts away passions and their recurring influences. He gives sharp wisdom sword to the beings, which severs their bonds. He holds a wisdom sword in his right hand and a lotus supporting Prajñāpāramitā-sūtra in the left. The sūtra contains the essence of the Pāramitā of Wisdom.

11. Vajrahetu

Vajrahetu represents wisdom functioning in the preaching of *dharma* as the cause of the transformation of beings. He is identified with Maitreya who will necessarily attain awakening and turn the Wheel of the *dharma*, which is the cause of awakening others. Vajrahetu holds the wheel of the *dharma*, the wheel he turns when he preaches the *dharma* of wisdom. His left hand is closed and is held at the waist level.

12. Vajrabhāṣa

He is the Bodhisattva who reveals wisdom by preaching a subtle, esoteric and wordless doctrine which, unlike verbal teaching, is not an idle discourse. The wordless teaching of the Law reveals true form of all the *dharmas*, as seen in the meditation that gives birth to wisdom. His right hand holds Tathāgata's tongue, topped by a three pronged vajra, symbolizing his wordless preaching of the doctrine.

Vajra-dharma and Vajra-bhāṣa are the manifestations of wisdom. So they are called Prajñā-Bodhisattvas in Vajra-Śekhara-sūtra.

Around Amoghasiddhi

Amoghasiddhi embodies the virtue of entry into nirvāṇa, at this stage all the passions have been cut away and the practices of benefit for self and benefit for others have been completed. He symbolizes the completion of all rituals and actions. The four Bodhisattvas who attend Amoghasiddhi are four aspects of the virtues of entry into nirvāṇa, which is the completion of all actions, attained as a result of the perfection of the Pāramitā of Exertion, Vīrya-pāramitā. They are:

13. Vajrakarma

The term action, *karma* in his name has a two-fold meaning: it is the upwardly directed action of making offering to all the Buddhas; and it is the downwardly directed action of the Buddhas in aiding and protecting sentient beings. Since he personifies the actions that lead to liberation and bestow benefits on beings throughout the four quarters of the universe, he is called Viśvakarmā,

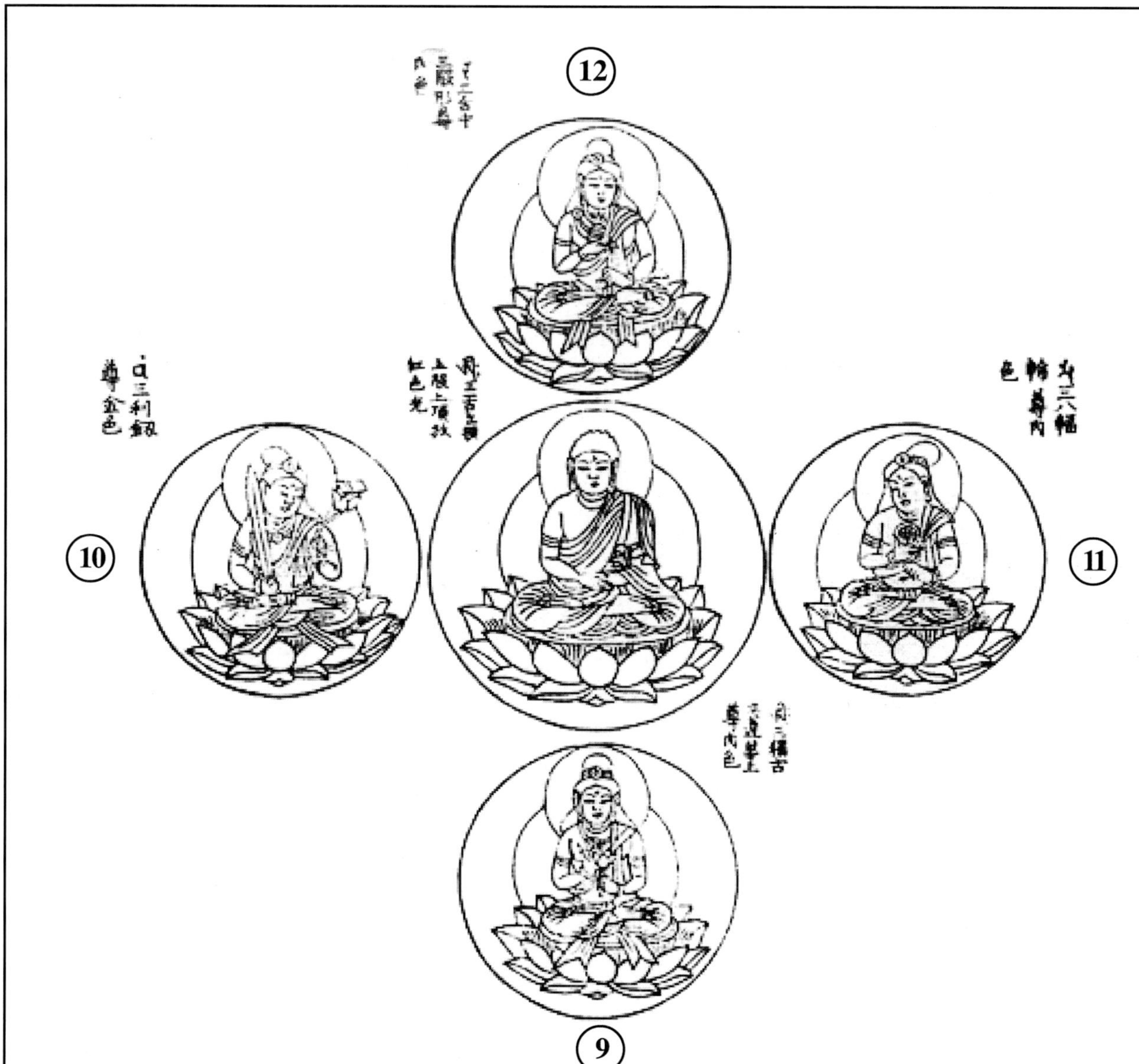
12
10
11
9

which is the name of the cross form vajra, the symbol of the action of the Buddhas spreading out to fill the extremities of the cosmos. He holds his joined hands raised above his head, a gesture that is said to represent the completion of action.

14. Vajrarakṣa

He embodies action and the Pāramitā of Exertion, Vīrya-pāramitā. He acts to protect the *sādhaka* from indolence that arises as a hindrance to the actions of making offerings to the Buddhas and of bestowing benefits on beings. He protects beings by covering them with the armor and helmet of the Great Mercy of all the Tathāgatas. His hands are in the gesture of tying the ribbons securing the helmet of Great Mercy.

15. Vajrayakṣa

The Bodhisattva resorts to expedient means, *upāya* to conquer the *sādhaka's* strong resistance to the performance of action of service. The Yakṣa is a violent and evil demon and Vajrayakṣa assumes the fearsome form of a Yakṣa to subdue the four demons and to convert and liberate beings who are difficult to influence by more specific means. Vajrayakṣa holds his two fists in front of his chest, sometimes his extended little fingers are hooked and touch the mouth, representing the upward pointing fangs of a Yakṣa.

16. Vajrasandhi

He represents completion of the sixteen stages of progress. At this final stage the *sādhaka's* three actions of body, speech and mind, merge with the three actions of the Tathagāta. He is the fist that grasps and contains the virtues of the previous fifteen stages. It is also the fist that expresses the Pāramitā of Exertion, Vīrya-pāramitā, the Bodhisattva's energetic activity in benefiting beings and bringing them to awakening. Vajrasandhi holds both hands as diamond fists in front of the heart and with the wrists slightly bent. The diamond fists here represent the attainment of Buddhahood. (for details see Snodgrass 1997:602-617)

Seven Bodhisattvas out of these sixteen, of the Vajradhātu-maṇḍala, are correlated with the system of debate developed by Asaṅga, as given below:

1. Vajrdharma	debate	(*vāda*) message of *dharma* preached in a
2. Vajratīkṣṇa	sharpness of words	sharp manner
3. Vajraketu	courtroom of the debate	establishment of *vadādhikāraṇa* in Asaṅga
4. Vajrabhāṣa	foundation of debate	*vādādhiṣṭhāna,* establishment of two kinds of theses and eight kinds of proof
5. Vajrahetu	adequacies for debate	*vādālaṅkāra*, the eight kinds of truth
6. Vajrahāsa	points of defeat in debate	*vādanigraha*, laughter after victory
7. Vajrasādhu	getting out of debate	*vādaniḥsaraṇa*, acclamation by the assembly

Defense of the state was seen as a prerequisite of the welfare of the people by many kings and emperors. They took religious steps for protection of the state and wellbeing of the people. The story of combining meditation with martial arts goes back to Amoghavajra who translated the text

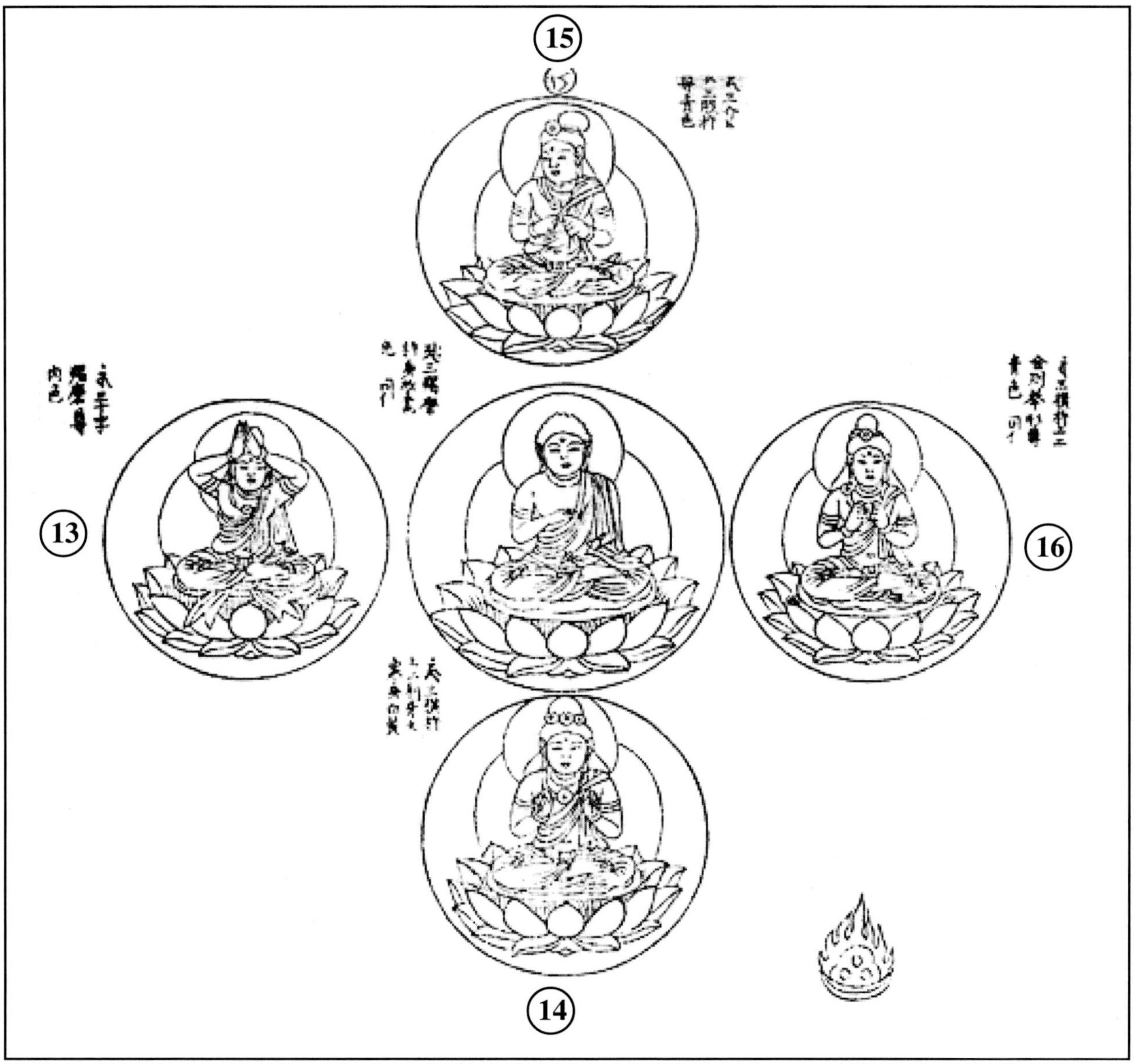
15
13
16
14

of Sarvatathāgata-tattvasaṅgraha (Shashibala 1986:26-29). His translations became popular as Kongo-cho-kyō, Vajraśekhara-sūtra. He was a prominent scholar who had introduced esoteric Buddhism into China. He seems to be familiar with the practice of movement arts and often refers to the dynamic aspects and sequences of ritual movement. It is recorded that in AD 750 he went to live in a military camp for five years and there he taught and initiated its commanders and officers into the esoteric method.

Later in AD 761 a great maṇḍala ritual was staged by Emperor Tai Tsung under Amoghavajra's guidance, as a part of the series of practices to learn more about the character and potential of those around the Emperor. It was organized in the temple, built in the Imperial palace. During the ritual, Emperor's immediate advisors took on the role of the tutelary deities, the bodyguards took the places assigned to the Vajra Bodhisattva Protectors, and all the other members of the court were also involved in the ritual. Art and skills of the Bodhisattvas around Amoghasiddhi were performed there. The whole event is an echo of the statement of the Roman poet Virgil in the Aeneid 1.405: *Vera incessa potuit deo* (the true goddess was known by her gait). From that time onwards Chüan Fa began to emphasize a dual practice of Yogācāra meditation and esoteric teachings. Thus the Buddhist principle of Vajramukti was transmitted under its Chinese title Chüan Fa. Meditation generated students who were both fine warriors and individuals.

The Four Bodhisattvas of the central section of the Vajradhātu-maṇḍala : Vajra-karma, Vajra-rakṣa, Vajra-yakṣa and Vajrasandhi, attending Amoghasiddhi are called Mahākarmasattvāḥ in the Gobushingan in place of Bodhisattvas. Others in the group are called Sarvatathāgata-mahā-samaya-sattvāḥ, -mahābhiṣeka-sattvāḥ and -mahājñāna-sattvāḥ.

They are identified as Bodhisattvas of defense by Shifu Nagaboshi Tomio (Tomio 1994: 209-218). According to him the maṇḍala illustrations express various teachings in symbolic forms. The northern quarter of the central section of the Vajradhātu-maṇḍala is related to the art of Chüan Fa because its tutelary Buddha Amoghasiddhi is the embodiment of the Buddha wisdom concerning enlightened activity and creation. It combines the physical and the spiritual value system.

Amoghasiddhi is surrounded by four Bodhisattvas, each of whom holds his arms in classical and dynamic *vajramukti* poses of both mystical expression and physical defensive readiness. These positions and gestures are described in the second part of the Vajraśekhara-sūtra. This contains ritual for initiation of disciples that includes sounds and thunderbolt dances.

The four Vajra Bodhisattvas are:

Vajra-karma	hands raised to chest, *ipponken* (dangerous bodily weapon)
Vajra-rakṣa	fists raised to heart with wrists slightly bent
Vajra-yakṣa	hands raised above head and clasped
Vajra-sandhi	hands held parallel to each other

Knowledge is power and power needs prajñā, as described in the Muṇḍakopaniṣad (3.2.4): *nāyam ātmā bala-hīnena labhyo,* this ātmā cannot be perceived by the weak and Chāndogyopaniṣad (7.8.1): *balena vai pṛthivī tiṣṭhati balenantarikṣam balen dyauḥ| balena lokstiṣṭhati balamupasveti||*

It is the power, the force that stations the earth and heaven and the inter-mediary space. The world is sustained by force which should be venerated. Awakening is self-realization, which is self-benefit. Beyond this lies the attainment of the virtue of transforming others which is benefit for others. Thus these Bodhisattvas play a philanthropic function and are identified as Bodhisattvas of debate and defence.

LITERATURE CITED

Lokesh Chandra 1997

Lokesh Chandra *Cultural Horizons of India,* vol. IV, Aditya Prakashan and International Academy of Indian Culture, New Delhi, 1997

Shashibala 1986

Shashibala, *Comaparative Iconography of the Vajradhātu-maṇḍala and the Tattva-saṅgraha,* Aditya Prakashan, New Delhi, 1986

Snodgrass 1997

Snodgrass Adrian, *The Matrix and the Diamond World Mandalas in Shingon Buddhism,* International Academy of Indian Culture and Aditya Prakashan, New Delhi, 1997

Tomio 1994

Tomio Shifu Nagaboshi, *The Bodhisattva Warrior,* Samuel Weiser, York Beach, 1994

Yamada 1981

Yamada Isshi, *Sarva-tathāgata-tattva-saṅgraha,* Śatapiṭaka Series, International Academy of Indian Culture, New Delhi, 1981

5

BUDDHIST COLOSSI IN JAPAN

Lord Kṛṣṇa manifested himself in *virāṭ rūpa*, a colossal form, as the last resort to inspire Arjuna to fight in the battlefield of Kurukṣetra during the Mahabharata war. 11th chapter of Śrīmadbhagavadgītā gives a detailed description of the soul stirring, awe inspiring magnificent and majestic form of Kṛṣṇa. Arjuna beholds and says: *Dṛṣṭvādbhutam rūpamugram tadevam lokatrayam pravyathitam mahātman*| All the three worlds are alarmed by looking at you in this form. *kecidbhītāḥ prañjalayor gaṇanti*| Some of the gods have begun to pray, being terrified. *Vīkṣante tvām vismitā-ścaiva sarve*| All of them are looking at you, stunned. Monumentality of size is reminiscent of greatness; it attracts the deepest of one's mind imperceptibly. Whatever is splendid or looks eminent, is called *virāṭ*, *viśeṣeṇa rājate iti virāṭ*.

The form of *virāṭ* described in Śaṅkaravijaya (prakaraṇa 6) says: *Ākāsá* is his head, Sun and Moon are the two eyes, directions are his ears, *anatarikṣa* is his nose, mount Meru is the backbone, three peaks are neck and arms, mountains are his back, sides and chest, oceans are his blood, creeping plants are nerves, grass is his pores, earth his belly, islands are bracelets etc. (Śabdakalpadruma 4.418).

Over the ages colossal images were made by rulers all over the world to exhibit their power, their political or religious strength and will. The colossal statue of Apollo Helios, made from the melted down weapons of defeated enemies, one of the Seven Wonders of the World, symbolized victory (Carter 1986:129). Roman empire erected colossal statues all over to impress the might of Rome. In the Buddhist world they were meant to inspire the devotee by the grand personality of Śākyamuni who was so majestic, overwhelming and strong, yet serene and humane. In the Northwest enormous images of the Buddhas suggested supra terrestrial power (Lokesh Chandra 1993:3.74). Likewise, in Japan Emperor Shomu portrayed himself as a counterpart of Vairocana/Rocana through a colossal image of Daibutsu at Todaiji monastery at Nara.

Beauty was joined to magnitude, size became a symbol of status, the bigger was the image, the higher was the position. So the highest in rank are made the largest in size. Colossus does not only merely mean huge, extremely large, gigantic or titanic but also great, grand, spectacular, extravagant, overwhelming, awe inspiring, imposing and monumental. It evinces that 'size matters'. Buddhism introduced the philosophy of grandeur in image making in Japan. It gained acceptance for its novel visual appeal because indigenous religion of the Japanese, Shinto lacked such a philosophy. Shinto shrines retained simpler architectural characteristics, even in later centuries while in Buddhist temples overwhelming size of images overwhelmed the viewer. Popularity of various sūtras at different points of time led to a variety of images made on a grand scale. But only the major divinities were sculpted large in size, i.e. Śākyamuni, Bhaiṣajyaguru, Maitreya, Avalokiteśvara, Amitābha and Vairocana/Rocana. At Sanjusangendo it is not size but number of images that attracts.

Life-size images often correspond to the measurements of donors or sponsors. In China many stone sculptures were made to the likeness of the Emperors. To arrive at colossal statues measurements were raised to their multiples (Lokesh Chandra 1993:3.74). *Shaku* is a Korean unit of measurement known in Japan as *komajaku* used for construction and image making. One *shaku* is equal to 35 cms. Five meters was accepted as the traditional height for statues of Buddhas and Bodhisattvas from base to the forehead hairline. Joroku or sixteen *shaku* was halved when applied to seated images (Fukuyama 1976:76).

The First Daibutsu of Japan

The Japanese, moved by the stormy entry of Buddhist philosophy accepted it as the religion of peace and grandeur, of political, social and spiritual advancement, as one of the most grandiose edifices of the human spirit. Emperor Kimmei of Japan received a gilt bronze Buddha with other gifts along with sculptors, architects and artists etc. in AD 552, sent by the Korean king of Paekche. He had strongly recommended to accept Buddhism as the state religion. Soon the advice of the Korean King was given an assent. Buddhism was seen as the most excellent of all the teachings that can bring endless blessings to the believer. Soon Buddhism was established as the state religion. The Japanese began to produce notable works of art and construct temples, working in collaboration with the Korean architects and sculptors in the sixth-seventh centuries. The Japanese casters, architects, technicians and painters etc. were trained by the Koreans.

The bronze statue of Śākyamuni, generally known as Asuka Daibutsu is the first native colossal image sculpted by the Japanese. They were impressed by the teachings of Lord Buddha who was seen as the epitome of Six Perfections (charity, fortitude, morality, patience, meditation and intutive wisdom) and Eightfold Path (right beliefs, right aspirations, right speech, right conduct, right mode of livelihood, right effort, right mindedness and right meditation). He was seen as the enlightened one who taught Four Noble Truths, impermanence, Twelve chains of causation, nirvāṇa, spiritual insight, the doctrine of *karma* and transmigration of soul etc.

Asuka Daibutsu is a symbol of complete revolution in Japanese civilization, a symbol of a religion of the highest wisdom, of a doctrine that can create religious merits and retribution without measure and without bounds. The first native production was meant for Hōkōji or Gangoji, also known as Asukadera, named after the village, Asuka. Soga-no-umako was passionate for a grandiose scheme to worship his forefathers. He thought of connecting it to worshipping the remains of the Buddha. Thus a sacred place was created. The temple was built in AD 595. Empress Suiko ordered Kuratsukurino-tori in AD 605 to cast a *joroku* image of Buddha measuring sixteen *shaku*, a monumental one. An ancestral house was destroyed and a temple was built on the site. A team of artists undertook the project. The king of Koguryo in Korea sent gold as gift for gilding the statue. Torii Busshi, a Korean sculptor was given the responsibility to cast the image in a short period of just one year. By AD 606 Buddha image was ready but was found to be too big to be shifted inside the hall. But Tori is said to have found a way and thus he emerged as the towering personality of the period.

At that point of time, the Koreans and the Japanese were familiar with blocky and visually effective style of the Chinese. Asuka Daibutsu is close to the Chinese models used by the Korean artists, especially the images at the Yun-kang caves in Shansi province, which were representative of the style of the Wei dynasty, who were strong patrons and promoters of Buddhism. Though the image is misshapen by blaze in AD 1196, making it difficult to judge the original style but the importance of the work also lies in its size. The image is now kept at the Anguin monastery. Another seated bronze image of Śākyamuni (262 cm. in height) is housed at the Kanimanji temple constructed during Early Nara period. Śākyamuni at Muroji (238 cm.) is also a similar work.

Buddha Head, Yamadadera/Kōfukuji

A 97cm. head of Buddha, a part of a sculpture of monumental proportions, the first Japanese sculpture with aristocratic bearing, was found from the Kōfukuji monastery. It is a part of a huge bronze image of Bhaiṣajyaguru that originally belonged the Yamadadera monastery at Asuka, founded by Soga Kurayamada Ishikawamaro, who was falsely accused of treason and so committed suicide. After his death members of his family and supporters continued to complete the monastery in order to placate his fretting spirit. A triad with impressive dimensions was housed at the Yamadadera. Its casting was initiated in AD 678 and installed in AD 685 in the Lecture or the Golden Hall. The image is placed in Early Nara period on the basis of the style suggested by the features such as clean, crisp and stout surface of the head and a kind of fresh adolescence prevailing on the face. No trace of gilding has survived.

According to a story told by one of the monks at the Kōfukuji monastery, the triad was commandeered by the monks of Kōfukuji in AD 1180 because they were not given substitute statues that were lost in fire. Lightening destroyed Kōfukuji in AD 1411. It was assumed that nothing salvaged, but by accident in AD 1937 the head was discovered from under the Buddha platform during the course of repairs.

Bhaiṣajyaguru Flanked by Sun god and Moon god, Yakushiji

Bhaiṣajya or Yakushi, the Healing Buddha in the Yakushiji monastery, witnesses in silence the devotion of Emperor Temmu, who was crowned in AD 673 and the encouragement given by him to the T'ang style monumental bronzes, dry lacquer and unbaked clay images. In Japan devotion to Bhiṣajyaguru can be traced back the 6th century when the first image was housed in the main hall of worship at the Hōryūji monastery. In AD 680, the wife of Emperor Temmu was suffering from eye disease. For her fast recovery he ordered construction of a temple dedicated to Bhaiṣajyaguru. Originally the temple was constructed in Fujiwara but was shifted to the present site in AD 710 when the capital was shifted to Nara. The temple was rebuilt exactly in the same style and on the similar scale as it stood at Fujiwara. A late seventh century text says that these statues were cast by Priest Gyogi at Kanaokiyama in the Yoro era (AD 717-724).

The seated image of Bhaiṣajyaguru is 255 cms. And his standing attendants are 312 cms. in height, each. The image is cast in one piece except for the head and right arm and the falling drapery in front of him; these were brazed to the body. Heads and pedestals of both the Bodhisattva images are carved separately and attached.

Long life was a pervasive theme, so tortoises, Sun and Moon were represented as its symbols. In the Yakushiji monastery Bhaisajyaguru is flanked by Sun and Moon standing on both the sides. Their body stances are mirror images as each of them holds up the inside hand. The Emperor passed away in AD 686 prior to the completion of the work. Empress Jito his consort continued the building of the temple and finally the consecration ceremony was held in AD 697.

Diabutsu, Todaiji

Nara Dai Butsu or the Great Buddha at the Todaiji monastery is 53 ft. in height. It is a symbol of political will and visualizes the vision of Emperor Shomu who commissioned the grand image of Rocana as an apt symbol of unification of the country under him as the controlling head of the state. He saw himself as an earthly counterpart of Rocana. It was an age when Buddhist art was revolutionized by Chinese stimulation. Emperors vied with each other in erecting temples and housing images. In AD 745 a ranked South Korean technician Kuninaka-no-muragi-kimimaro headed the team at Heijo and it took three years to cast the Great Buddha.

Rocana is the main deity of Avataṁsaka-sūtra, well known in Japan. Rocana and Abhyuccha-deva are used as synonyms; thus Rocana is the highest Buddha, who manifests infinite universe as Dharmakāya in the Kegon thought, which is based on the philosophy of Buddhāvataṁsaka-mahāvaipulya-sūtra. Buddha shifts from an individual to a cosmic personality (Lokesh Chandra 1993:3.61). Two available translations of the Avtaṁsaka-sūtra are by Buddhabhdra (AD 422) and Śikśānanda (AD 699). It made extensive cultural and philosophical contributions to the Japanese history. Its grand view of totality inspired Emperor Shomu to apply its philosophy to national politics and consolidate the nation. The sūtra is regarded as one of the most profound of Mahayana thought.

Emperor Shomu was driven in the direction of piety and religion because of epidemic, famine and plague and troubled by rebelliousness of factions. He felt the need of an efficacious protection for the people and the nation. He dispatched copies of Suvarṇaprabhāsa-sūtra, Nirvāṇa-sūtra, Avalokitésvara-sūtra and Saddharma-puṇḍarīka-sūtra, ordered to construct temples for Śākyamuni and to recite the sūtras. Finally he decided to do something that could be at par with Lung-men caves in China to guard the country from damage and disaster and avail happiness and blessings for the people.

Rocana had gained a widespread popularity all over the Buddhist world before reaching Japan. Afghanistan was the center of spiritual activities at that time. Religious steps for political gains had become fashion of the day. Steps for political unification were taken by Emperor Shomu by construction of kokubunjis all over Japan, to unite all the provinces under the Great Buddha at Nara.

According to the philosophy of the Kegon sect Historical Buddha, Śākyamuni is the only manifestation of the Cosmic and Omni present Buddha, Rocana. Rocana is from Sanskrit *ruc*, to shine, be radiant or resplendent or in the causative to enlighten, to illuminate or make bright. Philosophical speculations of the school believe that Rocana sits on a giant lotus seat with a thousand petals; each of these in turn has a myriad worlds. Engravings on the underside of the lotus petals bear scenes from Avataṁsaka-sūtra. According to a temple document, the base was not ready at the time of the dedication ceremony. Figures of Buddhas and Bodhisattvas engraved on the petals have round faces, broad shoulders, bare right shoulders and voluminously draped in florid folds, linear effects retain sprightliness of T'ang style.

The sūtra attained a notable position at the court because Emperor Shōmu was a follower of its philosophy that visualized emperor as the earthly counterpart of Vairocana sitting on a thousand petal lotus. Thousand is a symbol of power; thousand Buddhas on thousand petals of the lotus seat became the thousand Buddhas of the outer enceinte of the Vajradhātu-maṇḍala of Vairocana who unfolds the brightness of his wisdom through the power of these Buddhas.

Construction of Daibustsu Den or the hall to house the colossal image began when casting of the Buddha was complete. The hall is the largest wooden structure in Japan. By virtue of its size Tōdaiji monastery is enumerated among the seven Great temples of Nara: Tōdaiji, Daianji, Genkoji, Kōfukuji, Saidaiji, Yakushiji, Hōryūji and Tōshōdaiji.

Eye opening ceremony, performed in AD 752, was the most spectacular event of the life of Shōmu, because 10,000 delegates from all over the Buddhist world reached to attend it. Over the centuries, the image has been damaged many times. When the troops of Taira Shigemori attacked the monastery in AD 1180, the Buddha image was badly mutilated. Restoration was undertaken during the Kamakura period; the image was repaired and the hall was reconstructed but shortened from 11 bays to 7 bays.

Guardians/Niō, Tōdaiji

Niō or the two spiritual protectors, Misshaku-kongō and Naraen Kongō standing on both the sides of the entrance to the South Gate, Nandaimon of Tōdaiji, are gigantic in size. Their height is 26ft., and they were sculpted in AD 1203, jointly by the famous sculptors: Unkai and Kaikei, working in collaboration with twenty other craftsmen. Size of the figures could not be less than the existing one as they were to be sculpted in harmony with the scale of the temple. Their awe-inspiring size adds to their terrifying countenance. A similar pair of guardians is found at the Hōryūji monastery. That is made of stucco and is 378.8 cms. in height. Another notable example is the group of Four Celestial Guardians at the Sangatsudō hall of the Tōdaiji monastery. They are dry lacquer images measuring 363 cm in height.

Amoghapāśa-Avalokiteśvara, Sangatsudō, Tōdaiji

A grand image housed at the Sangatsudō hall of the Tōdaiji monastery epitomizes an austere and powerful appearance. The Amoghapāśa Avalokiteśvara statue is made from lacquer and is 14'5" in height. Among the multiplicity of manifestations of Avalokiteśvara, this seems to be very powerful. His lasso, *amoghapāśa* has the power to save all sentient beings without missing a single one. He has eight arms and a vertically placed third eye on his forehead, wears an elaborate diadem, and his two major arms are joint in front in prayer. Another image of Amoghapāśa Avalokiteśvara (372 cm.) that stands in the Kōfukuji monastery was made during the Kamakura period. Brahmā and Indra in Sangatsudō hall at Tōdaiji are 13'4. They are the earliest representations of these deities in hollow lacquer. Their giant size seems to be disproportionate to that of the main image because they stand as attendants, so their size should be smaller. Sun and Moon gods, known as Nikkō and Gakkō in this hall are stucco images measuring 224cms. each. The two guardian kings placed in the hall are 10' and 10'6¿ in height and are made in hollow lacquer technique.

Thousand-armed-Avalokiteśvara, Tōshōdaiji Monastery

The scale of Tōdaiji is echoed at the Tōshōdaiji. Thousand-armed-Avalokiteśvara popularly known as Senju Kannon (18 ft.), dated AD 759, the largest of the dry lacquer statues, is one of the finest examples of the scale of lacquer works produced during the Nara period. It symbolizes *karuṇā*, compassion leading to eternal peace. Thousand arms indicate his immeasurable power to save the mankind. 953 are the actual count of his arms creating an aureole around him. 911 are wooden arms with their spatular hands, 42 longer hollow lacquer arms holding the variety of attributes are attached to the statue. These are exquisitely carved and gold lacquered, the attributes that they carry are symbols of his power as a savior. Eleven heads express his omnipotent and all pervading nature. According to a legend a divine spirit descended to the earth to take its abode in the living body of Takeda Sakome and the spirit made the astounding image (Warner 1964:156).

Credit for construction of Tōshōdaiji goes to the Chinese priest Ganjin, the head of the Lu sect, who set out to take the responsibility of ordination ceremonies. Calamities, one after the other held him from reaching Japan for 14 years. Finally when he reached Nara he was almost blind due to shipwrecks. When he reached there, he was awarded land by the Japanese Govt. as a symbol of goodwill and imperial support.

Eleven headed Avalokiteśvara, Juichimen Kannon was one of the most popular forms during Nara and Heian periods. One of such images housed at the Shōrinji monastery made from dry lacquer, is 227.7 cm. in height. Another example from the Muroji monastery, made of wood is 212 cm. and dates from the Early Heian period. Still another is at the Hōrinji that surpasses all the above in dimensions, as its height is 357 cm.

Vairocana, Tōshōdaiji

Vairocana at Tōshōdaiji resembles Rocana of Tōdaiji. Hundreds of Transformation Buddhas on the mandorla of Vairocana are the Thousand Buddhas of the Vajradhātu-maṇḍala, carved in thirty three clusters. An 11' 2 image carved in hollow lacquer with lattice support sits on a huge lotus pedestal. Tradition attributes this colossal Buddha and the two gigantic wood core companions, Thousand-armed-Avalokiteśvara and Bhaiṣajyaguru to the year AD 759 when the Chinese scholar monk Ganjin founded the Tōshōdaiji monastery. His followers worked under his guidance. Names of two Chinese priests Jofuku and Ijo are inscribed on the lotus base of the image; other young

Chinese accomplished monk sculptors also worked there. It is an iconographically unique work surviving from the Nara period. Another statue of Vairocana, 330 cm. in height was carves in wood during the Early Heian period and housed at the Tōshōdaiji monastery. Kṣitigarbha, Jizō at the Fukuchuin monastery in the main hall is a seated figure made of wood during the Kamakura period. Its height is 276 cm.

Amitābha, Byōdōin

Amitābha became the most popular divinity with the rise of Pure Land sects in the whole domain of Japanese order. He presides over the Western paradise *Sukhāvatī*. The immeasurable light of the Buddha lights up the kingdoms of ten directions, so he is called Amitābha. Among all the Buddhas, Amitābha is the most frequently mentioned deity in the sūtras. With the propagation of the Pure Land philosophy by two famous exponents: Hōnen (1133-1212) and Shinran (1173-1262), Kamakura period witnessed the most important, novel and far reaching changes in the religious life. They preached an easy way to salvation, that is repetition of the name of Amitābha by heart. The practice was meant to bring salvation without fail because the Buddha had himself vowed. Simple faith in Amitābha sufficed for salvation. One's own merits or destruction of evil *karmas* were thought to be futile.

Art became an important mean to spread the faith in Pure Land sect. The philosophy of Pure Land in China is based upon Triple Sūtra. One of them is Larger Sukhāvatī-vyūha (Daimuryojukyō). Principle text of the Triple sūtra relates the story of Dharmākara Bodhisattva who created the most perfect Buddha lands for the benefit of sentient beings and made 48 vows to adorn his land. Amitābha-sūtra, Amidakyō translated by Kumārajīva in ca. AD 402 and later translated by Hsüan tsang in about AD 650 presents a description of Pure Land. (Matsunaga 1978:II.34). Amitābha is believed to be the saviour of the world.

A huge image of Amitābha is housed in the Phoenix hall of the Byōdōin monastery with twenty-five Bodhisattvas on the sides and a beautiful landscape painted at the back. This infinitely large statue was carved by Jōchō the famous sculptor in joint wood block technique. This popular form of Amitābha had taken reinterpretation of the concept of Pure Land; the monks preached the way to achieve it. Meditation and contemplation on the physical form of Amitābha was meant to eventually gain a total intellectual identity. So scholar artists produced grand images and paintings in a well-modulated idiom.

Amitābha, Jōruriji

The images of Amitābha produced during the Late Heian and Kamakura pds. were made as objects of intense observation and displayed the charm and grandeur that was never seen before. A nine-fold set of Amitābha images at the Jōruriji monastery derives its concept from the nine scenes painted at the bottom of the Taima-maṇḍala where Amitābha is envisioned as saviour of the nine classes of mankind. Among the three degrees multiplied by three classes, the top degree is attributed to saints, the second to the virtuous beings and the third to the sinners. Nine Amitābha images are dominated by a large central figure, seated in dhyāna mudrā. The image is made of wood and is 244cm. in height.

A similar example is found at the Hōkaiji monastery built in the Late Heian period. The wooden Amitābha statue measures 305cms. largest number of Amitābha halls were built during this time. One of the masterworks is housed at the Byōdōin monastery in its phoenix hall. Amitābha sits cross-legged and behind him is his retinue, twenty-five Bodhisattvas. Such examples visualizing Amitābha as a saviour in Raigō, were produced in painting form also. There they fly down to receive the soul of the dying person. Avalokiteśvara, sitting or standing in front brings an empty seat for the soul to be flown back.

Amitābha, Kōtokuin, Kamakura

The famous colossal image of Amitābha sitting in open is in Kamakura, the first warrior capital of Japan. The 42ft. high statue (including dais) was cast in AD 1252 for the Kōtokuin monastery. Stimulus came from restoration of great temples of Nara like Tōdaiji and Kōfukuji, destroyed during civil wars. Kamakura Buddha is heroic in scale, imperturbable in expression, looks downward and is full of compassion. He is the enlightened one sitting cross-legged in dhyāna mudrā and wearing monk's garments. The statue is an expression of the appeal of Buddhism to the masses. Dimensions heighten the calm majesty of Amitābha.

Huge size standing or sitting figures of Amitābha, flanked by Avalokiteśvara and Mahāsthāmaprāpta and a retinue of twenty-five Bodhisattvas descending down from heaven to receive the soul of the dying, attained immense popularity during the Kamakura period. One of the best examples is kept at the Konkaikomyoji monastery. Earthly scenes below the flying down group, are belittled in the presence of the glory of the triad looking overwhelmingly huge. In another style of painting Amitābha appears on the horizon like the Sun enlightening the dark zones. The two Bodhisattvas stand in front while devotees and guardians fill the lower portion. Such paintings were meant for a person to whom death was assumed to be approaching. Cords made of silk extending from the hands of Amitābha Buddha were given to him, believing that immediately after death he would enter Sukhāvatī (Munsterberg 1957:95). Such scenes were not restricted to Amitābha only. There are Śākyamuni and Kṣitigarbha Raigōs also, both coming down and flying back.

Production of Buddhist colossi in Japan does not cease with the classical age, they still have a fancy for the concept that thrives in their minds. A few years ago the Japanese sculpted a statue of Amitābha in Tokyo as a symbol of their devotion to Buddhism. It has an 80 ft. long hand. It is a valuable contribution of the present to the future generations.

Appendix

A few important colossal images in Japan

Image, Period	Monastery	Position	Material	Height
Śākyamuni, Asuka pd.	Asukadera	seated	bronze	275.7 cm.
Śākyamuni, Early Nara pd.	Kanimanji	seated	bronze	262 cm.
Maitreya, Early Heian pd.	Taimadera	seated	stucco	219 cm.
Bhaiṣajyaguru, Early Nara pd.	Yakushiji	seated	bronze	254.7 cm.
Sun & Moon, Early Nara	Yakushiji	standing	bronze	315.3 cm.
Head of Bhaiṣajya, Early Nara pd.	Kōfukuji		bronze	97.3 cm.
Four Celestial Guardians, Nara pd.	Taimadera	standing	dry lacquer	216 cm.
Four Celestial Guardians, Nara pd.	Tōdaiji	standing	dry lacquer	363 cm.
Brahmā, Nara pd.	Tōdaiji	standing	dry lacquer	403 cm.
Rocana, Nara pd.	Tōdaiji	seated	bronze	1484 cm.
Vairocana, Nara pd.	Tōshōdaiji	seated	dry lacquer	370 cm
Amoghpāśa-Ava., Nara pd.	Tōdaiji	standing	dry lacquer	394 cm.
Sun & Moon, Nara pd.	Tōdaiji	standing	stucco	224.7 cm.
Avalokiteśvara, Nara pd.	Shōrinji	standing	dry lacquer	227.7 cm.
Sahasrabhuja-Ava., Nara pd.	Tōshōdaiji	standing	dry lacquer	550 cm.
Indra, Nara pd.	Tōshōdaoiji	standing	wood	206 cm.
Vajradharas/Nio, Nara pd.	Hōryūji	standing	stucco	378.8 cm.
Vairocana, Early Heian	Tōshōdaiji	seated	wood	330 cm.
Avalokiteśvara, Early Heian pd.	Muroji	standing	wood	212.7 cm.
Avalokiteśvara, Early Heian	Hōrinji	standing	wood	357.5 cm.
Amitābha, Late Heian pd.	Byōdōin	seated	wood	306 cm.
Amitābha, Late Heian pd.	Jōruriji	seated	wood	244 cm.
Amitābha, Late Heian pd.	Hōkaiji	seated	wood	305 cm.
Amoghapāsá-Ava., Kamakura pd.	Kōfukuji	seated	wood	372cm.
Kṣitigarbha, Kamakura pd.	Fukuchiin	seated	wood	276 cm.
Vajradharas/Niō, Kamakura pd.	Tōdaiji	standing	wood	803 cm.
Amitābha, Kamakura pd.	Kōtukuin	seated	bronze	42 ft.

LITERATURE CITED

Terukazu 1961

Akiyama Terukazu, *Japanese Painting, Lausanne,* 1961

Lokesh Chandra 1993

Lokesh Chandra, *Cultural Horizons of India* vol. III, New Delhi, 1993

Matsunaga 1978

Matsunaga, Daigan and Alicia, *Foundation of Japanese Buddhism,* Tokyo, 1978

Munsterberg 1957

Munsterberg, *The Arts of Japan,* Tokyo and Rutland, 1957

Soper 1960

Paine and Soper, *The Art and Architecture of Japan,* Baltimore, 1960

Sabdakalpadruma, Chawkhambha Sanskrit Series, Varanasi, 1961

Sawa 1972

Sawa, T., *Art in Japanese Esoteric Buddhism,* Tokyo, 1972

Fukuyama 1976

Toshio Fukuyama, *Heian Temples: Byodoin and Chusonji,* Heibonsha, Tokyo, 1976

Warner 1964

Warner Langdon, *Art of the Tempyo Period,* Harward University Press, 1964

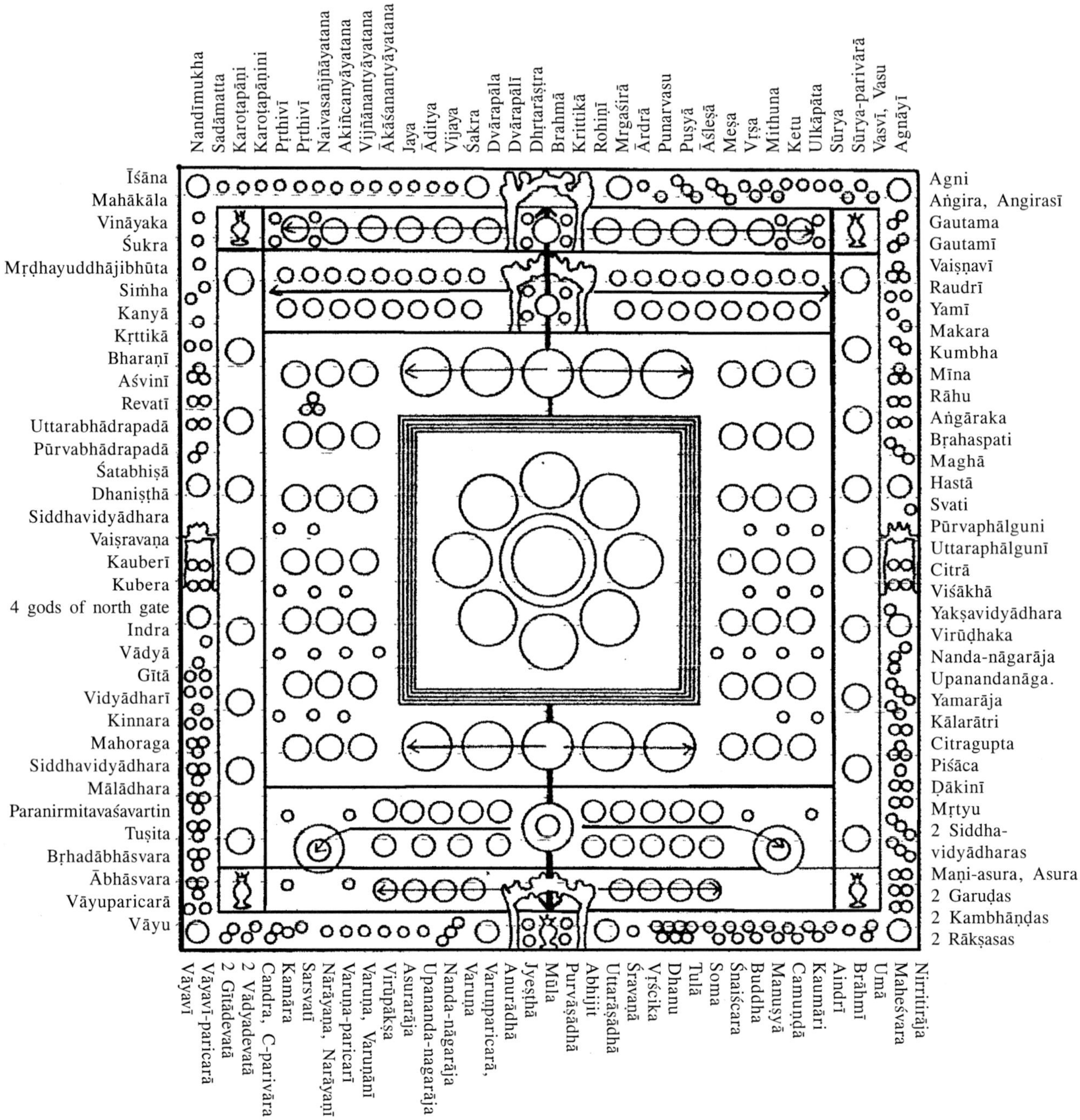

Deities sitting in the vajrakula of Mahākaruṇāgarbha-maṇḍala, genzu version.

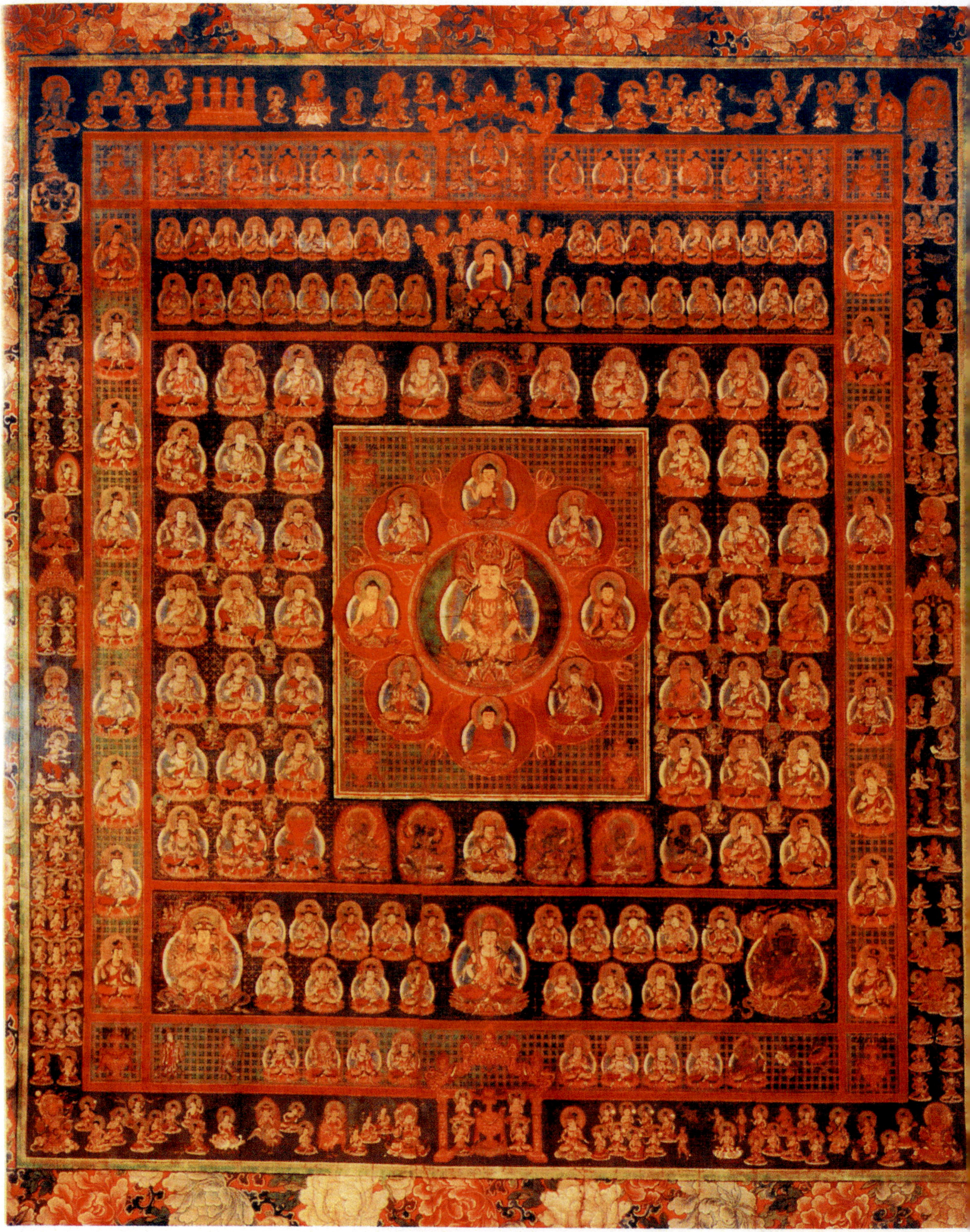

Mahākaruṇāgarbha-maṇḍala, genzu version, Japan.

6

MAṆḌALA AND MEDITATION IN JAPANESE ESOTERIC ART

The Vajradhātu- and Mahākaruṇāgarbha-maṇḍalas form the core in Japanese Esoteric Buddhism to translate profound truth, levels of meditation and emergence of the world from the Great source. As a psychophysical representation of the universe, they are used as a projection of interior life in meditation, a movement from multiple facticity of existence at the lowermost level to a focused concentration at the highest point. This also leads to realization of the outflowing enlightenment to penetrate every sphere of existence. The Mahākaruṇāgarbha-maṇḍala unfolds from its unitary center to the diversity of its extremes in the twelve sections. In ritual and symbolic form, the mystical circle is often drawn or painted on walls or on scrolls to be hung inside the Shingon temples. The *vajrakula* of Mahākaruṇāgarbha-maṇḍala represents the three realms: *Kāmadhātu*, *Rūpadhātu* and *Arūpadhātu*; beyond them is the world of Buddhas and Bodhisattvas in the eleven enclosures. Only on crossing these Six Levels of Existence and Eight *dhyānabhūmis* is one able to concentrate on Buddhas and Bodhisattvas and finally on Vairocana sitting at the center of the maṇḍala.

Levels of Existence

The central figure of Mahāvairocana is the great source and *dharmakāya* as it exists in the totality of phenomenal existence. He is the source of manifestation of the infinite world and yet is inherent in each and every existence. Being one with him is the goal of *samādhi*. Mahāvairocana is the body of principle, the supreme power in Esoteric Buddhism, preaches *dharma* in innumerable worlds in ten directions. He is the *Dharmakāya* inseparable from *rūpa* or form, and he has to reveal himself in formal modes in countless forms. Realization of Mahāvairocana's transcendental forms by an adherent requires the highest level of meditation. To reach that level one has to cross the Three Realms visualized in the Mahākaruṇāgarbha-maṇḍala: the Realm of Desire, the Realms of *Rūpa* and *Arūpa : Kāmadhātu*, *Rūpadhātu* and *Arūpadhatu*. They represent upward layers of the universe, the process of creation, the world in between the lowest and the highest levels of universe. The figures of Six Levels of Existence and Eight *Dhyānas* are depicted in the *vajrakula* of the Mahākaruṇāgarbha-maṇḍala:

1-4	Naraka, Preta, Tiryak and Asura	Kāmadhātu	*Durgati*	south
5.	Manuṣya	Kāmadhātu	*Sugati*	west
6.	Deva	Kāmadhātu	*Sugati*	divided

1-4	Dhyānas	Rūpadhātu	north
5-8	Dhyānas	Arūpadhātu	east

The Ttraidhātuka theory encompasses all the stages of existence and meditation. The Six Existences in the universe and Eight *Dhyānabhūmis* are a way to enlightenment, moving from the lowermost to the highest point through focusing on the spiritual symbol of strength at the center of the maṇḍala. The Three Realms lie below the world of Buddhas and Bodhisattvas who are above the Devas residing in the Devaloka. Gradually, through meditation on crossing these Three Realms, an adherent can enter their world.

Kāmadhātu: The Realm of Desire includes the six migratory states of existence generally accepted in Buddhism. They are a part of ten ascending stages of religious practice according to the Tendai sect. These stages are all mutually inclusive; each stage contains the other nine. The six migratory states can be further divided into two stages: *durgati* and *sugati*. *Naraka*, *Preta*, *Tiryak* and *Asura* fall in the *durgati* category, while the remaining two : *Manuṣya* and *Deva*, are placed in the *sugati* category. The Bodhisattva Kṣitigarbha (Jap. Jizō Bosatsu) saves all the sentient beings of the six existences (Kāmadhātu), who live in the period between the death of historical Buddha and the arrival of Maitreya (Matsunaga 1978:1.187). *Naraka* is the lowermost in the Realm of Desire; desire gives birth to sufferings and sufferings are given in hells. The gods who dwell in Kāmadhātu are known as *Kāmāvacara*. They can be divided in to two types: earth dwelling and sky dwelling.

Figures of the Six Levels of Existence: Man's existence is bound by earth and sky. The sky is the limit; beyond that is the world of Buddhas, which can be reached after crossing all the levels leading up to the twenty-eight heavens. The Six Levels of Existence are philosophically designed to represent the psychological states of human mind. Man ascends because of good deeds and descends to the lower levels as a result of his evil deeds. The Six Levels of Existence are known as *ṣaḍgati*. *Gati* signifies motion in general and is a mode of existence (Kaṭhopaniṣad iii.11). It represents the course of soul through numerous forms of life (Williams 1899:347). In Japanese, *ṣaḍgati* is known as *rokudō*, the Six Realms in which the souls of living beings transmigrate from one to another (JEBD, 1965). Rebirth is possible within the Six Levels of Existence. A brief summary of 5 or 6 *gati* is given in Abhidharmakoṣasaṅgraha, (iii,11), Divyāvadāna (300.10-11; 301.20) and Dharmasamuccaya (57). In the maṇḍala *ṣaḍgati* refers to various levels of human psychology which a person must transcend in order to be fit for meditation.

Gati is also the wheel of existence, *bhava-cakra*. *Bhava-cakra* is painted as a gigantic wheel inside the yoga rooms: *madhye yogagṛhasya atha likhet sansāramaṇḍalam* (Poussin 1894:842). It is also painted at the entrance of temples to instruct those who come to worship. *Bhava-cakra* symbolizes the endless cycle of birth and death and the beings of the world in the clutches of *karma*. It is a summation of Buddhist teachings in a pictorial form, a picture path to spiritual liberation. Three spiritual poisons and twelve *sānsāric* existences lead to the Six States of Rebirth (Lokesh Chandra 2000:2.551).

According to Nichiren, all the worlds from Hell to the realm of Buddhas exist in this five foot body. The condition of despair in which one is completely overwhelmed by suffering is Hell; the state of being dominated by deluded desires that can never be satiated is represented by eternally hungry ghosts in the world of Pretas; the instinctual state of fearing the strong and bullying the weak is animality represented by the world of Tiryak; the state of anger, characterized by an unrestraint competitive urge to surpass and dominate others, often on pretence of being good and wise, is represented by the world of Asuras. These four states of existence are said to be Evil Paths or *durgati* because they are characterized by destructive negativity. The world of humans has humanity, a tranquil state marked by the ability to reason and make calm judgements. The world of Devas is free from sufferings. It is a state of joy experienced when desires are fulfilled (Lokesh Chandra 2000:2.555). In sum, the first four are the realms of loss and woe.

1. Naraka (Jap. Jigoku): The lowermost level of existence is portrayed as Naraka, the realm of hells. Hells are infernal regions where different kinds of tortures are inflicted upon sinners. Buddha accepted the existence of heavens and hells for didactic purpose, but it was the later form of Mahāyāna Buddhism that propagated the idea because it was more laity oriented. The Buddhist concept of hell represents a psychological state of mind at the philosophical level in the present life. Naraka or niraya is called *jigoku* in Japanese, one of the six worlds in which unenlightened people transmigrate. Niraya means devoid of happiness. According to the Abhidharmakoṣasaṅgraha, the realm of hells is situated under Jambudvīpa *(Embudai)*, its descriptions vary according to scriptures (JEBD 1965:135).

The realm of tortures is visualized through Piśācas eating the limbs of a human body and drinking blood in the *vajrakula* of the Mahākaruṇāgarbha-maṇḍala below the figure of Chitragupta in the south. The figures drawn there are demons of dark places and privies. Śubhākarasiṁha says that *Piśāca* means supreme suffering and they belong to the rank of *Gaki,* the hungry ghosts. Sometimes they are named as attendants of Chitragupta (Snodgrass 1988:484). *Piśācas* look horrible with ugly postures, wildly grown hair and ill-shaped bodies. Hells are portrayed as future abodes of suffering in order to induce the practice of virtue. Inspired by Buddhist sūtras, monks painted a variety of hell scenes out of compassion aroused in their hearts to save the wicked from the path of evils and to lead them to salvation. Scrolls of hells, hungry ghosts and diseases served as warnings. In such works, people were confronted with different phases of hells, in which the damned are subjected to various ordeals. Such scenes are always gruesome and frightening, and are often accompanied by written commentaries. Examples are the scrolls from the Hara collection, now owned by the Commission for Protection of Cultural Properties in Tokyo. Here one can see the guilty being pounded and crushed in a huge mortar. Scenes of hell are often dominated by the gloomy atmosphere of the underworld symbolized by a grey background (Akiyama 1961: 87). The Gaki Zoshi is a picture scroll from late 12th century that depicts hungry ghosts in a Buddhist hell. The souls of the condemned men and women go to hell, looking horrible and monstrous, they wander around eternally hungry and thirsty, remaining invisible to humans but visible to themselves. They are often believed to go to graveyards to find food for themselves (Lee 1978:311).

2.Preta (Gaki): Pretas dwell in the realm of ghosts or evil spirits. A Preta is the body given to a person after death. They live in this form of existence so long as obsequial rites are not performed according to the Purāṇic tradition. Pretas are eternally hungry; not even a single grain of rice or drop of water enters their mouths or throats. Some of these suffering ghosts have huge bodies, but mouths are as small as eye of a needle. Others are very thin as there is no food to eat. They are so scrawny that not even a bit of flesh can be scraped off or a drop of blood can be squeezed. They consist of only bones and the layer of skin covering the bones; the skin of their stomachs is wrinkled and touches their backbones. Their eyes are deep and hollow and look as if they have been taken out. Their hair is nasty, and they do not have even a tiny piece of cloth to cover their bodies (Reynolds 1982: 96-97). They are devoid of any possessions, constantly seeking food to fill their distended bellies. The needle thin throats and wild hair add to the grim appearance. Hungry ghosts prefer to live in filthy places, eat impure food, and inflict sufferings, especially on children. Two Pretas kneel before Chitragupta in the south in *vajrakula* of the Mahākaruṇāgarbha-maṇḍala as if confessing or ready to listen to the judgement given by the king who attends Yama. Chitragupta keeps a record of the deeds of each person and passes judgement (Snodgrass 1988:484). Their world is called *Gakidō* in Japanese.

Apart from three types of Pretas, are powerful ghosts known as Yakṣas, Piśācas and Rākṣasas. Piśācas are placed in the same category as Pretas. They are depicted as malevolent and hungry, eating human arms and drinking blood with a corpse lying in front of them. Piśācī as a female imp appears among the retinue of Kālī. Ḍakinīs are their female counterparts, but are not represented in horrible shapes and appearances. Their hair is tied up, and they sit on lotus seats spread for them. Three Ḍakinīs are sitting below the Piśācas who are eating human arms. The two Dakinis sitting on the sides are holding bowls full of blood in their right hands, and one on the right side is holding a cleaver shaped sword in her left hand. Śubhākarasiṁha refers to them as being attendants in the retinue of Mahākāla, and also identified them as demons who devour the defilements found in the hearts of human beings. The ruler of the world of Pretas is Yamarāja, who holds a mirror reflecting the deeds of men. Chitragupta records their deeds and the assistants of Yamarāja punish the people for their sins and transgressions.

3.Tiryak (chikusho): The realm of birds, beasts, fishes, dragons, serpents, shells, worms and insects is the world of Tiryak. Animals do not have the sense of *dharma*, they do not till the land for living. *Tiryak gati* is the state of an animal in transmigration (Mahābhārata iii.1166). They live in a world of uncontrolled instincts. The life of animals is one *kalpa* in length at the most, and the animals that live the longest time live for one *antarkalpa*. These are the Great *Nagās*, *Nāga* kings, Nanda, Upananda etc. The Eight Great Nāga kings sustain the Earth (Paussin 1990: 2.473).

In the Mahākaruṇāgarbha-maṇḍala, the three Nāga kings represented in the *vajrakula* are Nanda, Upananda and Varuṇa. Nanda-nāgarāja and Upananda-nāgarāja sit in the west and south gates respectively. They are among the eight Nāga Kings (Jap. *hachidairyu*) who protect the Dharma. They sit opposite each other, *Nanda* means joy and *Upa* means near or lesser. They are the rulers of the Nāgas who dwell in the waters of the Great Ocean surrounding Mount Sumeru. They pour water over the infant Śākyamuni at the time of his nativity. Nanda represents the power of wisdom and Upananda the power of *samādhi* and of the quickening mind. They wear crowns of seven hooded snakes and hold swords in their right hands (Snodgrass 1997:479).

Varuṇa-nāgarāja, as ruler of the hydrosphere, sits in the west with Varuṇānī and Varuṇa-paricarā. He is shown with a frowning face, wears a seven hooded snake crown, holds a lance in his right hand and a snake noose in the left (Lokesh Chandra 1972:326-8).

4. Asura (Jap. Ashura): Asura is enumerated as the fourth level of existence and is visualized as chief of the evil spirits (Ṛgveda ii.30.4, vii.99.5) or demons or ghosts who are generally said to be enemies of gods (ibid viii.96.9). In the Purāṇic tradition they are said to be chidren of Diti by Kaśyapa, as such they are demons of the first order in perpetually hostile to the gods and must not be confused with Rākṣasas (Williams 1899:121). They are said to have been expelled from heaven because of their pride. They fight the gods for the fruits of the wish-giving tree, whose roots are in their realm but the fruit is in the world of gods (Lokesh Chandra 2000: 2.551). In Buddhism, *Asuras* are belligerant beings that make war on Indra. When the Asuras gain supremacy in the endless battle, evil and chaos prevail in the world (Snodgrass 1997:100).

In the *vajrakula* of the Mahākaruṇāgarbha-maṇḍala, Asura and Maṇi-asura sit below the Siddha-vidyādharas, wearing armour and shoes like Celestial Guardians. The figure identified as Maṇi-asura by Snodgrass is holding a sword in his right hand with the left placed on his thigh, and the one identified as Asura is holding a club with a jewel on the top. I would like to interchange these figures on the bases of their attributes. Two pairs of Asura Kings sit in the south and west gates of the *vajrakula* (Lokesh Chandra 1972: 271, 272, followed by 323). Identical to the Nāga Kings, they sit facing each other holding swords in their right hands with circles drawn as haloes.

5. Manuṣya (Jap. Ningen): Tathāgata Vairocana took the form of *Manuṣya* to preach in the world of humans to alleviate their sufferings. The Realm of humans (*manuṣya*) shows birth, disease, old age and death. It is located in the four great continents, *caturdvīpako-lokadhātu*, (Jap. *Shidaishu*) that surround Mount Sumeru in the four directions: 1.*Uttarakuru* is the "Excellent land" to the north of Sumeru (Jap. *Hokkuruji*), which is said to be square in shape, inhabited by square-faced people. 2. *Aparagodānīya* or *Aparagodāna* is to the west of Sumeru, is known as the "Western cattle giving land" because cattle are the medium of exchange. The continent is circular in shape and its inhabitants are also circular-faced. 3. To the south of Sumeru is Jambūdvīpa (Jap. *Enbudai*) named after the Jambū tree. It is triangular in shape and its inhabitants have triangular faces. 4. *Pūrvavideha* is believed to be located to the east of Sumeru (Jap. *Tohotsubadai*). It has a semicircular shape and its residents have the same shape of faces (Snodgraass, 1997:100).

In the *vajrakula* of Mahākaruṇāgarbha-maṇḍala, a Manuṣya sits in the west; after Manuṣyā, one of the nine mother goddesses. He represents the world of humans, which is one level higher than the Asuras. Man has the power to think and thus exists above the realms of Naraka, Preta, Tiryak and Asura and below the Devaloka. Here he is depicted sitting cross-legged with his right hand open flat almost raised to the chest level; the other hand rests on his lap. The halo behind the figure indicates his divine personality (Lokesh Chandra 1972: 309).The Mother Goddess Manuṣyā can be taken as one of the nine Mother Goddesses or as the female counterpart of Man.

6. Deva (Jap. Tennin): Devas fall into three large divisions: *Kāmāvacara* living in the *Kāmadhatu*, *Rūpāvacara* living in the *Rūpadhatu* and *Arūpāvacara* living in the *Arūpādhatu*. *Kāmāvacara* gods are: Caturmahārājika, Rājakāyika, Trayastriṁśa, Yama, Tuṣita, Nirmāṇarati and Paranirmitavaśavartin. They are divided into two categories: *Bhauma* and *Antarikṣavāsin*. (Edgerton 1977: 270). Devas born from lotus blossoms enjoy heavenly delight. They, too, are subject to the law of *anitayatā*, i.e. birth, life, death and rebirth. They may live for millions or billions of years in heaven but when their merits are exhausted they have to return to earth. Accumulated merits lead to birth in a higher realm and demerits in a lower realm.

According to Dharmasaṅgraha (127) the six categories of gods residing in the Realm of Desire are: *ṣaṭ kāmāvacarāḥ devāḥ tadyathā- caturmahārājikās-trayastriṁśas-tuṣitā yāmā nirmāṇaratayaḥ paranirmitavaśavartinaśceti* They are Caturmaharajikās, Trayastriṁśās, Tuṣitās, Yāmās, Nirmāṇaratayas and Paranirmitavaśavartinas. There are eighteen kinds of gods residing in the Realm of Form: *aṣṭādaśarūpāvacarāḥ devāḥ tadyathā- brahmakāyikāḥ brahmapurohitāḥ brahmapārṣadyāḥ mahābrāhmaṇāḥ parittābhāḥ apramāṇābhāḥ ābhāsvarāḥ parittaśubhāḥ śubhakṛtasnāḥ anabhrakāḥ puṇyaprasavāḥ bṛhatphalā asañjñisattvā abṛhā atapā sudṛśāḥ sudarśanā, and akaniṣṭhāśceti* (Dharmasaṅgraha 128). Four kinds of gods reside in the Realm of Formlessness: *catvāro rūpāvacarāḥ devāḥ: ākāśānantyāyatanopagāḥ, vijñānānantyāyatanopagāḥ akiñcanyāyatanopagāḥ, and naivasañjñāsañjñāyatanopagāḥ* (Dharmasaṅgraha 129).

Trayastrinśa: Trayastrinśa is the abode of thirty-three gods (Jap. *sanjusanten*) located on the summit of mount sumeru: the abode of Indra, the leader of thirty-three gods, is located at the centre. The way of Devas culminates in union with Brahmā. Indra preaches the *dharma* in the Trayastriṁśa heaven. The gods dwelling in the *Kāmāvacara*, the realm of desire are a group of six *ṣaṭkāmāvacarāḥ devāḥ dharmāḥ*. In iconography they are conceived of as dwelling upon the top of mount Sumeru in eight castles facing the four directions and one castle at the center containing their leader (Matsunaga 1969:52). Indra, the lord of Trayastriṁśa Heaven (Jap. *tori-ten*) sits cross-legged in full majesty in the north in the *vajrakula* to the west of the northern gate on a hill holding a vajra in his right hand. He is of golden color, wears a jewel crown with ribbons flowing down to the elbow level, has a third eye drawn on his forehead, and a double halo encircling his head. An attendant figure is kneeling in front below his seat and offering flowers.

Caturmahārājika, the Realm of Four Divine Guardian Kings: The group of four guardians or the celestial kings unknown in the Vedic literature believed to have played an important part in many events in the life of Śākyamuni, are collectively known in Japan as *Shitennō*. They are worshipped as guardians because of the pledge they took in the presence of the Buddha to protect the nation from all sorts of calamities, sorrows and pestilence. In their heaven, fifty years of human life is but a single day and the life span of these *devas* consist of five hundred celestial years composed of such days (Matsunaga 1969:51). In the Suvarṇaprabhāsa-sūtra they are called great kings: *Viśravaṇo mahārājo Dhṛtarāṣṭro mahārājo Virūḍhako mahārājo Virūpākṣo mahārāja* ....(Suvarṇaprabhāsa-sūtra p. 36)

Sanskrit	Direction	Japanese	Commander of
Dhṛtarāṣṭra	east	Jikokuten	Gandharvas and Piśācas
Virūḍhaka	south	Zōchōten	Kumbhāṇḍas and Pretas
Virūpākṣa	west	Kōmokuten	Nāgas
Vaiśravaṇa	north	Tamonten, Bishamonten	Yakṣas

Images of Four Divine Kings, often combined with Brahmā and Indra as maintainers of the Buddhist law and protectors of the state, complete with symbolic characteristic features and colours etc., are associated with four cardinal points of the compass and thus are placed in the corresponding four directions inside the halls of worship in Buddhist monasteries. As inhabitants of the lowest *Devaloka*, serving as guardians of the four quarters they are accompanied by large retinues on their travels. Protection of the Buddha was undertaken by this group from the moment of his conception; moreover in Āṭānāṭīyasutta they appear as protectors of Buddha's followers as well. The record of happiness in the assemblies of Devas is their responsibility, while their counsellors record righteousness and virtues of men. Their world is situated halfway up the mount or they preside over one of the slopes of Meru, assisted by twenty-eight or thirty-two generals presiding over the sun, the moon, the stars and the Eight types of Beings (Jap. *Hachibu:* gandharva, piśāca, kumbhāṇḍa, preta, nāga, yakṣa, rākṣasa and mahābhūta).

In the Mahākaruṇāgarbha-maṇḍala, Dhṛtarāṣṭra sits in the east wearing an armour and shoes and holding a sword in the left hand as protector or governor of the country. His body is red and has a wrathful appearance. Virūḍhaka is seated above the south gate attended by a Preta-like figure. He has a sword in his right hand and wears a helmet, armour and shoes. He is of ruddy skin colour. Virūpākṣa like the preceding guardians sits to the north of the west gate in the *vajrakula* holding a trident and wearing armor (Lokesh Chandra 1972: 325). Vaiśravaṇa is the protector of the North, so he is placed in the *vajrakula* above the north gate holding a stūpa placed on his left palm and a jewel sceptre in his right hand (ibid 362).

Twelve Celestial Beings of Space (Jap. *Juniten*):

1. Śakra (Taishakuten) E
2. Agni (Katen) SE
3. Yama (Emmatennō) S
4. Nairṛti (Rasetsuten/Nirritei-ō) SW
5. Varuṇa (Suiten) W
6. Vāyu (Futen) NW
7. Kubera (Kubira) W
8. Īśāna (Ishanaten) NE
9. Brahmā (Bonten) E
10. Pṛthivi (Jiten) E
11. Sūrya (Nitten) E
12. Candra (Gaten) W

Ṛṣis (sages): Sages or Ṛṣis are authors or singers of Vedic hymns for invocation of divine beings. They constitute a peculiar class, distinct from gods, men and asuras. Vedas are believed to be a result of their inspiration, introspection and spiritual vision. The word "*Ṛṣi*" is derived from "*ṛ*" meaning sound. In Vedic times, Ṛṣis communicated the sacred lore through their mouths. The voice of *Ārṣa Bhārata* is said to be the voice of Ṛṣis. They are regarded by later generations as saints and inspired personages occupying the same position in Indian history as heroes and patriarchs of other countries. According to the general belief, the number of Ṛṣis is forty-eight thousand. Several types of enumerations are given in Purāṇas, Brāhmaṇas, sūtras and epics. The Vedic tradition accepts their number to be seven, *saptarṣayaḥ*. According to Śatapathabrāhmaṇa (xiv.5.2.6) these seven sages are: Gautama, Bhāradvāja, Viśvāmitra, Jāmadagni, Vaśiṣṭha, Kaśyapa and Atri. The names given in Mahābhārata (xii) are different except those of Atri and Vasiṣṭha: Mārīci, Aṅgiras, Pulaha, Kratu, Pulastya, Atri and Vasiṣṭha. The large number of Ṛṣis are classified into three: Devarṣis, Brahmarṣis and Rājarṣis. According to Rāmāyaṇa, Vasiṣṭha was a Brahmarṣi, Viśvāmitra was a Rājarṣi and Kaśyapa was a Devarṣi.

According to the Japanese Buddhist pantheon there are five hermit ascetics who attend Agni: Vasiṣṭha, Gautama, Aṅgiras, Atri and Bhṛgu. Aṅgiras is replaced by Garga in Taizo-in-zu (TZ 241) illustrations of mudrās in Garbha-maṇḍala kept at Ninnaji, Kyoto. In the *vajrakula* of the Mahākaruṇāgarbha-maṇḍala Agni sits with Agnāyī in the southeast corner. Only three Ṛṣis are drawn with their consorts/attendants with Agni. Vasiṣṭha sits to the right side of Agni while the other two Aṅgiras and Gautama are sitting just below him.

Deities of Time

Twelve Zodiacal Signs: The Twelve Zodiacal signs are painted on a large number of scrolls over the past centuries after their adoption into the Mahākaruṇāgarbha-maṇḍala. In its *vajrakula* they are divided into four groups of three, and placed in the four directions of its *vajrakula*:

1. Meṣa (Yōkū) E
2. Vṛṣa (Gyukū) E
3. Mithuna (Nannyokū) E
4. Makara (Makatsukū) S
5. Kumbha (Gembyōkū) S
6. Mīna (Sōgyukū) S
7. Tulā (Hyōkū) W
8. Dhanu (Kyūkū) W
9. Vrśćika (Kachūgū) W
10. Karkaṭaka (Bōkaikū) N
11. Kanyā (Shōnyokū) N
12. Siṁha (Shishikū) N

Constellations: The twenty-eight constellations are divided into four groups of seven each to be accommodated in the four directions:

1. Kṛttikā (Bōshuku) E
2. Rohiṇī (Hisshuku) E
3. Mṛgaśiras (Shishuku) E
4. Ārdrā (Shinshuku) E
5. Punarvasu (Seishuku) E
6. Puṣyā (Kishuku) E
7. Āśleśā (Ryūshuku) E
8. Maghā (Seishuku) S
9. Hastā (Shinshuku) S
10. Svāti (Kōshuku) S

11. Pūrvaphalgunī (Chōshuku) S
12. Uttaraphalgunī (Yokushuku) S
13. Citrā (Kakushuku) S
14. Viśākhā (Teishuku) S
15. Śravaṇā (Joshuku) W
16. Uttarāṣāḍhā (Toshuku)W
17. Abhijit (Gyūshuku) W
18. Pūrvāṣāḍhā (Kishuku) W
19. Mūlā (Bishuku) W
20. Jyeṣṭhā (Shinshuku) W
21. Anurādhā (Bōshuku) W
22. Dhaniṣṭhā (Kyoshuku) N
23. Śatabhiśā (Kishuku) N
24. Pūrvabhadrapadā (Shinshuku) N
25. Uttarabhadrapadā (Hekishuku) N
26. Revatī (Keishuku) N
27. Aśvinī (Rōshuku) N
28. Bharaṇī (Ishuku) N

Nine Planets are drawn in the following manner:

1. Ketu, Nirghataketu/Ulkapata (Suisei, Ryūsei) E
2. Sūrya (Nitten) E
3. Rāhu (Ragosei) S
4. Aṅgāraka (Kayō) S
5. Bṛhaspati (Mokuyō) S
6. Budha (Suiyo) W
7. Śaniścara (Doyō) W
8. Soma (Getsuyō) W
9. Śukra (Kinyō) N

Trimūrti

Brahmā is the creator, Viṣhṇu is the sustainer and Śiva is the destroyer of the world. Vishṇu in his form of Nārāyaṇa rides on a garuḍa and holds a wheel in his right hand. Śiva as Nandīśvara rides a bull and is accompanied by his consort Umā. Gaṇapati the general of the Divine army popularly known as Vināyaka is the son of Śiva. Kārttikeya is his brother and is drawn in the west in the *vajrakula* of the Mahākaruṇāgarbha-maṇḍala, riding a peacock. Another important divinity is Mahākāla sitting below the northeast corner. Mahākāla means great time. He is transformation body and wrathful aspect of Maheśvara. Mahākāla has three aspects: god of war, wealth and dark realms. Thus Viṣṇu/Nārāyaṇa (Naraen-ten), Śiva (Daijizaiten), Umā, Gaṇapati/Vināyaka (Binayakaten), Kārttikeya/Kumāra (Kumaraten) and Mahākāla (Mahakara) fall into the group of Trimūrtti.

Goddesses

Saptamātṛ (*shichimoten*) is the collective name of the seven mother goddesses worshipped all over India since ancient times. They are believed to be divine mothers or personified energies or *śakti* of principal deities. They are said to be born from the bodies of Brahmā, Viṣṇu, Kārttikeya, Yama etc. According to a Purāṇic story when Śiva and Viṣṇu had created seven mother goddesses when they failed to kill Andhakāsura. An asura arose from each drop of blood of Andhakāsura that fell on ground. These mothers joined with Yogeśvarī, the creation of Śiva, drank the blood of the asura without allowing it to fall on the ground making it possible for Śiva to kill the demon. There are several stories in the purāṇas related to the creation of the Saptamātṛ (for details see Vettam Mani 1979:691); variations in enumeration and iconographic details are also found in various texts but their usual order is: Brāhmī, Maheśvarī, Kaumārī, Vaiṣṇavī, Vārāhī, Aindrī and Cāmuṇḍā. At some places their number is eight and sometimes they are known as "Navaśakti".

Saptamātṛ are mentioned in the thirteenth chapter of Rishukyō to have paid homage to the Buddha's feet and offered the hook, which gathers and brings sentient beings on to the path of the Buddha. The true essence of pledge enables the destruction of evils and attainment of enlightenment. Destruction refers to the elimination of unwholesome mind and attainment refers to the practice of esoteric teachings which quickly enables one to advance beyond mundane and acquire *siddhis*. In the *vajrakula* of Mahākaruṇāgarbha-maṇḍala they are:

1. Aindrī (Taishakunyō)	6. Vaiṣṇavī (Bichūnyo)
2. Brāhmī (Bontennyō)	7. Yamī (Yamanyō)
3. Kaumārī (Kyumari)	8. Manuṣyā (Manushanyō)
4. Cāmuṇḍā (Shamonda)	9. Kauberī
5. Raudrī (Jizaitennyō)	

Sky Dwelling Gods

Yama: In the heaven of Yama (*Emmaten*, time) the seasons are always good and inhabitants enjoy occasional pleasure (Snodgrass 1988:103). Mahāvairocana reveals himself in the form of Yama to preach in world of hungry ghosts. In the Mahākaruṇāgarbha-maṇḍala, Yama is sitting in the south in the *vajrakula* below the southern gate. He is regarded as the judge of the dead for holding a mirror in which a human face is reflected; but in the maṇḍala he holds a sceptre topped by a golden half moon supporting a man's head with a hair knot. He is sitting on his ride, a water buffalo and attended by Kālarātri holding the same attribute and looking towards him. The leader of this heaven Yama is frequently called Suyama, the name designated to the heaven. It is the place where times are always good because in Chinese "*su*" denotes goodness and "*yama*" was used for time. According to the Chinese accounts this heaven is always illuminated, there is no distinction between day and night, only the opening and closing of flowers regulate time. Two hundred years of human life is but one day to the Yama deva, and two thousand years composed of such days form their life span (Matsunaga 1969:52).

Tuṣita *(tosotsu)*: It is the heaven of contentment as the dwellers are contented with its pleasures. Bodhisattvas reside there before they are born as Buddhas. The heaven and its presiding deities are frequently termed as *San-tusita*, referring to the gathering of enjoyment or pleasure. To the Devas of this heaven one day is equivalent to four hundred years of human life and four thousand years composed of such days form their life span (Matsunaga 1969:52).

In Mahākaruṇāgarbha-maṇḍala, Tuṣita deva representing its inhabitants sits above Bṛhadābhāsvara and below Paranirmita-vaśavartin in the north in the *vajrakula* (Snodgrass 1988:523). He is holding a lotus in his right hand, going above the shoulder, attended by two, sitting on both the sides slightly behind him, holding the same attributes. The three have their separate halos, often identified as the three gods of Tuṣita but the smaller size of the two figures indicate their lower rank.

Nimāṇarati (Jp. Keraku): Nirmāṇarati is the heaven of joy in transformation where the inhabitants enjoy pleasures that they create themselves magically (*sunirmita*), mutual smiling produces impregnation and children are born on the knees by metamorphosis, at birth equal in development to a human child of twelve (Snodgrass 1988:104). The bondage of these devas is in being tied by desire to these creations. To the divinities of this heaven eight hundred years of mankind is but a single day and their lifespan consists of eight thousand such celestial years (Matsunaga 1969:53). The god residing in the Nirmāṇarati Heaven is most probably Mālādhara (Jimanten). Mālādhara is sometimes said to be the fifth heaven of world of desire, Nirmāṇarati, the heaven of joy in transformation (Snodgrass 1988:525). In the *vajrakula* Mālādhara sits in the east above Paranirmita-vaśavartin and below Siddhavidyādhara. He does not hold any garland as indicated by the name, there is a lotus in his left hand, ribbons from his jewel crown are hanging, face expression is extremely calm and peaceful. Two attending figures sitting on both the sides, looking towards him, are smaller in size and holding the same attribute, lotus flowers.

Paranirmita-vaśavartin (Jap. Takejizaiten): The name means heaven of free enjoyment of transformation by others where the highest class of *Kāmāvacara* gods live, controlling (enjoyment) magically, created by others. *Para* means other, *nirmita* is transformation, *vaśa* means freedom or autonomy and *vartina* is dwelling or abiding. This means that the inhabitants enjoy various types of pleasures in this heaven that are created by others. They rank higher than Nirmāṇarati who create their own magical enjoyment. King Māra (Ma-ō) the tempter lives in a separate locality in this heaven and he is accordingly called King Māra of the sixth heaven.

In the Mahākaruṇāgarbha-maṇḍala Paranirmita-vaśavartin sits above Tuṣita in the North in *vajrakula*. He represents the gods who dwell in the sixth heaven of the realm of desire. The central figure is attended by two, sitting on both the sides looking younger in age and smaller in size. Paranirmita-vaśavartin is holding a bow in his right hand and an arrow in the left; both the attending figures hold lotus flowers in their hands (Lokesh Chandra 1972: pl. 383-85).

Figures of the Eight Dhyānas

Samādhi is necessary for the exact knowledge necessary for salvation and concentration is application of pure minds on a single object with their concomitants, the five *skandhas*. Among the first four dhyānas the first three are three fold and the fourth is eight-fold. They are *adhicittaśikṣa*, the higher mental learning or the primary element in the purification of mind, *cittapariśuddhipradhāna*. Only the absorption that are filled with excellence are called dhyāna (Pousin 1990:4.1215-17). Absorption is the *samāpatti* form of dhyāna, the other is *upapatti* or existence.

An ascetic is fit to enter the basic dhyāna after abandoning all the defilements and obtaining detachment from *Kāmadhātu* and then obtain Four Immeasurables of the spheres of the basic dhyāna. Defilements are dispelled and made distant and the ascetic becomes invincible even when he encounters powerful causes of defilements (Pousin 1990:4.1268). Meditation is said to be of three types: *dhyānam trividha/ tadyathā- sadoṣāpakarṣa dhyānam sukhavaihārika dhyānam aśeṣ-avaibhūṣita dhyānam*, meditation by drawing out sins, by doing what is to be done and by residing comfortably (Dharmasangraha 59).

Beings are free from all desires and passions in the realm of form situated above Paranirmita-vaśavartin, the highest point of the realm of desire. The inhabitants have a pure and ethereal form. The realm of form is constituted of four *Dhyānabhūmis* as they are attained as a result of perfecting the four corresponding states of mind. Dhyāna, meditation, concentration or mystic trance has four levels in the realm of form, *rūpadhātu*. Various classes of *Rūpāvacara* gods occupy these four *dhyānabūmis*. So the gods who dwell there are divided into four, corresponding to four levels of meditation. Each of the four levels of meditation lead to rebirth in the successively higher stages among those gods. The last is the final stage and the highest. There the gods Śuddhāvāsakāyika are divided into five sub groups: Abṛha, Atapa, Sudṛśa, Sudarśa and Akaniṣṭha. In all, the levels of meditation are eliminated one by one.

Rūpadhātu**:** Rūpadhātu is made up of sixteen places. In the heaven of Brahmapurohitas there rises a lofty dwelling which is named the heaven of Brahmā inhabited by a single ruler (Paussin 1990: 2.366).

First Dhyāna: At this stage of meditation two types of consciousness are transcended devoid of sexual desire but possess sight, hearing, touch and mind. Meditation is hindered by *vitarka* and *vicāra*, by subtle and coarse intellections. *Vitaraka* (investigation), *vicāra* (reflection), *prīti* (joy), *sukha* (bliss) and *samādhi* are the five mental functions that exist. Through the First Dhyāna the ascetic obtains happiness in this world, *dṛṣṭadharmasukhavihāra*. The mind attains the level of Brahmaloka constituted by three heavens: Brahma-pāriṣadya, Brahma Purohita and Mahābrahmā.

Brahmā and his retinue is the creator of the world. The material beings different in bodies and ideas namely humans and certain gods are the first *vijñāna-sthiti*. The six gods of *Kāmadhātu* and the gods of First Dhyāna, the world of Brahmā have different bodies, because their colors, marks, garments, ornaments, figures etc. are not identical, their ideas of pleasure and displeasure are different.

In the Mahākaruṇāgarbha-maṇḍala Brahmā occupies a seat in the north in the *vajrakula*. As a representative of inhabitants of Brahmaloka he is sitting cross legged on a lotus with four heads and four arms holding a lance with the back right and doing *varada mudrā* with the front right. A lotus is given in his upper right hand while a vase is in the lower left. Two heads are drawn on both the sides and the fourth is put atop the three; all of them have a third eye on the foreheads indicating enlightenment (Lokesh Chandra 1972: pl. 223).

Second Dhyāna: *Vicāra* is eliminated at this stage. It contains joy, happiness, *cittaikāgratā* (concentration of mind on a single object) and *ādhyātmasamprasāda* (internal purity and faith). At this meditation only sixth sense, mind remains (*mano-vijñāna*), five types of consciousness corresponding to five senses, have been transcended, complementary of pleasure and pain are renounced, identity of persons and things is recognized, all the motivating activity of attraction and repulsion is overcome, only joy, *muditā* and renunciation, *upekṣā* are experienced (Snodgrass 1988:105). The ascetic acquires the seeing of knowledge, *jñānadarśana*, the supernormal knowledge of divine eye (Paussin 1990: 4.1263). Second Dhyāna corresponds to the following heavens: Parīttābha/limited luster, heaven of lesser light, Apramāṇābha/infinite luster, heaven of immeasurable light and Ābhāsvara/radiance, heaven of sounds of light, where light replaces sound as the medium of communication.

The inhabitants of this heaven are different in bodies but their ideas are similar. There is no difference of color, mark or figure. Ābhāsvara is the Pure heaven of supreme light where communication is possible through light. Ābhāsvara in the north in the *vajrakula* represents gods of the heavens of Second Dhyāna. He is sitting below Bṛhadābhāsvara with two attendants holding a lotus in his right hand and doing a mudrā with thumb, index and middle fingers flat and the other two folded. Next to him is the god of Bṛhādābhāsvara heaven holding a water pot in his right hand while the left is brought to the chest (Snodgrass 1988:522).

Third Dhyāna: Inhabitants of these heavens have only thought (*manovijñāna*) and experience only equanimity (not *vedanopekṣā* the sensation of indifference but *saṁskāropekṣā*), mindfulness (that is not losing sight of motive or reason for this equanimity, *upekṣānittasampramosa*), awareness (*samprajñānam*), happiness and stability (or *sthiti* a synonym for *samādhi*). Joy and renunciation like those of the second meditation. At the third stage of meditation the gods are called *śubhāḥ devāḥ*. The ascetic attains the excellent forms of *prajñā and prajñāprabheda*. The samādhi that produces these qualities is called *samādhibhāvanā*. The Third *Dhyāna* leads to the following heavens:

Parītta-śuddha/limited aura, heaven of lesser purity

Apramāṇa-śubha/infinite aura, heaven of immeasurable purity

Śubha-kṛtsna/steady aura, heaven of universal purity

Śubhakṛtasanas are of similar bodies and similar ideas because they have the sensation of pleasure. The *Śubhakṛtsanas* do not become fatigued with the pleasure of *Ābhāsvaras*, since they are calm. In contrast, the pleasure of *Ābhāsvaras* being mental pleasures, disturb the mind and thus the inhabitants are not calm.

Fourth Dhyāna**:** The fourth Dhyāna possesses of four parts: the sensation of indifference (sensation of neither suffering nor happiness), pure equanimity (*upekṣāparisúddhi*), pure mindfulness and samādhi. At the stage of fourth and the highest meditation in the nine heavens the *sādhaka* transcends joy and experiences only renunciation and possesses only thought. The first three dhyānas are *sa-iñjita* disturbed because of faults. But the fourth is free from faults and is undisturbed. The eight faults are *vitarka*, *vicāra*, happiness, suffering, satisfaction, dissatisfaction, inbreathing and outbreathing. The dhyāna is like a lamp in a sealed place not agitated by winds (Paussin 1990: 4.1239). The ascetic destroys all the defilement and attains:

Anabhraka: cloudless heaven, even clouds are not required to support the dwellings

Puṇya-prasava: heaven of auspicious birth having abundance of merits

Bṛhatphala: heaven of wide fruition

Asañjñinaya: heaven without thought because it is attained in meditation without thought, all mental functioning, feeling and perception ceases, resembling death except for the presence of warmth, life and consciousness. They can be entered by non-returners *anāgāmins*. But the beings who dwell there, will eventually be reborn into another level of existence, they have not escaped the wheel of becoming.

The next five heavens are the heavens of non-returners called Five Pure Abodes *Śuddhāvāsakāyika*. They are also states of existence but higher than the preceding six. They are:

Abṛha: passionless abode

Atapa: heaven without heat, devoid of fever of passions, distress and anxiety

Sudṛśa: heaven of clear vision

Sudarśana: well appearing heaven

Akaniṣṭha: heaven of the final limit of form

Akaniṣṭha, a heaven of non returners, of the most subtle and rarefied of forms, the highest of the eighteen heavens of the realm of form, is ruled by Maheśvara. It is located at the summit of Meru, and is known as the heaven of Sumeru assembly. Each of the heavens represents a state of existence that is subtle than the preceding. Bodhisattvas assemble there to hear the preaching of the sūtra. Probably this is the reason why Sarasvatī is painted next to Maheśvara in the west.

An adherent enters the Heavens of the formless world after crossing the *akaniṣṭha* heaven. The *arūpāvacara* gods dwell in the next four spheres *arūpadhātubhūmi*. The inhabitants live in an ecstatic state of pure spiritual existence, they do not possess the *rūpaskandha* which constitutes the body but retains the *skandhas* (aggregates) of perception, connotation, volition and consciousness, these four constitute the mind and its functioning. The four heavens of the realm of the formless or of void are formless but can be differentiated on the bases of hierarchy of corresponding meditations of the formless.

Fifth to eighth Dhyānas of Arūpadhātu: The paths by which the ascetic is delivered from the lower spheres are called *Anantyamārga* and *Vimuktimārga*. The idea of complete transcendence of physical matter is not there in Ākāśānantyāyatana but the next three are the abodes of those who have conquered the idea of physical matter, there is no *rūpa* in the sphere of Arūpadhātu (Pausin 1990: 4.1221-3). The mind is supported by mental states and the mental states by the mind. The ascetic leaves sensation, *vedanā* through the Arūpadhātu, as it is beyond sensation of lower spheres.

The first three dhyānas of Arūpadhātu: Ākāśānantyāyatana, Vijñānānantyāyatana and Akiñcanyāyatana are named after their preparatory exercise where one considers space, *āyatana*.

They are accompanied by only four *skandhas*; no *rūpa* or physical matter is accompanied. It arises out of separation from lower spheres. Each proceeds from separation from the lower sphere.

Fifth Dhyāna, Ākāśa-ananty-āyatana:

Meditation on the place of infinite space................................ Ākāśānantyāyatana-samāpatti

Sixth Dhyāna, Vijñāna-ananty-āyatana:

Meditation on the place of infinite consciousness..................... Vijñānānantyāyatana-samāpatti

Seventh Dhyāna, Akiñcanya-āyatana:

Meditation on the place of non-existence................................ Akiñcanyāyatana-samāpatti

Eighth Dhyāna, Naiva-sañjña-asañjña-āyatana:

The eighth dhyāna receives its name from the fact that *sañjña*, ideas is very weak in it, ideas are not active in it, but neither is it completely without ideas. It has the slightness of ideas in it.

Meditation on the place of neither thought nor non thought, Naivasañjñanāsañjñ-āyatana-samāpatti. This is called *bhavāgra* or the summit of existence.

Each level of meditation severs the mind of the *sādhaka* from the preceding level and unites with the upper (Snodgrass 1988:109). Finally the adherent attains tranquility, purity, uncreatedness essential to go up to the world beyond *Traidhātuka*, the world of Buddhas and Bodhisattvas. The heaven of neither thought nor non thought is the uppermost limit of the three worlds. Beyond this lies the adamantine world of Buddhas, totally unconditioned, immutable and eternal. According to esoteric Buddhism Buddhahood is beyond words and lies within the formless void, *arūpaśūnyatā*.

In the *vajrakula* of the Mahākaruṇāgarbha-maṇḍala these four stages of meditation are represented as four *stūpas* enshrining four Buddhas after Pṛithivī and followed by Jaya accompanying Sūrya.

An adherent raises himself above the five levels of existence, attains mentally the divine qualities that make him fit to begin meditation. He crosses all the eight levels of meditation one by one and concentrates on the Buddhas and Bodhisattvas and finally reaches the highest point, the great source of the world, Vairocana.

LITERATURE CITED

Akiyama 1961

Akiyama Terukazu. *Japanese Painting*. Albert Skira, 1961.

Lokesh Chandra 2000

Lokesh Chandra. *Dictionary of Buddhist Iconography.* (Vols. 1.5 published) International Academy of Indian Culture and Aditya Prakashan, New Delhi, 2000.

Chandra CH1

Cultural Horizons of India, Vols. 1-7. Aditya Prakashan, New Delhi, 1972.

Chandra 1972

Lokesh Chandra. *Esoteric Iconography of Japanese Mandalas.* International Academy of Indian Culture, New Delhi, 1972.

Dharmasangraha, ed., Muller, Oxford.

Edgerton 1977

Edgerton Franklin. *Buddhist Hybrid Sanskrit Grammer and Dictionary.* Motilal Banarsidass, Delhi, 1997.

JEBD 1965

Japanese-English Buddhist Dictionary. Daito Shuppansha 1965.

Kathopanisad, Upanishads. Kathopanisad, Varanasi, 1974.

Lee 1978

Lee Sherman E. *A History of Far Eastern Art,* London: Thames and Hudson, 1978.

Mani 1979

Mani Vettam. *Puranic Encyclopaedia.* Motilal Banarsidass, Delhi, 1979.

Matsunaga 1978

Matsunaga Daigan and Alicia. *Foundation of Japanese Buddhism.* Buddhist Books International, Los Angeles, Tokyo, 1978.

Matsunaga 1969

Alicia Matsunaga. *The Buddhist Philosophy of Assimilation.* Charles E. Tuttle Company, 1969.

Poussin 1894

Louis G. de la Poussin, *Journal of the Royal Asiatic Society,* London, 1894.

Poussin 1990

Abhidharmakosasangraha, translated by Louis Poussin, Paris and Louvain, 1923-31.

Reynolds, 1982

Frank E. & Mani B Reynolds. *Three Worlds According to King Ruang.* (Berkeley Buddhist studies series; 4) Berkeley, Calif.: Distributed by Asian Humanities Press / Motilal Banarsidass, Delhi, 1982.

Snodgrass 1988

Adrian Snodgrass. *The Matrix and the Diamond World Mandalas in Shingon Buddhism,* Aditya Prakashan, New Delhi, 1988.

Suvarṇaprabhāsasūtra, ed. Nobel, Leipzing, 1937.

TZ

J. Takakusu and G. Ono ed., *The Taisho Shinshu Daizokyo*, Picture Section, The Taisho Shinshu Daizokyo Kankokai, Tokyo, 1934.

Williams 1899

Monier Williams, *A Sanskrit-English Dictionary*, Clarandan Press, 1899.

7

INDIA AND EAST ASIA: A CULTURAL SYMBIOSIS

Since ancient times, the Indic religions are based on the philosophy of realization and freedom of thought. They are laden with rich treasures of arts, philosophy, science and literature etc. When they were accepted outside as vehicles of higher civilization, India became a perpetual giver of gifts, shedding effluence on the countries lying to its east, north and southeast. By supplying a basic script for developing new scripts to write historical chronicles or literatry works, a glorious pantheon to venerate, ceremonies to perform, systems of philosophy, rituals and festivals etc., India became a cultural leader. In these countries Hindu and Buddhist tenets were interwoven to such an extent that it became just impossible to draw a dividing line between them. The Buddhist pantheon assimilated a number of Hindu deities. Buddhist countries like Thailand adopted the ways to perform royal ceremonies according to the Śaiva system. The vast pantheon transmitted to the countries outside, over the past centuries has been developed into a variety of forms. Moreover local beliefs and customs were also taken into their folds, which resulted in a wide acceptance.

Indian culture reached Japan with the official introduction of Buddhism through Korea in AD 552. Although there is some evidence that it got its way to Japan at an earlier stage, but it is vague. By late sixth and early seventh century it was accepted as the state religion, sponsored by emperors, studied by scholars and above all embraced by masses out of a strong desire of fulfilment of their social requirements.

The credit for introducing Indian concepts and symbolism, rites and rituals, esoteric pantheon and practices into Japan, goes to the great monk scholar Kōbōdaishi, who went to China to study Buddhism and came back after a two years stay in AD 807. While returning he brought the twin maṇḍalas Mahākaruṇāgarbha-maṇḍala and the Vajradhātu-maṇḍala, which synthesize the transmission by Śubhākara-siṁha from Nālandā University and Vajrabodhi of Kāñchipuram. Kōbōdaishi established his headquarters at Kōyasan that later became a famous seat of Mahayana Buddhism, where over a hundred temples still exist.

Ceremonies

Today Indian religion, culture and traditions are so well absorbed into Japanese culture that they are no longer taken as imported from India. The Japanese modified and accepted whatever suited them to refine their lives. Hinduism has manifested itself in an expression of sentiments related to gods and semi-gods, goddesses and spirits etc. which takes various forms like rituals, worships, prayers, sacrifices and other such activities. Religion can be categorised in three ways – (i) religion of the rites; (ii) religion concerning asceticism; and (iii) religion related to knowledge. The first is to please the gods, the second is to purify the soul and the third aims at aquiring knowledge that is the means of salvation. The idea of incarnation and deification is quite similar to Indian religion in China and Japan. Performance of ceremonies to benefit the dead, *śrāddha* is common in these countries, In Japan, in the month of September, Koyasan city is thronged by visitors to perform the ceremony for their ancestors. People write names of their ancestors on wooden strips on one side and on the other they write a Sanskrit mantra and tie it near a sacred river flowing close to a temple so that the continuously flowing water keeps sprinkling on it and libation is automatically offered.

In the Shingon sect, propagated by Monk Kōbōdaishi, *abhiṣeka* ceremony, derived from consecration or anointment of kings upon their ascension to throne, came to symbolize attainment of Enlightenment. The ritual is called Kanjo. Besides this, countless other rituals form an integral part of the Shingon practice, performed for peace throughout the country, for prosperity, rain, good harvest and so on. They are viewed as *upāya*, means. One of the most important rituals used for spiritual and worldly purposes is *homa*, the fire ritual.

Homa

Homa, the fire ritual, known as Goma in Japanese shingon Buddhist tradition, considered to be the highest expression of ritual practice, was transmitted from Vedic India through China during the rule of the T'ang dynasty in the 8th century AD at the beginning of the Heian era in Japan. The ritual is an integral part of the contemporary Japanese religious life. During the long history *homa* has been refined and integrated into the ritual tradition of Buddhist Tantra. A large variety of rituals are present within the tradition. The training sequence of a Shingon priest culminates with *homa*. The pervasive impact of Shingon is known by the presence of Tantric ritual and symbolism through Japan today.

Four types of *homa* in Japan are:

1. Sokusaiho (Śāntika) – to calm the calamities as war, famine, diseases, accidental death and natural disturbance.
2. Zoyakuho (Pauṣṭika) – to increase or extend happiness and prosperity
3. Kushoho (Vaśīkaraṇa) – to invite the protection and compassion of the Buddhas and Bodhisattvas
4. Gofukuho (Ābhicārika) – to conquer evil

Altars and vessels for fire ritual: *Homakuṇḍas*

A large variety of *kuṇḍas,* vessels are known in the Japanese religious tradition used to perform six different kinds of fire rituals, dedicated to various divinities: *śāntika*, *vaśīkaraṇa*, *pauṣṭika, ābhicārika*, *āyuṣya* and *ākarṣaṇī*. Moreover, there is a different kind of *kuṇḍa* for offering an oblation to each divinity. Manuscripts, sheets, fascicles and scrolls are found from monasteries, illustrated with *kuṇḍas* and altars introduced by the Indian missionaries who sallied forth over mountainous crags, over tortuous streams, through deserts and snowy peaks, over long distances, mingled with foreign people, became one with them, captivated their hearts, moulded their conduct and gave them new ideas.

Brāhmaṇas in East Asia

According to the Japanese tradition Brāhmaṇas should be placed at the highest social level because they belong to the family that is pure since seven generations, they practise nobility, reject evil essences and are thinkers. Japanese literature abounds with references to Brāhmaṇas. The Generic term for a brāhmaṇa in Japanese is '*baramon*'. They are known as '*jogyo*' because of the purity that they practise; another term '*joshi*' means 'one who delights in purity; '*riyoku*' means without any worldly desire; and '*joei*' means descendent of a pure brāhmaṇa. The brāhmaṇa, who went to Japan in AD 736 was Bodhisena of Bhāradwāja *gotra*. He was cordially received by the court and presided over the eye opening ceremony of the Daibutsu at Nara in the presence of ten thousand delegetes from all over the Buddhist world. Vasiṣṭha, Aṅgiras, Gautama, Atri and Bhṛgu are the five Brāhmaṇa sages who are drawn, sitting in *vajrakula* of Mahākaruṇāgarbha-maṇḍala.

In China the word brāhmaṇa became a synonym of knowledge, the scientific works were known as '*brāhmaṇa* books'. Gautama Siddha was one of the great Brāhmaṇas who were responsible for the Bureau of Astronomy, calendrical science and mathematics etc.

Vasiṣṭha (Basosen, Vasu, an ascetic) is one of the five hermit ascetics who attend Agni and he is also one of the attendants of Sahasrabhuja Avalokiteśvara. Vasiṣṭha with matted hair and beard, holds a lotus in his right hand and a rosary in the left and Vasvī, his consort accompanies him.

Aṅgirasa (Akeirasen, body sweat), born from the mouth of Brahmā and husband of Maitreya and Dakṣa is one of the five hermit ascetics who attend Agni. In the form of a semi-naked hermit, with matted hair and beard, holds a vase placed upon a lotus with his left hand and performs a mudrā with the other. Aṅgirasī, his consort also accompanies him.

Gautama (Kudonsen), One of the five hermit-ascetics, Gautama, has a ruddy skin color and holds a water pot, sits with his right elbow resting on his raised right knee. Gautamī, his consort sits on his left side holding a single pronged vajra.

Astral Divinities

Astrology being an important science in ancient India was an attraction for the countries in East Asia. It played an important role in the social life of the East Asians after its transmission. The monks from these countries studied the influences of planets and stars in accordance with their positions at different places and times. Aspiration for a strong and stable Govt., and upliftment of nation, inspired the rulers to sponsor scholars of astrology. Several texts were translated into Chinese; the standard Chinese Buddhist canon includes sixteen such works. The Spencer Collection of manuscripts Kuyo Hirayaku details the mysterious astrological significance of the nine planets. (for details see John M. Rosenfield, Journey of the Three Jewels).

Mansion of the external, *vajrakula* is the fourth and the outermost layer of the Garbhadhātu-maṇḍala forming a border around it. It contains guardian deities who protect the dharma, the doctrine preached by the Buddha. This enclosure contains Hindu deities assimilated into the Buddhist pantheon. Over the centuries, these Hindu deities are illustrated in a large number of Japanese manuscripts, maṇḍalas on paper, silk or walls.

The astral deities that were introduced into Japan by Kōbōdaishi are positioned in this outermost enclosure in the four directions as well as individual maṇḍalas were painted for auspicious ceremonies.

Nine Planets

The Planets in the *vajrakula* of the Mahākaruṇāgarbha-maṇḍala, from the east gate to the south-east corner, are: Ketu (Keitosei, Comet), means pennant, lightening flash or commander; Ulkāpāta (Ryusei, Meteor) means falling star or meteor and represents fleeting transitoriness of existence; and Sūrya is translated into Sino-Japanese as Nichi (Sun), Nittenyō (Sunday), Nitten (Sun god) and Nittenyō (Sun god day). He rides three white horses and holds a sun disc in his right hand and the left is placed on the hip. The three planets of the south are: Rāhu (Ragosei, eclipse), Aṅgāraka (Katō, Fire day) and Bṛhaspati (Mokuyō, Wood day). The rest of the three planets: Soma (Getsuyō), Budha (Suiyō), Śukra (Kinyō) and Śani (Doyō), are depicted in the west.

Twenty-eight Constellations

Seven lunar mansions of the east, sitting from east gate to the south-east corner are: Kṛttikā (Bōshuku), Rohiṇī (Hisshuku), Mṛgasīras (Shishuku), Ārdrā (Shinshuku), Punarvasu (Seishuku), Puṣyā (Kishuku), Āśleṣā (Ryūshuku). Their left hands hold lotus flowers supporting red jewels and the right hands make various mudrās, but do not hold any attributes.

Seven lunar mansions of the south are: Maghā (Seishuku), Pūrvaphālgunī (Chōshuku), Uttaraphālgunī (Yokushuku), Hastā (Shinshuku), Citrā (Kakushuku), Svāti (Kōshuku), Viśākhā (Teishuku).

Seven lunar mansions of the west are: Anurādhā (Bōshuku), Jyeṣṭhā (Shinshuku), Mūlā (Bishuku), Pūrvāṣāḍhā (Kishuku), Uttarāṣāḍhā (Toshuku), Abhijit (Gyūshuku), and in the north are: Śravaṇā (Joshuku). Dhaniṣṭhā (Kyoshuku), Śatabhiṣā (Kishuku), Pūrvabhadrapadā (Shishuku), Uttarabhadrapadā (Hekishuku), Revatī (Keishuku), Aśvini (Roshuku), and Bharaṇī (Ishuku).

Zodiacal Signs

The three zodiacal signs sitting in the *vajrakula*, from the east gate to the south-east corner are: Meṣa (Yoku, ram), corresponding to Aries in the European zodiac, Vṛṣa (Mitsugoku, secret bull) corresponding to Taurus, and Mithuna (Nannyokū, man-woman) corresponding to a couple. Three zodiacal constellations of the south are: Makara (Makatsuku), corresponding to Capricorn, shown as an aquatic monster; Kumbha (Gembyōkū), corresponding to Aquarius and shown as a water pot; and Mīna (Sōgyokū, fish) and Siṁha (Shishikū), Kanyā (Shōnyokū) and Karkaṭaka (Bokaikū) are in the north. Zodiacal signs of the west are: Dhanu (Kyūkū), Vṛścika (Kachūkū) and Tulā (Hyōkū).

Hindu Pantheon

Gaṇeśa

Gaṇeśa is worshipped in Japan in a variety of forms. At the Jingoji monastery of Takao a special temple is consecrated to the esoteric twin Gaṇeśa and every year a celebration is held to worship him. Special shrines are dedicated to him in some monasteries of Mantrayana. Homes in Koyasan are hallowed by him. Gaṇeśa, the lord of good luck is known in Japan as Binayakaten or Shoden or Kangiten. Kangiten denotes the god of happiness, prosperity and well being.

The five manifestations of Gaṇeśa in the Vajradhātu-maṇḍala are:

1. Binayaka-ten or kangi-ten, the god of good luck, holds a radish in one hand and a *laḍḍu* (a sweet) in the other.
2. Vajracchinna or Kongo-zai-ten, sits in the east, holds a white umbrella, and is called Chatra-Vināyaka,
3. Vajrabhakṣana or Kongo-jikiten sits in the south and he is also called Mālya-Vināyaka. He is adorned with a garland of flowers.

The five symbolic forms of Gaṇeśa are :

Vināyaka, holding a *laḍḍoo*, Chatra-Vināyaka with a white umbrella, Mālya-Vināyaka with Garland, Dhanur-Vināyaka with bow and arrow, and Khaḍga-Vināyaka holds a sword. These attribute are placed on lotus leaves with rays of illumination issuing forth.

In the Mahakaruṇāgarbha-maṇḍala he is depicted with an axe and a radish. The Daigoji monastery at Kyoto preserves a ninth century scroll illustrating Gaṇeśa in this form. He occurs in five manifestations in the exterior circle of the central square of the Vajradhātu-maṇḍala brought by Kōbōdaishi in AD 805. This is the earliest reference to his worship in Japan. He attains a variety of forms holding different attributes. Four or six hands, three heads and four arms, Major attributes are a goad, a mace, a sword, a bowl, a noose, a tusk, a vajra, an axe, a *laḍḍu, a cakra*, and a radish.

Sarasvatī

Sarasvatī, the goddess of learning and eloquence is a divine power who can destroy darkness of ignorance, she is pure and white in color like moon and flakes of snow, the garments she wears are brightly white, she sits on a white lotus, a symbol of purity, knowledge and she carries a book and a *vīṇā*, a musical instrument as the major characteristic attributes. From east to west from north to south all over India annual festivals are celebrated in her honour, the manner although differs from place to place. During an annual festival, Kichijogekka in Japan, Sarasvatī and Lakṣmī are worshipped as a pair.

The second deity among Seven Lucky Gods, Shichijukujin in Japan, is Benzaiten. Benzaiten or Sarasvatī is worshipped in Japan for beauty, delightfulness, charm and generosity etc. Parents of young girls take their daughters to the temples to worship Sarasvatī for enhancing beauty.

Writers, painters, sculptors and architects etc. pray her on the New Year for fulfilment of their wishes. She attains a variety of forms. Many temples have preserved images and paintings portraying her, over the past centuries. A number of folk tales related to her are also popular in Japan.

In Japan in the Kokiji an annual *homa* ritual has been performed since the eighth century. Lakṣmī is worshipped as the goddess of good fortune and wealth, and the consort of Viṣṇu. According to the annals of Tōdaiji monastery Kichijogekka was first celebrated in AD 722. Ever since Goddess Sarasvatī reached Japan, she got a wide spread popularity not only among the Buddhists but also among the Shinto believers. She has also been worshipped to grant eloquence in speech, wisdom, longivity and victory in the battlefield, as well as to grant protection from natural disasters. *Vīṇā*, a stringed instrument, the chief attribute of Sarasvatī, is known as *biwa* in Japan. The ancient most *biwa* is kept in the Shosoin Repository in Nara.

Lakṣmī

Lakṣmī, the goddess of wealth is one of the seven lucky gods, Shichifukujin. She is worshipped as the goddess of beauty and fecundity and holds a wish granting jewel in her left hand. Her first and the most exquisite image painted with the native delicacy and a sensitive touch is preserved in the Yakushiji monastery since AD 771. A collection of ten scrolls illustrating selected figures "Zuzō-shō", kept at the Entsuji monastery at Kōyasan and "Besson-zakki", descriptions of divinities by Shinkaku, kept at the Ninnaji monastery, Kyoto, portray the goddess Lakṣmī sitting on a stool like throne flanked by two goddesses and backed by an elephant. Śrīdevī maṇḍalas are illustrated in Shika-shō-zuzō, Mandara-shū and Gensho-hitsu mandara-shū.

Yakṣa

Among the Seven lucky gods, Kumbhira or Kompira is a Yakṣa, worshipped by seafarers. The major temple of Kumbhira is said to be situated on the Shikoku island. According to the Indian tradition Yakṣa is a class of Demi-gods, described as attendants of Kuber: the god of wealth. Yakṣa is employed to guard the treasure and gardens of Kubera. It may be presumed that in ancient times sea routes were mainly used for trade, thus seafarers worshipped Yakṣa for gaining material wealth, but he is not a presiding divinity of water bodies.

Varuṇa

Varuṇa or Suiten presides over water bodies. He is one of the twelve Vedic divinities who constitute a group called 'Jūniten' in Japan. Varuṇa, the lord of water in India has been entrusted the responsibility of guarding atmosphere in Japan. He holds a lasso topped by snake as a symbol of being a justice who punishes accordingly. Those who aspire to get justice, worship him for good fortune.

Umā and Maheśvara

Goddess Umā and Lord Maheśvara or Śiva are the spiritual parents of Gaṇapati. In Japan Umā is known as Umahi and Maheśvara as Daijizaiten. They were first drawn in the Mahākaruṇāgarbha-maṇḍala by Monk Kōbōdaishi. Over the past centuries they were painted in a large number of manuscripts and scrolls kept at hundreds of monasteries like Ninnaji, Tōji, Entsuji, Kajuji, Daigoji etc. He attains the forms of Vṛṣa-vāhana, Paśupati-rudra, Maheśvara-rāja, Īśānarāja and Aṣṭabhuja-maheśvara. His *dhāraṇī* to be recited for invocation, symbolic form, seed syllable and maṇḍalas are also drawn in a number of manuscripts.

Mahākāla Śiva

The first among the group of seven deities worshipped for good luck in Japan is Daikokuten. Daikokuten is Mahākāla, the destroyer form of Śiva. In India Mahākāla takes a terrific form but in Japan he is represented as mild and placid, although his color is black. In olden times, Japanese houses used to have the major supporting pillar called *'Daikoku-bashira'* housing an image of Daikoku. It was believed to safeguard houses from evil eyes. But this form has been lost gradually, now he is worshipped as a powerful deity who bestows good luck.

Acala Śiva

Fudō-myō-ō, one of the most powerful deities in the Shingon pantheon, is a transformation of Acala Śiva. He emerges out of the fire of *homa* to subdue the evil-doers. He is portrayed in three different colors: red, yellow and blue. He is worshipped to take revenge against enemies or to conquer them. He is engulfed by flames of fire, swept to a side by wind.

Four Guardians

From the Purāṇic age there are four guardians of four directions: Virūḍhaka, Vaiśravaṇa, Virūpākṣa and Dhṛtarāṣṭra. These four guardian deities are sculpted for the Japanese temples from the very beginning. They occupy four corners of the central platform in the major halls of worship.

Dhyāna

Zen, that is *dhyāna*, was taken to China in the sixth century by the Indian teacher Bodhidharma, the youngest son of the king of Kāñchī and the follower of Prajñātāra whose manuscripts have survived in Japan. Zen is a school of East Asian Buddhism. Its philosophy of meditation is known as Ch'an in China. It underwent further developments there, got firmly rooted and blossomed in Japan. Both Japanese and Chinese monks propagated the meditative practices brought to Japan in the 7th century. They were Monk Dōshō, a disciple of Hsüan-tsang, Chinese priest Tao-hsüan, Gyokyo, a disciple of Tao-hsüan and teacher of Saichō. Emperor Soga's wife invited I-kung from China in the second quarter of the 9th century to preach the philosophy of Zen but effective plantation was done by the monks Eisai (1141-1215) and Dōgen (1200-1353).

When Zen reached Japan it was not just confined to the aristocratic class, serving painters, poets or sculptors but was also embraced by the masses who were unaware of the complications of the philosophy of popular sects, such as Shingon and Tendai. They could easily appreciate and adopt its one-pointedness in action, straight forwardness in presentation, strictness in discipline, heroic philosophy of life and death and masculine vigor and loyalty. They added their innate potential of delicacy and beauty. It penetrated deeply and widely into moral and aesthetic fields and became a great power not only in the artistic but also in the intellectual and political life of the Far

East. It moulded their character and became its expression itself. Zen has a following of around 10 million with 21000 temples. Sōtō and Rinzai, the two sub-sects vary in teaching and methods but meditation remains the foundation in both of them.

Twelve Vedic Deities/Jūni-ten

Indra (Taishakuten), Agni (Katen), Yama (Emmaten), Nirṛti (Rasetsuten), Vāyu (Futen), Vaiśravaṇa (Bishamonten), Īśāna (Isanaten), Brahmā (Bonten), Pṛthivī (Jiten), Sūrya (Niten) and Chandra (Gaten), the group of Vedic divinities reached Japan alongwith Tantrayana in the early ninth century when the great monk Kōbōdaishi came back from China to Japan in AD 805. They were painted in the outermost enclosure of the Mahākaruṇāgarbha-maṇḍala or Taizokai-mandara.

In most of the temples in Nara, Indra's images are enshrined along with Brahmā. He is the lord of heaven on the mount Sumeru while Brahmā is the ruler of the living world. His earliest extant image from mid eighth century is found from the Refectory of the Hōryūji monastery. It is a dry lacquer image, 404.6 cm. tall, wearing an armor under long flowing garments, a combination of the features of a guardian and a divine being. His left hand is holding a scroll and the right seems to be ready to hold something. The earliest representation of Indra as a Bodhisattva is seen in a Jātaka story painted on one of the side panels of the pedestal of a portable shrine produced in the 6th-7th century, Tamamushi-no-zushi, kept at the Hōryūji monastery. According to the story given in Konkyō-myō-kyō and Nehan-kyō Buddha was born as a brahmin and sacrificed himself to save a starving tigress. Indra came to test his virtue, recited half of a verse and then appeared in the form of a demon. Buddha listened and requested for the second half, but Indra as demon apologized as he was too weak. He craved for human flesh. Buddha got ready to sacrifice himself. The demon recited the second part, Buddha heard that, carved the verse on a rock, climbed up a tree and threw himself down. On this Indra relented and spared the Buddha.

Agni, the Fire born is one of the principal Vedic divinities taken into the fold of Buddhism. He is the fire born, but according to the esoteric philosophy he is the Tathagata's virtue of Wisdom that burns away the passions and ignorance, thus called Light of Wisdom. He is an adamantine protector of the law, known as *Goho-kongo*. As one of the eight guardians (*Happo-ten*) and Twelve Heavenly Beings (*Jūni-ten*) he presides over the southeast direction. He is described to be one of twelve different kinds in the chapter on maṇḍala devoted to six kinds of *homa* in the Mahavairocana-sūtra. He is represented as an aged hermit ascetic, whose colour is deep red and who has a triangle on his chest. To represent him symbolically three dots of ash are applied. He is always surrounded by flames and holds a rosary and a water pot.

In the Vedic age, Yama, the king, Yamarāja was venerated as the lord of death. Yamarāja is transliterated as *Emmarasha* or *Emma-ō* in Japanese. Long life was bestowed upon those who worshipped him. It is believed that every one is bound to be present in front of him for judgement after death, as Yama is responsible to keep an account of one's deeds. The Japanese term *Sosei* refers to his function as a judge. So in the post-vedic age Yama was portrayed as a judge. An account of sinful or the virtuous acts is kept in accordance with the law, *dharma*, thus he is called Dharma-rāja. After judgement he himself is responsible to punish the wicked, thus he is given a horrible appearance with burning red eyes and wearing red garments. *Kazai-funnu-ō* means a wrathful king who punishes the evil. *Dharma-rāja* is ascribed the highest position in Tibetan Buddhism because of being the lord of forefathers. Everybody goes to Yama to get justice by looking into the mirror held by him. By virtue of being the lord of forefathers he is also known as *śraddhā-deva*. He rides a buffalo, so he is called Mahiṣavān and Mahiṣadhvaja. In Japanese, he is also known as Emmara or abbreviated as Era. It comes from Yamala, meaning a pair. The word Yama also means restraint, binding, driver and observance.

In Japanese esoteric Buddhist tradition Varuṇa is placed in the Mahākaruṇā-garbha-maṇḍala twice in the west side of the Vajrakula once on the right side of the west gate and its north after Virūpākṣa. In the Sino-Japanese tradition his name is translated as "Suiten" and transliterated as "Baruna". He is one of the Twelve Celestial Beings and also one of the eight guardians. According to Subhākarasiṁha, Varuṇa is the king of serpents and guardian of the west. He rules over water that symbolises total knowledge. In esoteric Buddhism, he is the *honzon* of rituals for averting floods and other catastrophes caused by water. He is dressed in armour and crowned with snake-heads. He holds a serpent noose in his right hand, the left fist is placed on his hip and he sits to the south of the western gate. Varuṇa as the lord of hydrosphere, sits on the north side of the western gate attended by Varuṇānī and Varuṇa-paricarī in Mahakaruṇāgarbha-maṇḍala.

Vāyu or wind equates the cosmic breath. The intermediate space between the sky and the earth is occupied by the divine being Vāyu. Vāyu is one of the major Vedic divinities As the protector of the North-western direction he is said to have a thousand eyes; his chariot is driven by the horse called Rohit or Aruṇa. Vāyu is the fastest among all the divinities so he is the first to get the first drop of nectar. He can have two or four or even thousand arms. The colour of his garments is white his, eyes are red, his major attributes are a banner or a bag full of air and his ride is a deer. In the Japanese Buddhist pantheon he is counted among the Twelve Celestial Beings (*jūniten*) and the eight guardians (*happoten*). He is normally represented as an old man holding a wind flag or a blue flag and riding a roebuck.

Īśāna sits in the North-eastern corner in the *vajrakula* of the Mahākaruṇā garbha-maṇḍala as one of the Twelve Celestial Beings. He is the first among the five aspects of Śiva in his angry form. In the Dvādaśadeva-kalpa he is called Maheśvaradeva and Īśvaradeva (Tajima 210). He is also counted among the eleven rudras and eight forms of Śiva (aṣṭa-śiva). Īśāna is a symbol of knowledge and Īśāni of meditation. He is said to be dextrous (*kṣetrajña*), lord of all the spheres: *sarva-vidyā-swāmī Īśānaḥ sarva-vidyānām-iti-smṛtaḥ*, he helps the ignorant to be knowledgeable.

Brahmā (Dai-bonten-nō or Bonten) guardian of zenith and ruler of the heaven is refered to in the sūtras as a guardian of the *Dharma* when incorporated into Buddhism. In the Genzu maṇḍala he is shown with four arms and four heads, each of his four faces has three eyes.

Other Deities

Durgā is known as Juntei Kannon or Chuṇḍī Bhagavati. Hayagrīva transformed as Bato Kannon, is one of the famous forms of Avalokiteśvara. Apart from the group of twelve Vedic deities, Brahmā and Indra enjoy poupularity as important personalities in the Japanese pantheon.

Viṣṇu in the form of Nārāyaṇa sits on a Garuḍa in the *vajrakula* of the Mahākaruṇā-garbha-maṇḍala, known as Naraen-den. *Cakra* is his chief attribute. When he has three heads, the right side head is of a lion while the left is of an elephant. A large number of manuscripts illustrate him in various forms alongwith mudrās and mantras etc. Cāmuṇḍā in the Maha-vairocanābhi-sambodhi-pāṭha-kalpa and Taizo-in-zu kept at the Ninnaji monastery Kyoto illustrate the mudrās of Cāmuṇḍā. Kumāra Kārttikeya has also been worshipped as an individual apart from his placement in the maṇḍala as one of the major divine beings. One of his most beautiful sculptures, was produced during the Late Heian period by Kaikei in AD 1200. Brāhmī, Kaumārī, Cāmuṇḍā, Raudrī (Jizainyoten), Kauberi, Vaiṣṇavī (Bichu-nyōten) and Manuṣyā are the seven *mātṛkas* in Japanese pantheon. Raudrī, Vaiṣṇavī and Yamī form a group in south. Raudrī attains a terrific form as one of the Saptamātrkas and Navaśakti. She is said to be the *śakti* of Vidyeśvaras. It is also an epithet of Gaurī, so it may therefore be identical with the terrific aspect of Pārvatī as Durgā or Kālī. Raudrī sits below Gautama Ṛṣi in the south in Mahākāruṇāgarbha-maṇḍala with Vaīṣṇavī and Yamī. Her body is white, she has a double halo behind her head and holds a blue lotus in her upright right hand and the left hand is brought to the chest as if to carry something, most probably a vajra. Mahāvairocana-sūtra and Subhākarasiṁha assign Raudrī to be a part of the retinue of King Yama as one of the Seven Mother Goddesses, perhaps because Rudra is one of the names of Yama. Usually Raudrī is taken as a feminine form of Rudra, the name of wrathful aspect of Śiva, so she is taken as his consort. But in this context she is not sitting in that form.

Yamī is one of the Saptamātṛkā, Aṣṭamātṛka and Navaśakti. She is mentioned as twin sister of Yama and also as wife of Yama in the Purāṇic literature. She symbolizes '*paiśūnya*' malignity.

Yamī as one of the seven mother goddesses, sits with Raudrī and Vaīṣṇavī below Gautama in the southern vajrakula of the Mahākaruṇāgarbha-maṇḍala. The Shosetsufudōki details her form as consort of Yama Emmako but according to Genbōgiki and Shōryūgiki the consorts of Yama are Kālaratrī (Kokuyaten, "Black Night") and Mṛtī (Shikō, Queen of Death). But in this context she is not to be identified as any of them.

Vaīṣṇavī is also enumerated among Saptamātṛ, Aṣṭamātṛ and Navaśakti, as *śakti* or energy of Viṣṇu. She represents passion, *mātsarya,* envy or *lobha,* avarice. She is to sit in lalitāsana on garuḍa performing abhaya and varada mudrās, and hold *cakra*, *gadā*, *padma*, *śaṅkha* etc., as her attributes, and *pippala* is her sacred tree. Her images are prescribed to make her appear as a lovely woman with beautiful eyes, dark complexion, large breasts, pretty face and clad in yellow silken garments. She is said to have attacked demons with her discus and mace.

Brāhmī enumerated among Saptamātṛkā, Aṣṭamātṛkā and Navaśakti is said to be the *śakti* and consort of Brahmā. It is also an epithet of Sarasvatī. She rides a goose, in lalitāsana, performs varada and abhaya mudrās and holds *akṣamālā, kamaṇḍalu,* book, *triśūla* etc. She symbolizes *mada*, pride. According to Āgamas her complexion should be golden, she should have four hands and four faces. She is the one who made the enemies powerless. She is also regarded as the mother of Vedas, Vedamātā, she resides under *brahmavṛkṣa*.

In the western direction of the vajrakula of Mahākaruṇāgarbha-maṇḍala, she sits after Maheśvara and Umā with Aindrī. Rishukyō dose not include Brāhmī among the seven mothers. Taizō-zuzō locates her in north of outer vajrakula Mahāvairocana-sūtra and Śubhākarasiṁha call her "Daibon-myōhi" (mantra queen Mahabrāhmī). The maṇḍala transmitted by Śubhākarasiṁha also shows Brāhmī among seven mothers in the south. Her body is said to be of skin color, she holds a full blown lotus in her left hand and gesture of right hand is not clear. Aindrī is enumerated as one of the Saptamātṛkā and Aṣṭamātṛka, she is the energy of Indra and symbolizes *krodha*, anger or *matsarya*, envy.

Thus esoterism forms the core of cultural symbiosis between India and Japan which was transmitted from China to Japan by the great monk scholars like Kōbō Daishi and Denggō Daishi who had chosen the transcendental path. The unique personalities had contributed enormously to search the path of the Dharma. Chinese translations of the basic Buddhist texts, commentaries accomplished by the great teachers of India and China, the vast pantheons rituals and ceremonies brought and introduced by them served as the core and culmination of Buddhism in Japan.

8

BODHISATTVAS IN BUDDHIST ART AND THOUGHT

The first sight of sufferings in the world moved the heart of Prince Siddhārtha, the Buddha to be. He left the palace and went into the search of the ways of saving humanity from all sorts of sufferings. The would-be *cakravartī*, took the path of an ascetic to work for the welfare of the people—*bahujanasukhāya*, *bahujanahitāya*, the ultimate goal of his life. And this is the message that he gave while addressing the first gathering of sixty Arhats. He asked them to go, meditate and get enlightenment to work for the people. This led to the evolution of the Bodhisattva ideal that is embedded in the teachings of the Buddha: a harmonious combination of intellect and emotion, of theory and practice, of head and heart. During a later phase, Buddha was seen as a divine teacher whose personality became a combination of royalty and divinity.

Śākyamuni always associated himself with this world and not with the world beyond. He discouraged mere philosophy and speculation if it had no practical value. Gautama Buddha was not an escapist and wanted no one to be. And it is the pure social life that the Bodhisattva ideal rightly recommends (EB pp. 224-233). Nirvāṇa was sought within the worldly life. A Bodhisattva lives in this world and postpones his nirvāṇa to be able to work for benefit of humanity. But in contrast to this, his followers later began to make mere academic studies as an end in itself. Mahayanists reacted against the ideal.

The Bodhisattva doctrine was a result of two movements of thought: the growth of *bhakti* (devotion, faith and love) and idealization and spiritualization of the Buddha. The evolution of the stage of *bhakti* in Buddhism is represented by the Saddharma-puṇḍarīka- and Sukhāvatīvyūha-sūtras. Buddhavaṁśa, Caryāpiṭaka, the Pali commentaries and the Mahayana sutras developed the Bodhisattva concept in such a way that a Bodhisattva became an object of devotion and his human nature began to disappear.

The deep-rooted feelings found an outlet in the invention and adoration of the Bodhisattvas (Dayal 1932:31). The Mahayanists turned in their need to the earlier history of Gautama Buddha when he was a charitable, patient and wise Bodhisattva. As a Bodhisattva he had helped many men and women with gifts of wealth and knowledge. He was a more humane and lovable figure at that stage. The pious worshipper could pray to a Bodhisattva for health, wealth and mundane blessings, and that was all that they really wanted. Ordinary men and women are more anxious to secure welfare and happiness in this world than to strive for distant goal of Buddhahood. The Bodhisattvas endowed with super human qualities were thus chosen for worship and adoration in order to satisfy needs of the devout and pious Buddhists.

The analogy of other religious movements also proves that uneducated men and women require some attributes of human personality in the superhuman beings whom they are willing to worship (Dayal 1932:31-35). The earliest usage of the term Bodhisattva is found in Mahāvyutpatti (645) when it gives a list of ninety-two Bodhisattvas.

A variety of interpretations are given to the meaning of the word Bodhisattva, but the most acceptable one, is that Bodhisattva is the one, who aspires for enlightenment, *bodhi+sattva*, Buddha to be. '*Bodhi*' means enlightenment, but '*sattva*' has been explained in many ways-

- essence, nature, true essence (Monier Williams 1899)
- substance (Rhys 1925)
- one, who has '*bodhi*' or perfect wisdom as essence
- he, whose essence is becoming enlightened
- '*sattva*' means any living or sentient being
- a being seeking for *bodhi* or destined for enlightenment (Dayal 1932:4-5)

The term Bodhisattvayāna was also framed (SP 79,6, 416,14) but rarely used because it was replaced by the term Mahāyāna (the vehicle of Bodhisattvas, SP 183.8, 285.8, Edgerton 1977:403). It is some times called Tathāgatayāna "O Lord, in this manner this Mahayana belongs to the great beings, Bodhisattvas" (SSPP:1530,6). At another place (p. 552) it is the *Arhad-dharma* and *pratyekabuddha-dharma*. The other related terms found in the Buddhist literature are: Bodhisattvayāna (SP 79.6, 416.14), Bodhisattvayānikā (SP 183.8), Bodhisattvayānīyā (SP 224.4, 285.8).

The Bodhisattva Concept Under Influence

Hindus established the cult of certain devas and deified heroes and the Buddhists endowed their Buddhas and Bodhisattvas with similar attributes and powers. The Buddhist leaders popularized Buddhism by inventing compassionate Bodhisattvas as Buddhist counterparts of Hindu deities and their incarnations (Dayal 1932:37).

Zoroastrianism also contributed to the rise of Bodhisattva doctrine. It influenced more directly through the cult of Sun worship that was introduced into India in the 3rd century BC. Dīghanikāya (1.11.line 21) refers to Sun worship. Many familiar names in Mahāyāna are suggestive of Sun worship—Amitābha, Vairocana, Maitreya, Dīpaṅkara. The solar myth penetrated deep into every sphere of Buddhism and many Bodhisattvas were endowed with solar attributes.

Like the Hellenic gods Buddhists invented their own pantheon of Bodhisattvas in order to worship half divine and half human beings.

Assimilation of Deities of Tribes

Buddhists absorbed new ideas in the Northwest of ancient India. Semi barbarian tribes were converted to Buddhism. Their deities were adopted as Bodhisattvas. The Bodhisattva doctrine exalted love and activity and peopled the heavens with gracious beings who could be worshipped (Dayal 1932:39-40). Such deities should be identified as Lokeśvaras, but they gained popularity as Bodhisattvas.

Spiritual Life of a Bodhisattva

A Bodhisattva crosses the ten stages of spiritual progress called *bhūmis*, described in the Mahayana works such as Mahāvastu, Bodhisattvabhūmi and Daśabhūmika-sūtra. These *bhūmis* are the gradations of spiritual life. The glory and power of a Bodhisattva gradually increases as he passes from one stage to another. Finally he is seen as almost equal to a Buddha.

Pāramitās are related to the practical side of the spiritual life of a Bodhisattva. Jātakas and Avadānas illustrate these perfections. These stages distinguish a Bodhisattva from an Arhat. Śāntideva, a 7th century theologian has left a work "Introduction to the Career of the Bodhisattva", on spiritual life of a Bodhisattva. The virtues that make him a Buddha are a combination of merit and knowledge. He participates directly or indirectly in the first seven stages being generous, moral, patient, energetic, meditative, studious and skilled in the means to be employed in saving others. Beings in possession of these stages are: Bodhisattvas, Mahābodhisttvas, Mahāsattva Bodhisattvas and Daśabhūmīśvara Bodhisattvas. They are all protecting and helpful. When they are grouped around the Buddha, they constitute the third jewel, that is *saṅgha*. They are more merciful and active.

When a Bodhisattva is in possession of the perfect qualities of a Buddha, he is superior to the Arhats and the Pratyekabuddhas. The intentions or aspirations of a Bodhisattva even when he is only on the threshold of his career are pregnant with *bodhi* and salvation of all beings. Therefore he is superior to the Arhats and the Pratyekebuddhas. But it happens only when he enters the seventh *bhumi* out of the ten *bhumis* (Mādhyamakāvatāra 18-20, Encyclopaedia of Religion and Ethics pp. 747-753).

Bodhisattvas: Different from Arhats and Pratyekabuddhas

Śākyamuni was a Bodhisattva before becoming a Buddha. He himself has used this term. His career as a Bodhisattva, spans from his renunciation to enlightenment because he was a man who perfected himself by realizing his self to the highest degree possible for a man. He was a teacher and the Arhats were his disciples who followed his teachings. They were taught the Four Noble Truths and the Eightfold Path. The concept of Arhatship was later gradually widened and elaborated. An Arhat was absolutely free from the three or four Āsravas. He was liberated, he was not to be reborn. Such an Arhat was sent as a preacher to preach the truth for the welfare and liberation of the multitude, as he loved his fellow creatures and has pity on them: *caratha bhikkhave cārikam bahujanahitāya bahujanasukhāya lokānukampāya atthāya hitāya sukhāya deva manussāṇām* (Vinaya 1.21).

The Buddhist texts like Dhammapada, Theragāthā and Milindapañha laid emphasis on self-control, meditation and personal salvation. But there were those who aspired to be enlightened in preference to merely becoming Arhats, they were Bodhisattvas. According to Dayal (1932:3) the rise of the Bodhisattva concept was against the Arhats who had turned cold and aloof. Some monks began to neglect certain important aspects in the 2nd century BC. They became self centered and cared only for their own liberation. Some Buddhist leaders protested against this lack of spiritual fervour.

Har Dayal further says that a Bodhisattva is primarily and emphatically one who criticizes and condemns the spiritual egoism of Pratyekabuddhas. The idea of Pratyekabuddhas evolved in the second century BC. He is the one who was enlightened by himself; one who has attained the perfect and supreme insight, but died without proclaiming the truth to the world. The duty of teaching and helping others was not fulfilled. So the Bodhisattva ideal counteracted this tendency. A Bodhisattva was defined as the one who strove to gain *bodhi* and scorned nirvāṇa as he wished to help and succour his fellow creatures in the world of sorrow, sin and impermanence.

Bodhisattvas are distinct from and opposed to Arhats and Pratyekabuddhas. A Bodhisattva is regarded superior to them. The word Arhat seems to have disappeared in the later literature. The words often used are 'śrāvaka-bodhi' and 'śrāvaka-yāna'. A Bodhisattva aims at acquisition of *bodhi* and *Buddha-jñāna* while a Śrāvaka and a Pratyekabuddha is content with nirvāṇa (Dayal 1932:10).

Buddhas as Bodhisattvas

Śākyamuni bore the name of Sumedha in Dīpaṅkara Jātaka, a famous story of Buddhist literature. He discovered the ways of nirvāṇa through attainment of Arhatship at the sight of the Buddha Dīpaṅkara. Thenceforward he was a Bodhisattva. This was his vow, *praṇidhāna* or supplication, *prārthanā*, *abhinīhāra*. (Encyclopedia of Religion and Ethics p. 739). Buddhavaṁśa, life stories of 25 Bodhisattvas, describes the Buddha's decision to postpone his entry into nirvāṇa. The term Bodhisattva developed as a concept in Buddhavaṁśa and in later commentaries. It describes the ten Pāramitās, eight conditions necessary for fulfillment of Buddhahood and the Bodhisattva's decision to postpone his entry into nirvāṇa. 1st-2nd century BC text Mahavastu describes a Bodhisattva's career and Jātakas illustrate the selfless nature of Bodhisattvas.

The other Buddhas who are adored as Bodhisattvas are: Maitreya, the Buddha of past and Bodhisattva of present, Amitābha, who vows as a Bodhisattva in Sukhāvatīvyūha-sūtra and Bhaiṣajyarāja Bodhisattva in Saddharma-puṇḍarīka-sūtra.

Bodhisattvas based on Buddha's Power and Personality

The universal practice of saint worship shows that it has satisfied certain fundamental needs of human nature at a certain stage of intellectual development. The Buddhists invented their class of saints (Bodhisattvas) chiefly by personifying the different virtues and attributes of Gautama Buddha's personality. Bodhisattvas derive their existence and attributes from the central historical fact of Buddha's life and works. They also took up certain epithets that were applied to Gautama Buddha and converted them into the names of Bodhisattvas. Mañjuśrī and Avalokiteśvara are personifaications of *prajñā* and *karuṇā* of the Buddha. Maitreya typifies *maitrī,* friendliness. Many of such Bodhisattvas became a special kind of Godlike character.

Some Bodhisattvas owe their names to the adjectives that were first employed to describe the great teacher. Buddha is spoken of as Samantato-bhadraka and Samanta-bhadra-kāya (auspicious and excellent in all ways) in the Avadāna-śataka and Lalitavistara and Samantabhadra is a name of a Bodhisattva (Dharma-saṅgraha section 12, Mahāvyutpatti, section 23, Avadānaśataka, 1.3.7). Another Bodhisattva, Mañjuśrī may perhaps has been derived from Mañjughoṣa and Mañjusvara, the epithets used to describe the voice of the Buddha. (Sukhāvatīvyūha-sūtra 76.8, Lalitavistara 366.19).

Sūtra-based Interpretation

In Hīnayāna, there could be only one Bodhisattva at a time but in Mahāyāna the celestial Bodhisattvas were multiplied.Their number is innumerable because most of the sūtras contain different lists of names in different chapters. A classification of these groups requires an analysis of the Mahāyāna sūtras. Saddharma-puṇḍarīka-sūtra gives various lists of names of Bodhisttvas in its chapters. The first chapter says that there were eighty thousand Bodhisattvas but it gives a list of only twenty-five Bodhisattvas who were present in the assembly of Lord Buddha:

1 Mañjuśrī (Mahāsattva Bodhisattva)
2 Avalokiteśvara (Mahāsattva Bodhisattva)
3 Mahāsthāmaprāpta (Mahāsattva Bodhisattva)
4 Sarvārthanāma
5 Nityādi
6 Anikṣiptadhura
7 Ratnapāṇi
8 Bhaiṣajyarāja (Mahāsattva Bodhisattva)
9 Bhaiṣajyasamudgata (Mahāsattva Bodhisattva)
10 Vyūharāja
11 Pradānasūtra
12 Ratnacandra
13 Ratnaprabha
14 Pūrṇacandra
15 Mahāvikrāmin
16 Anantavikrāmin
17 Trailokyavikrāmin
18 Mahāpratibhāna
19 Satatasamita
20 Dharaṇīdhara
21 Akṣayamati
22 Padmaśrī
23 Nakṣatrarāja
24 Maitreya (Mahāsattva Bodhisattva)
25 Mahāsattva Siṁha

SIXTEEN BODHISATTVAS OF A TIBETAN MAṆḌALA

Sixteen Bodhisattvas of the Tibetan maṇḍala from the Ṅor monastery correspond to the Bodhisattvas of Sapta-tathāgata-pūrva-praṇidhāna-viśeṣa-vistara. They are as follows:

East

Bodhisattva	Attribute	Emphasis
Mañjuśrī (Mahāsa.Bo.)	sword and book	knowledge and virtue
Avalokiteśvara (Mahāsa. Bo)	lotus	-
Vajrapāṇi (Mahāsa.Bo)	vajra	-

Sūryaprabha	sun	eternity
South		
Candraprabha	moon	eternity
Mahāmatī	eye	wisdom
Maitreya (Mahāsa.Bo.)	lotus	-
Trāṇamukha	book on lotus	liberation through knowledge
West		
Pratibhānakūṭa	incensoir	power/fighting
Vikrāmin	sword	power/fighting
Darśanīya	book on lotus	enlightenment
Sarvatamonirghātamati	jewel stick	-
North		
Adhimukti	vase of *amṛta*	*tarpaṇa*
Merukūṭa	crescent on lotus	power
Gadgadasvara	thunderbolt	power/fighting
Meruśikhara	vase of *amṛta*	power

(Lohia 1994:13-20)

Only four among them are said to be Mahāsattva Bodhisattvas: Avalokiteśvara, Mañjuśrī, Vajrapāṇi and Maitreya. A number of sūtras are important sources of information for a study of the development of the Bodhisattva concept. Such as:

- Daśabhūmika-sūtra
- Bodhisattvabhūmi
- Bodhicaryāvatāra
- Saddharmapuṇḍarīka-sūtra
- Brahmajāla-sūtra
- Bodhisattva-prātimokṣa-sūtra
- Śrīmālādevi-sūtra
- Avalokiteśvara-sūtra
- Lalitavistara
- Sukhāvatīvyūha-sūtra
- Sarvatathāgata-tattva-saṅgraha

Different Bodhisattvas have different functions in sūtras. Saddharmapuṇḍarīka-sūtra and Avalokiteśvara-sūtra have very long lists of Bodhisattvas that are to be reassessed. But characterization of two types of Bodhisattvas based on two chapters of the Saddharmapuṇḍarīka-sūtra, Gadgadasvara-parivarta and Samantamukha-parivarta exemplify that they are bodhicentric/dhyānasattvas like Gadgadasvara and philanthropy-centric beings/Bodhisattvas like Avalokiteśvara. But it should be made clear that even meditation by the Bodhisattvas was meant for the well being of the people. Gadagadasvara Mahāsattva Bodhisattva attains seventeen types of samādhis.

In the light of sūtras, it can be presumed that at various stages of development, Bodhisattvas had to play various functions such as:

- The Bodhisattvas who lay emphasis on meditation
- Those who are portrayed as saviours
- Bodhisattvas of defence
- Bodhisattvas of polemics (*sāstrārtha, upāyakauśalya,* debate)
- Dhyāni-bodhisattvas
- Jñānasattvas
- Vajrasattvas
- Śrībodhisattvas
- Vajrabodhisattvas
- Samvaraśīlas (aim at suppressing all evil acts)
- Kuśaladharma-saṅgrāhaka-śīlas (cultivation of virtues)
- Sattvārthakriyā-śīlas (inculcate compassion and mercy)

(ER 2.265)

Mahāsattva Bodhisattvas

As a result of the Buddhists' emphasis on moral and spiritual qualities, Avalokiteśvara and Mañjuśrī were seen as personifications of kindness and knowledge. Sometimes Bodhisattvas were also seen as active agents of the Buddhas who had produced them. But a distinction between Bodhisattvas and Mahāsattva Bodhisattvas can clearly be seen in the sūtras. In Saddharmapuṇḍarīka-sūtra, some of them are called Bodhisattva Mahasattvas, e.g.:

Akṣayamati-Bodhisattva-mahāsattva (SP 443)

Samantabhadra-Bodhisattva-mahāsattva (SP 469)

Avalokiteśvara-Bodhisattva-mahāsattva (SP 443)

Mañjuśrī-kumārabhūta-Bodhisattva-mahāsattva (SP 2)

For a comparative study, the following texts should also be consulted:

NSP 19 Vajradhātu-maṇḍala

NSP 22 Durgatipariśodhana-maṇḍala

NSP 20 Mañjuvajra-maṇḍala

NSP 21 Dharmadhātu-maṇḍala

SM 83, 280, 283

The eight popular Mahāsattva Bodhisattvas in the Buddhist pantheon are according to different texts:

SM 18	SM 83	SM 280	NSP 26	Dharmas 12
Kṣitigarbha	Kṣitīśa	Kṣitigarbha	Kṣitigarbha	Kṣitigarbha
Khagarbha	Ākāśagarbha	Khagarbha	Khagarbha	Khagarbha
Vajrapāṇi	Kuliśa	Vajrapāṇi	Vajrapāṇi	Vajrapāṇi
Maitreya	Lokeśa	Lokeśvara	Lokeśvara	Maitreya
Viṣkambhin	Skambhin	Viṣkambhin	Sarvanīvaraṇa-viṣka.	Sarvanīvaraṇa-viṣkambhin.
Mañjughoṣa				Mañjuśrī
Gaganagañja				Gaganagañja

(Lokesh Chandra 1992:2.240)

The eight prominent Bodhisattvas given in the beginning of the Sarvatathāgata-tattvasaṅgraha are:

1. Vajrapāṇi
2. Avalokiteśvara
3. Ākāśagarbha
4. Vajramuṣṭi
5. Mañjuśrī
6. Sahacittotpādadharmacakrapravartī
7. Gaganagañja
8. Sarvamārabalapramardī

Bodhisattvas as Acolytes

Following Bodhisattvas come as acolytes, attending the four Buddhas:

Samantabhadra and Mañjuśrī with Śākyamuni

Avalokiteśvara and Mahāsthāmaprāpta with Amitābha

Sūrya and Candra with Bhaiṣajyaguru

Ākāśagarabha and Kṣitigarbha with Maitreya

Analysis of the Bodhisattvas of Pure Land Tradition

Devotion to Pure Land philosophy in Japan can be traced back to the 6th century AD. The known reference to the sūtra Daimuryōjukyō (Larger Sukhāvatī-vyūha) appears in the writings attributed to Prince Shōtoku taishi. Tenjukoku-mandara (the Land of Heavenly longivity) was produced after the death of the Prince, making a vow that the soul of the prince may rest in the heaven of Amitabha. During the early Nara period priests of Kegon, Hosso and Sanron sects used to study the Pure Land sūtras. Monk Chiko of the Sanron sect is said to have created a Pure Land maṇḍala after AD 640. Although the sect flourished during the late Heian and Kamakura periods but the rise was not sudden, it developed gradually. Thus during this long span of time Bodhisattvas of Jōdo tradition were sculpted and painted over and over again as:

(a)2 Bodhisattvas, Avalokiteśvara and Mahāsthāmaprāpta, flanking Amitābha

(b)8 Bodhisattvas with Amitābha in his paradise

(c)25 retinue Bodhisattva in the Raigō tradition in Japan, flying down from the heaven to receive the soul of the deceased

(d)2 + 32 Bodhisattvas of the Taima-maṇḍala based on Amitāyurdhyāna-sūtra

Analysis of the 25 Bodhisattvas depicted in Raigō Scenes from Japan

	Bodhisattva	**Attributes**	**Emphasis**
1.	BS Avalokiteśvara	Lotus throne	bears to paradise
2.	BS Mahāsthāmaprāpta	prayer	non-duality of wisdom and mental concentration
3.	BS Samantabhadra	banner	points out the path to perpetually obedient humanity
4.	BS Yakuō	banner	waves the massage of agelessness and deathlessness
5.	BS Yakujo	jade flag	indicates the ranks of rebirth in distant land
6.	BS Hojizai	flower garland	expresses the meritorious power of Amitabha's infallible salvation
7.	BS Shishiku	boisterous	cavorting taps out edification, reaching downward for unenlightened folk
8.	BS Darani	swaying sleeves	exhorts to seek upward for spiritual awakening
9.	BS Ākāśagarbha	hip drum	sounds aloud the power to fulfil merit and wisdom
10.	BS Tokuzō	reed pipe	reverberates with eighteen excellences of Budhas
11.	BS Hōzō	flute	blows cool breeze of the three gates to enlightenment
12.	BS Konzō	lyre	manifests thirty seven deities
13.	Kongozō	lyre	resounds with the oneness of the ten worlds
14.	BS Komyoō	lute	lightens perplexity of oppressive knowledge
15.	BS Sankai-e	harp	teaches principal of quiescence and Absolute Reality
16.	BS Kegon-ō	instrument	fills up the whole universe as object of mind
17.	BS Shuho-ō	gong	extols the one Buddha vehicle

18. BS Gakko-ō	swaying drum	causes the world of ten quarters to reverberate
19. BS Nissho-ō	hand drum	extols the four realms embraced in eternally tranquil light
20. BS Sammami-ō	scattering	flowers, dispersed in the realms of empty space and sea
21. BS Jojizai-ō	large drum	sounds like a great assembly of non discrimination
22. BS Daijizai-ō	flower banner	soars up towards absolute non-duality
23. BS Hakuzo-ō	jeweled flag	flutters in the heaven of Ultimate Truth
24. Daitoku	jewel	imbued with the teaching free of any taint of illusion
25. BS Muhenshin	incense	offers to Amitabha

(Okazaki 1977:114-5)

Among the above twenty-five Bodhisattvas there are four Pūja-devīs (6,8,20,25), five pennant bearers (3,4,5,22,23), twelve deities of music and dance (9-19, 21), two Mahāsattva Bodhisattvas (1,2), and two of them (7,24) could not be classified.

Bodhisattvas of the Gaṇḍavyūha Tradition

Bodhisattvas of the Gaṇḍavyūha tradition are different from those of the Pure Land. The Kegon sect is based on the Buddhāvataṁsaka Mahāvaipulya-sūtra (Jap. Daihokobutsu Kegonkyō) popularly known as Kegonkyō. The Kegon sect made extensive cultural and philosophical contributions to Japanese history. Philosophers, artists and devotees were inspired by its grand view of totality, which exerted a considerable influence on the development of Buddhist art. The bodhisattvas of the Kegon sect are as follows :

(a) 10 Bodhisattvas of the 10 directions, (same as in Avataṁsaka-sūtra) coming from the heaven,

(b) Bodhisattvas with Daibutsu, Tōdaiji, (Roshana Daibutsu)

(c) 10 Bodhisattvas in the Hōryūji pagoda witnessing the mahāparinirvāṇa scene (Lokesh Chandra 1992:2.240)

Bodhisattvas of the Healing Cult

Saddharmapuṇḍarīka-sūtra is the earliest text wherein the concept of the Healing Bodhisattva personified as Bhaiṣajyarāja Bodhisattva, is found. In later times Buddha of healing was venerated as Bhaiṣajyaguru, who cures physical as well as spiritual illnesses. He resides in his paradise of pure emerald situated in the east. As a Bodhisattva he vowed to cure diseases, so his cult centers around life in this world to achieve health and longevity. Devotion to the Bodhisattva spread fast. Innumerable Bodhisattvas are said to dwell in his paradise, chief among them are Sun and Moon, symbols of eternity. Moreover there are eight Bodhisattvas of Bhaiṣajyaguru, according to various traditions –

	Lalitavistara	Chinese	Tibetan	Hōryūji
1.	Avalokiteśvara	Avalokiteśvara	Avalokiteśvara	Lokeśvara
2.	Vajrapāṇi	Mahāsthāmaprāpta	Vajrapāṇi	Vajrapāṇi
3.	Samantabhadra	Akṣayamati	Samantabhadra	Samantabhadra
4.	Mañjughoṣa	Mañjuśrī	Mañjuśrī	-
5.	Kṣitigarbha	Pao-t'an-houa	Kṣitigarbha	Kṣitigarbha
6.	Ākāśagarbha	Bhaiṣajyarāja	Ākāśagarbha	Khagarbha
7.	Maitreya	Maitreya	Maitreya	-
8.	Sarvanīvaraṇa-viṣkambhin	Bhaiṣajyasamudgata	Sarvanīvaraṇa-viṣkambhin	Viṣkambhin

Bodhisattvas of the Naya-sūtra Tradition

Rishu-kyō or the Naya-sūtra has functioned on many levels of activities of esoteric sect, from the political to the popular. Recitation of this sūtra is a regular event in its temples throughout Japan. It is also an important part of the rituals performed on various special occasions. The teachings of Naya-sūtra are condensed into chapters. The first eight of the nine central divisions of the text are devoted to the virtues of the eight great bodhisattvas. Chapters III-X, deal in detail with the specific teachings of these bodhisattvas.

(a) 8 Bodhisattvas: Trailokyavijaya, Avalokiteśvara, Ākāśagarbha, Vajra-muṣṭi, Sacittodpāda, Gagangañja, Sarvamāra

(b) Four Bodhisattvas of the east, west, north and south

(c) Four primary Bodhisattvas

(d) Four Bodhisattvas of offering

(e) Four inner and four outer Bodhisattvas

(g) Bodhisattvas of adamantine love, pride, desire, joy, flower, fragrance, dance, song, vow, lamp etc.

These Bodhisattvas require a reinterpretation in the light of the interpretations of the Bodhisattvas of the Vajradhātu-maṇḍala.

Avalokiteśvara Mahāsattva Bodhisattva: A Saviour

Avalokiteśvara was worshipped to win favour because with the evolution of the cult of devotion the altruistic motives were greatly emphasized. Avalokiteśvara was seen as an embodiment of compassion who aims at delivering all human beings from sufferings. Sukhāvatīvyūha (Nanjio 25, T vol. 12, p.2902), Purṇaprabhāsa-samādhimati, (Nanjio 381, T. vol. 15, p. 451), Vimalakīrti (Nanjio 147, T. vol. 14, p. 519) and Pañcaviṁśati-sāhasrikā-parajñāpāramitā (Nanjio 2, T. vol. 8, p. 1, Nanjio 4, T. vol. 8, p. 147). Saddharmapuṇḍarīka-sūtra contains an entire chapter on Avalokiteśvara, which portrays him as Samantamukha, as a saviour, one, whose face is turned in every direction in order to see all things and save all beings. There is no shape or form that he does not assume to preach the *dharma*. With its translation into Chinese a new sect evolved around him. According to the Saddharmapuṇḍarīka-sūtra he assumes the following forms to preach the *dharma* and convert the sentient beings:

Manifestations in the SP

1. Buddha
2. Bodhisattva
3. Pratyekabuddha
4. Disciple
5. Brahmā
6. Indra
7. Gandharva
8. Goblin
9. Īśvara
10. Maheśvara
11. Cakravartin
12. Imp
13. Kubera
14. Senāpati
15. Brāhmaṇa
16. Vajrapāṇi

33 manifestations often listed

1. Buddha
2. Śrāvaka
3. Pratyekabuddha
4. Upāsaka,
5. Upāsikā
6. Brahmā
7. Indra
8. General
9. Īśvara
10. Maheśvara
11. King
12. Vaiśarvaṇa
13. Rich man
14. wealthy woman
15. Gṛhapati,
16. Gṛhapati woman
17. Brāhmaṇa,
18. Brāhmaṇa woman
19. Vajradhara
20. Official,
21. Woman official
22. Bhikṣu
23. Bhikṣuṇī
24. Boy
25. girl
26. Deva
27. Nāga
28. Yakṣa
29. Gandharva
30. Asura
31. Garuḍa
32. Kinnara
33. Mahoraga

(Nos. 26 to 33 are the eight types of being called aṣṭayami. They should not be considered as manifestations of Avalokiteśvara.)

Avalokiteśvara as a Saviour in Saddharma-puṇḍarīka-sūtra

According to Saddharma-puṇḍarīka-sūtra if one calls upon the name of Avalokiteśvara at the time of danger, he will be saved from the following perils:

1. If one falls into a great mass of fire, he will be delivered by virtue of the luster of the Bodhisattva.
2. If one is carried off by currents of rivers, the rivers will afford him a fort.
3. If those sailing in a ship lose their treasures, and the ship is cast on the island of Giantesses, they will be saved.
4. If a man is given capital punishment, the swords of the executioners will snap asunder.
5. The goblins and giants will lose faculty of sight in their wicked designs.
6. Wooden or iron manacles, chains or fetters shall give way if one pronounces the name of Avalokiteśvara.
7. Merchant leader of a caravan rich in jewels, will be saved from knaves, enemies and robbers.
8. Creatures acting under the impulse of impure passions, hatred or infatuation can be freed from them.
9. A woman desirous of a male child will get a male offspring and the one who desires to have a girl child will be blessed with the same.

The person who adores Avalokiteśvara will derive unfailing profits. Avalokiteśvara comes as a saviour in the gatha in the chapter Samantamukha-parivarta. A devotee shall be saved from the following dangers if he contemplates on the name of Avalokiteśvara:

1. Hearing, seeing regularly (*darśana*) and constantly thinking [of Avalokiteśvara] will infallibly destroy all suffering, (mundane) existence, and grief of living beings here on the earth.
2. If one is thrown into a pit of fire, the fire shall be quenched as if sprinkled with water.
3. If one is thrown into the dreadful ocean, abode of *nāgas*, marine monsters, and demons, he will not sink.
4. If a man is hurled down from Meru, he will stand firm in the sky like the Sun.
5. If rocks of thunderstorms and thunderbolts are thrown on man, he will not be hurt.
6. The enemies with swords who intend to kill will be kind hearted.
7. The swords of an executioner who is ready to execute, will go into pieces.
8. If a man happens to be fettered in shackles of wood or iron, the bonds shall be speedily loosened.
9. Mighty spells, witchcraft, ghosts, and specters, perilous to life will revert thither whence they come.

10. Goblins, *nāgas*, demons, or giants, who are in the habit of taking away bodily vigour, shall not be able to hurt.
11. Fearful beasts with sharp teeth and claws will quickly fly in all the directions.
12. The snakes, malicious and frieghtful, on account of the flames and fires they emit, shall quickly lose their poison.
13. If a heavy thunderbolt shoots from a cloud pregnant with lightening and thunder, the fire of heaven shall quickly, instantaneously be quenched.
14. Avalokiteśvara is a saviour of the world that is full of troubles and afflictions.
15. Avalokiteśvara quells the wicked troops of foes in quarrel, dispute, war, battle or any great danger.
16. Avalokiteśvara is a refuge, a recourse in death, disaster and calamity.
17. He possesses all the virtues and beholds all the beings with compassion and benevolence.
18. He, so compassionate for the world, shall become a Buddha destroying all dangers and sorrows.

Thirty-three Bodhisattvas

The group of Thirty-three Bodhisattvas are different manifestations of Avalokiteśvara. In China, foundation of the cult of Thirty-three Bodhisattvas was laid when Saddharmapuṇḍarīka-sūtra was propagated (though Avalokiteśvara manifests himself in 16 forms and not thirty-three according to the sūtra). During the Sui and T'ang dynasties a concept of thirty-three forms of Kwanyin / Kannon / Avalokiteśvara Bodhisattvas developed as a popular cult that suited well to the Chinese social system. These Bodhisattvas enjoyed popularity individually also, serving special interests of the people, e.g. to gain power, to be cured from illness, to gain wisdom, to escape downfall, longivity, protection from poisonous snakes etc. Although some of them are placed high in the Japanese Buddhist pantheon.

Some of them are Bodhisattvas of various professions, some are Bodhisattvas of power and virtue, while some of them are manifestations of Avalokiteśvara, and some of them can be portrayed as saviours.

1. Bodhisattva holding a willow branch: He made a vow to cure illness and holds a spray of willow branch in the right hand as a symbol of his power. Often the willow branch is seen in a vase of holy water placed near him on a rocky ledge. Kwanyin with a willow branch is often portrayed as a female deity in China. Originally this Bodhisattva was a male deity, a chief Bodhisattva attendant of Amitābha. But after translation of the Lotus-sūtra into Chinese the name was mistranslated from "The Seen Lord" to "One who Hears the Cries". This personification rapidly came to represent the quality of mercy and compassion that the Chinese mind associated with a female. Some of the religious systems have nurtured the concept of supreme mother or the queen of heaven. This Bodhisattva was seen as the most suitable to characterize the ideal, which could appeal to the suffering masses. Taoists in

China also fostered the concept of Queen Mother of the West. So this deity was seen as an answer to the Queen Mother. The male origin of this deity can be traced through slight moustache and beard.

2. Dragon headed: Since the dragon is considered to be the king of animals, this Bodhisattva, who rides on the head of a dragon, symbolizes the power of the divinity. He should be identified as a Lokeśvara and not as Bodhisattva Avalokiteśvara.
3. Sūtra holding Bodhisattva: The deity is characterized by the sūtra that it carries. Thus he should be a Bodhisattva of the Śrāvakas or those who listen to the teachings of the Buddha and attain enlightenment. He is adored for his philanthropy-centred character.
4. Bodhisattva of complete light: He symbolizes the completeness of the Bodhisattva's compassion. He is also venerated for the qualities that are philanthropy centred.
5. Bodhisattva of enjoyment: In his enjoyment of preaching and converting, there are no hinderances. Through preaching, he aims at the welfare of others. Thus the category in which he is to be kept, is philanthropy centric.
6. White-robed-Avalokiteśvara Bodhśattva/Pāṇḍaravasinī: Originally the deity appears in Garbhakoṣadhātumaṇḍala. He is identified by the white robes that he wears, sits on a white lotus and carries the same in the left hand. The white colour symbolizes purity, hence the mind of enlightenment.

   It should be identified as Pāṇḍaravasinī because of the colour of her clothes. Prior to becoming a manifestation of Avalokiteśvara, the deity had an independent existence, and in Indian Tantrism appears as the spiritual consort of Amitābha. In China after the rule of the T'ang dynasty popular figures of this deity appeared with full-length white robes apparently unrelated to the Buddhist sūtras. Thus it should be taken as a Lokeśvara and not as Avalokiteśvara.
7. Lotus-leaf-Avalokiteśvara Bodhisattva: He has been identified on the basis of his chief attributes.
8. Waterfall-viewing Bodhisattva: He sits on a rock and gazes at a waterfall or a river flowing nearby. This form shows an affinity to the form of Avalokiteśvara, venerated in Zen temples in Japan.
9. Bodhisattva who gives medicine: The Bodhisattva who gives medicine to sentient beings in order to cure both the psychological and physical aspects of human suffering, may be identified as Bhaiṣajyarāja Bodhisattva whose function is philanthropy-centric.
10. Fish basket-Bodhisattva: The Bodhisattva is identified after his attribute, based upon a legend of a Ch'an believer and his daughter Ling-chao, who was believed to be a manifestation of Avalokiteśvara, and carried a bamboo basket. This should be taken as a Bodhisattva of profession.

11. Bodhisattva as King of Merit: The Bodhisattva, appearing as Brahmā, the king of the Rūpadhātu, has distinguished merits, hence he receives the title 'King of Merit'.

12. Bodhisattva of Water and Moon (Jap. Suigetsu-Kannon): The name of the Bodhisattva is derived from the images portraying him as gazing at the reflection of the moon in water, considered as a personification of concentration and meditation. The earliest example was found by Aurel Stein at the Dun-huang caves in 1906-8. Five basic elements in such paintings are: halo and nimbus, figure of Buddha on tiara, vase containing embrosia of immortality, willow branch of healing, outdoor setting of Potala mountain.

13. One Leaf Avalokitśvara Bodhisattva: He is painted as floating on water on a single leaf. He enjoys meditation and protects those who fall into the depths of the ocean as promised in the Lotus sūtra: "if one happens to fall into the dreadful ocean, the abode of Nāgas, marine monsters, and demons, he has but to think of Avalokiteśvara, and he shall never sink down in the waters (Kern 1909:413).

14. Bodhisattva Nīlakaṇṭha (Blue throat Bodhisattva): Nilakaṇṭha is identified as a Loeśvara among Lokeśvaras in Sādhanamālā (16), and in the hymn to 108 Lokeśvaras, popular deities assimilated into the Buddhist pantheon. In that list Nīlakaṇṭha is No. 49 (Lokesh Chandra 1988:38-9).

15. Bodhisattva of Power and Virtue: Power symbolizes the ability of the divinity to embrace sentient beings, and virtue depicts love and compassion of the Bodhisattva. Thus he is placed in the category of philanthropy-centric Bodhisattvas.

16. Bodhisattva of Extending Life: The Bodhisattvas is known for his ability to grants longivity. Bhaiṣajyarāja and Bhaiṣajyaguru are also adored for the fulfillment of similar kind of wishes.

17. Bodhisattva of Various Treasures: Portrayal of the Bodhisattva is based upon the story given in the Lotus Sūtra, where it is promised that if a group, sailing in ocean should lose all their treasures and during a gale be cast upon an island of Giantesses, if single one of them invokes Avalokiteśvara, all will be saved (Kern 1909:413).

18. Bodhisattva of Rock cave: He sits in a cave to protect beings from the poisonous snakes that frequent there. Thus the Bodhisattva has a philanthropic function to perform.

19. Bodhisattva who calms (the ocean): He protects sailors, grants calm seas for boats, and saves them from shipwrecks. The form should be taken as a Bodhisattva of profession.

20. Anu : Anu is an abbreviation of Anotatta (Skt. Anavatapta), it is personification of a lake existing, according to Indian legend on the Northern side of the Himalayas (Kailāśa Mānasarovara?). From this lake four sacred rivers issue forth, and its shores are decorated with gold, silver and emerald, while its beaches are covered with golden sand. The waters of the lake are crystal-pure like mirror. But Anavatapta means 'not heated' or not radiating heat. In the Lotus Sūtra it is mentioned that a devotees who falls into a great mass of fire

will be delivered by virtue of the luster of Avalokiteśvara if he recites his name. So the Bodhisattva is a saviour here.

21. Bodhisattva of fearlessness: The Bodhisattva believed to enter the hells to save sentient beings, when adored. Thus he is also a saviour.

22. Parṇaśabarī: This particular form of a Bodhisattva is based upon the Parṇaśabarī dhāraṇī. He offers protection from pestilence, insects, illness and grants longivity. So he should be taken as a philanthropy-centric Bodhisattva.

23. Vaidūrya Bodhisattva: The Bodhisattva saves those who are suffering and are in danger. If someone would chant the Vaidūrya-rāja-sūtra, a thousand times even the dead would rise to life.

24. Tārā: The Bodhisattva is described as Blue-white in colour, wearing white robes, and holding a lotus between its two hands. Being a goddess, it should not be taken as a Bodhisattva.

25. Bodhisattva of the Clam: During the T'ang dynasty Emperor Wen-tsung once tried to eat a clam, but he refused to open, so he burnt incense and prayed. Finally the shell took the human form. The Emperor invited a monk to explain this miracle, and he replied that he was a manifestation of Avalokiteśvara Bodhisattva. The Emperor then had temples housing his images built throughout the land.

26. Bodhisattva of Six Hours: The Bodhisattva is based on the Indian division of one day into six hours. This Bodhisattva symbolizes Bodhisattva's constant flow of compassion and protection towards sentient beings, day and night.

27. Bodhisattva of Universal Compassion: The Bodhisattva who grants sympathy and compassion for sentient beings that extends throughout the three thousand great worlds. This form is of Avalokiteśvara as the most compassionate Bodhisattva.

28. Bodhisattva called the Wife of Ma-Lang: Once during the year 817 of the T'ang dynasty, there was a beautiful girl living in the countryside who was sought after for marriage by all the eligible young men. At that time to eliminate some of the competition, she declared to marry the man who could memorize the Kwayin chapter of the Lotus Sūtra within a single night. The next morning twenty men appeared who had complied with her command, so once again she set forth a new challange. This time she asked to learn Chin-kang-ching by the next morning. The number of eligible young men was cut down to ten, but it was still too far many, so she set forth a final challenge to marry the young man who could memorize the entire Lotus Sūtra within the period of three days. Only a young man named Ma-Lang was able to accomplish this feat, so a marriage was planned. Just as the marriage ceremony was about to begin, the girl suddenly fell ill and died. Shortly after she was buried. An old priest visited the house of Ma-Lang and suggested the girl's grave to be opened. On doing that they found only golden pieces of bone kept in the coffin. The old monk then explained that she had been a saint to lead others to salvation and was a

manifestation of Kuan-yin. Upon saying this, the priest promptly vanished. People began to worship Kuan-yin who carries a lotus in the right hand, and in the left holds a female skull (Mallmann 1975:134).

29. Bodhisattva of Prayer (in añjali mudrā): It is believed that the Bodhisattva will appear only to those who worship with detachment from the worldly things.

30. Bodhisattva of Oneness: The Bodhisattva sits upon a cloud, flies through air and conquers thunder. He symbolizes oneness, that is not duality, or the Absolute Truth that fills the whole *dharmadhātu*.

31. Bodhisattva of Non-duality: The Bodhisattva symbolizes that *pen* and *chi* are not two, even though *pen-men* and *chi-men* may appear to be two designations. He is similar to the above mentioned.

32. Bodhisattva holding a lotus: He symbolizes the original vow, this Bodhisattva is also known as Padmapāṇi Bodhisattva.

33. Bodhisattva of Pure Water: He carries a vase full of water to symbolize the act of purification. (Matsunaga 1969:134).

Lokeśvaras/Independent Bodhisattvas

The independent Bodhisattvas hold the power to be worshipped of their own. They enjoyed independent popularity. They were worshipped for religious, virtuous, social or political gains. Carving of the six forms of the so-called Avalokiteśvara became popular in the mid Heian period, in Japan and in AD 1024 Fujiwara Michinaga held a special service for such dedications. These Lokeśvaras are sometimes confused with Avalokiteśvara.

1. Ārya-Avalokiteśvara-Bodhisattva (Ch. Sheng-kuan-yin, Jap. Shō-kannon): The Bodhisattva presides over the inhabitants of hell. He has a single face and two arms, sometimes held together in the *añjali mudrā*. The figure is either seated or standing upon a lotus pedestal. In some instances his left hand holds a lotus and the right is in *varada mudrā,* or the left hand is holding a vase and the right is in *abhaya mudrā* (Matsunaga 1969:123).

   The form has to be re-assessed. The one that is *in añjali mudra* should be equated with no. 29, among the 33 Bodhisattvas. The other that holds a lotus and performs *varada mudrā* is Padmapāṇi Avalokiteśvara. And the third that holds a vase and performs *abhaya mudrā* is Pitṛsantarpaṇa-lokeśvara according to Sādhanamālā.

2. Ekādaśa-mukha-Avalokiteśvara Bodhisattva (Jap. Juichimen Kannon): He presides over the realm of Asuras. The form of this Bodhisattva is based upon Bussetsu-juichimen-kanzeon-jinju-kyō (Nanjio 327, T. vol. 20, p. 149), translated into Chinese by Yashogupta of the Northern Chou dynasty (557-81). According to the accepted hypothesis the form had developed in India during the fifth century under the influence of Indian god Rudra, with whom the number eleven is frequently associated, e.g., the eleven Rudras and the Rudra as Eleven faced fearful god, Ekādaśamukha-rudra. Eleven faces are mounted upon the crown

of the Bodhisattva. Sometimes there are three faces of compassion, three faces of anger, three faces with fangs and one laughing face topped by a Buddha's face. The faces that are full of compassion look at the virtuous sentient beings and save them. Those full of anger, deliver evil creatures; and the faces bearing fangs encourage people to enter into the Buddhist way. The single face of laughter looks at the disillusionment of the world and converts to a right view; and finally the face of the Buddha on top preaches the philosophy of Mahāyāna to lead human beings to enlightenment. Numerous theories are advanced concerning the symbolism of these faces:

1. Eleven stages of enlightenment.
2. Ten Pāramitās and the Tathāgata.
3. The twelve links of Pratītyasamutpāda (including the Bodhisattva's own face).
4. Eleven faces of *upāya* and one true face representing Absolute Truth.
5. Eleven ignorances (*avidyā*) of sentient beings illumined by the light of wisdom (Matsunaga 1969:123-4).

3. Sahasrabhuja-Avalokiteśvara-Bodhisattva (Jap. Senju kannon): He presides over the realm of Pretas. Iconographical representations were needed for adoration. Thus a number of Bodhisattva images were especially created in Mahāyāna countries. Buddhist art became richer through these artistic creations. In the subsequent phases of the Bodhisattva cult these deified personages were given various forms to symbolize their multifarious functions. The most powerful among them is Thousand-armed, thousand-eyed and eleven headed Avalokiteśvara. Its emergence is linked with interiorisation of Śiva/Īṣvara into Avalokita as Viśvarūpa. It recalls the myth of the Cosmic Man (*Puruṣa*) of the Ṛgveda. He is also the prototype of Viṣṇu with thousand arms and thousand eyes, Indra and Śiva with thousand eyes. They have served as models for the deity. It is linked with the security of the state.

4. Horse-headed-Avalakiteśvara-Bodhisattva (Jap. Bato kannon): He presides over the realm of animals. The concept of a deity with the head of a horse can be traced back to ancient India in the representation of Viṣṇnu as taking the form of Hayagrīva. In Buddhist pantheon horse symbolizes power; it is able to crush people's evil passions and desires. The horse headed deity always looks angry and has a third eye on his forehead. His hair stands upright. Sometimes he has three heads, one on either side. Moreover above his central head there is a horse's head.

   In Tibet Hayagrīva is the protector of horses and is supposed to frighten away demons by neighing like a horse. In Japan his chief task is to protect the valuable horses from illness and injury and to look after the souls of the departed horses.

5. Cintāmaṇi-cakra-Avalokiteśvara-Bodhisattva (Jap. Nyoirin Kannon): He presides over the realm of the Devas. The Bodhisattva was worshipped for protection of the state.

6. Cuṇḍā Bhagavatī-Avalokiteśvara-Bodhisattva (Jap. Juntei Kannon): He presides over the realm of Men. It is the deity called Butsumo in Japan. Butsumo is a translation of mother of

Buddha, but Butsumo should be translated as Buddha-mātṛkā, a Buddhist goddess. Being a goddess it should not be identified as a Bodhisattva.

7. Amoghapāśa-Avalokiteśvara-Bodhisattva (Jap. Fukukenjaku-kannon-bosatsu): Often it is worshipped by sea farers.
8. Cintāmaṇī-Avalokiteśvara-Bodhisattva (Jap. Guze-kannon-bosatsu): He was worshipped as a Lokeśvara who is a *Kāmadhenu,* one who yields all the desires including defeating enemies. A number of such images were sculpted in Japan during the Heian period when a struggle was going on among the powerful clans.
9. Shichigutei Bosatsu: The term is a transcription of '*Koṭi*', meaning supreme and '*shichi*' means seven. Thus this is Saptakoṭi Bodhisattva.
10. Needle and Thread Avalokiteśavara Bodhisattva: The form can be presumed to be a deity of profession in China.

Bodhicentric Bodhisattvas

Virtue of knowledge is sustained by energy and nourished by meditation or contemplation, dhyāna, samādhi (Dayal 1932:35-6). Awakening through concentration is self-realization for a Bodhisattva, which is self-benefit. Beyond that is the sphere of helping others, the major role of a Bodhisattva. There are certain Bodhisattvas who aim at samādhi, e.g. Gadgadasvara Bodhisattva Mahāsattva attained seventeen kinds of samādhis as described in the Gadgadasvara-parivarta of the SP:

1. Dhvajāgrakeyūra
2. Saddharmapuṇḍarīka
3. Vimaladattā
4. Nakṣatrarājavikrīḍita
5. Anilambha
6. Jñānamudrā
7. Candrapradīpa
8. Sarvarutakauśalya
9. Sarvapuṇyasamuccaya
10. Prasādavatī
11. Ṛddhivikrīḍita
12. Jñānolkā
13. Vyūharāja
14. Vimalaprabhāsa
15. Vimalagarbha
16. Apakṛtsna
17. Sūryāvarta

After attaining a state of these samādhis he vows to see (*darśana*) of Kumārabhūta Mañjuśrī and six Bodhisattvas:

1. Bhaiṣajyarāja
2. Pradānaśūra
3. Nakṣatrarājasaṅkusumita

4. Viśiṣṭacāritra
5. Vyūharāja
6. Bhaiṣajyarāja (the name reoccurs)

Gadgadasvara declares that he will go to the Sahālokadhatu by the grace of the Tathāgata and his power etc. vested unto him. This is visualization of the Transcendent being through meditation, without leaving the Buddha field and his seat, he plunged into deep meditation, he could see eighty-four thousand myriads of *koṭis* of lotuses, on gold stalks with silver leaves with cups of the hue of rosy lotuses. The chapter narrates further the journey of Gadgadasvara. Finally it is described that he manifests himself in the following forms to preach the Saddarmapuṇḍarīka-sūtra:

1. Brahmā
2. Rudra
3. Śakra
4. Īśvara
5. Senāpati
6. Vaiṣravaṇa
7. Cakravartī
8. Kottarāja
9. Śreṣṭhī
10. Gṛhapati
11. Naigama
12. Brāhmaṇa
13. Bhikṣu
14. Bhikṣuṇī
15. Upāsaka
16. Śrāvaka
17. Upāsikā
18. wife of Śreṣṭhī
19. Wife of Gṛhapati
20. Wife of Naigama
21. Boy
22. girl
23. Yakṣa
24. Asura
25. Garuḍa
26. Kinnara
27. Mahoraga
28. Naraka
29. Tiryak
30. Yamaloka
31. Woman
32. Tathagata
33. Animals

Gadgadasvara preached *Saddharma-puṇḍarīka-sūtra* after attaining the samādhi called Sarvarūpasandarśana. Finally he comes back to the Buddhakṣetra.

Such Bodhisattvas have little to work for the benefit of humanity. Thus they may be called 'bodhicentric'.

Generalisation of the Term 'Bodhisattva'

Centrality of the concept of the term Bodhisattva was lost and was defused in different conceptions. The term Bodhisattva seems to have been over used in the Japanese Buddhist tradition. To exemplify the following Bodhisattvas are selected for the present paper:

Four Pāramitā Bodhisattvas of the Vajradhātu-maṇḍala: Pāramitās are apotheosis of transcendental virtues. They are called Pāramitā Bodhisattvas who sit in the Vajradhātu-maṇḍala, around Vairocana, in the Japanese tradition-Shi-haramitsu-bosatsu:

1. Vajra-pāramitā (Kongōharamitsu Bosatsu)
2. Ratna-pāramitā (Hōharamitsu Bosatsu)
3. Dharma-pāramitā (Hōharamitsu Bosatsu)
4. Karma-pāramitā (Katsumaharamitsu Bosatsu)

(Lokesh Chandra 2003: 249)

Etymologically Pāramitā means: supremacy, mastery or perfection. They are the supreme virtues of the Buddhas or are to be cultivated by the Bodhisattvas (Edgerton 1977:2.341). Usually they are six, sometimes ten, rarely five or seven. They are: *dāna, śīla, kṣānti, vīrya, dhyāna* and *prajñā.*

In Sarvatathāgata-tattvasaṅgraha the four Pāramitās that surround the Great Buddha are in their feminine forms and symbolize the four samādhis entered by the four Buddhas:

Tathāgata	**Samādhi**	**Mudrā**
Akṣobhya	Vajrapāramitā-samayodbhava-vajrādhiṣṭhāna	Sattva-vajrī
Ratnasambhava	Ratnapāramitā-samaya-sambhava-vajrādhiṣṭhāna	Ratna-vajrī
Lokeśvararāja	Dharmapāramitā-samaya-sambhava-vajrādhiṣṭhāna	Dharma-vajrī
Amoghasiddhi	Karmapāramitā-samaya-sambhava-vajrādhiṣṭhāna	Karma-vajrī

(Yamada 1981:43; Shashibala 1986: 218)

Four Goddesses of Music

The four goddesses of music and dance are called Mahādevīs in the Sarvatathagata-tattvasaṅgraha (Yamada 1981:47). Vairocana enters the four kinds of samādhis and utters the names of the four Sarvatathāgatakula-mahādevīs:

Samādhi	**Mahādevī**
Ratipūjāsamaya-sambhava-vajram	Vajralāsyā
Ratnamālābhiṣeka-samayodbhava-vajram	Vajramālā
Sangītisamaya-sambhava-vajram	Vajragītā
Nṛtyapūjā-samayodbhava-vajram	Vajranṛtyā

(Yamada 1981:47; Shashibala 1986:230)

In the Sino-Japanese tradition they are called Inner Offering Bodhisattvas (Nai-kuyô Bosatsu). They sit inside the diamond circle. Gobushingan identifies them as goddesses, *Guhyadevīs* and not as Bodhisattvas:

Vajralāsyā	Kāmarati, Guhyarati, Jñānarati and Ratiratā
Vajramālā	Mālā, Guhyābhiṣekapūjā, Jñānamālā, Bodhyaṅgavatī
Vajragītā	Gītā, Gītapūjā, Jñānagītā, Gītasukhā
Vajranṛtyā	Nṛtyā, Nṛtyapūjā, Jñānanṛtyā, Nṛtyasukhā

(Shashibala 1986:230)

Goddesses of Offering

Out of the five goddesses of offering — Puṣpā, Dhūpā, Dīpā, Gandhā and Naivedyā, four occupy four corners of the second enclosure of the Vajradhātumahā-maṇḍala. Dhūpā symbolizes virtue and removes impurities; Puṣpā symbolizes decoration of perfection; Ālokā symbolizes light of knowledge and Gandhā symbolizes purification of heart. In Gobushingan they are called as Vajradhūpā, Vajrapuṣpā, Vajradīpā and Vajragandhā. The same identifications are given in the Sarvatathāgata-tattvasaṅgraha (Shashibala 1986:247-267). According to this, four Tathagātas enter the following samādhis to worship Vairocana:

Tathāgata	Samādhi	Attending Figures	Godess of Offering
Akṣobhya	prahlādana-samayodbhava	gaṇikā	Vajradhūpā
Ratnasambhava	ratnābharaṇa-pūjā-samayasambhava	pratihārī	Vajrapuṣpā
Lokeśvararāja	ālokapūjā-samayodbhava	dūtī	Vajrālokā
Amoghasiddhi	gandhapūjā-samayasambhava	cetī	Vajragandhā

(Yamada 1981:51; Shashibala 1986:247)

Only in the Sino-Japanese tradition, they are identified as Four Offering Outer Bodhisattvas:

Vajradhūpā Bodhisattva	Kongō-kō Bosatsu
Vajrapuṣpā Bodhisttva	Kongō-ke Bosatsu
Vajrālokā Bodhisattva	Kongō-tō Bosatsu
Vajragandhā Bodhisattva	Kongō-zukō Bosatsu

(Snodgrass 1997:626)

Identification of the four deities need reinvestigation, as to when and why were they first identified as Bodhisattvas.

Four Forces of Attraction

The Four Forces of Attraction are called Mahāsattvas in Tattvasaṅgraha and not Bodhisattvas:

Deities		Attributes	Characteristics
Aṅkuśamahāsattva	Gaṇapati	Vajrāṅkuśa	samākarṣaṇa

Praveśamahāsattva	praveśapratihāra	Vajrapāśa	praveśa
Sphoṭamahāsattva	dūta	Vajrasphoṭa	sarvabandhamukti
Āveśamahāsattva	ceṭa	Vajrāveśa	sarvapati (king)

(Yamada 1981:55; Shashibala 1986:266)

The Forces of Attraction sit in the four gates of the second enclosure *catvāri saṅgrahavastūni* (Shashibala 1986:266). Nowhere in Gobushingan or Tattvasaṅgraha they are called Bodhisattvas. Hence require reinterpretation.

In Tattvasaṅgraha their philanthropic and royal powers are described as follows:

> *Aho hi sarva-buddhānām vajrāveśamaham dṛḍhaḥ* |
> *Yat sarvapatayo bhutva ceṭāpi bhavanti hi* | |

"Oho, I am the strong entrance of all the Buddhas who become servants after becoming kings". (Yamada 1981:58)

Sages and some of the Hindu deities are also called Deva Bodhisattvas. They also should be reinterpreted. Moreover nine female Bodhisattvas in the Lamaist pantheon are not to be taken as Bodhisattvas as they are goddesses:

1. Parṇaśabarī
2. Uṣṇīśavijayā
3. Sitātapatrā
4. Mahāmāyūrī
5. Sarasvatī
6. Cuṇḍā
7. Vasudhārā
8. Marīcī
9. Prajñāpāramitā

Bodhisattvas of The Mahā-Karuṇā-Garbha-Maṇḍala

(The manḍala taken up here is Omuro edition of the Takao maṇḍala, Yamamoto 1980:pl.6)

Mahākaruṇā-garbha-maṇḍala is divided into the following sections:

1. Central quarter: Samantabhadra, Mañjuśrī, Avalokiteśvara, Maitreya
2. Quarter of Universal Knowledge: 4 Bodhisattvas (to be reassessed)
3. Quarter of Padmapāṇi : 21 Bodhisattvas
4. Quarter of Vajrapāṇi : 21 Bodhisattvas
5. Quarter of Śākyamuni : Eight Buddhoṣṇīśas, eight Śrāvakas and four Pratyeka Buddhas, 12 Bodhisattvas and others, (total number of deities:39)
6. Quarter of Mañjuśrī: Avalokiteśvara, Samantabhadra, Candraprabha, Mañjughoṣa, Jāliniprabha, Ratnaketu, Vimalaprabha, (total number of deities:25, to be reassessed)

7. Quarter of Kṣitigarbha: Sarva-śoka-tamo-nirghātamatī, Amogha-darśana, Ratna-mudrā-hasta, Ratnākara, Kṣitigarbha, Ratnapāṇi, Dharaṇīdhara, Dṛdhadhyāsáya, Sūryaprabha,
8. Quarter of Sarva-nīvaraṇa-viṣkambhin: Paritrāṇāśaya-mati, Apāyañjaha, Abhayamdada, Bhadrapāla, Acintyamati-datta, Mahāmaitreyābhyudgata, Karuṇā-mṛḍita, Sarva-dāha-praśamita, Sarva-nīvaraṇa-viṣkambhin,
9. Quarter of Ākāśgarbha : ten Pāramitās, Aṣṭottara-sahasrabhuja-Avalokiteśvara, Sahasrabhuja-Avalokiteśvara, Ākāśagarbha, and others (total number of deities:28)
10. Quarter of Susiddhi: Ekādaśa-mukha-Avalokiteśvara and seven other deities

To the left of the viewer is the mansion of Avalokiteśvara, complimentary to the Vajrapāṇi mansion on the opposite, occupies a symmetrical position. The Avalokiteśvara mansion symbolizes Great Compassion, *karuṇā,* while the Vajrapāṇi mansion symbolizes Great Knowledge, *prajñā*, or they may represent virtue and power in perfect equilibrium, a combination of *śāstra* and *śastra*, *śastre śāstre ca kauśalam*.

The number of Bodhisattvas, twenty-one in each mansion is the same. The significance of each Bodhisattva in one mansion is analogous to that of the corresponding Bodhisattva in the other (Snodgrass 1997:284). Avalokiteśvara (Padmapāṇi) and Vajrapāṇi are placed in the middle in the inner rows. On the top of the inner rows are Padmakulodbhava and Vajrakulodbhava. At the bottom of the inner row are Hayagrīva and Krodhacandratilaka, the two wrathful Bodhisattvas.

21 Bodhisattvas of Adamantine Power in the Vajradhara Mansion

Identification of all the Bodhisattvas of the quarter of Vajrapāṇi of Mahākaruṇāgarbha-maṇḍala (Genzu version) indicates their adamantine desire or power. Several interpretations are given to the Bodhisattvas sitting in the Vajrapāṇi mansion of Mahākaruṇāgarbha-maṇḍala of the Genzu version. They are the Bodhisattvas of adamantine power that pave the way to salvation and becoming *cakravartī,* to be enlightened and to spread the message of the Buddha, combination of power and political will with religious aspirations. Their sequence according to Snodgrass (1997:314-334) is:

	Bodhisattvas	Attributes	Characteristics
1	Krodhacandratilaka	looks wrathful	wrathful conqueror, destroys hinderances
2	Vajramuṣṭi	vajra-daṇda	destroys hinderances, doubt and karma
3	Vajrāgradhārī	sharp vajra point	speed and sharpness of knowledge
4	Vajrapāṇi	vajra and muṣṭi	liberating action of wisdom innate within beings
5	Vajrahasta/vajradhara	varada and vajra	energy or power of wisdom
6	Vajrāṇkuśī	varada and vajrahook	draws all beings by means of nirvāṇa
7	Vajrakulodbhava	vajra in lap	single true form of Bodhicitta
8	Vajrāgra-dhāraka	varada and vajra	cuts away difficulties and destroys the indestructrible
9	Vajradhara	vajra and vajra	eternally and firmly holds the Tathāgata's wisdom
10	Vajraṣṛṅkhalā	chain and muṣṭi	chains the sādhaka to prevent from slipping back to the saṁsāra

11 Gaganāñtaka-vikrama	varada, vajra	causes the sādhaka to step beyond the limits of the sensible world
12 Vajrāgradhara-vajradhara	varada, vajra	crushes the hinderances of delusion
13 Sivajradhara	varada, vajra	hardness ?
14 Gaganāmala-vajradhara	varada,vajra	unlimited and undivided like the sky
15 Mahācakra-vajradhara	rosary, vajra	?
16 Suvajradhara	vajra, vajra	governs the subtle, excellent and incomparable virtues of the Tathāgata
17 Niḥprapañcavihārī	fist, vajra	cuts away idle arguments
18 Vajradaṇṣtra	fist, lotus	devours the causes of ocean of suffering
19 Surata-vajradhara	fist, vajra	embodies the bliss of the self-enjoyed Dharma
20 Vikhyāta-vajradhara	mudrā, vajra	?
21 Cakravajradhara	wheel, muṣṭi	crushes the enemy with the wheel

21 Bodhisattvas of the Padmapāṇi (Avalokiteśvara) mansion

east

21. Śvetabhagavatī	14. Mahāpratisarā	7. Padmakulodbhava
20. Parṇaśabarī	13. Stūpamahāśrī	6. Mahāsthāmaprāpta
19. Bhagavatī	12. Yaśodharā	5. Bhṛkuṭī
18. Amoghapāśa	11. Cintāmaṇi	1. Avalokiteśvara
17. Ḍākaśrī	10. Mahāśrīmahāvidyā	2. Tārā
16. Lakṣmīmahāvidyā	9. Śrīmahādevī	3. Gaurīmahāvidyā
15. Pāṇḍaravāsinī	8. Śivāvahavidyā	4. Hayagrīva

(deities are numbered according to their placement in the maṇḍala)

Among these Bodhisattvas, five are Mahavidyās (3,8,9,10,16), nine are goddesses (2,5,13,14,15,17,19,20,21), so they are not Bodhisattvas. As Tārā is 'compassion of Avalokiteśvara', Bhṛkuṭī is associated with Hayagrīva, Yaśodharā is the wife of Śākyamuni as a Bodhisattva, Bhagavatī is the female power of Śiva/Viṣṇu and Pratisarā is the name of a Rakṣā. Thus Bodhisattvas of all the sūtras await a comprehensive study and reinterpretation in the light of their symbolism, form and function.

LITERATURE CITED

Avadanaśataka

J.S.Speyer ed., *Avadanaśataka,* St. Petersburg, 1906, 1909, 2 vols., Bibliothica Buddhica 1.3.7.

Bhattacharyya 1958

Benoytosh Bhattacharyya, *Indian Buddhist Iconograhy,* Calcutta. (K.L. Mukhopadhyay), 1958.

Chandogyopanṣad

Dayal, 1932

Dayal, Har, *The Bodhisattva Doctrine in Buddhist Sanskrit Literature,* London, 1932, Motila Banarasidas, Delhi, 1978

DS

Dharma-Saṅgraha, F. Max Muller ed., H. Wenzel and K. Kasawara, Oxford 1885

Dīghanikāya

Edgerton

Edgerton, Franklin, *Buddhist Hybird Sanskrit Grammar and Dictionary,* Motila Banarasidas, Delhi 1977

EB

Encyclopedia of Buddhism, G.P. Malalsekara, Colombo, (Government Press) 1961

The Encyclopedia of Religion, Mircca Eliade, Macmillan Publishing Company, New York, 1987

ERE

Encyclopedia of Religion and Ethics, James Hastings, Edinburg, T+T Clark, 1932

IDIR 1976

Liebert Gösta, *Iconographic Dictionary of Indian Religions,* Hinduism, Buddhism and Jainism, E.J. Brill, Heiden, 1976.

Kaṭhopaniṣad

Kern 1909

F. Max Muller ed., *Saddharampuṇḍarīkāsūtra,* tr. H. Kern, Oxford 1909

Lalitavistara

Lalitavistara, S. Lifmann ed., Halle 1902-8

Lohia 1994

Lohia, Sushma, *Lalitavajra's Manual of Buddhist Iconography,* New Delhi, 1994

Lokesh Chandra 1986

Lokesh Chandra, *A Ninth Century Scroll of the Vajradhatumandala,* Śatapitaka, Vol. 343, International Acdemy of Indian Culture, New Delhi, 1986.

Lokesh Chandra 1988

Lokesh Chandra, *The Thousand Armed Avalokitesvara,* Indira Gandhi National Center for Arts, New Delhi, 1988.

Lokesh Chandra 1992

Lokesh Chandra, *Cultural Horizons of India,* Vol. VI, International Academy of Indian Culture and Aditya Prakashan, New Delhi, 1992.

Lokesh Chandra 2003

Lokesh Chandra, *The Esoteric Iconography of Japanese Mandalas,* International Academy of Indian Culture and Aditya Prakashan, Delhi 2003

Mahavyutpatti

Mādhyamakāvatāra

Mallmann 1975

Mallmann, *Introduction a l'iconographie de Tantrisme Bouddhigue,* Labrairie Adrien - Maisonneuve, Paris, 1975.

Matsunaga 1969

Matsunaga, Alicia, *The Buddhist Philosophy of Assimilation,* Tokyo, Charles E. Tutle Co. 1969.

Monier Williams

Monier Monier Williams, *Sanskrit-English Dictionary,* Clarendon Press, Oxford 1899

Muṇḍakopaniṣad

Nanjio 1883

Nanjio, Bunyiu, *A Catalogue of Chinese Translation of the Buddhist Tripiṭaka,* Clarendon Press, Oxford, 1883.

NSP

Niṣpannayogāvalī

Okazaki

Joji Okazaki, *Pure Land Buddhist Painting,* Tokyo, 1977

Rhys 1925
T.W. Rhys Davids and W. Stede, *Pali dictionary,* Chipstead 1925.
SP
Dr. Ramamohan Das, *Saddharmapuṇḍarīka-sūtra,* Bihar Rāṣṭrabhāṣā-Parishad, Patna, 1966.
SSPP
P. Ghosh ed., *Śata-sāhasrikā-prajñā-pāramitā,* Calcutta, 1902-13, Bibliotheca Indica
SM
Sadhanamālā
Shashibala 1986
Shashibala, *Comparative Study of Tattva-Saṇgraha and The Vajradhātumaṇḍala,* Satapitaka series, International Academy of Indian Culture, New Delhi, 1986
Snodgrass 1997
Snodgrass, Adrian, *The Matrix and the Diamond World Mandalas,* International Academy of Indian Culture and Aditya Prakashan, Delhi 1997
Sukhāvatīvyūhasūtra
Max Muller and Nanjio ed., *Sukhāvatīvyūha-sūtra* 76.8, Oxford, 1883
Taishō
Taishō Edition of *Chinese Trīpitaka,* ed, Takakusu Junjirō and Watanabe Kaigyoku, Tokyo, 1924-1929
Tajima
Tajima, Ryujun, *Les deux grands maṇḍalas et la doetrine de l'esoterism-e Shingon,* Tokyo, Maison Franco-Japonaise, 1959.
Tomio 1994
Tomio Shifu Nagaboshi, *The Bodhisattva Warrior,* Samuel Weiser, York Beach, 1994.
Vinaya
H. Oldenberg ed., *The Vinaya Pitakam,* London 1879-83, 5 vols.
Yamada 1989
Yamada, Isshi, *Sarva-tathāgata-tattva-saṅgraha nāma mahāyāna-sūtra,* Śatapiṭaka series 262, International Academy of Indian Culture, New Delhi, 1981.
Yamamoto 1980
Yamamoto, Chikyo, *Introduction to the Maṇḍala,* Dōhōsha, Koyto, 1980.

9

FROM AJANTĀ TO HŌRYŪJI

Creation of magnificent centres of learning and meditation in solitude was in great demand when Buddhism became a thriving religious force in and around India, vibrating the hearts and minds of the devotees and scholars, of kings and masses. Thousands of such centres were constructed during the age of splendour but destroyed later over the centuries. A few still stand to relate the saga of past glory, thronged by pilgrims and tourists, historians and art lovers. Two of them are focused here, one from India and the other from Japan.

Murals in Ajantā and Hōryūji

Ajantā a spectrum in the lap of darkness: a complex of rock cut caves is one of the oldest monasteries and meditation centres of India. Hōryūji, *dharma-varadhana-vihāra*, a magnificent complex, ten kilometers away from the Nara city, is the oldest Japanese monastery standing intact. Both of them lie alone amidst nature, full of power, grandeur, beauty and serenity. They served as retreats from the din of the daily busy life, filled with the spiritual resonance of prayers chanted by thousands of people through hundreds of years. Mural paintings at Ajantā and Hōryūji are wonders for the modern world. They were painted by the artists who had Buddhist scriptures in their minds and faith in their hearts. The brush with a spiritual motivation has successfully brought spirit on the walls. The artists are silent beyond their works, their paintings are the immortal signatures. A tender touch of an outstanding artist is felt all over, especially in the eyes. Buddhas and Bodhisattvas are painted with an idealistic approach, with a view of the world beyond. Buddhas with their down cast eyes are full of love and compassion for the welfare of mankind. Bodhisattvas portrayed with a charming personality are living to enlighten others and not for nirvāṇa for themselves.

Art of Ajantā flourished as Ajantaism all over the Buddhist world. Its impact can be traced in paintings in the monasteries and temples in Sri Lanka, Nepal, Tibet, Mongolia, China and Japan. It remained a source of inspiration for its technique, style, colour and theme. Ajanta paintings illustrate Jātaka stories and other Buddhist philosophical ideals.

Cultural contacts of India and Japan have a historical background of over fourteen hundred years. Buddhism was first introduced into Japan officially in AD 552, when the Korean king of Paekche sent a statue and scriptures as a gift for the Japanese Emperor with a strong advice to accept the new religion. Buddhism because of its polytheistic nature received a warm welcome on the Japanese soil. Unlike other religions it caused no conflicts with the indigenous faith, called Shintō. Within a couple of years it got state patronage; soon priests and architects migrated from Korea in order to undertake large scale construction of temples; painters and sculptors were invited to guide and sculpt images to be enshrined in the newly constructed shrines, artists came to decorate their interiors. 46 temples were erected during the reign of Prince Shōtoku Taishi, the most devout patron of Buddhism who himself transcribed the three Sanskrit texts: Saddharamapuṇḍarīka-stūra, Vimalakīrtinirdeśa- and Śrīmālāsiṁhanāda-sūtras. Shōtoku Taishi is responsible for drafting the first Japanese constitution based on fundamental Buddhist principles of *pañcaśeel*, *triratna* and the idea of "*bahu-jana-hitāya bahu-jana-sukhāya*". A 7th century Sanskrit manuscript of Uṣṇīśavijayā-dhāraṇī was brought from India for recitation on the occasion of promulgating the Constitution. Recitation of this *dhāraṇī* leads to the supreme victory. The palm leaf manuscript of the *dhāraṇī* is till today preserved at the Hōryūji monastery. Hōryūji, the oldest wooden structure all over the world, preserves a valuable treasure of Buddhist artifacts in a surprisingly good condition. Bhaiṣajyaguru, Śākyamuni and Avalokiteśvara, besides a number of secondary gods are enshrined there.

Hōryūji, founded by Prince Shōtoku Taishi is one of the most significant and remarkable Japanese Buddhist temples. It received Buddhist art styles passing from India to Central Asia, China and Korea, reaching Japan with some modifications. Japanese art during the Nara period was highly influenced by the T'ang creations after a direct exposure to Chinese art. Japan set up a painters' bureau in AD 701 in the capital, while groups of painters, other than those of the bureau were called upon whenever required for large-scale undertakings. Great temples of Nara were lavishly decorated with hanging embroideries, tapestries and paintings, under state patronage.

Hōryūji monastery belongs to the Hosso sect which subscribes to the veneration of four Buddhas — Śākyamuni, Bhaiṣajyaguru, Maitreya and Amitābha. These four became the choice to decorate the walls of the main hall, called Golden hall at Hōryūji. These wall paintings are the finest examples of pictorial art of the Nara period, having no forerunner.

Frescoes of Indian Buddhist temples served as models which were copied and taken to China by a Chinese pilgrim Wang-Hsüan-se during the 7th century AD. Evidently the style and technique of these murals are very close to paintings in Ajantā caves. Sensual *tribhaṅga* posture, given to the bodies and profusion of ornaments is derived from Indian art. Transparent clothes are Indian but wire like lines are essentially a Chinese mode of drawing. No low of light and shade is followed in the arbitrary shading. Red outlines are called wire lines because they create tension and sharpness and give a self-contained volume to the bodies. Red, purple, yellow, green, blue, black and white colours are so skillfully combined as to provide a variety of vivid and serene effects. Bodhisattvas are richly bedecked with diadem, necklace, earrings and bracelets, the many-patterned brocade recall the costumes of early T'ang Chinese style.

Paradise scenes of the four Buddhas on large surface of walls were executed around the beginning of eighth century. Each wall has distinctive features and varied handling. Composition is grand in scale, figures are noble in grace and face expressions are full of spiritual depth. An offering table and two lions are shown in the foreground. But the layout does not impose a monotonous convention as each wall has the distinctive features of its own with a varied handling of figures and background. Principal deities sit at the centre of each paradise, surmounted by a large baldachin with flying angels on both the sides. Śākyamuni is depicted on the east, Amitābha on the west, Maitreya on the left of the north wall and Bhaiṣajyaguru on the right side of the north wall. Eight corners of walls are filled by Bodhisattvas acting as attendants of the main divine beings facing each other two by two. Arhats, meditating on mountain tops occupy upper part of the entire wall-space. Flying angels decorate under-space of the ceiling between shafts of inner column. The smallest of details of the composition is brilliantly decorated.

Style and Technique

A Chinese envoy Wang-Hsüan-tse who came to India thrice in the 7th century on diplomatic missions, copied frescoes of Buddhist temple walls during his sojourn. Seventy volumes of travelling record and political documents along with forty volumes of painting were compiled from the material brought by him. A Korean artist Kibumino-miya suko-hojintsu took these paintings from China to Korea after his stay there in AD 658-671. These copies are supposed to have served as models for Hōryūji murals. A centrally controlled style was fostered by the Imperial workshop of artists who were trained in decorative arts and copying sūtras. Thus the style was hardly affected by differences in technique. T'ang style seems to be highly influential because of decorous distribution of forms, fullness of figures and substantial quality of costumes. The art of painting had touched the heights. The drawings are smooth and fluid, colours are rich and workmanship is advanced. But the process of advancement cannot be traced because of scarcity of material on the art of Hakuho painting from late 7th Century.

Red outline in the paradise scene of Amitābha is sharp. The bodies are shaded reddish brown. Red, purple, yellow, green, blue, and white – simple and unsophisticated colours are used skillfully. The Bodhisattvas wear diadem, necklace, earrings and bracelets. Their rich patterned brocades are in the early T'ang fashion. The flying angels above, drawn by a pouncing pattern are as charming as the Bodhisattvas. They are lucky to have escaped the disastrous fire.

According to a scientific examination by Prof. Yamazaki Kazuo the pigments employed are cinnabar, red lead, yellow ochre, litharge, malachite for green, azurite for blue, white clay for white and ink for black. First the surface of the walls was coated with fine clay and then the design was transferred by pouncing pattern. Outlines were done in black and red and the artists added colours a secco. These mineral pigments are altogether different from those used previously in Japanese tomb paintings.

The new technique and materials were introduced with Buddhism and are still used by the Japanese painters. The technique was mastered by them prior to the execution of Hōryūji decorations. Most of the artists came from families of Chinese and Korean origin who had settled there for a couple of generations. Use of reddish brown and scarcity of black brings forth Indianness. Red and green are the two main colours used symmetrically like Ajantā. Colouring method and shading emphasizing three dimensionality again goes close to Ajantā. Compass is used to draw halos and some kind of rule for long and straight lines. Besides their similarity some differences are also visible. The compositions are ideally balanced, static and inverse. Emphasis in Ajantā is on Jātaka stories to encourage liveliness except in cave no. 16, which has a formal arrangement which could have served as prototype for the paradise scenes. Sensual *tribhaṅga* posture of the standing figures and profusion of ornaments are derived from Indian art but firm outline and vivid colouring are in contrast. Wire-like line should be a Chinese mode of drawing but translucent drapery seems to be Indian in character.

Paradise of Amitābha

Sukhāvatī, the paradise of Amitābha occupies western wall with an overall dimension of 313 x 260 cm. Amitābha as the presiding divinity, sits cross-legged on a lotus pedestal with his hands kept at chest level in *dharma-cakrapravartana-mudrā,* the mudrā of preaching or turning the wheel of Law. A chair like back of his throne derived from far West Asia is visible at the back. Amitābha is positioned a little higher in the frame which suggests his position on a lotus with a long stalk. Both of his attendants, Avalokiteśvara and Mahāsthāmaprāpta are standing on lotus flowers flanking him. They wear coronets with a small Buddha image and hold a phial. Their smaller size is an indication of lower rank; other lower ranking inhabitants of the paradise sit on lotus flowers behind the main figures. Sukhāvatī paradise was considered the most outstanding of all the Hōryūji murals. Their fluent line and beautiful colours with harmonious movement ruling the entire composition point to the perfection attained by the Japanese art during Nara period.

Paradises of Bhaiṣayaguru and Maitreya

Paradise of Bhaiṣajyaguru depicted on the east section of the north wall has an overall dimension of 313 x 255 cm. Bhaiṣajyaguru Buddha at the centre is attended by four Bodhisattvas, two monks, 12 heavenly generals, Vajradharas and celestial maidens flying through air. The painting was darkened by smoke but still was in a fairly good condition before destruction. Bhaiṣ ajyaguru is seated in *yogāsana* on a lotus seat supported by a hexagonal dais bearing four atlas like dwarfs, each corner of the dais is decorated with a small figure recognized as twelve generals of Bhaiṣajyaguru. Paradise of Bhaṣajyaguru is astonishingly similar to the Maitreya triad bringing forth a special kind of balance. Paradise of Maitreya is called Tuṣita where he sits on a rectangular lion throne in *bhadrāsana* with both of his legs pendant. The style in which this panel is painted, again goes close to Ajantā because of its drapery, lines, colouring and shading technique.

Bodhisattva Figures

Mañjuśrī and Samantabhadra, Ārya-Avalokiteśvara and Ekādaśamukha Avalokiteśvara, Sungod and Moongod, Avalokiteśvara and Mahāsthāmaprāpta are the eight Bodhisattvas depicted in the eight corners. Out of these eight, four Bodhisattvas seem to be ranking higher as they are seated and surmounted by special canopies, Mañjuśri and Samantabhadra are graced by triangular canopies, Sungod and Moongod by flat canopies while those of Bhaiṣajyaguru and Maitreya are flat as well.

The most appreciable of all the Bodhisattva figures is Avalokiteśvara standing as an acolyte of Amitābha. Avalokiteśvara, the spiritual son of Amitābha, full of compassion for humanity is one of the masterpieces of far eastern art. Unluckily the lower part of the figure is damaged but the well preserved upper part is an example of Nara period painting at its best. A thick, strong and flowing red line delineates the contours. Sparingly used shading is suggestive of roundness of body. Curved bow like beautiful eyes are done in an Indian fashion. Half closed eyes look down to the devotee out of compassion, nose is sharp and strongly modelled and lips are full. Black curles of hair, symbol of a Bodhisattva, of a prince who has not yet attained *bodhi* and renounced the world, fall on his shoulders. A small image of Amitābha bedecked in his crown is an indication of his being the father of Avalokiteśvara. He holds a branch of willow tree. According to a legendary evidence he brushed away small insects that he does not wish to kill even unknowingly. The Bodhisattva attains a *tribhaṅga* posture, which adds to his spiritual and dreamy gentleness.

Flying Angels

Twenty panels depicting flying angels coming from heaven scattering flowers decorate the upper part of the golden hall. These are the best preserved murals as they were out of the hall at the time of fire because renovation was not yet complete. They are so similar to each other that presumably the same basic designs were used for all of them. They are very important because they represent technique and style and above all give an idea of the damaged masters. The downwards flight, pose of the figures, garments and ornaments and moreover the idea is well known in Chinese cave art. Five angels each, of dance, music and worship decorate the walls of Chinese cave temples especially in the Tun-huang caves in a well organized manner.

Disastrous Incident

Hōryūji along with other temples of Nara and Kyoto were spared from bombing in the second World War. But the winter of the new year, 26th January 1949 brought tears rolling down the cheeks of the Japanese, when the news of burning of the Golden Hall of the Hōryūji mononastery was broadcast. It was shocking for art lovers all over the Buddhist world. The cause of fire was traced to faithful reproduction of paintings. They had damaged over the centuries by earthquakes and climatic conditions, colours had chipped off and breaks had appeared. It was decided to make original size copies in order to preserve them for posterity. A number of top artists were engaged for several years for the task. The work was finished by 81 per cent. An exhibition was scheduled at the National Museum, Tokyo. The artists were rushing at the top speed working during wintry nights using heating appliances. Owing to the carelessness, one of the heating pads caught fire. Next morning all the leading newspapers cursed the incident, a number of responsible officers had to resign and the minister begged a public excuse but the treasure once lost can never be repossessed. Almost one third of these paintings is preserved today in its original form and for the rest of the panels we have to rely on extremely faithful reproductions and copies done before the disaster.

10

A SANSKRIT MANUSCRIPT OF THE GUPTA PERIOD AT THE HŌRYŪJI MONASTERY IN JAPAN

Japan has preserved a rich literary treasure in Sanskrit, consisting of *dhāraṇīs, tantras, sūtras* and other texts, from the sixth century onwards. Prajñāpāramitā-hṛdaya-sūtra (hannya-shinkyō), Uṣṇīśavijayā-dhāraṇī (Sonshi-darani) and Vajracchedikā-prajñāpāramitā (Kongōkyō) can be heard in daily recitation of a Japanese. Vajracchedikā and Hṛdaya-prajñapāramitā are a class by themselves and deservedly renowned throughout the world of Northern Buddhism. Both have been translated into many languages and have often been commented upon. The title Varacchedikā-prajñāpāramitā means 'perfection of wisdom which cuts like a thunderbolt of Indra' (Conze 1973:p.ii).

The Prajñāpāramitā-hṛdaya-sūtra generally followed by Uṣṇīśavijayā-dhāraṇī, exists in two recensions – the longer one in twenty-five *ślokas* and the shorter version in fourteen ślokas. The shorter version is the earlier of the two. It is attested by the translations of Kumārjīva (*c*. AD 400) and Hsüan Tsang (AD 649), the translation from Tun-huang (before AD 600) and the palm-leaf manuscript in the Hōryūji monastery (AD 609), whereas the longer text makes its first appearance with the Chinese translation (AD 741) by Darmacandra (Conze 1973: p.ii).

Prajñāpāramitā-hṛdaya and Uṣṇīśavijayā-dhāraṇī, attributed to Kāśyapa are in the possession of the monastery of Hōryūji ever since the year AD 609. The grand monastery of Hōryūji stands in a quiet rural neighbourhood in the western part of the Yamato plain, some distance from Nara, the eighth-century capital of Japan. The entire Yamato distric is rich in historical monuments of great importance. Hōryūji is one of the most significant monasteries in Japan. It was founded in the early seventh century by Prince Shōtoku Taishi AD 574-622) who was regent to Empress Suiko and one of the most remarkable personages in Japanese History (Mizuno 1974:9).

Now these two palm-leaf manuscripts are transferred to the Imperial Government. They existed at Hōryūji till AD 1727, where they were seen by Zakumio and copied, in fourteen leaves, by Ziogon in AD 1964. The first of them is called Shin-jio-bon-hon, means the text of the Hṛdaya-sūtra. It gives the most valuable help for resorting the texts.

These leaves were brought to Japan from China in AD 609. Moreover, probably in China they belonged to the Monk Yashi who died in AD 577. Before that we can say that they were in the possession of Ācārya Bodhidharma who emigrated from India to China in AD 502. Certainly the manuscripts cannot be dated later than the first half of sixth century being evidently written by an Indian scribe. In spite of their transmission from India to China and from China to Japan and a long span of time of thirteen hundred years, they are mostly legible, but have suffered partly on the margins and partly by the fading of ink.

They are primarily valuable for their palaeographical antiquity. They show the same writing materials as were used in the India later on. Technical contrivances used by the writer and the method of forming the letters resemble the Indian style.

The text of the Prajñāpāramitā-hṛdaya-sūtra scribed in the palm leaf manuscript at the Hōryūji monastery reads as follows:

(1)* *Namaḥ sarvajñāya. Āryāvalokiteśvaro Bodhisattvo gambhīrāyāṁ*$_1$ *Prajñāpāramitāṁ*

caramāṇo vyavalokayati sma: pañca skandhās tāṁśca svabhāv$_2$*aśūnyān paśya* (2) *ti sma.*

Iha Śāriputra rūpaṁ śūnyatā śūnyatāiva rūpam, rupānna pṛthak śūnyatā śūnyatayā na pṛthag rūpam yad rūpaṁ sā śunyatā, yā śūnyatā tad rūpam.

(3) *Evameva vedanā-saṁjñā-saṁskāra-vijñānani.*

Iha Śāriputra sarvadharmāḥ śūnyatā-lakṣaṇā anutpannā aniruddhā amalā na vimalā nonā na paripūrṇṇāḥ. Tasmāc Chāriputra śūnyatā$_3$ (4) *yāṁ na vedanā na saṁjña na saṁskāra na vijñānāni, na cakṣuḥ-śrotra-ghrāṇa-jihvā-kāya-manāṁsi, na rūpa-śabda-gandha-rasa-spraṣṭavya-dharmāḥ, na cakṣurdhātur yāvanna mano* (5) *dhātuh, na vidyā nāvidyā, na vidyā-kṣayo nāvidyākṣ ayo, yāvanna jarāmaraṇaṁ na jarāmaraṇakṣayo, na duḥkha-samudaya-nirodha-mārgo, na jñānaṁ na prāptitvam.*

Tasmādaprāptitvād bodhisttvānāṁ prajñāpāramitām (6) *āśritya viharatyacittāvaraṇaḥ. Cittāvaraṇa-nāstitvād atrosto viparyāsātikrāntaḥ niṣṭhanirvāṇaḥ. Tryadhyavasthitāḥ sarvabuddhāḥ prajñāpāramitām āśritya anuttarāṁ* (7) *samayak*[4]*-sambodhimabhisambuddhāḥ.*

T[4]*asmāj jñātavyo prajñāpārmitā mahāmantra mahā-vidyā-mantro*

'nuttaramantro (8) *'samasama-mantraḥ sarva-duḥkha-praśamanaḥ satyam amithyā-tvātprajñāpāramitāyām ukto mantraḥ. Tadyathā gate gate pāragate pārasaṅgate bodhi svāhā.*

Iti prajñāpāramitā-hṛdayaṁ samāptam.

This manuscript was copied by Jiun Sonja, last of the Sanskritists of Japan in the traditional style in the eighteenth century. He lived from 1718 to 1803 AD. A saint of great learning and noble virtue, he stands unique in the history of Mantrayāna as the doyen of traditional Sanskrit studies in Japan, and in recognition thereof he had the honorific title Sonja which means Ārya or Arhat; none had been thus called in Japan. It is said of him that the Goddess Sarasvatī has manifested Herself to teach him Sanskrit (Lokesh Chandra 1972: p.iv). His writings on Sanskrit comprise a thousand fascicules (*kwan*). Some of them were published by the 'Jiun Sonja One Hundred Fiftieth Death Anniversary Commemoration Society' in Japan in four volumes in 1953. The International Academy of Indian Culture, New Delhi published some of his works in two volumes in 1972. his complete works in Japanese were edited by Hōshū Hase of Shingonshū University, Kyotō and published by the Kokiji temple in 19 volumes (Ishihama 1953:pp.1-2). The Sanskrit studies by Jiun Sonja were not included in them.

The copy by Jiun Sonja has only two variations if compared with the manuscript at Hōryūji: 1. Instead of *manodhātu* in the fifth line of the first leaf he says *mano-vijñādhātu*. 2. The same line has *prāptitvam*, while Jiun writes *na prāpti nāprāptitvam.*

From AD 400 onwards there are several translations and commentaries on the sūtra in Chinese, Tibetan and other languages, (for details see Conze 1960: pp.70-75). Kumārajīva's translation of the *Prajñāpāramitā-hṛdaya-sūtra* is recited daily to this day in Japan. This version is given below in Sino-Japanese pronunciation, transliterated into Roman followed by its English translation and by Sanskrit equivalents:

Kan-ji-zai (*Avalokiteśvara*) bo-satsu (*Bodhisattva*) gyō-zin (deep, *gambhīra*) han-nya-ha-ra-mitt-ta-ji (in the *Prajñāpāramitā, Prajñāpāramitāyām*) shō-ken (looked down, *avalokayati sma*) gō-on (five *skandhas, pañcaskandhāḥ*) kai-kū (them, *tāṁśca*) do-it-sai-ku-yaku (take away all agony and misfortune).

Sha-ri-shi (*Śāriputra*) shiki (form, *rūpam*) fū (no,*na*) i (different) kū (emptiness, *śūnyatā*) fū (no, *na*) i (different) shiki (form, *rūpam*), shiki (form, *rūpam*) soku (equal) zē (by all means) kū (emptiness, *śūnyatā*). kū (emptiness, *śūnyatā*) soku (equal) zē (by all means) shiki (form, *rūpam*).

Jū (perception, *vedanā*) sō (name, *saṁjña*) gyō (conception, *saṁskāra*) shiki (knowledge, *vijñāna*) yaku-bu-nyo-ze (the same applies to, *evameva*).

Sha-ri-shi (*Sāriputra*) ze shō (all nature, *sarva*) hō (religious objects, *dharmāḥ*) kū (emptiness, *sūnyatā*) sō (have the character, *lakṣaṇāḥ*), fu-shō (without beginning, *anutpannāḥ*), fu mestu (no end, *anirudhāḥ*) fu ku (no fault, *amalāḥ*) fu jhō (not faultless, *na vimalāḥ*) fu zō (no imperfect, *nonāḥ*) fu gen (not perfect, *na paripūrṇāḥ*). Ze-ko (hence, *tasmāt*) kū-chū (in this emptiness, *śūnyatāyām*) mu shiki (no form, *na rūpam*) mu ju (no perception, *na vedanā*) sō (name, *saṁjñā*) gyō (conception, *saṁskāra*) shiki (knowledge, *vijñāna*), mu (no, *na*) gen (eye, *cakṣuḥ*) ni (ears, *śrotra*), ki (nose, *ghrāṇa*) zestu (tongue, *jihvā*) shin (body, *kāya*) i (mind, *manas*), mu (no, *na*) shiki (form, *rūpa*) shō (sound, *śabda*) kō (smell, *gandha*) mi (taste, *rasa*) soku (touch, *spraṣṭavya*) hō (religious objects, *dhaṛmāḥ*) mu (no, *na*) gen-kai (sight-organ element, *cakṣurdhātu*) nai-shi (until we come to, *yāvan*) mu (no, *na*) i-shiki (mind-consciusness, *mano*) kai (element, *dhātu*) mu (no, *na*) mu-myō (ignorance, *avidyā*) yaku (or) mu (no, *na*) mu-myo-jin (extinction of ignorance, *avidyā-kṣaya*), nai-shi (until we come to, *yāvan*) mu (no, *na*) rō (old age, *jarā*) shi (death, *maraṇa*) yaku (or) mu (no, na) ro (old age, jarā) shi (death, maraṇa) jin (extinction, *kṣaya*), mu (no, *na*) ku (suffering, *duḥkha*) shū (origin, *samudaya*) metsu (stoppage, *nirodha*) dō (path, *mārga*), mu (no, *na*), chi (knowledge, *jñāna*) yaku (or) mu (no, na) toku (obtaining *(of nirvāṇa)*, *prāptitvam*) i (more than this) mu (no, *na*) sho-toku (income, *prāpti*).

Ko (hence) bo-dia-satsu-ta (of Bodhisattvas, *Bodhisattvānām*) e-han-nya-ha-ra-mitsu-ta (having approached the *Prajñāpāramitā*, *Prajñāramitām āśritya*) ko (hence) Shin (consciousness, citta) mu (annihilation) Kei-ge (envelopment, āvaraṇa) mu (non-being, *nāstitvāt*) kei-go (envelopment, *cittāvaraṇa*) ko (hence) mu (free of, a) u-ku-fu (fear, *trasta*), on-ri (beyond the reach of, *atikrānta*) itsu-sai (all, *sarva*) ten-do-mu-sō (change, *viparyāsa*) ku-kyo (ultimate, *niṣṭha*) ne-han (liberation, *nirvāṇa*). San-ze (three worlds, *tryadhvavyavasthitāḥ*) Sho-butsu (all Buddhas, *sarvabuddhāḥ*) e-han-nya-ha-ra-mitsu-ta ko (after approaching the *Prajñāpāramitā*, *Prajñāpāramitām āśritya*) toku-a-noku-ta-ra (highest, *anuttarām*) san-mikaku (perfect, *samyak*) san-bo-dai (knowledge, *sambodhim*).

Ko-chi (therefore, *tasmāt*) han-nya-ha-ra-mitsu-ta (*Prajñāpāramitā*) ze-dai (great, *mahā*) jin-shu (*mantraḥ*) jin-shu (*mantraḥ*) ze-dai (great, *mahā*) myō-shu (verse of wisdom, *vidyā-mantraḥ*) ze-mu-jho (unsurpassed, anuttara) shu (mantraḥ) ze-mu-tō-dō (incomparable, *asama*) shu (*mantraḥ*) nō-jhō-itsu-sai-ku (appeases all pain, *sarva-duḥkha-praśamanaḥ*) shin-jitsu (true, *satyam*) fu-ko-ko (not false, *amithyātvāt*) setsu (*so*) han-nya-ha-ra-mitsu-ta (*Prajñāpāramitā*) shu (*mantraḥ*) soku-setsu-shu watsu (thus the verse is proclaimed, ukto mantraḥ) e-gye-tei (gone, *gate*) gya-tei (gone, *gate*) ha-ra-gya-tei (gone to the other shore, *pāragate*) ha-ra-sō-gya-tei (landed at the other shore, *pārasaṅgate*) bo ji (*bodhi*) so-wā-kā (*svāhā*).

Han-nya-ha-ra-mistu-ta-shin-kyo (the heart *sūtra* of *Prajñāpāramitā*, *iti Prajñāpāramitā-hṛdaya-sūtra*).

In the *dhāraṇī* at the end of the *sūtra*, *Ga* is pronounced as *gya*, *pa* as *ha*, *san* as *so*, *dhi* as *ji*, *s* as *so* and *ha* as *ka*.

Sanskrit manuscripts available in India generally belong to the eleventh-twelfth centuries and thereafter (Nakamura 1961: p.3) Till recent times it was known as the oldest Sankrit manuscript. The German Catalogues of Sanskrit manuscripts have brought to light the existence of seven Sanskrit manuscripts of the Kuṣāṇa period (AD 48-220):

1. An *Abhidharma* text, (Waldschmidt 1965: 10.1, no.15)
2. Three plays, in the first play we come across *Buddhi*, *Dhṛti* and *Kirti,* the second play is *Śāriputraprakaraṇa* and the third is unknown, (Waldschmidt 1965:10.1, no.16).

3-4. Abhidharma texts, (Waldschmidt 1965:10.3, nos.809,920).

5. Commentary on some *sūtra*, (Waldschmidt 1965:10.1, no.649).
6. *Āyurveda* text, (Waldschmidt 1965:10.1, no.17).
7. A *Kāvya* in *Upajāti* meter, (Waldschmidt 1965:10.3, no.921).

Footnotes

1. Ms. Gambhīram.

2-2. Ink faded.

3. Illegible.

4-4. Illegible.

LITERATURE CITED

Conze 1960
Conze, Edward, *The Prajñāpāramitā Literature,* 'S-Gravenhage, 1960.

Conze 1973
Conze, Edward, *The Short Prajñāpāramitā Texts,* London, 1973.

Ishihama 1953

Ishihama, Juntaro, *Jiun Sonja, Selected Works,* Japan, 1953.

Lokesh Chandra 1972

Lokesh Chandra, *Sanskrit Texts from Japan,* New Delhi, 1972.

Max Müller 1884

Max Müller, *Buddhist Texts from Japan,* Oxford, 1884, (New York, 1976).

Mizuno 1974

Mizuno, Seiichi, *Asokan Buddhist Art: Hōryūji,* Tokyo, 1974.

Nakamura 1961

Nakamura, Hajime, *Japan and Indian Asia,* Calcutta, 1961.

Waldschmidt 1965

Waldschmidt, Ernst, *Orientalische Handshriften in Deutscland, Sanskrithand schriften aus den Turfanfunden,* Wiesbaden, 1965.

11

ZEN BEARINGS ON JAPANESE ARTS

Zen is a practice that can not be bound by time and space. It is a product of Chinese and Japanese soil from an Indian seed. It has penetrated into the Japanese life far more deeply and widely than the Chinese. Zen as a Buddhist sect, lays emphasis on stern spiritual discipline. The idea was near and dear to the hearts of the warrior rulers who gave patronage for its propagation. Over the past nine centuries it has become a warm reality of Japanese culture. The Influence of its philosophy on their arts and taste, attitudes and perceptions has been profound. Its sway on the masters of garden design, tea ceremony and flower arrangement, pottery and poetry, Noh plays and swordsmanship, architects, painters and sculptors has been pervasive.

Meditation and Zen

Zen, as a Buddhist sect was propagated by the Chinese and the Japanese monks, during the warrior regime when their capital was at Kamakura. Its philosophy is different from all other Buddhist sects. It was born in India, went to China and from there travelled to Korea and Japan. In Japan it is vibrantly alive as a part of the daily life at almost all the levels of society. The Japanese go to Zen monasteries, to practice Zen, to learn self-reliance, physical and spiritual discipline, refinement and advancement through concentration, purity of mind and essentiality, inner quest, patience and obedience. It is steeped in its fundamental concepts of *śunyatā* and simplicity, beauty and purity, harmony and grace; it advocates futility of nonessentials, worldly trappings and human passions, The conceptual basis of its philosophy is *satori* or suudden enlightenment, that is possible through concentration and meditation. Through *satori* the inner most wisdom becomes free from misconceptions and is awakened.

Importance of meditation is paramount in Zen because action after meditation with an unwavering mind and soul is the Zen spirit. Meditation is *dhyāna* in Sanskrit and the word Zen is literally derived from it. *Dhyāna* is the seventh step in Yoga. Meditation is literally translated as thinking quietly, ponder, contemplate, mystic trance or collecting one's thoughts etc. But while speaking explicitly it should be explained that meditation is preceded by contemplation, *chintana*, thinking deeply about an object, which is possible through concentration, *ekāgracitta,* an inward gaze of the senses. It brings the whole mind to one point: the object of meditation. Concentration enables to take the consciousness to its deeper and deeper levels that further leads to a state of meditation, which leads to a vast ocean of silence, that opens up doors of knowledge and power, that fills one's mind with joy and ecstasy, purity and devotion, that serves as an instrument to accomplish that is aspired for. And thus one gets peace of mind and composure, a basic requirement of life that is full of desires and passions, lust and greed, anxiety and confusion, full of mental and physical illnesses.

The final stage of mind according to Yoga philosophy is *samādhi* that comes after *dhyāna*. It is the control of subtleties of mind and its movements that are beyond calculations. Attaining this, is a wonderful experience but it demands perseverance and confidence or else one might give up in despair. Mind becomes purer and stronger, it gets illuminated, thoughts are not diversified; soul gets lost into the spiritual world in a calm, serene and joyful manner. Then there is no movement, no interruption, no limitation, no darkness and no contrary things exist. Thus mind and body are improved and hidden talents are manifested. Apparently a sort of intoxication comes upon the practitioner; his face becomes red, eyes are tearful, he is not able to speak; sometimes such a person starts trembling.

Final stage in Zen is the state of illumination which can be achieved after a regular practice. Zen practice is termed as *zazen*. During *zazen,* riddles arising normally in a human mind regarding one's own existence, impermanence of life, reality of death, action and inaction etc. can also be solved. Talking about death, a Zen monk Takuan Soho said that when one dies timely and leaves his body, he can go freely wherever he likes. But it needs time and labour to realize it, there is no royal road to achieve this state. Mental and physical discipline is the basic requirement, senses should not be let loose, though they are made so, that they go outward, eyes and ears, all the senses are eager to contact their objects. Only a wise person can control his senses and turns them inward. Meditation is not fun, it is a period of struggle, it means disciplining one's energy, checking it from flowing in a wrong direction, but even that struggle gives joy if a person does it regularly. The process may be slow but the underlying gain is infinitely valuable and eternal.

Meditation enables a practitioner for *satori*. *Satori* is the sudden feeling of being enlightened. Enlightenment means realization of the highest spiritual values and the ultimate truth which is not an object of the practical knowledge but personal experience and practice. For practice one has to struggle hard to concentrate his mind on an object or on *śūnya*, the mind gets activated and wakes up resulting in a sudden feeling that he has experienced a reality that was never before done. That feeling is more interior than exterior, it is infinitely superior. But one has to be adamantine as nothing may happen for months, though by trying more and more often, the experience can become frequent.

In Zen pratice, breath control or *prāṇāyāma* is used as a means of concentration and to direct all the senses and the mind. According to Patañjali breath is of five types: *prāṇa* is inhalation, *apāna* is exhalation, *samāna* is the breath that maintains a balance in the working of *prāṇa* and *apāna*, the fourth is *vyāna* that spreads the life giving force to the entire body system, the fifth form of breath is *udāna* that goes up to the throat and enters the head. *Prāṇāyāma* helps to train the mind to think creatively and make one's life more meaningful. It gives relaxation from tension, clarity of perception and deep insight.

In Zen, asymmetrical balance is carefully maintained. Asymmetry means being irregular, imbalanced, uneven or informal. Zen monks are unconcerned with an apparent perfection. Zen abhors media, it does not explain but affirms as it is a discipline primarily and an experience. To be fit for Zen, mind should be free from all entanglements and attachments such as words, ideas and desires. Its ideals can be transmitted from mind to mind, learnt through insight, not through words implanted from outside. Zen instills a craving to come to light from darkness "*tamaso ma jyotir gamay*". Once a practitioner is out of spiritual and mental darkness he can transcend individual ego and attain personal attitudes and social values.

Zen monasteries are open for imparting training to anyone who is an enthusiast, an earnest explorer of truth. Zen practice is permitted even for laymen and women, no age bar, no prerequisites exist in the system of the centers. The only requisite is an adamantine desire, a resolute mind, a strong body and patience, which is tested before giving permission for training. Once permission is granted, one has to leave behind status consciousness and transcend individual ego, he is supposed to honour value of labour, adopt a regulated and collective way of living without any superiority or inferiority complex. He is taught to listen attentively, to see one-pointedly, to realize the ever-renewing world, sit quietly and meditate. According to Zen, quietness and emptiness are enough to pass through life without error.

Transmission and Propagation

The credit for transmitting the philosophy of meditation from India to China goes to the great monk of Kāñcīpuram, Bodhidharma. He is commonly known as Bodai-daruma, abbreviated as 'Daruma'. This teacher was the youngest son of a king of Kāñchī and went to China during the sixth century. According to a historical record discovered from Tun-huang caves in China, the first patriarch of Laṅkāvatāra-sūtra, one of the basic texts of Zen, was Bodhidharma. He propagated its philosophy, and revealed the hidden meaning of the sūtra. During his stay in China he handed down the doctrine to a Chinese monk, Hui-kuo (AD 487-593), then to four others followed by Hui-neng (AD 639-716). In China it became famous as Ch'an.

This contemplative tradition of Ch'an was brought to Japan by the Japanese monk Dōshō, founder of the Hosso sect, who had gone to China in AD 653. On coming back he established the first meditation hall in Japan, to introduce teaching of the way of meditation. The tradition was further followed by a great monk of the ninth century, Saichō, posthumously entitled as Dengyō-daishi. He is the founder of the Tendai sect. In between, a Chinese monk Tao-Hsüan went to Japan in the eighth century for propagation of the philosophy. There Gyokyō became his disciple who was the teacher of Saichō. Wife of a Japanese emperor Soga invited a Chinese monk I-kung in the second quarter of the ninth century to establish the doctrine. When Zen came to Japan it was aristocratic on one hand. It served poets, painters, sculptors and architects. On the other hand it got rooted among the masses, who were ignorant of the Mahayanic philosophy, those who were not able to read and write.

Shofukuji is the first Zen temple of Rinzai Zen sect in Hakata, in Fukuoka prefecture, founded by Eisai. Kenninji at Kamakura is the first large scale monastery constructed in AD 1202. Zen was rapidly becoming popular during the Kamakura period. The Shogunal govt. invited Eisai to Kamakura, there he undertook the erection of another temple, Jūfukuji which later became the cradle of Zen activities. Then onwards, sixty-six temples were built to pacify the country.

Promotion of Zen was meant for protection of the nation. It has a following of around ten million with twenty-one thousand temples. Sōtō and Rinzai are the popular sub-sects. They vary in teaching and methods, but meditation remains their foundation. Sōtō was founded by monk Dōgen.

Political Patronage by the Samurais

Fuedal lords of the Kamakura period appreciated the Zen ideals of loyalty, modesty, service, discipline, respect for brevity and contempt for death. They also loved the way the Zen monks who painted scenes of nature with small huts of monks, devoid of any restlessness and displeasure. The Samurais had a passion to resort to a place where they could get solace, as the period was full of confusion and political unrest. They were coming direct from fields of war, they were not men of sophistications and learning. So they liked the Zen idea of realization of truth through introspection in place of tedious book learning.

Literary works were esteemed highly. Writing, commenting and speaking on them by the Zen monks vibrated the minds of the Samurais who took pleasure in patronizing them. Due to patronage given by the Shogunal government to Zen activities, monks became ideals in the society. They worked as active advisors to domestic and foreign affairs and were sent as envoys to Ming government of China. Thus the Zen way of life and thought grew rapidly in the political capital at Kamakura and the cultural capital at Kyoto.

Zen monks were sent to China to study and to visit the five mountains and ten famous monasteries there. On coming back they settled as monks, painters, philosophers and writers etc. Notable contributions were made in the fields of education, calligraphy, pottery, decorative and theatrical arts. Zen concept of '*mu-ni*', non-duality, oneness of life and death became dear to the hearts of warriors, an inspiration for going to a field of war. The Zen monks preached fearlessness from death; they said that death breaks the shackles of being confined, after death one can easily move wherever he likes. Monk painters painted cherry blossoms. In a very short span of life they are blown away by wind like the soul of a warrior that flies away suddenly in a battlefield with a blow of a dagger. Zen gives will power that is urgently needed by the warriors.

Will power was another requisite of the warriors, eager to capture the political sphere. Zen training increases will power and helps in the betterment of health, mental and physical both. It needs a resolute mind to join the practice and in return the strict discipline during training enhances the quality of life. Again a passion of warriors.

Fundamental Principles of Zen

Fundamentally science and Zen spiritualism have no points to contradict as Zen is a religion of realization, realization of isness, of what is happening around us; this isness of things is science. Science has no place for blind faith and superstitions; Zen also detests all that had gained ground to some extent after the propagation of esoteric sects like Tendai and Shingon.

Seven fundamental characteristics of Zen are: asymmetry, simplicity, austere sublimity, naturalness, subtle profundity, freedom from attachment and tranquility. There is no sequence, each of them are equally important. Aloneness, familiarity, refinement, inwardness, commonness, minimalism, purity and *śūnyatā* – are fundamental in Zen. Asymmetry means imbalance, irregularity and informality. By definition it means being uneven. It is implied in architecture, painting, flower arrangement and interior decor. It would be more difficult to bring out beauty in an asymmetrical arrangement, so asymmetry has to be very carefully calculated. Portraits of Bodhidharma and Hakuin are the best examples, unconcerned with perfection. Simplicity in designing a room means empty space topped by thatched roofs; no grandeur of Chinese temple architecture exists there. In painting simplicity means using least of strokes to bring out the best of effect; colours are unobstrusive. The simplest colour is used in Zen painting, that is ink.

The concept of aloneness taken from the Laṅkāvātara-sūtra leads to refinement of life. It needs pure and serene mind to enjoy its essence. It is followed in most of the forms of art like landscape gardening, tea ceremony, ikebana. Inwardness needs an unperturbed mind. Minimalistic approach teaches to express the plentitude of form through least of means. *Śūnyatā* is appreciation of absolute poverty and non-attachment and purity means freedom from defilements.

Zen as Training and Practice

The essence of Zen training lies in practicing single-mindedly without aspiring for any results. People from any walk of life aspiring for higher goals can go for training under a qualified monk or a lay teacher who has received sanction (*inka*) to get insight and peace of mind following a very strict time table; getting up at three in the morning working till nine O'clock at night, reciting sūtras, doing meditation, sitting on straw mats spread along the walls and carrying out other monastic responsibilities.

Large monasteries have Zendō or meditation halls with Mañjuśrī Bodhisattva at the center, venerated for knowledge. Smaller monasteries combine the Buddha and the meditation halls with Śākyamuni as the principal object of worship. Preparation for *zazen* is done by reciting sūtras, paying homage to Mañjuśrī, Nīlakaṇṭha, Avalokiteśvara and the Buddhas. During training students go to offer prayers to them, to help them, in getting strength and to lead to enlightenment. A short period of meditation each day can make a person more attuned to one's environment. Training in Zen gives a mind that is resolute and a body that is powerful. *Zazen* or seated meditation quietens the mind and solves difficult questions. It trains to concentrate, concentration of insight aids to accumulate energy, together they inspire for action, unparalleled.

The practice of Zen is forgetting the self in the act of uniting with something. An aspiring monk might have to wait for three days at a monastery gate to get admission. Then he has to enter into a demanding schedule of meditation, chanting of sūtras, manual labour and even begging.

Daily schedule of a Zen temple is strict. Students under training shoulder responsibilities and strictly follow table etiquettes. During Zen training there is little time for sleep or rest and none for personal activities. Seriousness, perseverance, absolute silence and simple meals are the basic requirements of training period. Uninterrupted meditation gets animated through a daily discourse by a Zen master, themes can be selected from Buddhist sūtras, from the lives of Zen patriarchs or stories. A Zen master also tries to moderate unrelenting severity of twenty-two points, plus triple-word-score, plus fifty points for using all letters. The monastic life encourages so that the mood of the participants becomes full of excitement, enabling them to enter a peculiar frame of mind.

One of the objects of Zen training is to transcend ego in order to achieve *satori*. Once having embarked upon the way of enlightenment one gets determined to undergo austerities. Will to succeed is the basic disposition. The more difficult and stubborn is the teacher, it is more likely that the pupil would break through to enlightenment.

Sitting posture, breath control and concentration are the techniques, the outer process of the exercise without involving the inner personality. These techniques are to be accompanied by personal devotion. Sitting in full or half lotus posture, normally leads to pain, but one gets used to it in two or three days. Life gets harder with aching limbs, bodily fatigue due to reduced time to sleep and soar throat because of recitation of '*mu*' for hours at the top of the voice. Slackening of zeal is not permissible, the adapt is beaten with a stick to stir up his zeal. The body of the trainee calms through perfectly regulated breathing, mind is exerted on the themes known as '*koan*'.

Relevance of Zen Training

Meditation has permeated the psycho-sphere of the Japanese; it has become the warm reality of their culture, given a new dimension to all the forms of art. After being trained one can practice meditation anywhere anytime, even spare time can be utilized while one is on his way to office. Meditation trains both physically and spiritually and leads to deepening and strengthening of insight. So industrial management technology lays stress on Zen philosophy. Concentration leads to refinement and refinement leads to advancement.

Character building is another important factor that is possible through Zen education, through regulated collective living, resulting in a chance to shine forth. It teaches value for labour being taught through the concept of intense labour during Zen training. Work is not toil or trouble. Thus Japanese have a reputation of being hard workers, rate of employee absentees is extremely low in Japan. Positive attitude for hard work is taught in Zen, no value is given to rest and repose. Leisure does not fill lives with meaning and purpose for a Zen trainee.

Zen teaches democratization of peoples' way of living, superiors and subordinates work in co-operation; tea is sipped together at the Zen monasteries. Due to a sense of communal consciousness, a company becomes a one big family, where co-operative attitude and active participation are paramount. Harmony among workers increases work efficiency, saves the workers from tension, confusion and restlessness, gives relaxation, clarity of perception and trains the mind to think creatively.

Literary Basis

Zen abhors media, the written word in favour of an unwritten doctrine, a doctrine that can be transmitted from mind to mind. It is a matter of realization. But this does not mean that Zen ignores the value of sūtras that provide a base for its fundamental principles. There are three basic scriptures of Zeṇ: Laṅkāvatāra-sūtra, Vajracchedikā-prajñā-pāramitā and hymn to Nīlakaṇṭha-lokeśvara. Chinese translation of Laṅkāvatāra-sūtra by Guṇa-bhadra was used by Bodhidharma for propagation. It has given a base for transcendental intuition, inner realization and enlightenment. Embracing the philosophy of Laṅkāvatāra-sūtra, Zen has become more introvert than extrovert. Buddha mind exists in each of us but we are ignorant, but once we come to know about it, we are enlightened. This requires inner quest and an urge for knowledge of the self. This idea is also derived from the same sūtra.

Non vegetarianism is strictly prohibited in Zen monasteries, food served to the trainees is pure vegetarian. Laṅkāvatāra-sūtra forbids eating meat recounting eight reasons to abstain from it. Taking animals' lives are like eating our own flesh. Eating meat causes spiritual pollution. They say that the skin of a meat eater emits offensive odour, eating meat is not good for physical health and a meat-eater is not trustworthy. The Buddhist concepts of reincarnation and compassion also denounce killing of animals and eating their flesh.

The philosophy of *śūnyatā* contained in the Prajñā-pāramitā has exerted a profound influence on Zen. Zen believes in void. So the space should be uncluttered, non essentials are to be eliminated from a work-place, Least of means should bring out the best of effect. In Japan it may be a painting, a garden, a hall for meditation, a living room or an emperor's workplace, a factory or a monk's hut, they are all steeped in the philosophy of *śūnyatā*.

When Zen reached Japan it was not just confined to the aristocratic class, but was also embraced by the masses who could appreciate and adopt its one-pointedness in action, straight forwardness in presentation, strictness in discipline, heroic philosophy of life and death, masculine vigour and loyalty. But the Japanese added their innate potential of delicacy and beauty to it. Zen penetrated deeply and widely into moral and aesthetic fields and became a great power not only in the artistic but also in intellectual and political life of the Far East. It moulded their character and became its expression itself.

Impact on Architecture

Domestic, monastic, temple or palace architecture in Japan is a combination of simplicity, beauty and elegance. Space inside is filled except the unavoidables. Artificial trappings are stripped off. The interiors are devoid of anything that would deviate one's mind from concentration. Not even a particle of dust is allowed that can cause distraction. An area is carefully selected for construction of a Zen monastery, favourably with a natural surrounding, if possible with a hill to serve as a backdrop because harmony with nature is paramount.

With the coming of Zen during the Kamakura period most of the temples were constructed in accordance with the Zen ideals and to fulfil the requirements of the monks living there. The style of temple architecture bearing enormous influence of Zen is termed as '*kara-yo*'. They are abodes of silence, their windows are arched, pillars stand on stones, ceilings are mirror ceilings, lattice work under eves is sloping and doors are on pivots. Their meditation halls have images of Bodhidharma or other patriarchs. '*Somon*', the main gate can even be a three storey construction, '*sanmon*'.

Surviving examples of Zen temples are: Daitokuji, Nanzenji, Tōfukuji and Sōfukuji in Kyoto, Engakuji at Kamakura, Jufukuji, Eiheiji and Kenchoji, Kozanji in Yamaguchi prefecture, Ginkakauji, Kinkakuji, Kenninji at Kyoto. Nanzenji is a detached palace converted into a temple by Kageyama-tennō in AD 1293 and Kyoto imperial palace is one of the best examples of Zen style architecture.

Zen Gardens: Aid to Meditate

Japanese gardens, shimmered in Zen ideals, are the most symbolic and abstract. Garden is the first to welcome a guest to a house, a devotee to a temple or a trainee to a monastery. It is a link between the space for meditation and the world outside or to say the other way, separating the world of passions from that of eternal bliss. It serves as a gateway to *satori* or sudden enlightenment. Every plant and tree, grass and bush, stone and gravel has a meaning behind. It represents the Japanese reverence for nature: mountains, rivers, rocks and trees.

Unlike a formal garden it is a symbolic reproduction of a view of nature compressed into a limited space in a domestic, public, monastic or a palatial garden. All the constituents in a Zen garden have their own relevance, it can be a small rock representing a rock, sand and gravel substituting slow moving water or a waterfall, a wooden bridge, a stone lantern and a replica of a pagoda; trees and bushes, plants and grasses everything grows in a natural manner. It is a pleasure for the eyes to visit a garden that is planned according to the Zen standards of taste. In such a garden nature is utilized to lend support for meditation.

A Zen garden corresponds to architecture. Planning is wonderful. Something is planted while something is left for imagination of the visitor. Each component is planned according to the taste of the user, his age and requirements. A Zen garden can be realistic, symbolic or abstract. They may represent a landscape, an island or symbolize a paradise. Tea gardens are intented to create an atmosphere of *'wabi'* and *'sabi'*, presenting a secluded rural atmosphere or meant for strolling.

Veneration for nature, mountains, rivers and rocks gave birth to dry landscape, abstract kind of gardens with white sand substituting water, with stones big and small, standing as hurdles for the waves of ocean, ripples of water coming and striking them is a symbol of the ocean of existence that is to be crossed before going to the heaven. It also symbolizes the ocean of illusions that lie on the way to enlightenment or illumination. Such gardens represent refined simplicity, no flowers or trees are found witnin their bounds; quiet atmosphere quietens the mind and aids to meditate. This simplicity is a result of the Zen concept of using least of means to acquire the most. Some of the famous Zen gardens are at: Ginkakuji, Kinkakauji, Ryoanji and Daitokuji.

Japanese Aestheticism and the Cult of Tea

Tea ceremony and Zen are intimately connected. It became a rigid cult, an exercise in taste and a symbol of later Japanese aestheticism. Serving tea ceremoniously is a product of elite Ashikaga culture. Tea is served in an artificially and ritualistically simple manner. Fundamental ideas of tea are taken from Zen, fostered by the monks for relief from knotty discussions, severe meditation and betterment of life. The ceremony is very formal, involving a series of actions like a dance performance, also incorporating works of art, a kakemono, a tea kettle, bowls, dishes, ikebana etc, everything is important. Architecture of a tea house is simple, garden is set in accordance, everything is in harmony. In China during T'ang and Sung periods literati used to judge the colour and savour of tea along with discussions on history, poetry and works of arts.

Zen monks are trained in conducting a tea ceremony to get a lesson on the essential constituents of an orderly life. It is not merely the practical side but principally also they are supposed to observe the spirit that runs through it. The ceremony is conducted in harmony (*wa*), with reverence (*kei*), purity (*sei*) and in tranquility (*gaku*). Gentleness of spirit, and tenderness of touch govern the atmosphere. Simplicity is fundamental. A tea room is empty except a few required utensils, carefully selected and arranged. Windows and screens are a source of gentle charm. Light inside is gentle, restful and conducive for meditative mood. The whole atmosphere is a reflection of the personality of the planner. External emptiness is filled with internal richness.

To absorb the spiritual benefits of Zen, tea seeds were brought by the monk Eisai from China when Emperor Minamoto Sanemoto (1192-1219) was ill. Thus he is honoured as father of tea cultivation. Later priest Dai-o brought it as a ceremony. Finally Ikkyu was established as the first tea master. Gradually tea ceremony became an artistic custom adopted by Zen monasteries, where tea is sipped with aestheticism of primitive simplicity under a thatched roof, sitting on tatami mats. On entering a tea room one is supposed to cast off the garb of his social status, no earthly distinctions or restraints are allowed inside. So the door height is too low that a guest literally bows and crawls into a tea room in a humble manner.

Zen and the Art of Painting

Sung Chinese style filtered into Japan in the 13th century in the form of ink monochrome painting which gradually emerged as the finest expression of spirit and the minds of monk philosophers, as a creation of meditation and visualization of ideals. It is not meant for art's sake but for awakening. A Zen painting symbolizes deep insight and self determination. There is no space for a second thought; a stroke of brush once done is done. Each stroke is a reflection of the personality of the painter, a result of his long silent meditation, plus physical and emotional control. Thoughts of the Zen painters are given form through empty spaces, ink washes and diaphanous water colours. The beauty of such paintings do not reside in line or precise details but it is manifested in the minimalistic approach, in unfilled spaces, in merging of rocks and trees into mist and mist into sky. Paintings are abstract but abstraction is not felt. The technique is known as Suibokuga which was imported from China but was modified by the Japanese according to their own skills and sensibilities to such an extent that today there is no parallel.

Painting became a forte of Zen, a teaching tool, to speak directly to the viewer. Non attachment to the worldly comforts is visualized through painting a small hut of a monk, busy in meditation or study. Though the huts are small but they are focal points. They stand in harmony with natural surroundings in such a way that it looks like a part of the scene without being touched by human hands; it is solitary and inconspicuous, provides peace of mind, which is essential for meditation. The message portrayed, is withdrawal from the world.

In a Zen painting there is more space for imagination than visualization following the concept of elimination of the non essentials and use of least of strokes. The space left empty is eloquent in itself. A solitary bird on a dead branch is done in appreciation of transcendental aloofness in the minds of multiplicity, this is '*wabi*'. '*Wabi*' also means worshipping poverty. It instills an innate longing for primitive simplicity, this further means going close to the nature and feel its pulsation. Complexities that lie on the surface of life became immaterial.

Concentration on the tip of the brush, calculation of the ink filled in, length of brush, density of ink, one pointedness towards pressure exerted, are fundamental in Zen painting. A rhythmically moving brush can give a dry brush effect even when it is filled. The thrifty brush tradition of the Zen painters is associated with one corner style. Such painting are asymmetrically balanced.

Zen paintings are known for portraying a variety of ideals. For example, sincerity towards a teacher is of prime importance in Zen. A Chinese Zen patriarch, follower of Bodhidharma came to him to express his earnestness. He knelt before him to seek instruction, cut off his left arm with a knife. The story is painted on a scroll kept at the Kozanji monastery. Blood is gushing forth, cut off arm and the knife are lying on the ground; people standing there, are stunned to look at. Many Japanese painters have painted Bodhidharma crossing the Yangtse river on a reed. Bodhidharma became a legendry figure in Zen. Sesshū, a leading artist of the Muromachi period painted Bodhidharma in meditation facing a rock for nine years at the Shaolin monastery. Other Zen master artists are: Mokuan, Mincho, Josetsu, Shubun, Sesshu, Takuan, Ikeno Taiga, Hakuin, Suito etc.

A painter prepares his own ink artistically and skillfully. He obtains a fine black soot by burning pine branches and mixes it with gelatin to make sticks of ink. A stick is dipped into water and rubbed on the slanting stone up and down with a meditative mood. The dish required for preparation of ink is called '*suzuri*'. Half of it holds water and the half contains that hard and smooth stone of fine texture. Sumi mixture should have a creamy consistancy. Then brush moves on a soft and absorbent paper, made up of vegetable fibers, mounted and stretched. A felt is spread on *tatami* to give a non sticky undersurface called *'mosen'*. *'Fude'* or sumi brushes have long handles and are circularly composed. Lines created thus, have a life of their own while paintings are powerful to stir the emotions.

Ikebana: The Zen Way of Arranging Flowers

Flowers with light and incense are arranged by the Japanese in the best possible and the most beautiful way for offering to the divine beings, to express devotion, since the advent of Buddhism in the 6th century AD. Buddha himself reiterated in his sermon that plants and flowers serve as vital elements to assist in spiritual awakening and enlightemment. But with the coming of Zen, the Japanese started utilizing its ideals for various concepts of *'kado'* or the way of flowers. Gradually it emerged as a creative art, an art that brings the outdoor beauty of nature, charm of a landscape or a seashore, inside a room. Now arranging an ikebana means recreating a scene from nature on a reduced scale. Variety of flowers symbolizing different seasons along with other plant material gathered from a garden, a river, a hill or a valley arranged together enables us to learn about the essence of nature. These arrangements sometimes look like paintings. The concept of a symmetrical balance is discarded in an ikebana arrangement.

By watching an ikebeana one can appreciate seasonal changes, so dear to the Japanese. These seasonal changes symbolize an ever changing life which is continuous, which goes on and on, but finally it is destined to die. Pine and crytomaria are evergreen. They do not change colour; the quality symbolizes immutability of truth. Over the past centuries masters of ikebana have taught hundreds of different ways to arrange, to suit various occasions and places.

Martial Arts and Zen Philosophy

'*Kendo*', the way of swords derives its spiritual nutrition from Zen principles of stern discipline, intense concentration, physical power and love for hard work. Spiritual training is far more important than technical. This is the reason why martial arts of swordsmanship, judo and archery are priced as meditative techniques. Drawing a bow, aiming and shooting at the target are conducive to the achievement of spiritual concentration.

Relationship between Zen and sword, exercise and judo etc. is significant. Judo is a physical and spiritual training for character building. According to a Japanese saying "*ken-zen ichi*" sword and Zen are one. A person should wield wisdom and power both as Zen ascribes equal importance to them. A master of sword is called Osho and the hall where swordsmanship is practised is called '*dojo*', a place of enlightenment. A great number of Zen masters are also famous teachers of swordsmanship. Chiyo Nagahite studied martial arts under the guidance of Zen priest Jion of Jufukuji temple at Kamakura.

Modern Japanese Life and Zen

Though the Japanese do not follow religions with clearly defined world views but traditions are woven into the fabric of their daily lives. Zen has entered into almost every sphere of cultural life of the Japanese giving it a new dimension. They enjoy a reputation of being hard workers. Hard work is considered to be a virtue. This positive attitude is based on centuries old customs and traditions. *Zazen* is valued as the most highly perfected techniques to achieve a higher spiritual state along with related activities like tea ceremony, flower arrangement and copying sūtras etc.

Zen training instills a sense of equality and communal consciousness. It inspires the employees of a company to look at it as a big family where they work for its benefit without regarding hard work as toil or trouble. Cooperative attitude, active participation and harmony among workers increases their efficiency. The Japanese society does not put a high positive value on rest and repose; they feel guilty about resting. More work means being more lively which makes their lives meaningful and a purposeful.

Veneration for the Divine

Zen negates image worship but when it comes to the teacher-disciple relationship, it prescribes the worship of the ideal and eternal teacher Mañjuśrī. Mañjuśrī holds a scroll of Prajñāpāramitā-sūtra in his left hand. The followers of Zen believe that its ideals can be transmitted from mind to mind, prescribing the value of role of a teacher. In his right hand Mañjuśrī holds a sword. The sword is not meant for annihilation, it is not a weapon of destruction but an object of inspiration to cut away the entanglements of ignorance and evils that lie in the way of peace, justice and humanity. Kannon-bosatsu or Avalokiteśvara-Bodhisattva is worshipped by almost all the Haiku poets in order to be fearless. Their morning service includes homage to Nīlakaṇṭha. Thus sometimes Zen seems to be full of paradoxes.

12

FOUR DIVINE GUARDIANS IN JAPANESE ART

The group of four guardians or the celestial kings[1] unknown in the Vedic literature believed to have played an important part in many events in the life of Śākyamuni is collectively known in Japan as Shitennō[2]. They are said to be present to listen to the sermon delivered by Śākyamuni at Vaiśāli. Popularly they are worshipped as guardians because of the pledge that they took in the presence of the Buddha to protect the nation from all sorts of calamities, sorrows and pestilence. Their images often along with Brahmā and Indra, as maintainers of law and protectors of the state, complete with symbolic characteristic features and colours etc., are associated with four cardinal points of the compass and placed in the four directions inside the halls of worship in Buddhist monasteries. As inhabitants of the lowest Devaloka, dwelling as guardians of the four quarters they keep large retinues[3] to accompany them on their travels.

Protection of the Buddha was undertaken by the same group of guardians from the moment of his conception; moreover in Āṭānāṭīyasutta they appear as protectors of Buddha's followers also. A record of happiness in the assemblies of Devas is their responsibility while their counselors record righteousness and virtues of men. Their world is situated halfway up the mount[4] or they preside over one of the slopes of Meru, assisted by twenty-eight or thrity-two generals given a command over the sun, the moon, the stars and the Eight types of Beings (Hachibu: gandharva, piśāca, kumbhāṇḍa, preta,nāga, yakṣa, rākṣasa and mahābhūta). Grotesque demons crouching obligingly, acting as their pedestals, displaying a weird expression on their faces symbolize their role of subduing wickedness. Halos are drawn to represent their divine personalities and crowns their royalty[6]. Large shoes and tight fit armours of the Northwestern style are sometimes associated with helmets and Chinese style long sleeve garments under their armours.

Shotoku Taishi, a scholar statesman devoted to the Buddhist philosophy wrote commentaries on Buddhist sūtras and delivered lectures. He worked hard to elevate the power and prestige of the Imperial line and set the country on the course of centralized reform. He is accredited as the first Japanese Prince to vow to construct a temple for the Four Guardians, if victorious, when a short civil war broke following the death of Emperor Yomei. According to the tradition Hokoji and Shitennōji monasteries were built by Prince Shōtoku Taishi and Soga no Umako as an act of thanks giving for their victory over the anti Buddhist faction. Shōtoku was in his mid teens when he made the vow. Shitennōji, dedicated the Four Divine Kings, is located in the Naniwa area[7].

Worship of the Four Divine Guardians

Suvarṇaprabhāsa-sūtra ascribes to the worship of the Celestial Guardians which was elevated to a prestigious position by early seventh century in Japan and was kept in high esteem in China specially by the T'ien T'ai priests, translated into their languages as a result of the royal solicitude[8]. It was first expounded in the Japanese palace and various Buddhist monasteries in AD 680. Again in AD 686 one hundred priests were invited to read it, in 692 an imperial order was given by the Empress Jito on account of floods that the sūtra should be expounded in the capital and the four home provinces. She sent its one hundred copies to various provinces to be read without fail when moon of the first month was in its first quarter. In AD 696 an imperial order was issued to expound the sūtra and it was recommended that every year on the last day of the 12th month ten persons of pure life should be made to enter the religion (Visser 1945: I.14-16). Thus Suvarṇaprabhāsa became the most popular sūtra during the eighth century when national peace, its protection from disaster and damage, national unity and divine security were the prime concerns for the emperor[9]. Recitation of the sūtra was ordered as Shitennō guard the country and avail happiness and bliss[10]. In AD 741 the Japanese Emperor Shōmu himself intended to make its copies in gold characters. Provincial temples constructed during the eighth century were called Konkyōmyō-shitennō-gokokuji, 'monasteries for protection of the country by the Four Deva Kings'. Twenty monks were given responsibility to expound this sūtra on the 8th day of every month.[11]

Guardians as Kings

Seventh chapter of Suvarṇaprabhāsa (*Caturmahārāja-parivartaḥ*) is devoted to the Four Guardians as Great Kings, as they promise to protect the kings together with their families and their countries who listen to the sūtra attentively and make offerings respectfully[12]. The Suvarṇaprabhāsa was given the most important place as it guarantees an all round protection for a country[13].

For many centuries the sūtra was supposed to be the most powerful expedient both for the emperor and the state. In AD 1281 when Kublai Khan attacked Japan dangerously, Priest Eison (AD 1201-1290) explained and propagated it and the Emperor Go Uda himself copied the sixth chapter devoted to the protection of the country by the Four Divine Kings. A special attention was paid to propagate it by the Tendai priests Ryogeon (1742-1814) and Ryo-a (1800-1882). Ninno hannya-kyō is another sūtra of the Benevolent Kings expounded to remove calamities, to promote felicity and protect the head of the state (Visser 1945: I.419)

The earliest images of the Divine Guardians sculpted in wood during the mid seventh century stand on the central altar of Hōryūji monastery, distinctive in style from all the other existing sets, schematically arranged garment edges, natural proportions, softening of angularity puts the set in a more advanced stage than the earlier Suiko group. Another remarkable set of seventh century clay images of the Four Guardians from Jikidō, Hōryūji is kept at the Nara National Museum[14]. The figures present a stodgy appearance, with leather armour like hot woolen and with helmets as heavy as those of Jogan period (Warner 1964 105-6).

On the front door panels of Tamamushi shrine two of the four Guardians standing, facing each other are representative of their earliest forms known in Japan (Mizuno 1974: pl. 39). They can not be identified as Niō, as all the characteristic features like haloes, crowns, long flowing garments, armours etc are like the group kept at the Golden Hall of the Hōryūji monastery. They are standing on dwarf demons, swaying in space as though stepping forward indicated by their postures and scarves swinging out behind them. They are also painted on the outside of the four leaves of side doors of the Lady Tachibana shrine kept at the Hōryūji monastery. The portable shrine displays a mature fullness of flesh, natural postures, wire like flowing lines etc. reminiscent of the early Nara period style.

Unlike the group at the Hōryūji monastery, the guardians at Tōdaiji[15] monstery, in the Kaidan-in hall are full of action displaying a variety of movements, suggesting great artistic accomplishment and profundity of emotional expression. Clay has given enough freedom to bring out texture of their clothing and armour and a realistic expression on their faces.

In Mahākaruṇāgarbha-maṇḍala Dhṛtarāṣṭra sits in the south of the eastern gate in the vajrakula (Lokesh Chandra 1972:224). He rules over the Gandharvas and Piśācas who dwell on the east of mount Meru. But in the maṇḍala, Piśācas are placed in the south, below Chitragupta and Preta, the retinue of Yama. He and his unlimited number of Gandharva attendants guard the eastern direction. He is said to have been present at the time of preaching the Mahāsamaya-sutta and Āṭānāṭīya-sutta. He has a daughter called Siri and numerous sons[16] (Malalasekera 1998:I.1128). His body is red and appearance is wrathful, hightened by wide open eyes and wild growth of hair. He is wearing an armour and long shoes, carrying a sword in his left hand while the right palm is placed on his thigh; he is sitting cross legged with his upper garment fluttering around (Snodgrass 1997:459).

Dhṛtarāṣṭra as one of the four Divine Guardian Kings who stands straight on a demon. In the Sangatsudō hall of the Tōdaiji monastery[17] he stands on two demons crouching under his feet with right hand holding a long staff and the left resting on the hip. He does not wear any crown or helmet, his shoes are long, armour is tight fit with a raised collar, forehead is wrinkled, mouth is wide open and eyes add to his terrible look. Animal faces are hanging on his arms (Kobayashi 1975:pl.57). But Dhṛtarāṣṭra figure standing in the Kaidan-in hall of the Tōdaiji is wearing a helmet (ibid pl. 61).

Virūḍhaka is the ruler and guard of the southern side of mount Sumeru joined by innumerable Kumbhāṇḍas as his retinue. That is the realm of Kumbhāṇḍas and Pretas. In the Mahākaruṇāgarbha-maṇḍala Preta is placed below Yama and Kumbhāṇḍa below Garuḍa. Virūḍdhaka as one of the Four Celestial Guardians sits above the south gate holding a sword, in the vajrakula accompanied by a demon attendant kneeling on his left. The figure can be identified as his *āyudhapuruṣa* because of holding the same attribute, a sword. Virūḍhaka's helmet, tight fit armour and long shoes indicate his personality as a guardian. In place of a fluttering garment, a scarf is tied on his shoulders; he looks angry and vigilant with eyes opened wide. He is holding a sword in his right hand and the left fist is placed at his hip (Snodgrass 1997:477-8)

Virūḍhaka in the Sangatsudō hall of the Tōdaiji monastery displays all the characteristic features of a guardian looking vigilant, standing attentively, holding a long staff with both of his hands, and a scarf is tied over his shoulders.

Literally Virūpākṣa means one who has deformed eyes but Snodgrass (1997:507) has translated the name as "Universal Eye", as '*viru*' means multi or universal and '*pākṣa*' means opinion, statement or subject of conversation.

Regent of the western quarter and lord of Nāgas. In the assembly of the Devas he sits facing east, all the Nāgas visit him regularly and wait on him and any question of dispute arising among them would be refered to him for solution (Malalasekera 1998:II 894). As one of the four Celestial Guardians he guards the western direction as a leader of Nāgas and Pūtanas in the vajrakula of the Mahākaruṇāgarbha-maṇḍala he is placed to the north of the west gate (Snodgrass 1997: 507). It is believed that hundreds and thousands of Nāgas join him as his retinue to protect the western direction. Moreover he is also said to be a transformation of the body of Maheśvara, born from the third eye in the middle of his brows. The colour of his body is red, appearance is wrathful, ribbons hanging from his crown are fluttering up, there is no helmet, his armour and shoes are like the preceding figure of the guardian, sitting cross legged with *triśūla* in his right hand and the left fist is placed on his thigh.

In the Kaidan-in hall of the Tōdaiji monastery the group of Celestial Guardians is like the one in the Sangatsudō hall. Virūpākṣa is holding a brush in his right hand and a scroll in the left (Kobayashi 1975: pl. 60).

References

1. In the *Suvarṇaprabhāsa-sūtra* they are called great kings: Vaiśravaṇo mahārājo Dhṛtarāṣṭro māhārajo Virūḍhako mahārājo Virūpākṣa mahāraja ....(Suvarṇaprabhāsa-sūtra p.36).

Sanskrit	Direction	Japanese
Dhṛtarāṣṭra	east	Jikokuten
Virūḍhaka	south	Zōchōten
Virūpākṣa	west	Kōmokuten
Vaiśravaṇa	north	Tamonten/Bishamonten

2. Tib.: Hjig-rten-skyong, Ch. Hu-shih-chieh (guardians of the universe or protectors of the world)
   Tib.: Rgyal-chen (mahārājas, great kings)
   Ch.:T'ien Wang, Jap.:Tennō (kings of the devas)
3. Dhṛtarāṣṭra - gandharvas Virūḍhaka - kumbhāṇḍas
   Virūpākṣa - nāgas Vaiśravaṇa - yakṣa
4. Meru (Malalasekera 1998:2.861-2
5. Catvāro mahārājaḥ sārdhamaṣṭāvimśati-yakṣa-senāpatibhiranekaiśca yakṣa-sahasraiḥ.... (Suvarṇaprabhāsa-sūtra p.36)
6. In Tibetan Lamaist style they are portrayed as giants wearing an elaborate antique armor with their faces displaying awe inspiring expression. Their identity as kings is portrayed by five lobed crowns bearing five Dhyānī Buddhas or their seed syllables and the martial personality is marked by helmets (Lessing 1942:38)

7. Although the original temple was destroyed by fire its main foundations remain intact and the temple has been reconstructed on them.
8. According to Kao-sang-chw'en (Kosoden AD 519) Kāśyapa Mātaṅga (Shomoto), who arrived in China in AD 67 expounded the sūtra in a small country (?) attached to India.
   Chinese translations:
   Dharmarakṣa II, 414-423 (Nanjio 127)
   Pao-kwei. 597 (Nanjio 130)
   Jñānagupta (Nanjio 130)
   Paramārtha, 548-557 (Nanjio 130)
   Yaśogupta, 561-578 (Nanjio 130)
   I-tsing, 700-712 (Nanjio 126)
   Japanese translations: three or four renderings into Japanese by Jinamitra, Śilendrabodhi and others.
9. In AD 702 when Emperor Mommu was ill, 100 men became monks and expounded the *sūtra* in four provinces, in 703 it was read by an imperial order to pray for rain in four great temples of Nara, Yakushiji, Gangoji, Kōfukuji and Daianji. Emperor ordered to read it in AD 705 to save the people from drought and for peace in the state, it was again ordered to be read in AD 728.
10. Vayam catvāro mahārājaḥ .... Vyavalokayiśyāmi ārakṣayiṣyāmi paripacayiṣyāmi. Tena hetuna bhadanta bhagavānnasmākam caturṇām mahārājānām lokapāla iti sañjñotpādita (*Suvarṇaprabhāsa-sūtra* p.36)
11. Visser, 1935, II.448.
12. Vayam bhagavānścatvāro mahārāja..... deva-nāga-yakṣa-gandharvāsura-garuḍa-nāga-mahoragāṇām rājatvam kārayiṣyāmi. ......
13. Sarva-sattvānām parama-sukha-dāyakaḥ sarva-naraka-tiryagyoni-yamaloka-duḥkha-saṁśodhakaḥ vyādhikāntara-praṇāśako jñāna-prakāṣakaḥ parama-śāntikaraḥ śokāyaśa-praśamanaḥ vividha-nānopadrava-śata-sahasra-praṇāśayita (*Suvarṇaprabhāsa-sūtra* p. 36).
14. According to Honzon Reiho Catalogue clay for making the images was brought by Tori Busshi from China (Warner 1964: 105), height 3'3" - 3'7".
15. AD 755, clay, average height 170.5 cms.
16. Dīghanikāya ii.207, 220,257, iii.197.
17. Painted, dry lacquer, 363.3 cms..

LITERATURE CITED

Dighanikāya

Kobayashi 1975

Kobayashi Takeshi, *Nara Buddhist Art: Todaiji,* in the series of the Heibinsha Survey of Japanese art, Weatherhill/Heibonsha, Tokya, 1975.

Lessing 1942

Lessing F.D., *Yung-ho-kung,* Stockholm, 1942,

Lokesh Chandra 1971

Lokesh Chandra, *Esoteric Iconography of Japanese Mandalas,* International Academy of Indian, Culture, New Delhi, 1971

Malalasekera 1998

Malalasekera, G.P., *Dictionary of Pali Proper Names,* Munshiram Manoharlal, New Delhi, 1998

Nanjio

Bunyui Nanjio, *A Catalogue of the Chinese Translation of the Buddhist Tripitaka,* Clarendon Press, Oxford, 1883

Snodgrass 1997
Snodgrass Adrian, *The Matrix and the Diamond World Mandalas in Shingon Buddhism*, International Academy of Indian Culture and Aditya Prakashan, New Delhi, 1997
Suvarṇaprabhāsa-sūtra
Visser 1945
Visser M.W.de, *Ancient Buddhism in Japan,* E.J. Brill, Leiden, 1935
Warner 1964
Warner Langdon, *Japanese Sculpture of the Tempyo Period,* Harvard University Press, 1964.

13

INDIA AND JAPAN: ACADEMIC RELATIONS IN EARLY 20TH CENTURY

Japan is the land of devotion to action, grandeur of thought and depths of philosophy expressed in the beauty of gardens, Haiku poetry, painters' brush and vibrations of Zen. Devotion of the Japanese people for Buddhism make them pilgrims to tread on the footsteps of Kōbō Daishi leading to the heights of Shikoku hills. They climb with great effort to visit the places that are sacred to their hearts but can offer prayers only from the outside of the halls of worship because doors of the temples are opened for the monks or on very special occasions. They are kept closed in order to preserve the treasure for the coming generations with loving care. The devotees don't mind, they stand and recite Sanskrit sūtras. Sanskrit for them is the divine language. It is the sacred language for all the Asian countries, the language that carried them to higher levels of thought and the light of wisdom.

Journey of Sūtras

Thousands of Buddhist sūtras written in Sanskrit were translated into Chinese and from China they were taken to Japan first during the period of Prince Shōtoku Taishi. He drafted the Seventeen Article Constitution, first in the world, based on the philosophy of '*bahu-jana-hitāya*' and '*bahu-jana-sukhāya*'. On the auspicious occasion of its promulgation the Sanskrit *dhāraṇī* of Uṣṇīṣavijayā was brought from India. Its manuscript in Gupta script is still kept at the Hōryūji monastery.

In the early ninth century, the great monk scholar, Kōbōdaishi brought a number of Sanskrit Buddhist scriptures from China to Japan. He also invented a new script for Japan, Hiragana, on the basis of Sanskrit sound sequence. He was the first Japanese to give training for writing Sanskrit *dhāraṇīs* and seed syllables. Siddham characters, known as *Shittan* in Japan, became dear to the hearts of the Japanese. Monk Kōbō Daishi must have written a lot in Sanskrit but only forty pages in his handwriting are preserved. After him the Japanese scholars continued to visit China and Chinese regularly went to Japan. This resulted in a continuous flow of Sanskrit texts from China to Japan. The monk scholar Ennin brought a Sanskrit dictionary from China to Japan. Sage Jiun Sonja, the last of the traditional Sanskrit scholars of Japan undertook an encyclopedic work of Sanskrit texts in 1000 fascicules, Bongaku-shinryo in the 18th century. Tradition says that Goddess Sarasvatī had herself appeared to the sage to initiate him into the mysteries of the divine language.

In recent past the Japanese scholars Bunyui Nanjio and Kasawara had gone to Oxford to study Sanskrit because the universities of England and Germany had become outstanding centres of Sanskrit studies. But the dream of the Japanese to study Sanskrit in India came true when Late Prof. Raghu Vira began to invite them to study and undertake research in collaboration with him. He was the first Indian to work on the higher levels of academics for exploring and deepening cultural ties among the Asian countries. The ambitions of Japanese scholars for learning Sanskrit worked at deeper levels to bring India and Japan closer in 1930s.

The history of Indo-Japanese cultural friendship goes back to the 1934-5 when Late Prof. Raghu Vira, a great indologist, philosopher, visionary, linguist and cultural activist began to teach the Japanese language in Lahore in Pre-partition India. He sent invitations to scholars in Japan to work in various fields of Buddhism. His students from Japan undertook research in India and on going back worked for the enhancement of our friendship.

Prof. Raghu Vira was fascinated by Sanskrit *dhāraṇīs* in Japan when he listened to their recitation by the Japanese in England. They were partly clear, partly unclear; partly correct partly incorrect. Prof. Raghu Vira was amazed, he had a question in his mind, as how and when did they reach Japan, who carried them and in what form. He went to see an exhibition of Sanskrit manuscripts from Japan brought to England. A manuscript of Uṣṇīṣvijayā-dhāraṇī from the Hōryūji monastery was the earliest among them. Till then, this was the earliest known Sanskrit manuscript in the world. He was so full of enthusiasm that soon, when he was still in England, he began to study the Japanese grammar written by Chamberlain to learn the language.

On coming back to India he began to teach the Japanese language. The British government got suspicious. Prof. Raghu Vira was put behind bars as the government sensed some conspiracy behind his Japanese language teaching program. But this could not put any hurdles on his way, he went on and on. In 1933 he met Prof. Suenaga of the Kanazawa University, Tokyo, in Poona. He was the first Japanese Sanskritist in India. Both of them had long meetings to discuss the future plans. Prof. Suenaga was so impressed by the vision of Prof. Raghu Vira that he decided to accompany him to Lahore. In Lahore he began to translate the great epic Mahābhārata into Japanese, in collaboration with Prof. Raghu Vira. During his stay there he advised him to establish an international centre, where foreign scholars could come and undertake research on various fields of Indology. The idea appealed to Prof. Raghu Vira. Soon he wrote letters to several scholars of world fame for joining hands in the noble endeavor. Prof. Suenaga was the first Japanese to donate for the cause. He donated fifty rupees. An academic institute began to take form. It was named 'International Academy of Indian Culture' in English and 'Sarasvati Vihar' in Hindi. Prof. Suenaga was busy translating the great epic. The work was enormous and ambitious, but Professor fell ill and he had to go back to Japan without completing the project.

Thus International Academy of Indian Culture was founded by Late Prof. Raghu Vira in 1934 in co-operation with several other scholars. Prof. N. Fukushima from the Imperial University, Tokyo, was one of the members of the Academy. Dr. A. C. Woolner, Vice Chancellor, University of Lahore, Punjab, was the first President. Mahārājā of Mysore, His Highness Shri Shri Krishnarāja Wadiyar Bahadur, Rājā Saheb of Aundh, Shrimant Bala Saheb Pant Pratinidhi and Rājā Saheb of Miraj Senior, His Highness Shrimant Sir Balasaheb Patwardhan were the patrons. Prof. Dr. Louis

Rénou, from Paris, Prof. Dr. R. L. Turner from London, Sir D. B. Jayatilak from Colombo, Sir Richard Burn from Oxford, Dr. V. S. Sukathankar from Poona, Prof. Dr. S. K. De from Dacca were the members of the executive. Prof. Raghu Vira was the Director and convener. Later other professors also joined the Academy as members, e.g. Prof. Sylvan Lévi, Sir John Marshall, Prof. Sten Kono, G. Tucchi, Prof. Winternitz etc.

Prof. Raghu Vira was the first Indian to create scholarships for the foreign students to come to India and study at the International Academy of Indian Culture. Foreign universities and governments were intimated. In response to his invitation the Japanese Govt. sent two state scholars, Mr. Shodo Taki from the Taisho University and Mr. Chikyo Yamamoto from the Kōyasan university. They arrived on 29th September 1936. During the first term both of them were given a course in Indian philosophy by Prof. Raghu Vira.

Works on Tantrism

Mr. Shodo Taki began to work on an unknown Tantric dictionary, the Uddhāra Koṣa of Dakṣiṇāmūrtī. It is the first work to give an insight into the secrets of the darkest sections of Indian literature, the Tantra. The Tantras once flourished all over India and beyond, up to the farthest limits of the Buddhist world. It provides a key to the monosyllables that conceal the whole world in them. The monosyllables are no longer gibberish. They have a meaning. Their combinations as mantras or dhāraṇīs are not merely a string of isolated items, but they form an organic whole. It is at once a primer and a reference book indispensable for the scholars of Tantrism. Mr. Shodo Taki finished editing it under guidance of and in collaboration with Prof. Raghu Vira, in 1938. His work was sent to Prof. Otto Schroder from Kiel, Germany and Prof. Louis Rènou from Paris for examination. On their warm appreciation and recommendation Mr. Shodo Taki was granted the degree of Doctor of Philosophy in Sanskrit on the 29th January, 1939. The project containing text, exegetical notes, appendices, Sanskrit and English glossary, was published by the International Academy of Indian Culture as Vol. No. 4 of the Sarasvati Vihar series in June 1938. After a stay of two years and four months he left Lahore for his motherland, Japan.

Studies on Buddhist Sculptures

Mr. Yamamoto began statistical studies of the Buddhas and Bodhisattvas in Indian sculpture. In the summer term he also went through a course in Indian philosophy. He carried on field work for a detail study up to the last day of his sojourn in India, that was February 1940. He also worked under the guidance and co-operation of Prof. Raghu Vira. The research project extended over three volumes. It contained the result of his study of all the important museums and sites lying between Kabul and Colombo. It was an absolutely new approach to the study of sculpture. Different schools had been studied in their minute details. An accurate objective basis for comparative study of the various schools had been established. He covered different aspects of sculptor's techniques and aesthetics. The work was published as Vols. 5,10,11 of the Sarasvati Vihar series entitled "The Buddhas and the Bodhisattvas in Indian Sculpture (from Central Asia and Afghanistan to Ceylon and Java)".

The project was submitted for examination to R.B. Dayaram Sahni, the Late Director General for Archaeology in India. Mr. Yamamoto was granted the degree of Doctor of Philosophy, in Indian Art and Archaeology on the 22nd November 1939.

Dr. Chikyo Yamamoto worked on Rāmāyaṇa in China in collaboration with Prof. Raghu Vira. Two texts were discovered from China— Jātaka of an unnamed King and Nidāna of King of "Ten Luxuries". The first was translated into Chinese from an original Indian text by K'ang-seng-hui in AD 251 and the second by Kekaya in AD 472. No trace of the Sanskrit originals is left in India or anywhere else. Both the works were translated into English. The first is the 46th story of Roku-do-jik-kyō, Six Pāramitā collection sūtra, No. 152 of the Taisho edition of the Chinese Tripiṭ aka. The second story is No. 203 in Taisho Tripiṭaka. Both of them were published by the academy as No. 8 of the 'Sarasvati Vihar Series' at the Ārya Bhāratī Press in Lahore.

Encyclopaedia of Indian Historical Geography

Encyclopaedia of Indian Historical Geography was another ambitious task undertaken by Dr. Chikyo Yamamoto in collaboration with Prof. Raghu Vira. Fan Fan Yu is a Chinese dictionary of the Indian geographical names compiled in AD 517 from literature and accounts of travellers. It contains the names of kingdoms, countries, cities, towns, villages, monasteries, shrines, mountains, rivers, ponds, islands, gardens and forests. It begins from the earliest and goes up to the 12th century AD. The dictionary was transcribed into Devanāgarī and rendered into Sanskrit for the first time. Corrections were suggested for badly handed down names and meanings were supplied. It was to appear in several volumes but could not be published so far due to financial constraints.

Chikyo Yamamoto left for a tour to Eastern India, on his way back to Japan. In Japan he was offered the post of Assistant Professor at the Kōyasan University. Later he joined as a curator at the Kōyasan Museum. Throughout his life he was constantly in touch with the academy. He paid several visits to India for his research projects. Later International Academy of Indian Culture published more books written by him.

Throughout their stay at the academy both the scholars were allowed the benefit of free board, lodge and tuition. Every year they used to go on tours with Prof. Raghu Vira to visit important Indian Buddhist places. On the eve of departure Mr. Yamamoto presented Taisho Issaikyo edition of the Chinese Tripiṭaka, along with several other books as his *gurudakṣiṇā* to Prof. Raghu Vira.

Hideo Kimura from the Ryukoku University was another great scholar of Sanskrit who had come to India. Prof. Raghu Vira affectionately used to call him Hṛdaya Kumāra. He had translated the two works by poet Kālidāsa: Ṛtu-saṁhāra and Meghadūta into Japanese.

Prof. Genjun Sasaki from the Otani University was another Japanese scholar who worked at the Academy. He prepared a Sanskrit-Chinese catalogue based on the Saddharma-puṇḍarīka-sūtra. He was so impressed by Prof. Raghu Vira during his stay that when he went back he introduced Hindi programs on the Japan Radio. He was very much upset after the news of India's partition because Lahore had gone to Pakistan where his dear teacher's institute was situated. He kept on trying to know about his whereabouts. In 1954 he came again to the academy for research.

The Japanese scholars who had come and stayed under the shade of fatherly affection of Prof. Raghu Vira loved India to the deepest of their hearts. India was another home for Shodo Taki. He was sad when all his books on India were burnt during the world war. Once he wrote in a letter that whenever he closes his eyes he beholds the flowing rivers and mountains, temples and monasteries, ancient monuments of India. When he had gone back to Japan, he delivered a number of lectures on India and its culture, religion and philosophy. Prof. Shoson Miyamoto, an eminent scholar on Indian philosophy in Japan and director of Japanese Association of Indian and Buddhist studies and Prof. Hajime Nakamura were also associated to Prof. Raghu Vira. They had visited the academy in 1954. Whosoever used to come to India, tried to meet him or else their visit to India was incomplete.

Teaching the Japanese language was seen as a tool to understand the Japanese mind, their character behind amazing achievements and patriotism. When the Academy was shifted to Nagpur in 1946, the Japanese studies were once again resumed. Prof. Raghu Vira's daughter Dr. Sudarshana Devi Singhal and son Dr. Lokesh Chandra began to teach Japanese language. A large number of Indians joined as students from various fields. They were ministers, advocates, secretaries, justices, principals and teachers. The programmes of the academy included viewing of films on Japan, playing Japanese music and lectures on Japanese culture.

Prof. Raghu Vira was very famous in the Japanese scholarly world. He had uninterrupted connections with them. Whosoever required anything from India, on any subject, Prof. Raghu Vira was there to help them. If he required any book from Japan it was made available to him by his students or other scholars. For example once Prof. N. Tsuji sent some books to him but he sent them back after studying. Once Soichi Adachi asked for some books on Sanskrit prosody from the then Governor of Madhya Pradesh, HE Pattabhi Sitaramaiya. The request was directed to Prof. Raghu Vira and he responded immediately.

A number of Japanese scholars visited the academy in Delhi, stayed there, studied and took part in teaching also. It is a matter of detail study as how far the academy founded by Late Prof. Raghu Vira has worked for the deepening of our friendship. His son Prof. Lokesh Chandra has continued the unfinished task and it is carried on further by others. He outstands as a visionary, a philosopher, art historian and an expert on Buddhism. Interaction with a number of Japanese organisations and scholars are a part of the programme of the Academy founded by Prof. Raghu Vira, an important step towards enhancement of the academic relations between the two countries.

Documents in the Raghuvira Archives at the International Academy of Indian Culture, New Delhi are used as the sources material.

14

STRUCTURE OF GOBU-SHINGAN AND THE GRAPHIC VAJRADHĀTU-MAṆḌALA IN THE LIGHT OF THE SARVA-TATHĀGATA-TATTVA-SAṄGRAHA

The Sarva-tathāgata-tattva-saṅgraha is of signal importance for the historic development of philosophic speculation in India, Nepal, China, Japan, Tibet and Mongolia. In the eighth century it was transmitted to China along with Mahāvairocana-sūtra. From there they were taken to Japan and became two basic sūtras of Japanese Shingon.

Sarva-tathāgata-tattva-saṅgraha is divided into five parts: the first four parts correspond to the four *samayas* and the conclusion is given in the fifth. The four *samayas* are: *abhisamaya, vajra-samaya, dharma-samaya and karma-samaya*. The fifth part is called the Tantra, Uttara-tantra and Anuttara-tantra. The first four parts have four chapters each, dealing with the maṇḍalas of Tathāgata-kula, vajra-kula, dharma-kula and karma-kula. The four *kulas* correspond to the four maṇḍalas: mahā, samaya, dharma and karma maṇḍalas. The fifth chapter in each part gives the Caturmudrā and Ekamudra-maṇḍalas.

The text of STTS (Sarva-tathāgata-tattva-saṅgraha) is represented as a visual dharma as a maṇḍala in the form of painted scrolls and also as sculptures in three dimensional form. Thus it exerted an influence on the fine arts of several countries. It was expressed as Vajradhātu-maṇḍala in the Sino-Japanese tradition (Hakeda 1972:147-8).

Configuration of the graphic Vajradhātu-maṇḍala has been a problem for the historians of Japanese art on several counts: (i) which textual tradition do the prevalent twin maṇḍalas represent; (ii) if they do not conform to texts, are they a synthesis of different transmissions; (iii) was it Amoghavaraja who integrated the two maṇḍalas for the sake of his disciples or Hui-kuo; (iv) what is the relationship of Vajradhātu-maṇḍala in six parts in the scroll, Gobu-shingan and in nine parts in the Genzu maṇḍala. Scholars have debated these and other aspects of the problem. These questions have been sought to be answered on the basis of the abridged translation for recitation by Vajrabodhi (Nj.534, T.866) or by recourse to Amoghavajra's translation of the first chapter (Nj.1020, T.865) which were the only orthodox sources for the Shingon tradition. Dānapāla's translation of the complete text was not taken into consideration. Without the complete text of the STTS and its classification in the Tibetan exegesis it is not possible to explain the complimentarity of the twin maṇḍalas and the nine sections of the Vajradhātu-maṇḍala. In Japan the four-fold Tibetan classification of the classes, the two classes of *caryā* and *yoga* have Vairocana as the central deity. Hence they constitute the pair or *ryobu* maṇḍala, the maṇḍala of both (*ryo*) the classes (*bu*).

The earliest Sino Japanese representation of the Tattva-saṅgraha is known as the Rita-sogyara-gobu-shingan meditation on five sections of the Rita-saṁhāra (Tattva-saṅgraha) done on the orders of Subhākarasiṁha (AD 637-735). The Chinese colophon at the end says that it was given in AD 855 by the Chinese teacher Fa-chüan to his Japanese desciple Enchin, whose Sanskrit name was Jñānavajra. The text has full six maṇḍalas (Lokesh Chandra 1972: 53). Six complete or incomplete copies are known. The best is the one written by Zenkaku of the Onjoji in AD 1194.

The six maṇḍalas of Gobu-shingan are the six coordinates of the first part of the Tattvasaṅgraha method by which the yoga wheel of law was set in motion (Lessing/Wayman 1968:214-249).

The first part of the Tattva-saṅgraha contains five chapters:

1.	Vajradhātu-mahā-maṇḍala	pp. 1-99
2.	Vajra-guhya-vajra-maṇḍala	pp. 100-115
3.	Vajra-jñāna-dharma-maṇḍala	pp. 116-129
4.	Vajra-kārya-karma-maṇḍala	pp. 130-141
5.	Caturmudrā and ekamudrā maṇḍalas	pp. 142-152

Now let us take up the six sub-maṇḍalas of the Gobu-shingan. The six are:

1.	Vajradhātu-mahā-maṇḍala prathamaḥ pādaḥ (colophon on illus.37)	1-37
2.	Vajradhātu-guhya-dhāraṇī-maṇḍalam (colophon on illus.71)	38-71
3.	Vajradhātusūkṣma-maṇḍalam	72-104
4.	Vajradhātu pūjā-maṇḍalam (colophon on illus.137)	105-139
5.	Vajradhātu catur-mudrā-maṇḍalam	140-144
6.	Vajradhātu ekamudrā-maṇḍalam. Samāptam	145.

Vajradhātu-mahā-maṇḍalam

All the deities of Gobu-shingan in its six maṇḍalas are named, classified and arranged according to the Tattvasaṅgraha. Their attributes, mudrās and mantras are also indentical with the text. The teachings of the yoga school of tantras are set fourth in two works: the fundamental or the mūla-tantra, Tattva -saṅgraha (Toh.479) and the explanatory tantra Vajraśekhara (Toh.480, Lessing/Wayman 1968:25).

The chief disciple of the great Tibetan teacher Tsoṅ-kha-pa in his analysis of the fundamentals of Buddhist tantras, systematizes the yoga tantra literature into fundamental and explanatory tantras. The explanatory tantras are divided into two from the viewpoint of *prajñā* and *upāya* (Wayman 1973:236-7). Fifteen texts (Toh. 479-493) and 161 commentaries on them (Toh. 2501-2661) are classified under this scheme (Wayman 1973:236-7). Here below is a conspectus of the classification as it applies to the Sino-Japanese tantras:

Yoga tantras

1. Mūla or Fundamental tantra

Tattva-saṅgraha (Toh.479)

a. T.866, Nj.534, Vajrabodhi, AD 723, abridge translation for reciation called=nenju-kyō=japa-sūtra

b. T.865, Nj.1020, Amoghavajra, worked AD 746-771, translation of the first chapter.

c. T.882, Nj.1017, Dānapāla, worked AD 980-1000, translation of the complete text.

2. Vyākhyā or Explanatory Tantras

i. Prajñā:

Ārya-prajñā-pāramitā-naya-pañcaśatikā (Toh.489, T.220(10)=Nj.I, T.240=Nj.1033, T.242=Nj.862, T.243=Nj.1034.)

ii. Upāya

Trailokyavijaya-mahā-kalpa-rāja (Toh.482, explanatory of the second part of Vajrākula)

The nine sub-maṇḍalas of the graphic Vajrādhātu can be devided in to three groups:

1. The six sub-maṇḍalas of the Tattva-saṅgraha:

i. Vajrādhātu-mahā-maṇḍala

ii. Samaya-maṇḍala

iii. Sūkṣma-maṇḍala

iv. Pūjā-maṇḍala

v. Caturmudrā-maṇḍala

vi. Ekamudrā-maṇḍala

2. vii. Naya-maṇḍala

3. The two sub-mandalas of the second section of the Tattva-saṅgraha pertaining to Trailokyavijaya:

viii. Trailokyavijaya-mahā-maṇḍala

ix. Trailokyavijaya-samaya-maṇḍala

Scholars have debated the raison d'eter of the nine maṇḍalas on one painted scroll. While practical considerations guided the novenarrian formulation of the Vajradhātumaṇḍala, the philosophic basis for the concatenation is not clearly provided by the Sino-Japanese texts. It is only when we take into account the Tibetan taxonomy and topical analysis of the tantras that the three groups fall into a coherent picture. Thus the Sino-Japenese Vajrādhātu-maṇḍala compromises the six sub-maṇḍalas of the Tattva-saṅgraha, the seventh maṇḍala represents the exegesis from the *prajñā* standpoint, and the eight and the ninth maṇḍalas betoken the *upāya* viewpoint. Thus this type of graphic maṇḍala is all embracing in its inclusion of the explanatory perspectives of *prajñā* and *uapāya* on a single scroll.

Kōbō Daishi had brought with him the following four types of the graphic Vajradhātu-maṇḍala:

1. Vajradhātu-maṇḍala consisting of nine small maṇḍalas, one sheet in seven sections, 1 to 6 shaku long.
2. Mahā-maṇḍala made of cotton cloth representing 447 deities
3. The central maṇḍala with 81 deities, one sheet in 3 sections
4. samaya-maṇḍala of the Vajradhātu made of cotton cloth representing 120 deities.

The original paintings were lost. In AD 821 Kōbō Daishi ordered duplicates to be made. Even these duplicates have been lost but they are available in the copy known as the Takao maṇḍala kept at the Jingoji monastery.

Kōbō Daishi in his memorial presenting a list of newly imported sūtras and other items submitted to the Japanese emperor in AD 806 says that after due concentration he received instruction in the mantras and mudrās of the five divisions of the Vajraśekhara-sūtra (= Tattva-saṅgraha). The abbot informed him that the Buddhist scriptures are abstruse that their meaning cannot be conveyed except through art. For this reason he ordered the court artist Li Chen and about a dozen other painters to execute ten scrolls of Garbhadhātu and Vajradhātu-maṇḍalas and assembled more than twenty scribes to make copies of the Vajradhātu-sūtra and other important esoteric Buddhist scriptures (Hakeda 1972:147-8)

The second possibility for drawing only the first part of the Tattva-saṅgraha in the graphic Vajradhātu-maṇḍala can be:

Only the first part of the graphic of the Tattva-saṅgraha was drawn by Śubhākarasiṁha (AD 637-735) (TZ 54-56) may be to avoid repetition. He probably intented to translate the tantra into Chinese but he did not do so. Vajrabodhi had carried the text on his voyage to China but it was lost on his way when the flotilla was engulfed by a raging storm. He could save its portions for recitation which he translated into Chinese in AD 723 under the title of Chin-kang-tingyu ch'ieh chung liao-ch'u nien-sung ching (Jap. Kongō-cho-yuga-churyaku shutsu nenju-kyō) which means an abridged *japa sūtra* for recitation from the Vajraśekhara-yoga (Nj.534, T.866). Here Vajraśekhara yoga refers to the Tattvasaṅgraha. In Japan this text is known as the Ryaku-shutsukyō or abridged sūtra. Later Vajrabodhi's disciple Amoghavajra translated the first chapter into Chinese during the years AD 746-771 under the title Ching-Ting I-ch'ieh julai chen-shin she ta-sheng heien-ching ta-chiao wang ching (Jap.Kongōchō-issiai-nyorai-shinjitsu-shō-daijō-gensho-daijō-ō-kyō) Vajrāśekhara-sarva-tattāgata-tattavasaṅgraha-mahāyānābhisambuddha-mahātantra-rāja-sūtra (Nj.1020,T.865). In Japan it is most popularly referred to as Kongō-chō-vajra-śekhara-sūtra (Lokesh Chandra 1972:3).

It is retained in the Chinese Tripiṭaka in three versions: the first translated by Vajrabodhi in four chüan, the second by Amoghavajra in three, and the third by Dānāpala in thirty (Kiyota 22-23). The abridged translation of the first chapter is the only orthodox textual source for the Shingon tradition. Dānapāla's translation of the complete text was never used.

The Tantric tradition waned in China and for more than two centuries the remaining Tattva-saṅgraha was not translated. The Chinese translation of the complete text was done by Dānapāla between AD 980-1000 (var. AD 1012-1015, Yamada1973) under the title Fe-shuo-I-chich-ju-lai-chen-shin-she-ta sheng-hsien-cheng-san-mei-ta-chiao-wang-ching (Jap. Issai-nyorai-shinjitsu-shō-daijo-genshō-daikyō-ō-kyō) Sarva-tathāgata-tattva-saṅgraha-mahāyāna-abhisamaya-abhisambhudha-samādhi-mahā-tantra-rāja-sūtra (Nj.1017, T.882).

LITERATURE CITED

Hakeda 1972

Hakeda Yoshito S., *Kukai, Major Works,* Columbia University Press, New York and London, 1972.

Kiyota

Kiyota Minoru, *Shingon Buddhism: Theory and Practice,* Buddhist Boooks International, Los Angeles and Tokyo.

Lessing/Wayman 1968

Ferdinand D. Lessing and Alex Wayman, *Klhas grub rje's Fundamentals of Buddhist Tantras,* The Hague, Mouton, 1968.

Lokesh Chandra 1971

Lokesh Chandra, *Esoteric Iconography of Japanese Mandalas*, International Academy of Indian Culture, New Delhi, 1971.

Nanjio

Bunyui Nanjio, *A Catalogue of the Chinese Translation of the Buddhist Tripitaka,* Clarendon Press, Oxford, 1883.

T

Takakusu Junjiro and Watanabe Kaigyoku ed., *Taishō edition of Chinese Triitaka,* Maison Franco-Japonaise, Tokyo, 1924-29.

Toh.

Hukuju, Ui et la, *A Complete Catalogue of Tibetan Buddhist Canons,* Sendai Tohoku Imperial University, 1934.

15

ICONOGRAPHY OF VAIŚRAVAṆA IN JAPANESE ART COMPARED WITH SANSKRIT LITERARY SOURCES

Mount Sumeru, the centre of the universe is protected in all the directions from evil spirits and goblins by guardian deities (Edmunds 1974: 240). Vaiśravaṇa presides over the northern direction. Mahāvaipulya-mahāsannipāta-sūtra (T 397.52, Nj 64) mentions that Vaiśravaṇa safeguards the north of Jambūdvīpa in the south of Mount Sumeru. According to this sūtra jambūdvīpa is the birthplace of Lord Buddha. Vaiśravaṇa with his ninetyone sons, Yakṣas, Rākṣasas, Kumbhāṇḍas, Pretas, Piśācas, Nāgas, gods and constellations etc. was indoctrinated by Lord Buddha himself. He defends Buddhism and reprimands the bad, to the pious he assures five advantages: increment of life, riches, health, pleasure and fame (Hobogrin 79).

He is known by another epithet: Kubera. Skandapurāṇa, giving an account of Kubera states that Kubera means a deformed figure. *'Ku'* means ugly and *'bera'* means body. He is portrayed with eight teeth, green beard, pointed ears, small arms, three legs, big chin, large head and reddish-brown colour. Vṛddhi is his wife and Nalakūbara is one of his sons (Skandapurāṇa 7.1.20.21-24):

Aṣṭadantaṁ haricchmachruṁ śaṅkukarṇaṁ vilohitam|
Svapādaṁ hrasvabāhuṁ ca piṅgalaṁ śucibhūṣaṇam||
Tripādaṁ tu mahākāyam sthūlaśīrṣam mahāhanum|
Evam vidham sutam dṛṣṭvā virūpam rūpatastadā||
Tadā-dṛṣṭvābravīt taṁ tu kubero'yamiti svayam|
Kutsāyām kviti śabdo'yam śarīram beramucyate||
Kuberaḥ kuśarīratvan nāmnā tena ca soṅkitaḥ|
Tasya bhāryā abhavad Vṛddhi putrastu Nalakūbaraḥ||

Chief of Yakṣas

According to the purāṇic tradition Vaiśravaṇa received a boon from Lord Śiva after practicing penance on the confluence of rivers Narmadā and Kāverī, to become the chief of the Yakṣas. His name has two variations in Mahāmāyūrī—Vaiśravaṇa and Vaiśramaṇa (T 982,984,985; Nj 306-308). He is the head of the multitude of Yakṣas (T 279.67). The same form is mentioned in the Avataṁsaka-sūtra also (T 279; Nj 88). All the yakṣas residing from mountain Yugandhara up to northern Cakravāda, depend upon Vaiśravaṇa according to Lokasthiti-abhidharmaśāstra (T 1644.5;

Nj 1297), translated by Paramārtha in AD 558. Vaiśravaṇa's same position is dealt with in Saptatathāgatapūrvapraṇidhānaśāstra (T 1331.4; Nj 167), translated by Śrīmitra, where he tells that he occupied the position as the chief of the Yakṣas to eliminate the darkness of ignorance. Those who are ignorant, are saved from transmigrations and elevated towards liberation. It is said that reading Vaiśravaṇa-sūtra, given in the Dīgha-nikāya can protect all his devotees from vile Yakṣas (Hobogirin 80).

God of Wealth

Dhanada, distributor of wealth, an epithet of Vaiśravaṇa, itself explains his position as a god of wealth. A story given in the Uttarakāṇḍa of Rāmāyaṇa relates that he was the son of Brahmā's son Pulastya. Being pleased by his devotion, Brahmā himself sent him to Śrīlaṅkā with a boon of immortality and lordship of treasures. But after a while he was defeated by Rāvaṇa and left for Gandhamādana hills. Another tradition ascribes him to be a son of Ṛṣi Viśravas.

In Buddhist tradition Vaiśravaṇa is often identified with Kubera. In Taishō (390.50) he is regularly designated under the double name Kubera Bishamon or Kubera-Vaiśravaṇa. Aśokāvadāna (T 2082.6) calls him Bishamon and the corresponding passage of Aśokasūtra (T 2043.6) names him as Kubira. His wealth is proverbial. In Taishō (703) he is compared to a houseowner of a Rājagṛha. Elsewhere (T 279.76) he is compared to Jennu or Kalyāṇamitra, his treasures to dharma and his practices to good fortunes. He is also attributed the name Daikozōshu or the proprietor of the grand depositary of treasures (T 190.12). Along with Vaiśravaṇa, Indra is also cited as an affluent (T 201.2). In one of the many stories about Vaiśravaṇa in Taishō, he appears to a lay woman, Upasenā (T 202.4) when she was reciting loudly the Dhammapada upon the roof of her house. All of a sudden she heard to a voice in air. Vaiśravaṇa was going to Virūpākṣa accompanied by his thousand Yakṣas. He asked her as what would she do if he would give her celestial joys. Furthermore he uttered a word of blessing for her...

Ekottarāgama (T 125.26) narrates the story of a Brāhmin, named Keizu. He was too poor to offer food to Buddha and his followers, invited to Kapilavastu. So he was expelled by the local confraternity of Brahmins. He borrowed money from a notable person and in exchange promised himself to be sold as a slave. The Brāhmins accepted his money but refused to lift the pronounced expulsion.

Indra and Vaiśravana descended to assist him on Lord Buddha's command. Vaiśravaṇa set up in a forest of sandal wood, a grand cuisine where his five hundred Yakṣas prepared meals for the Buddha. Then he sent a golden bar to the Brāhmin, which transformed into a million ounces of gold when flung to the floor. He purchased the food cooked by the Yakṣas and offered a magnificent feast to the Buddha with all the monks and arhats who were miraculously present there. Ekottarāgama narrates many such stories.

God of War

In Chinese and Japanese traditions he is generally venerated as a god of war. In a *dhāraṇī* in Taishō (1248) he is said to be a guardian of the dharma who has a ferocious form, is dressed in an armour, holding a lance in his left hand and offers a stūpa to Lord Buddha with the other. He treads on two black Yakṣinīs. Just on recitation of the *dhāraṇī*, Vaiśravaṇa sends his third son to assist him and if one recites it a million times, covers his armour with gold powder and offers him perfumes, flowers and other offerings Vaiśravaṇa himself comes as a commander with his celesteal troops for his victory. A non-stop reading of the *dhāraṇī* results in the arrival of Vaisravaṇa's successor Dokke as a head of the celestial troops. Beside all this, if someone desires to conquer, he should suspend a statue or a portrait on a staff as a banner, which will make the enemy powerless (Hobogirin 81).

Taishō (2043.6, 2042.6) mentions that he received the mission from Indra to protect Buddhism against the attacks of Śakas, Yavanas and Pahlavas. A number of fragments can be seen in Taishō dealing with the same aspect, showing the position of Vaiśravaṇa as a guardian deity.

Dīgha-nikāya (218-19, 257-58) names him as Vassavana or Kubera among Chaturmahārājika or the Four Divine Guardian Kings. According to Ādiparva (198.6) of Mahābhārata, Kubera has another epithet, Vaiśravaṇa (Sharma 1971: 481). The descriptions given by Getty (1962: 85) and Suzuki (1937: 209) also represent the same aspect of Vaiśravaṇa. Suzuki writes that the original name of Bishamon or Vaiśravaṇa, is Kubera.

Till the sixth century AD, Vaiśravaṇa was not much popular in Japan. For the first time Prince Shōtoku Taishi installed four images of the Four Divine Guardian Kings in Shitennōji monastery, yearning for victory in a war with Moriya (Matsunaga 1969:253), and he got their pictures engraved on his helmet. On the occasion of war Vaiśravaṇa appeared as an old *bhikṣu*, saved the life of the emperor and gave a word for his conquest. After that Shōtoku Taishi built a temple in Osaka, named Shitennōji (Edmands 1974:263-4). Till today we can see him being portrayed as a guardian deity (Matsunaga 1969:253).

All the Japanese translations of the word Vaiśravaṇa are based upon the root *śrū*, meaning to listen. His popular names in Japan are: Bishamon and Tamon. Tamon means one who has listened much. According to Taishō (1721-12) he is called Tamon because he always listens to the teachings of dharma. Other names of Vaiśravaṇa are Fumon, Hemmon and Rimon. Fumon means much-listened; Hemmon means one who has listened everywhere and Rimon means one who listens specially. Eonongi gives a different interpretation: once Kukotsura or King Kubera went to listen to the teachings of Lord Buddha. As he entered the hall, the *śrāvakas* spoke mutually: *vai śramaṇa, vai śramaṇa*. so he is called Vaiśramaṇa (Hobogirin 79).

Iconography

(1). Vaiśravaṇa, holding a halberd with a cintāmaṇi jewel atop, in his right hand and a stūpa in the left (TZ 87.257) is the frequently portrayed form. The same attributes are given to him in a number of drawings and paintings in different texts, manuscripts, scrolls and screens etc. representing him with minor variations.

a. Among Four Guardian Kings: Vaiśravaṇa in the given picture is an extract from Besson-zakki (TZ 87.257) followed by Dhṛtaraṣṭra, Virūḍhaka and Virūpākṣa, the guardians of four cardinal points called Shitennō in the Japanese language. Treasures are considered to be in the northern direction, so Vaiśravaṇa is the lord of north (Daniélou 1963:130). He

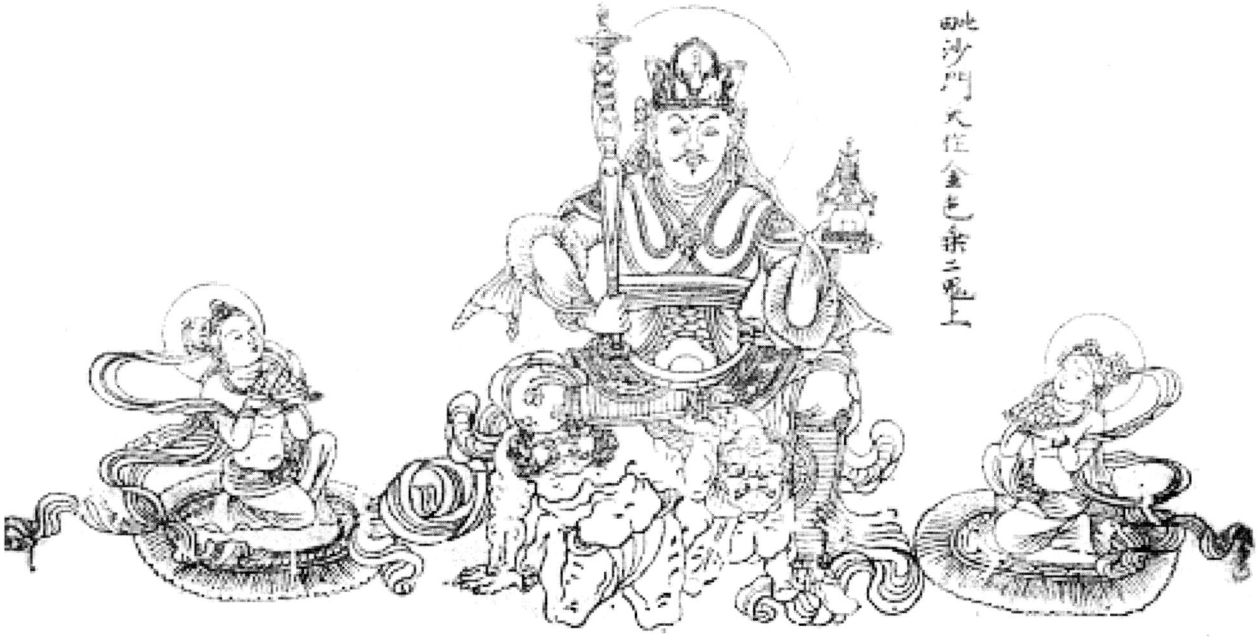

TZ.87.297

looks at the stūpa in his left hand with an angry face expression as has been mentioned by Buddha-bhāṣita-divya-rāja-sūtra (T 1244, Nj 849). He rides a goblin sitting on a rock while another is supporting from the right hand side. Jurokuzenjinno-gyotai (T 1293) translated by Vajrabodhi, says that Vaiśravaṇa has a blackish blue colour and puts on red garments. He is called Tamon-ten in this form. Various sūtras give different names for his dwelling places. According to Kisekyō (T 24.6, 25.6) he dwells on the top of Yugandhara mountain to the north of Sumeru, 42000 li away from the earth; Lokasthiti-Abhidharma-śāstra (T 1644.5), translated by Paramārtha in AD 558, says that it is situated in between the two summits of Yugandhara; according to Abhidharma-koṣa-bhāṣya by Vasubandhu, translated by Hsüan-tsang, it is on the fourth part of Sumeru, parallel to the height of Yugandhara; Dīrghāgama (T1, Nj 545) says that it is a thousand li away to the north of Sumeru and Loka-dhātu-sūtra (T 23, Nj 551) says that it is at a distance of 4000 li from Sumeru. He protects the place where Lord Buddha had preached. He is worshipped among the Seven Lucky Gods, Shichi-fuku-jin (Hobogirin 79 JEBD 17).

In the given illustration Vaiśravaṇa is flanked by two attending figures. One of them is holding a lance with a flag and the other, a cakra. They are his *āyudha-puruṣas*. He is represented in a same form in Shika-shō-Zuzō (TZ 89.172). Being slightly different he is sitting upon two demons in *lalitāsana*, but the flanking figures are not there.

b. The same form of Vaiśravaṇa is portrayed when he figures as one of the group of twelve deities, Juniten, carrying the same attributes. In Jit-ten-gyō-zō (TZ 212.8) he is flanked by two goddesses. Vaiśravaṇa in a scroll, kept at Daigo-ji looks similar (TD 14). Dvādaśadevakalpa mentions that two goddesses sitting on both the sides offer flowers to

Vaiśravaṇa who has a golden body, wears an armour and is trampling on two demons (T 1298). Kakuzenshō (T 6.2244) and Asabashō (T 6.2026) contain the same form but in the drawing in Asabashō the two goddesses are missing. Vaiśravaṇa in Besson-zakki, among Jūni-ten has no variations in iconography (TZ 87.297). In Zuzō-shō, Vaiśravaṇa is drawn alone (TZ 86.117). In all the above mentioned collections Vaiśravaṇa comes as the seventh among twelve deities.

c. According to Hindu mythology, Kubera as the god of wealth is related to goddess Śrī. Goddess Śrī presides over fortunes, happiness, prosperity and eight treasures (Banerjee 1956:560). Śrī is portrayed with Vaiśravaṇa as his sister, bestowing wealth (Edmunds 1974:264).

   In Asabashō Vaiśravaṇa is depicted with Śrī riding upon two demons carrying all the attributes as mentioned before. He never attains an angry posture in this form because with goddess Śrī, he is portrayed as a god of wealth, instead of a warrier or a defender. There he is named as Vaiśravaṇa Devarāja, Vaiśravaṇa, the lord of lords.

d. According to Alicia Matsunaga, Vaiśravaṇa generally appears either as one of the four Devarājas or two kings, where he is usually accompanied by Virūḍhaka or Dhṛtarāṣṭra.

e. Vaiśravaṇa accompanied by Dhṛtarāṣṭra and five guardian Yakṣas is portrayed in To-hon-Shi-tennō-zō (TZ 199.5). He is still worshipped in Japan as one of the Shichifukujin or Seven Lucky Gods. A stūpa or a pagoda in one of his hands indicates his quality as a protector of the *dharma* and a halberd in the other, bestows treasures of faith, duty and honour (Matsunaga 1969:253-54).

f. The collection Kakuzen-shō contains different forms of Vaiśravaṇa. One of them in which (TZ 102.380) he is flanked by two deities is very similar to the one given in Zuzō-shō (TZ 86.117).

Vaiśravaṇa holds a sword in his right hand and a stūpa in the left, in Bishamonten-zō kept at Daigoji, Kyōto (TZ 203). To-hon-Bishamon-ten-zō, a sheet is a section of a scroll (TZ 204). Vaiśravaṇa comes after Four Guardian Kings in Shōson-zuzō-shū (TZ 298.38), being a bit different from the preceding, he holds a lance in place of a halberd and rides upon two demons with goddess Pṛthivī in the middle. Vaiśravaṇa-mantra (T 1249) mentions him as holding a lance topped by a trident in the right hand and a flag in the left. Riding two black Yakṣaṇīs, he offers a stūpa to Śākyamuni Buddha. In Dhāraṇīsaṅgraha, translated by Atikūṭa (AD 653-4), he holds a stūpa in his right hand and a lance in the other (T 901.11). This form can also be found in Kakuzen-shō (T 6.2242). Hōryūji also has an image with the same attributes. The form that is denoted in Vaiśravaṇa-dhāraṇī (T 1246), translated by Prajñācakra (AD 847-860) is portrayed in a drawing in Asabashō (T 6.2026) and a sculpture kept in Kuramadera monastery, Kyōto.

Sometimes visual depictions and textual descriptions vary in their sequence of attributes. Hūm-kaḍaya-kalpa (T 1251) translated by Vajrabodhi mentions Vaiśravaṇa with a stūpa in his left hand, riding Jiten or Pṛthivī flanked by two demons: Biramba and Niramba (Hobogirin 1929:83). According to Coomaraswami (1971: 6-7) the idea of four guardian deities comes from Khotan. Aśokarājasūtra (T 2043.6, Nj 1343), translated by Saṅghapāla in AD 512 mentions that the mission was received by Vaiśravaṇa from Indra to protect Buddhist religion in the region of North, especially against the attacks of three cruel kings: Śaka, Yavana and Pahlava. Hsüan-tsang encountered the cult of Vaiśravaṇa in the north-western countries. The great monastery of Bulkh was protected by an image of Vaiśravaṇa which had miraculously warded off the armed attack of a Turk Khan. The kings of Khotan claimed themselves to be the descendents of Vaiśravaṇa, as their first ancestor was born in front of a statue of Vaiśravaṇa (T 2087.1,2). The collection of Vinaya and other sūtra literature by Sang-min Pao-chang (AD 516) (T 2126.2) insists on close connections that existed between Vaiśravaṇa and Khotan and claims that this name Bishamon is derived from the name of the country of Khotan Bishabu. The point can also be compared with Mahāmāyūrīvidyārājñī, translated by Amoghavajra (T 982, Nj 307) and by Saṅghapāla and Itsing (T 984.985, Nj 308, 306), which assigns the country of Tukhar as his residence (Hobogirin, 1929: 80).

The descriptions given in Dharmakośasaṅgraha (Lokesh Chandra 1973: 55) of the image of Vaiśravaṇa in the temple of Hārīti on mount Gopuchha corresponds to the form mentioned above. He is depicted with a frown face and has two arms: *Kuberaḥ ekāsyaḥ dvikaro bhrūbhaṅga-karālanetraḥ*...(Bhattacaryya 1974:58-9). He is a Devarāja in Hayaśīrṣa Saṁhitā (25.10-11, Smith 1969:245), wearing necklaces and armlets etc., is strong bodied, a lord of Yakṣas, holding a halberd and a conch in his hands, sinless, splendid with precious stones, crowned, short statured, two handed and riding human beings:

Supīnadeho yakṣeśo hārakeyūrabhūṣitaḥ |
Sarvalakṣaṇasampūrno gadā-śaṅkhadharo 'nagha ||
Nānāratnojjvalenātha makutena vibhūṣitaḥ |
Karttavyo vāmanākāro dvibhujo naravāhanaḥ ||

Matsyapurāṇa (261.20-22) describes him to be big bellied and corpulent, wearing earrings necklace, armlets and a crown etc, endowed with eight treasures, putting on white garments, holding a halberd and making a posture of conferring a boon. And he should sit in a cart with a human being:

Kuberaṁ ca pravakṣyāmi kuṇḍalābhyamalaṅkṛtam |
Mahodaram mahākāyaṁ nidhyaṣṭasamanvitam ||
Guhyakairbāhubhiryuktaṁ dhanavyayakaraistathā |
Hārakeyūrarachitaṁ sitāmbaradharam sadā ||
Gadādharaṁ ca karttavyaṁ varadaṁ mukuṭānvitam |
Narayuktavimānasthamevaṁ rītyā ca kārayet ||

According to Viṣṇudharmottara-purāṇa (3.55.1-2) his lustre is like that of a lotus leaf. Four handed Vaiśravaṇa wears a dress in north-western, *āpīcya* style, an armour, has a big belly but a charming personality. Posture of conferring boon and sitting on a human figure, is described as it has been done earlier:

Karttavaḥ padmapatrābho varado naravāhanaḥ |
Cāmīkarābho varadassarvābharaṇabhūṣitaḥ | |
Lambodaraścaturbāhu... ... ... |
Āpīcyaveṣaḥ kavacī hārabhārī manoharaḥ | |

In Pūrvakāraṇagama (14) he is a lord of Yakṣas and all the treasures. He looks lustrous like gold, purified by fire. His four hands hold a conch, a lotus, treasures and a halberd. Other characteristics are similar to those, as described earlier:

Makuṭī kuṇḍalī hārī keyūrī naravāhanaḥ |
Yakṣarājaḥ Kubero'yam taptakāñcanasannibham | |
Śaṅkhapadmanidhīyukto gadāhasto nidhīśvaraḥ | (Rao 1968: II II 265)

According to Anśumadbhedāgama (49, Rao 1968: II II 263) one of his hands should be in a posture of conferring boon or safety and the other should hold a halberd. With a crown named karaṇḍa and white upper garments, he shines like gold purified by fire:

Dhanadassarrvayakṣeśas sarvābhāraṇabhūsitaḥ |
Tapatakāñcanasaṅkāśo hastadvayasamanvitam | |
Varadābhayahastaśca gadām vai vāmahastake |
Karaṇḍamakuṭopetas sitavāsottarīyakaḥ | |

While Anśumadbhedāgama identifies his crown as karaṇḍa, Śilparatna (Rao 1968: II II 264) says that it is *kirīṭa*. The latter describes him to have an attractive personality, with long arms, eight treasures, and his hands are eagerly occupied in money (*draviṇa-vyagra-pāṇi*) and he is surrounded by Guhyakas. But Suprabhedāgama (48, Rao 1968: II II 263) describes a different form; it says that he causes fear, has a black complexion and red eyes, wears red garments and had red color hands:

Yakṣeśaṁ tu gadāhastaṁ śyāmarūpambhayāvaham |
Dvibāhuṁ raktavastrāḍhyaṁ raktakeśaṁ raktapāṇinam | |

Gadī is an epithet of Vaiśravaṇa in *Agni-purāṇa* (51.15, Mallamann 1963: 134) because of holding a gadā or halberd: *Gadī Khaḍgī Kubera meṣastha*. He rides a human being according to other two references given in Agni-purāṇa 260.22 and 96.29 (Mallmann 1963: 134) :

Narayuktavimānasthaṁ evaṁ rītyā ca kārayet |
Kuberaṁ mānuṣasansthitam | |

Rūpamaṇḍana (2.37) describes him as riding an elephant or a human being and holding a halberd, treasure, citron and a *kamaṇḍalu* in his hands:

Gadānidhībījapūrakamaṇḍaludharaḥ karaiḥ |
Gajārūḍhaḥ prakarttavyaḥ saumyayo naravāhanaḥ | |

Coomaraswami (1971: 8) identifies the ride of Vaiśravaṇa as a Guhyaka and not as a human being. Gukyyaka is the name of a class of demigods who like the Yakṣas are attendants of Kubera and guardians of his treasures (Apte 1976: 190).

A cintāmaṇi over his halberd symbolizes fortunes, and a stūpa in the other hand is a symbol of the top of the stūpa where Nāgārjuna's Buddhist texts are found (Getty 1962:167). The iron tower in South India was called Nan-ten-no-tet-to, where Mahāvairocana- and Vajraśekhara-sūtras were preserved. Nāgārjuna received the sūtras from Vajrasattva, according to the Shingon tradition (JEBD 210).

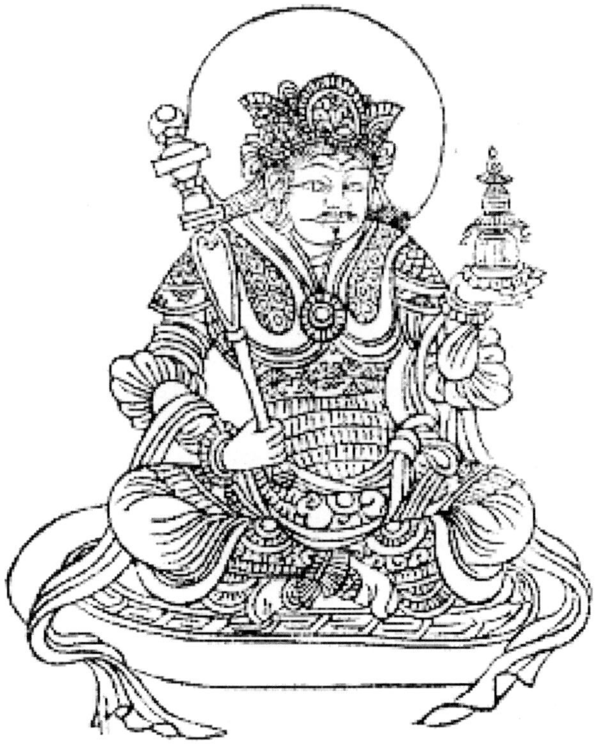

2. The drawing given above is taken from the northern side of the outer circle of Mahākaruṇāgarbha-maṇḍala (Lokesh Chandra 1971:362, Tajima 1959: 19). Halberd and stūpa in his hands are the same as before but here he is sitting on a lotus. Cintāmaṇi atop his halberd and stūpa can be compared with the previous drawing. To the east of Vaiśravaṇa are Siddhavidyādhara and Siddhvidyādharī in the maṇḍala. Hase-dera at Nara (TD 16) and Daigō-ji monastery at Kyōto (TD 32) also have preserved the same drawings. A scroll of AD 1213 kept at Daigō-ji monastery (T D.32) has the same form of Vaiśravaṇa flanked by two attendants *anucaras*. Vaiśravaṇa in Taizō-kyō-zuyō (T D.13), among the divinities of Mahākaruṇāgarbha-maṇḍala has two maid attendants to his left. The same form is portrayed in a hanging scroll from Tōji monastery, now kept at the National Museum, Kyōto (TD 1). Vaiśravaṇa among twelve deities in Shika-shō-zuzō (TZ 89.194) is similar to the one which is kept at the Daigō-ji, drawn by monk Chisen (TD 15).

Vaiśravaṇa with a halberd and a stūpa, stands upon a lotus flower, in the paintings kept at Kyō-ō-gō-koku-ji (TD 3), Shōju Raigō-ji (TD 4) and Jingō-ji (TD 5) monasteries, National Museum, Nara (TD 8), Kōryu-ji (TD 9) and Saimyō-ji (TD 10) and a hanging scroll of 13th century (TD 11).

According to Chiba Vaiśravaṇa is worshipped as a lord of warriors, so he wears an armour, halmet and holds a halberd. Only the tower that he carries in his other hand, reveals his nature and virtues. The tower represents stronghold of faith and at the same time a treasure tower of wealth. Vaiśravaṇa, as he is more formally known, bestows happiness and fortune as represented by the tower that he carries (Chiba 1972: 25.6). As one of the Four Guardian Kings he defends Buddhism. To do away with evils he carries weapons and wears halmet and armour. He is a god of healing as well, because sickness comes from evil (Chiba 1972: 25.6).

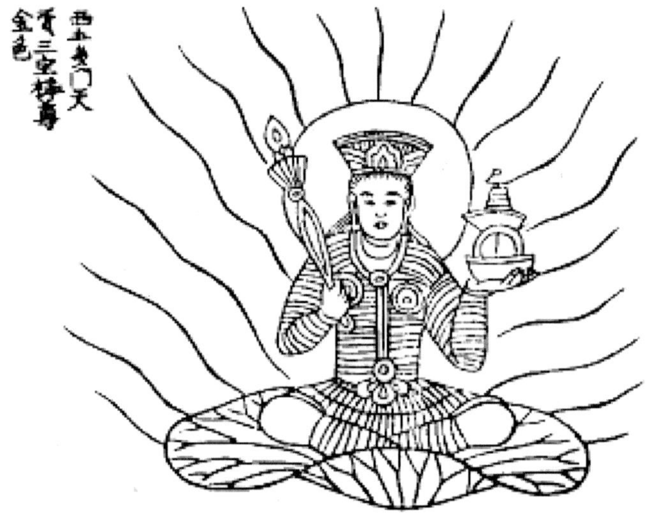

3. Vaiśravaṇa in Vajradhātu-maṇḍala sitting on a lotus leaf does not differ much from the one that is drawn in Mahākaruṇāgrabha-maṇḍala. His armour looks different in both the maṇḍalas. According to the Chinese description given with this drawing he is the fifth in the western outer circle holding a three treasure stick (*tri-dhana-daṇḍa*) and is of golden colour. Here (Lokesh Chandra 1971:458) in the Vajradhātumaṇḍala he is the lord of Yakṣas according to Hobogirin (1929: 82). Vaiśravaṇa is drawn in the same form in the outer circles of Sūkṣma-maṇḍala (Lokesh Chandra 1971:604), Pūja-maṇḍala (Lokesh Chandra 1971:681) and Trailokya-vijaya-karma-maṇḍala (Lokesh Chandra 1971:780) of Vajradhātumaṇḍala. According to Tajima (195) Vaiśravaṇa is of golden colour in this form.

4. Four guardian deities are depicted twice in Horokaku-mandara or Maṇi-vimānanamaṇḍala (TZ 130.323). In the first painting only a stūpa in his left hand is visible. In both the cases he stands upon a mountain. It may be mount Kailāśa because it is considered to be his abode (Sahai 1975: 64-5, Leibert 1976: 143-4). His garments and armour are the same as in Vajradhātu-maṇḍala. Vaiśravaṇa is depicted in this form as one of the different incarnations of Vaiśravaṇa in Zuzō-hokke-kyō-bō or collected paintings of Saddharma-puṇḍarīka-kalpa (TZ 137.9). Vaiśravaṇa sitting on a mountain in lalitāsana is gazing at the stūpa placed upon his palm.

5. Vaiśravaṇa is sitting with his consort and a goddess offering flowers on the right in Taizō-zuzō (TD 12) drawn in AD 1194. He is depicted in three forms in Besson-zakki (TZ 87.287-9).

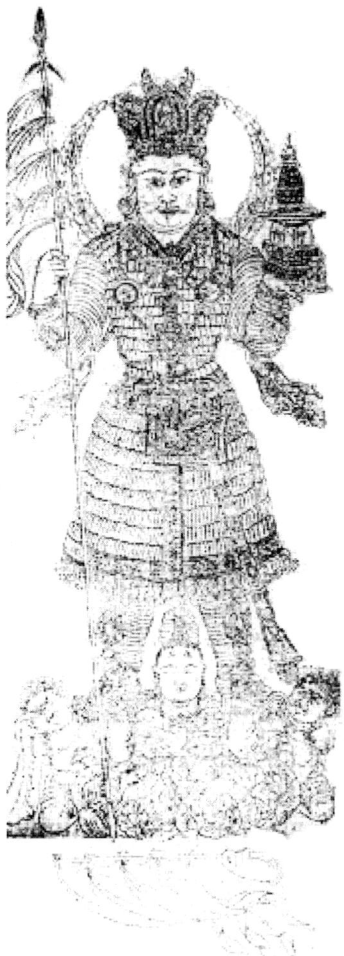

6. In the drawing extracted here Vaiśravaṇa is treading on a demon lying on a mountain. He is holding a three pointed lance with a flag atop in his right hand and a stūpa upon his left palm. A cintāmaṇi is drawn in his crown. In another (TZ 87.287) collection Vaiśravaṇa is riding on two demons with goddess Pṛthivī in the middle. Shōson-zuzō-shō (TZ 298-37) depicts the same form. According to Getty (1962:168) Vaiśravaṇa has a stūpa, a trident or a flag when he is counted among twenty-eight deities with Bodhisattva Kannon. He holds a flag and a stūpa in Butsu-bosatsu-tō-zuzō (TZ 297.6). The collection contains different forms of Buddhas and Bodhisattvas. Here his armour looks different in style.

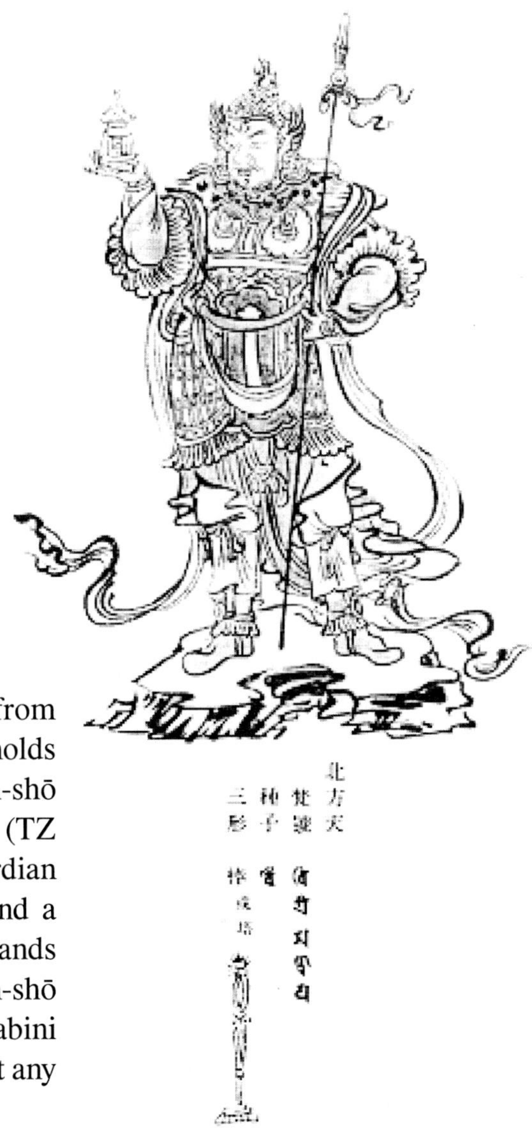

7. The drawing of Vaiśravaṇa given here is from Zuzō-shō, a collection of ten scrolls (TZ 86.110). He holds a stūpa in his right and a lance in the left. Kakuzen-shō (TZ 102.378a) illustrates the same form. Besson-zakki (TZ 87.246) portrays Vaiśravaṇa as one of the Four Guardian Kings, holding a three pointed lance in his right and a stūpa in the left hand. Vaiśravaṇa in the same form stands upon a lotus flower instead of a mountain in Kaku-zen-shō (TZ 102.379). In the collection Nizu-hachibu-shu narabini jūni-shinshō (TZ 198-16) Vaiśravaṇa is drawn without any ride.

8. As a guardian deity of the north in Besson-zakki (TZ 87.250), Vaiśravaṇa holds a stūpa in his right hand and a three pointed lance in his left, as shown here. He stands upon a demon holding a baton in his right hand, lying upon a rock. The picture neither shows a fierce face expression nor he is looking at the stūpa. In this context all the four guardians deities have the same ride.

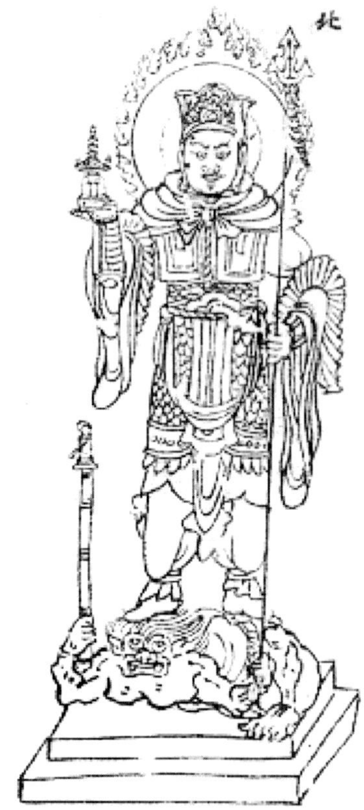

9. Asabashō contains different forms of Vaiśravaṇa. In one of them he looks like an old monk (TZ 264.70). His right hand rests on his waist and the left holds has a lance. Standing upon a mountain he is looking towards his right.

10. Shōson-zuzō-shū gives different forms of Vaiśravaṇa. In the last drawing (TZ 298.39) his right hand is resting upon his waist and the left holds a stūpa. He is treading on two demons.

11. The last among the nine forms of Vaiśravaṇa given in Tōji-bon-daigen-myō-ō-zuzō (TZ 192.16) is drawn according to the Āṭavaka-maṇḍala. Daigo-bon-daigen-myō-ō-zuzō also illustrates the same drawing.

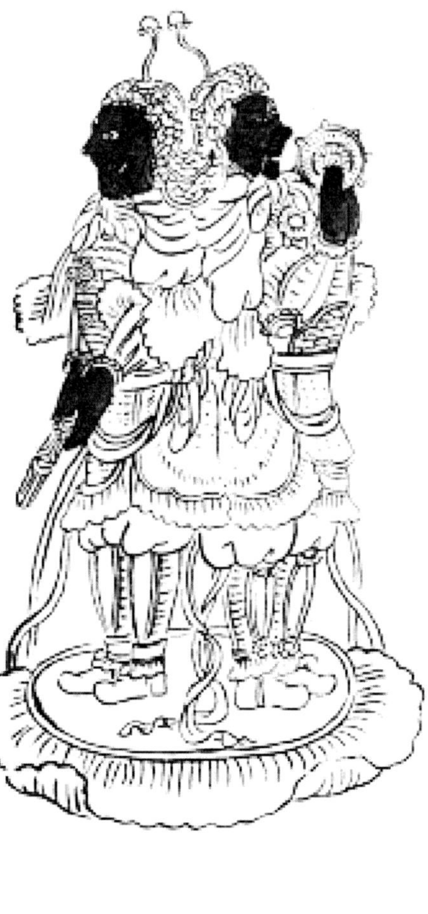

12. In Taimitsu, an esoteric branch of Tendai sect the rite called Hūm-kaḍaya is celebrated in honour of double bodied Vaiśravaṇa and goddess Śrī (cf.T 2151). According to Asabashō (T 6) the two figures are represented back to back with red faces and three eyes. He wears black garments and an armour. One of his hands holds a vajra while the other, a cakra (fig. Asabashō 6.2046). The figure given here is from Asabashō in Taishō-zuzō (TZ 264.71). This iconographic type, known in Japan since AD1264, seems to be connected with Suvarṇaprabhāsa-sūtra (T 665.6, Nj 126) translated by I tsing where Vaiśravaṇa and Śrī figure frequently side by side in the esoteric texts, for example Shōdaiki (T 850) and Vaiśravaṇa-kalpa (T 1249) etc. Later the two figures were considered as metamorphoses of Vaiśravaṇa in the Garbhadhātu and on the other hand in Vajradhātu. Their combination symbolizes the identity of the two *dhātus*.

Viṣṇudharmottara-purāṇa (3.53.3) mentions that Vaiśravaṇa has a beard, two teeth and two faces: *dve ca danṣṭre mukhe tasya karthavye śmaśru-dhāriṇaḥ*.

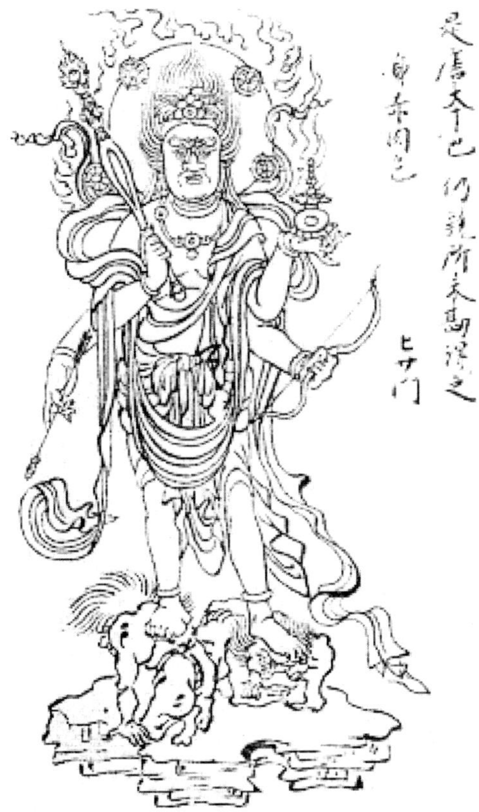

13. In this four armed form of Vaiśravaṇa taken from Besson-zakki (TZ 87.288), he is holding a halberd and an arrow in his right hands and with the left hands he holds a stūpa and a bow. Tōji-bon-daigen-myō-zuzō (TZ 192.8) and Shōson-zuzō-shū (TZ 298.36) have the same drawings.

14. In the second form of Vaiśravaṇa given in Tōji-bon-daigen-myō-ō-zuzō (TZ 191.15) he is sitting on a rock and is holding a sword in his upper right hand and a stūpa in the upper left. In other two forms his hands are in *namaskāra* posture. Daigō-bon-daigen-myō-ō-zuzō (TZ 192.15) has the same form. According to Viṣṇudharmottara-purāṇa (3.53.2), he is four handed: *Lambodaraścaturbāhur vāmapiṅgalalocanaḥ*. Vaiśravaṇa in the eight *śmaśānas* of the Ugratārā chapel, as described in Dharmakoṣasaṅgraha (50) has four hands, but the attributes are different. They are: a wheel, a club, a mongoose and treasure. *Uttarakalaṅka-bhairava-śmaśāne Kubero yakṣādhipaḥ, ekamukhaḥ svarṇaḥ caturbhujaḥ dvābhyāṁ cakragade dvābhyāṁ nakulanidhanau sarvālaṅkāra śmaśrula ratnataupikaḥ aśvapadma-vajrāsanaḥ* (Lokesh Chandra 1973:50, Bhattacharyya 1974:56-7).

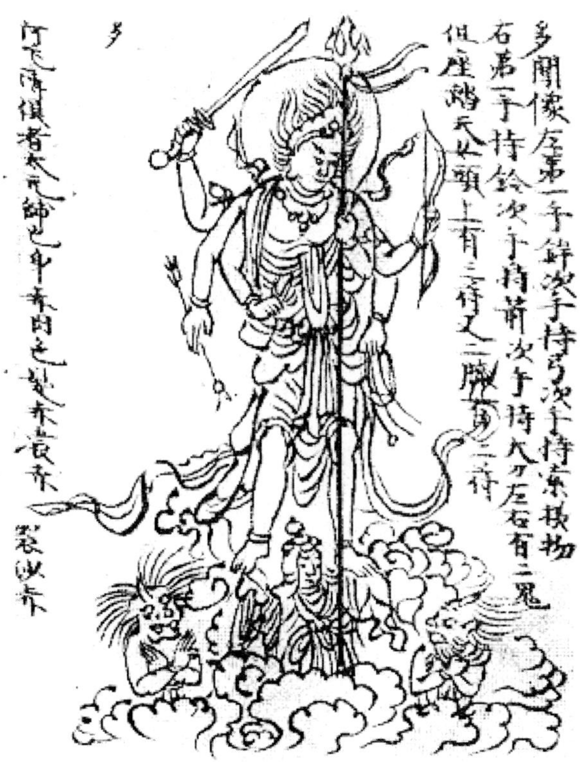

15. This six armed figure of Vaiśravaṇa is taken from Tōji-bon-daigen-myō-ō-zuzō (TZ 191.9). A sword, an arrow and a bell are in his right hands and a bow, a triple pointed long lance and a noose in his left hands. Vaiśravaṇa without an armour is supported by goddess Pṛthivi, flanked by two demons. Daigō-bon-daigen-myō-ō-zuzō (TZ 192.9) has the same drawing.

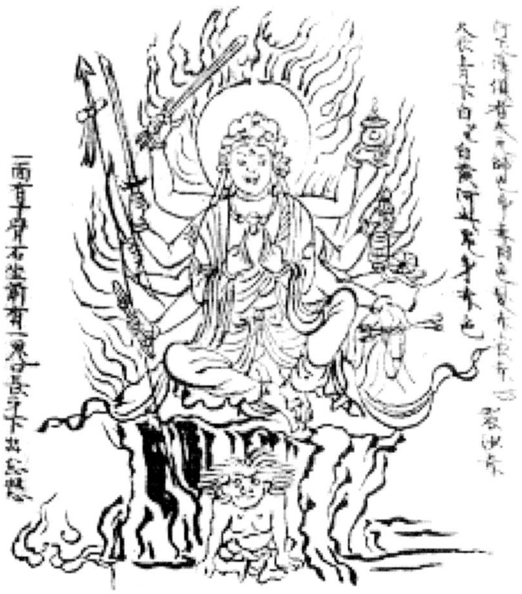

Bīja maṇḍalas

The given maṇḍala depicts the bīja form of Vaiśravaṇa–maṇḍala (TZ 89.173). In another bīja maṇḍala Vaiśravaṇa is surrounded by eight guardian deities in seed syllable forms (TZ 88.174). In some of the maṇḍalas only Chinese names of the deities are given (T2 89.175)

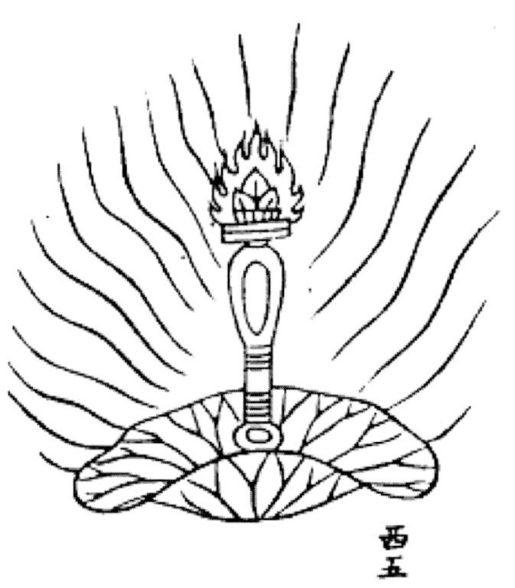

16. This ten armed Vaiśravaṇa is from Tōji-bon-daigen-myō-ō-zuzō (TZ 191.11-14). In his right hands he has a sword with a vajra like handle, sword, bow and vajra while in his left hands he has a stūpa, a bell, a wheel and a noose with two arrows. Front two arms are in a *mudrā*. According to Hōbōgirin (p.83) it should be *namaskāra mudrā*. Five drawings of ten armed Vaiśravaṇa in Daigō-bon-daigen-myō-ō-zuzō (TZ 192.10-14) are similar to the five given in the Tōji-bon-daigen-myō-ō-zuzū.

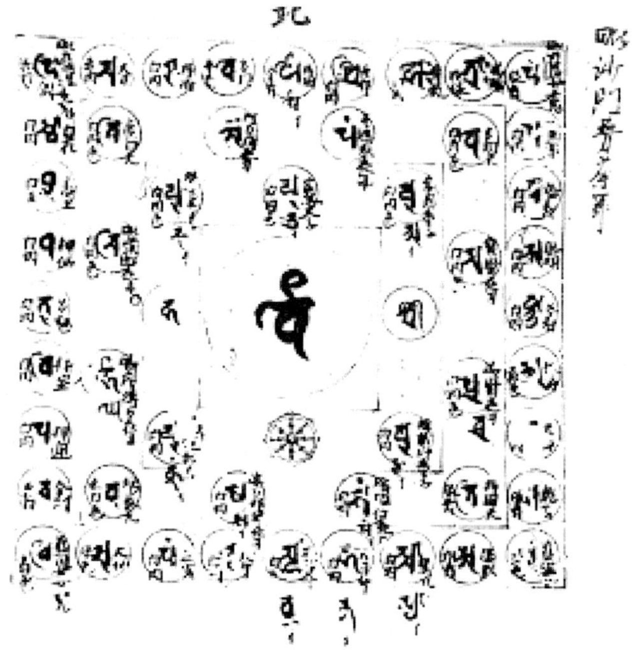

Symbolic form

Vaiśravaṇa is generally drawn holding a halberd with a cintāmani or three jewels atop. So in his symboic form in the sūkṣma-maṇḍala of Vajradhātu he is drawn as a halberd (Lokesh Chandra 1971: 531, 851). Vaiśravaṇa attains the form of *'vai'*, an *akṣaradevatā* as shown in the seed syllable maṇḍalas. This *'vai'* in Siddham script is taken from Shū-shi-ji, a collection of seed-syllables.

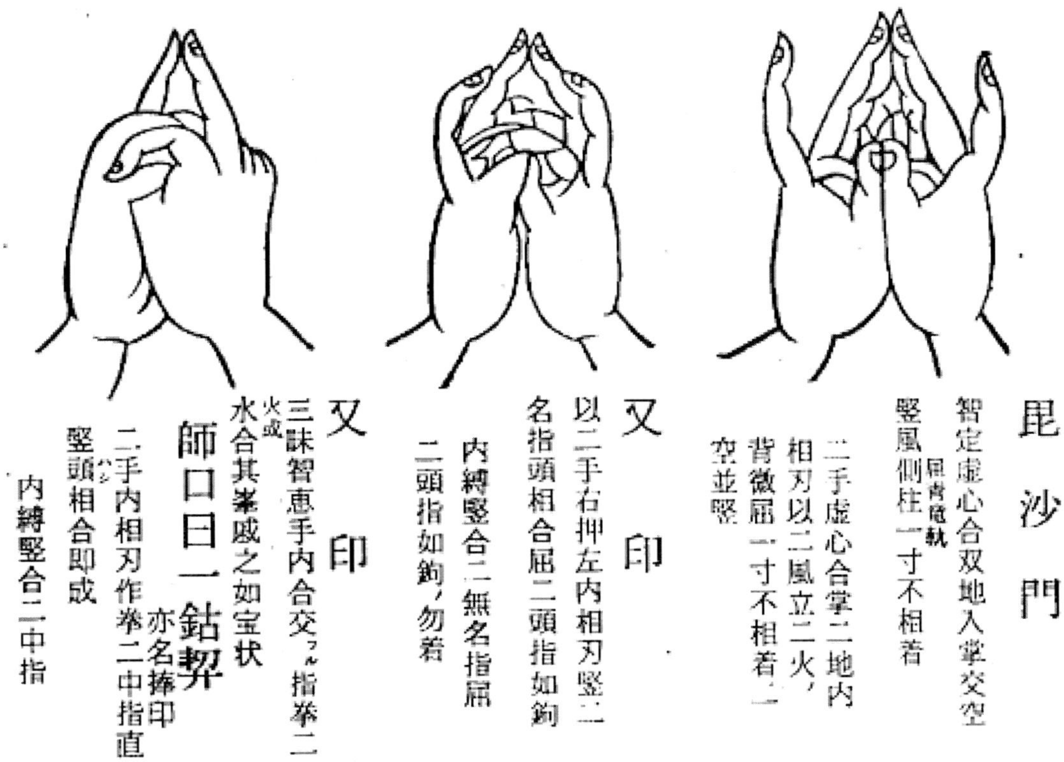

Mudrās

Mudrās of Vaiśravaṇa are illustrated thrice in Shingon-mikkyō-zū-in-shū. The picture given here is from its fourth part (Lokesh Chandra 1978: 220): Vaiśravaṇa and Śrī are together here. Secondly he is eighth among twelve deities (Lokesh Chandra 1978: 4.246). Thirdly we come across a *mudrā* of Vaiśravaṇa in its third part among the deities of the outer circle of Mahākaruṇāgarbha-maṇḍala (Lokesh Chandra 1978: 3.181). It is the same as the first given above.

Mahāvairocanābhisambodhi-mahā-maṇḍala-pāṭha-kalpa or Bus-setsa… Nenju-giki (TZ 240.230) a collection of mudrās, gives the mudrā and the mantra along with its Chinese transcription.

The table of Various forms of Vaiśravaṇa is given below:

S.	Attributes		Ride	Reference
No.	**Right hand**	**Left hand**		
1.	halberd	stūpa	goblin	TZ 87.257, 89.172, 212.8, TD 14, TZ 86.117, TZ 87.297, 199.5, 264.69, 102.380,203, 204, 298.38.
2.	halberd	stūpa	lotus	Lokesh Chandra 362, TD 16, 32, 13, 1 TZ 89.194, Tz 15, 2, 3, 4, 5, 8, 9, 10, 11

3.	halberd	stūpa	lotus leaf	Lokesh Chandra 458, 604, 681, 780
4.	halberd	stūpa	mountain	TZ 130.23, 137.9
5.	halberd	bag	lotus	TD 12
6.	three pointed lance	stūpa	demon	TZ 87.289
7.	stūpa	lance with a flag	mountain	TZ 297.6, 86.110, 102.378a, 102.379, 198.16.
8.	stūpa	three pointed lance	demon	TZ 87.250
9.	resting on waist	lance	mountain	TZ 264.70
10.	resting on waist	stūpa	two demons	TZ 298.39
11.	mudrā	lance	demon	TZ 191.16, 192.16
12.	cakra	vajra		TZ 264.71
13.	mudrā	lance	lotus	TD 12
14.	halberd	stūpa		TZ 87.288, 191.8, 192.8, 298.36
15.	sword namaskāra-mudrā	stūpa	rock	TZ 191.15, 192.15
16.	sword, arrow, bell	bow, tripple pointed lance, noose	Pṛthivi & two demons	TZ 191.9, 192.9
17.	sword, sword, bow, vajra	stūpa, bell, wheel, noose, two arrows		TZ 191.10-14, 192.10-14

LITERATURE CITED

Apte 1976

Apte, V.S. *Sanskrit-English Dictionary*, Motilal Banarasi Dass, Delhi, 1976

Banerjea 1956

Banerjea, Jitendranath, *The Development of Hindu Iconography,* University of Calcutta, 1956.

Bhattacharyya 1974

Bhattacharyya, Dipak Chandra, *Tantric Buddhist Iconographic Sources,* Munshiram Manoharlal, New Delhi, 1974.

Chiba 1972

Chiba, Reiko, *The Seven Lucky Gods of Japan,* Charles E. Tuttle Company, Tokyo, 1972.

Coomaraswamy 1971

Coomaraswamy, Ananda K., *Yakṣas,* Munshiram Manoharlal, New Delhi, 1971.

Daniélou 1963

Daniélou, Alian, *Hindu Polytheism,* Routledge and Kegan Paul, London, 1963.

Edmunds 1974

Edmunds Williams H. *Pointers and Clues to the Subjects of Chinese and Japanese Art,* Sampson Low, Marston and co., London Minkoff Reprint, Geneva, 1974.

Getty 1962

Getty, Alice, *The Gods of Northern Buddhism,* Charles E. Tuttle Company, Tokyo, 1962.

Hōbōgirin 1929-1967
Sylvain Lévi and J. Takakusu, Hōbōgirin, *An Encyclopaedic Dictionary of Buddhism,* Compiled from Chinese and Japanese Sources, fascicules 1-4, fascicule Annexe, Maison Franco-Japonaise, Tokyo, 1929-1967.

JEBD 1965
Japanese English Buddhist Dictionary, Daitō Shuppansha, 1965.

Liebert 1976
Liebert, Gosta, *Iconographic Dictionary of the Indian Religion,* E.J. Brill, Lieden, 1976.

Lokesh Chandra 1971
Lokesh Chandra, *Esoteric Iconography of Japanese Maṇḍalas,* International Academy of Indian Culture, New Delhi, 1971.

Lokesh Chandra 1978
Lokesh Chandra, *Mudrās in Japan,* International Academy of Indian Culture, New Delhi, 1978.

Mallmann 1963
Mallmann, Marie-Therese de, *d'Agni-Purāṇa,* les Enseignements Iconographiguesde, Presses Universitaires de France, Paris, 1963.

Matsunaga 1969
Matsunaga, Alicia, *The Buddhist Philosophy of Assimilation,* Sophia University and Charles E. Tuttle Company, Tokyo, 1969.

Matsyapurāṇa 1895
Matsyapurāṇa, Veṅkaṭeśvara press, 1895.

Nanjiō 1883
Nanjiō Bunyiu, *A Catalogue of the Chinese Translation of the Buddhist Tripiṭaka,* Clarendon Press, Oxford, 1883.

Rao 1968
Rao, T.A. Gopinath, *Elements of Hindu Iconography,* Motilal Banarsidass, New Delhi, 1968.

Rūpamaṇḍanam
Upendramohan, Sāṅknyatīrtha, *Devatāmūrti Prakaraṇam and Rūpamaṇḍanam,* Metropolitan Printing and Publishing House, Calcutta Sanskrit Series XII, Calcutta, 1936.

Sahai 1975
Sahai, Bhagwant, *Iconography of Minor Hindu Deities,* Abhinav Publications, New Delhi, 1975.

Sharma 1971
Sharma, Rāṇāprasada, *Paurāṇic Koṣa,* Jñānamaṇḍala Ltd., Varanasi, 1971.

Skandapurāṇa
Skandapurāṇa, S.V. Press, Bombay, 1953.

Smith 1969
Smith H. Daniel, *Vaiṣṇava Iconography,* Pāñchrātra Pariśodhan Pariṣad, Madras, 1969.

Suzuki 1937
Suzuki, Beatric Lane, *Shingon School of Mahayana Buddhism,* Part II, The Eastern Buddhist, vol.VII.2, June 1937. Eastern Buddhist Society, Kyoto.

TD
Twelve Devas, A special Exibit, Kyoto National Museum, Kyoto, 1977.

16

CULTURAL INTERFLOW BETWEEN INDIA AND CENTRAL ASIA

Buddhism reached the Central Asian kingdoms situated along the Silk Route two thousand years ago which soon became important centers of art and culture. In and around those centers, caves were excavated, temples and monasteries were built to house a rich treasure of images that smiled in dreamy postures and elegant looks. Walls of these monastic complexes were covered with murals in glorious colours, visualizing the essence of Jātaka stories, Avadānas, heavenly scenes, fabulously flying goddesses, maṇḍalas for meditation, and themes of the highest spheres of religious life. Libraries attached to these centers, preserved a rich treasure of invaluable literary works. They served as important centers for Sanskrit studies and translation works. Manuscripts discovered from there, in Indian scripts and languages stand as the most valuable for studies in linguistics and epigraphy. The texts found during excavations play a significant role in writing the history of Buddhist literature and in an in-depth study of art and iconography.

The Buddhist monasteries were built under the patronage given by the local rulers and religious community. Seventh century portraits of such donors in the murals of Central Asia are the most important relics to tell the story of varied inhabitants who sponsored Buddhist arts. The art of Kucha flourished in the second half of the first millennium AD, under four representative races. Tokharian knights of Indo-European origin have short reddish brown hair parted at the center. Their eyes are light coloured. Others wear dresses of Parthian, Uigurian and Sassanian style. All of them carry daggers and swords with unusually long hilts hanging from their belts. Donors are generally portrayed inside the caves on the walls of the side passages, to the right and left niches of the main image. In Bezeklik also, portraits of princesses were painted in the 9th century. The paintings give an insight into the story of people migrating from one place to another and their life styles and customs of the time. Eastern Turkestan also possessed a rich and flourishing culture right up to the end of the first millennium.

All these kingdoms situated on the Silk Route contributed towards propagation, preservation and advancement of Buddhist art and thought. The art reflects extraordinarily varied aspects of the influence of the neighbouring China, India, and West Asian cultures. The artifacts discovered from Central Asia are important specimens for the history of Indo-Chinese cultural relations also because Buddhism was transmitted via this route, from India to China. Most of the treasures were ruined during the invasions by Islamic community; those now preserved in various museums as magnificent collections of the relics, comprising of manuscripts, woodcuts, coins, seals, terracotta, and other figures, were found from the sites buried in sand drifts.

India and the kingdoms of Central Asia shared cultural efflorescence for centuries in the first millennium. A culture of higher aspirations of life flourished in the ancient cities that once graced the Silk Route from China to Rome and to India around the vast expanses of deserts, with rivers flowing from the surrounding mountain ranges. Habitation began in the oasis cities, and on the mountain and glacier fed rivers and streams, especially Tarim, being the most notable.

Silk and jade, horses and valuables commodities changed hands, but the most lasting treasure that travelled along the route was Buddhism. These cities were halting places for monks and missionaries, for pilgrims and merchants, and later became famous centres of Buddhist learning. Thus a trade route transmitted religion and philosophy, ideas and beliefs, languages and literature, art and culture.

The route was named after silk, one of the chief mercantile commodities of China. It ran through the vast deserts of Taklamakan, Lop and Gobi, bound by long chains of Tien Shans and Kunluns to the north and south, and Pamirs to the west. A travel through it meant deadly perils of the deserts. But they could not deter the pilgrims and the monks, carrying the Buddhist sūtras. For centuries main traffic between China and the West circulated along these routes. The Silk Route thus later became Sūtra Route. The oasis cities and kingdoms were established as great centres of Buddhist art and learning.

The Silk Route bifurcates at Kucha and meets at Dunhuang. The northern route goes via Samarkand, Kāśgarh, Tumshuk, Aksu, Kucha, Karashahr, Turfan and Hami and the southern route via Yarkand, Khotan, Keriya, Cherchen and Miran. Chinese and Indian scholars travelled through these routes in search of wisdom and propagation of Buddhism, and western explorers went in search of invaluable cultural treasures.

History

How did Buddhism gain its foothold in such a remote part of the world and what forms of expression did this religion develop in these out of the way places? A precise chronology of the important events and achievements of the great scholars, active in the kingdoms of Central Asia provides mile-stones for a study of their cultural heritage and chronology of their relations with India. Sequence of movements of traders and pilgrims, scholars and missionaries, their major activities, their travelogues provide a broad base to the study in historical perspective. Inscriptions and art styles are equally important for a comprehensive study of evolution and development of various sects in Central Asia and beyond.

Power struggle went on for centuries among the Chinese, Uigurians, Turks, Tibetans and others. In the ninth century Chinese Central Asia was predominantly controlled by the Uigurians. Around the beginning of the second millennium the monasteries began to become victims of destruction. Arabs were threatening. Khotan was attacked several times. With the decisive victory of Islam in the tenth century, Kāśgarh was converted to Muhammadanism. This marked a death knell to the classical traditions and arts of Central Asian kingdoms. In a few centuries beauty of paintings, elegance of sculptures, wisdom contained in the scriptures was buried under sand. Sand in the desert preserved the cultural heritage and history of Indo-Central Asian cultural intercourse for centuries.

Explorations

Suddenly by the end of nineteenth century, scientific and archaeological expeditions to the regions along the Silk Route in Chinese Turkestan led to the discovery of numerous cave temples and monasteries on the slopes of T'ien Shan and Kunlun ranges of mountains. Great adventurers, archaeologists and explorers began digging the deserted and devastated kingdoms, glorious cities enlivened by the activities of Buddhist community. Art historians in the east and the west got amazed and began to toil hard to excavate more and more of the art treasures.

They collected artifacts in large numbers, preserved them in museums and opened up a new avenue for the art historians. Whatever they collected was fragmentary. But still a missing chapter on the history of India's cultural relations with Classical Central Asia began to be documented.

Experts left from British India, Sweden, Russia, Germany and Japan: alone or in teams, to survey the land and to study archaeological sites. The first serious information was brought in 1860-1875 by British officials Montgomerie, Forsyth and Johnson. Their reports were supplemented by Russians: Nicholai Prejevalsky and Albert Regel who found Buddhist relics in the form of images and temples in Kocho near Karakhoja.

Swedish geographer Sven Hedin began a series of planned expeditions in 1895 to the lost cities of Taklamakan. Sir Aurel Stein set out from Kashmir in 1900. His contributions on research on Khotan, rediscovery of Dunhuang and the excavations in Innermost Asia were amazing. Almost at the same time Russian scholar Dimitri Klement began his investigations. They were followed by German expeditions in 1902-14.

Achievements of Western explorers and archaeologists are the most valuable. The caves of Bezeklik were first explored by von Le Coq in 1905, by representatives of Baron Otani in 1908-9 and finally by Aurel Stein at the end of 1914.

Richness of cultural efflorescence was studied through fragments of manuscripts, mural paintings, architectural styles of the destroyed monasteries, sculptural treasure, linguistic heritage, customs and beliefs, traditions and ceremonies, performing arts and music. Exploration of deserted Buddhist sites in Central Asia has illuminated the dark zones of the history of dissemination of Buddhist art and thought from India to the East Asian countries. Relics of temples and monastic complexes, sculptural treasures, paintings and manuscripts discovered from the cities on the southern and northern route, bear witness to a very powerful tradition of religious art and thought and its dissemination.

Works of Art and Architecture

Works of art and other materials discovered from various sites, give us invaluable information about their contemporary culture. The findings show that Kucha was a centre of Hīnayāna Buddhism and Turfan of Mahāyāna school of Buddhism. The monasteries were treasure houses of works of art that dotted the cities of Central Asia. Fahien has stated that each family of Khotan had its own domestic chapel with a stupa. According to Fahien the king's New Monastery, which was one of the grandest monasteries of Central Asia was constructed in eighty years. Six kings of Eastern Turkestan had donated all their valuables for them.

One hundred and sixty cave temples discovered from there often had subterranean elements. Many of these temples were adorned with Chinese, Turkish and Indian inscriptions and magnificent frescoes. At the time of discovery many manuscripts were found written in unknown scripts and languages. Sculptures and paintings illustrated association with the art of China, India and Persia and indeed with that of Greece, Rome and the Near East.

Sculptures discovered from ancient cities, and once flourishing oasis kingdoms illuminate in many ways, the crosscurrents of iconography and style. They relate the history of Buddhism traversing the path from the Northwest frontiers of the then-India to China, Korea and Japan. The images are of divine beings, of Buddhas and Bodhisattvas, of protectors, benefactors, guardians, Eight Classes and Śrāvakas etc., symbolising purity and perfection resulting from *puṇya* (merits) and *jñāna* (knowledge).

Paintings and drawings were done on paper, silk or walls. An eighth century fragment of a drawing on silk found from the manuscript room at Toyok is reminiscent of the tradition. Inside the caves, paintings and sculptures intermingle to create glorious scenes. Empty niches of today, once housed images of great beauty. Hell scenes were awe-inspiring, they were meant to instill a sense of virtue in the minds of the devotees. Buddhist texts served as source books for such paintings.

As early as AD 647/48 the second emperor of the T'ang dynasty, T'ai-tsung (r. AD 616-649) brought Eastern Turkestan under Chinese hegemony. Artistic influence of China can be seen from this date onwards, particularly in the Turfan region.

Language and Literature

Sanskrit was the most important language taught at the monasteries. After learning Brāhmī alphabet, a student had to study Sanskrit grammar according to the Kātantra system and then learn to translate Sanskrit into Kuchean. An extensive literature is found translated from Sanskrit original into Kuchean or Tokharian.

People with multilingual skills translated the sūtras into classical languages of Central and East Asia. Cultures of the east and the west blended to create an intellectual aura of high order. Fragmentary Sanskrit manuscripts were first found from Kucha written on birch bark dated fifth century AD. They were older than any other Sanskrit manuscripts known till then. An interesting document of Indian cultural heritage in Central Asia is the so-called Bower manuscript that contains seven medical texts written by four different persons, all of them were residents of Kuchan monasteries. Sanskrit played the same role in Khotanese medicine, as Latin in the European.

One of the most important and extensive works: Maitreyasamiti was translated by Āchārya Prajñārakṣita from Tokharian. A Mahayana text of Avataṁsaka-sūtra was translated from Sanskrit into Chinese in AD 421 by the Indian monk Buddhabhadra. It was a source for the iconography of Vairocana, which was popular in Central Asia especially along the southern Silk Route in the kingdoms of Khotan, Kucha and Karashahr. Another Mahāyāna text Amitāyturdhyāna-sūtra was translated into Chinese in the fourth century. Scenes based on the sūtra were painted in several caves. A Sanskrit text of Mahāparinirvāṇa-sūtra found from Central Asia has its parallels in Pali, Tibetan and Chinese. A library of very old manuscripts on palm leaf, birch-bark and paper and inscriptions on wooden tablets were among the Sanskrit documents found from Kizil.

Bhaiṣajyguru-sūtra was recited for prolonging one's life and was known in China in the fourth century AD, the date of the first pictorial representation of Bhaiṣajyaguru's paradise. A number of offering banners are found from Kocho from 8th-9th century.

Cave of Red Dome in Kizil contained a large number of manuscripts of superb quality, written on palm leaf, birch bark or paper in many different scripts and languages. Another interesting document is an inscription in Tokharian language and Brāhmī script with a Buddha figure painted on a wooden board. Fragments of painted figures can be seen carrying Indian style manuscripts. Sometimes texts written in various languages, bear illustrations. These book illustrations were done with the help of wood blocks, in black and white or lightly coloured drawings.

Khotan emerged as an important centre, a place of cultural confluence for the Chinese and the Indians. Coins from the first century AD, discovered from Khotan, bear Chinese on the obverse and Prākṛt in Kharoṣṭhī script on the reverse. A large number of Sanskrit manuscripts, translations and transcriptions of Sanskrit Buddhist texts are discovered from the sand buried monasteries. Bilingual texts in Sanskrit-Khotanese and Chinese-Khotanese for conversation are eloquent in their silence.

Most of the texts discovered from Khotan are Buddhist, twenty-six with known titles and eleven without them; among the non Buddhist texts, Rāmāyaṇa is of prime importance. Among the texts related to medicine are—Jīvaka Pustaka, Siddhasāra and others. Apart from them there are three documents other than literary and medical: Chronology of the Khotanese kings, Khotanese administration and bilinguals like Sanskrit-Khotanese, Chinese Khotanese and Turkish-Khotanese. Prākṛt was the administrative language of a nearby kingdom Shan-shan in the 3rd century, Khotanese rulers continued to bear Indian titles till the tenth century.

Script and Calligraphy

Libraries were built for the community living around the monastic extablishments in Central Asia. They kept huge collections of Buddhist texts copied and translated from Indian manuscripts written in different scripts and languages. At times, the texts are bilingual or even multilingual. Buddhist texts in Sanskrit, Prākṛt or local languages, are largely written in Indian scripts—Brāhmī and Kharoṣṭhī. Sanskrit dramas and texts on medicine, astronomy and astrology, written in Brāhmī have also been discovered from Central Asia. Besides them, hundreds of documents are of administrative, commercial, and legal use, drafted in Sanskrit, Prākṛt or Central Asian dialects, and written in Indian scripts, as well as common alphabets of the Brāhmī script have been found from various sites.

A text of Dhammpada, written on birch bark, in Kharoṣṭhī script of 1st-2nd century in Prākṛt language was discovered from Khotan. The ancient sites at and near Khotan have also yielded

Khotanese texts of Vajracchedikā-prajñā-pāramitā and Amitāyurdhyāna-sūtra, besides quite a few fragments in the Late Gupta script. Inscriptions in the 'Cave of the Painters' are written in Turkestanian Brāhmī of 5th-6th century.

Performing Arts

According to the Chinese sources people of Kucha were fond of Indian music and musicians. Indian music was taken to Kucha in ancient times. Many musical subjects decorated the walls of the Central Asian monasteries. Early Chinese records speak about the tradition of music in Khotan: Emperor Wu-ti sent Chang Ch'ien to the west in 138 BC to bring musical instruments and melodies from Kucha. Most probably this melody was of Indian origin. Son-in-law of the Emperor wrote twenty-eight new tunes based on the melody—Mo-ho-tou-le. The tunes were played as military music. Kucha continued this unbroken tradition for centuries.

The Chinese General Protector, Lu Kuang carried away groups of performers, actors, musicians and dancers to China as war booty in AD 382. This resulted in popularity of Indian music in China. Records say that once one of the lute teachers in China, was a Brahmin. Another teacher was Sujīva from the royal family of Kucha. He taught the seven keys of music that can be traced back to India. The Indian goddess of music, Sarasvatī was also worshipped in Central Asia. An 8th-9th century painting of Sarasvatī on a wooden penal is discovered from Yarkhoto. Kucha thus loomed large as a veritable outpost of Indian culture.

Rituals and Ceremonies

Fahien, a Chinese pilgrim has stated that an annual car festival was celebrated in Central Asia as a national event, for fourteen days. Each day was allotted to a particular monastery on which the monastery used to take out its images in a procession. Hsüan Tsang says that every five years a religious assembly was held in front of the two colossal images of Buddha outside the capital town for ten days and the event was celebrated as a national festival. Religious festivals were a regular feature in Kucha as well as Khotan.

Dedication ceremonies was a fashion in Classical Central Asia. It was believed that by offering a banner with dedication the donor or his relatives would gain admittance to paradise more easily or they would be blessed with long life, or numerous children or prosperity. The offerings could also be presented as a thanksgiving for even a successful business trip. Due to a big demand a variety of offering banners were produced on a large scale in temple workshops. Eighth century banners from Kocho are among the most beautiful. Similar banners are found from Turfan, Yarkhoto and at Dunhuang caves in China.

Figures on the banners were drawn with stencils. Their use in monastery workshops was unavoidable due to a great demand and strict iconographic requirements. Simple and unpretentious stencil paintings reveal Chinese influence both in slightly modulated brushwork of the ink lines and in full bodied physique of the Bodhisattvas, reflecting T'ang aesthetic ideals.

Scholar Pilgrims

The history of Indo-Central Asian relationship is witnessed by a continuous flow of teachers and monks from India to Khotan, Kucha and other kingdoms and cities. Pilgrims and scholars continuously came to India in search of knowledge. Those who were destined to go to China from India, had stopovers on their way through the Northern or the Southern Silk Routes. These halting places provided them ample opportunities to study and train themselves or to upgrade their knowledge. Cities situated on the Silk Route were crossed by the west-bound Chinese travellers also. Travelogues of the Chinese pilgrims serve as the most important source of our knowledge today for a study of cultural life and monastic activities in Central Asia.

Scholars travelled to these distant lands from various parts of India for example Jinagupta was born in a Kṣatriya family in Gandhara. He left his home with nine companions in order to propagate Buddhism. The group travelled through Kapiśā, Badakshan, Tash-khurgan and Khotan and reached Si-ning in Kansu province and the Chinese capital in AD 559. Dharmagupta was born in south India. On his way to China he spent two years each in Kāśgarh, Karashahr and Turfan and another year in Hami. Kashmir is referred to as an important centre of Buddhism, a cradle of art and thought. Vairocana, the first monk who went to Khotan to propagate Buddhism was from Kashmir. He was followed by several monks and nuns. Many Kalyāṇamitras are said to have come from there; some of the Khotanese princes and princesses also came there in search of knowledge. Stūpas are said to have flown from Kashmir, probably architects would have been invited for construction. References are found in the biographies of Chinese monks. A famous missionary and translator is said to have visited Tuṣita in a trance when he was staying in Kashmir in AD 400. Kashmiri masters of meditation were famous. The most accomplished of the Chinese practitioners of meditation, Chih Yen also studied in Kashmir for several years.

Chinese pilgrims, Fahien and Hsüan Tsang have given glowing accounts of Central Asian kingdoms. Monks inhabiting the monasteries had contacts with Buddhist scholars in India in general and Kashmir in particular. They were engaged in studying and translating Sanskrit Buddhist texts. Gomatī vihāra in Khotan accomodated three thousand monks. Many Indians used to live there. The learned scholars of the monastery composed texts which were canonical and attracted students from China who used to stay there for higher studies.

Important Sites

Tumshuk

The main ruins at Tumshuk are discovered from above the hamlet of that name, on the ridge whose northern end divides into three spurs and parts of the sides of the massif between them, are covered with ruins of places of worship. A French expedition was led by Paul Pelliot to investigate these ruins of monasteries and temples. A German expedition went there under von Le Coq to study the complexes on the three cliffs to the south.

The art of Tumshuk was influenced by Indian and Iranian styles. Sometimes the figures reflect classical Indian art of 5th-6th century, especially of Mathurā and Sārnāth. Paintings found from there are earlier in date and different in style from Kucha. Many clay objects are also found from there. A variety of Buddha figures are richly painted and overlaid with gold. Some of them were made from moulds.

Kizil

One of the most famous sites in Central Asia, Kizil is situated on the Muzart river, where a multitude of Buddhist temples were discovered, hewn in the mountainsides. The local name for this site 'Ming-oi' (1000 cells or chambers) referred to the vague figure of great magnitude.

Approximately 300 caves at Kizil contained frescoes. Their style evolved in c. AD 500. The paintings look more western and older in comparison to those of Turfan oasis. Scenes portraying sermons delivered by the Buddha were among the famous episodes painted in the monasteries at Kizil. Paintings in the Maya cave display characteristic features of Indo-Iranian style at the peak of its development. Flying figures filling the upper sections exemplify the style found in the Chinese cave complexes.

Life size figures were parts of larger tableau consisting of several sculptures. Chopped straw, plant fibers or animal hairs were added to clay to add to their durability. Some of the 6th century painted clay images were shaped with the help of stucco moulds. Individuality of faces was heightened through treatment of crowns, hairdos and face expressions. Some of the figures are predecessors of their Chinese counterparts.

Kumtura

Kumtura is a small locality to the west of Kucha. The extensive complex of cave temples of Kumtura lie in a broad valley about twelve and a half miles southeast of Kizil caves on the lower reaches of Muzart river. Deep ravines cut into these mountains from the east. On their slopes a number of cave temples have been found.

Walls of Kumtura caves are covered by paintings in two different styles - Indo-Iranian and East Asian, without any tendency to merge. In some instances Indo-Iranian elements mingle with Chinese Buddhist features. Sometimes facial characterization reflects a distinctly oriental inspiration whereas borders, lotus flowers and portrayal of monks reflect a different style. Paintings in some of these temples belong to the early Indian influence phase while in others they are executed in later T'ang style. But the scenes depicted in paintings, discovered from there are so fragmentary that it is difficult to trace the legends that they represent.

Kucha

Kucha is situated on the banks of river Kucha Dariya. To its northeast is Simsim and on the two sides in the south of Simsim are Kirish and Achik-ilik. Another site Subashi is to the north of Kucha and Kizil Kargha to the Northwest on the Kizil Dariya. Caves and temples of outstanding artistic and architectural importance once existed in Kucha. Wall paintings depicted a variety of Buddhist subjects and legends.

Kucha was a leading city on the northern route, corresponding to Khotan on the southern route. Its kings bore Indian names, such as Haripuṣpa, Suvarṇapuṣpa, Haradeva, Suvarṇadeva etc. Valuable remains in substantial number have been traced from the great monasteries of Kucha. Like art and architecture, the local literature and curriculum also followed the Indian model. Sanskrit was methodically taught in the monasteries of Kucha.

The kingdom of Kucha built 1000 Buddhist stūpas and temples and numerous monasteries and nunneries in the fourth century. Hsüan Tsang has mentioned that there were five thousand monks in a hundred monasteries. The figures found from Kucha region are full of a soft and sensuous elegance, enhanced by mild face expression. These are reminiscent of paintings and sculptures found at Fondukistan in Afghanistan. A remarkable number of wooden sculptures of 5th century are also found from Kucha and Tumshuk. Their quality is often superb.

Shorchuk and Karashahr

Shorchuk is a small village to the east of Kucha, halfway towards Turfan. The town of Korla is to its west and Karashahr, known as Agni-deśa, to the east. At the foot of the mountains stood a whole row of temples in open, which were most probably destroyed by fire. The site is famous for the most interesting finds in clay. The figures are Buddhist deities with round faces, designed to fit into niches, left unmoulded at the back.

Karashahar was a leading center for spread of Buddhism in other countries including China. Its rulers bore Indian names such as Indrārjuna, Chandrārjuna etc. The Buddhist site Khora near Karashahr has yielded Sanskrit texts of Śatapañcāśikā and Catuhśataka, two stotras by Mātṛceta, written in the Gupta Brāhmī characters.

The nearby cave temples housed extremely interesting manuscripts, murals and clay images of great beauty. Inside the caves were paintings and sculptures, grouped together, around the main image. The figures are characterised by full and round faces with plump cheeks, occasionally with a double chin.

Turfan

Once Russian merchants reported to the Imperial Academy of Sciences in Petersburg about the riches of ancient times. Mr. Klementz and his wife discovered significant remains of Buddhist archaeology depicting ethnography and philosophy of Central Asia from near Turfan, north of the Terim river in the eastern foothills of the T'ian Shans. They found a whole series of cave temples, full of wall paintings, characterized by Indian, Chinese and Iranian styles. The pictures included Buddhas and Bodhisattvas.

Although the geographical position made Turfan region more susceptible to cultural trends from the east than from the west, but there are evidences substantiating the activities of Indo-Iranian artists. It was not exclusively the region of Chinese artists. Features of some of the images found from there verify the works of Indo-Iranian artists at work in Kocho.

The type of architecture often found in the Turfan region is particularly based on the so-called pillar or stūpa temple in tower form. In such structures there are several square plinth tiers built one on the top of other and topped by stūpa domes. Varying number of niches to house Buddha images were let into these tiers.

In the North of Karakhojo, Sengin, Bezeklik, Murtuk and Toyok, cave temples were cut in soft stone or the cave temples were given a projecting porch of bricks and wood or a combination of both systems was followed. The style of paintings is different in comparison to other sites. Bezeklik was a repository of caves. When the German expedition reached there in 1905, many of them were intact.

Near Murtuk, between the village of Bezeklik and the uppermost part of the Sengin gorge, to the west of the mountain ridge, is another settlement, called Chikkan-kul. It consists of a number of caves in a gorge near the large lake. Buddhist ruins have been found on the shores of the lake and on an island lying in shallow water. Besides a few damaged paintings, were some very fine heads of clay statues.

Bezeklik

Among the most important excavation sites in the Turfan region are the temples of Bezeklik situated to the south of the village of Murtuk. They are reached by following the gorge of Sengin northward as far as the point where Murtuk brook flows into the Sengin river. The high cliffs on the right bank have to be climbed in order to find a narrow, winding path that leads along the cliff top to the great monastic complexes of Bezeklik, protected from the unwelcome visitors. Temples and settlements were built as far as possible from the profane world. Altogether several hundred temples had been preserved. The majority was built in open and were originally joined together by means of wooden porches. Cave temples hewn in rock also existed there. A whole row of temples was buried in sand or covered by loess dust, yielded many well-preserved relics of early cultures.

By the tenth century the area from Gansu province to Khotan was controlled by Uigurs. Bezeklik flourished as a centre for Buddhist learning. Silk Route brought great wealth to its rulers. More than eighty caves have survived. Forty out of them were decorated with paintings. The best paintings date from ninth to thirteenth centuries. The paintings are in Indo-Persian and Chinese styles and represent the Uigur empire at its height. The murals celebrate cultural and economic riches of the epoch.

Some of the murals executed in 7th-8th century exhibit Indian styles. The wall of the hall of worship, bear paintings from the 9th century. A fragment of a wall painting from Bezeklik represents Tokharians, who once populated the oasis towns of the northern and southern sections of the Silk Route.

A number of large sized paintings were taken to Berlin by the Germans and kept at the ethnological museum by von Le Coq. They were lost during the second world war leaving behind only the photographic records.

Kocho

Kocho, a great but ruined city adjoining Karakhoja, was a forgotten Asian site of extraordinary interest. The inner holy city consisted only of temples and palaces and was surrounded by a wall measuring 7400 feet. There were hundreds of tiered temples and grandiose vaulted edifices. A large number of figures in wood and clay, woodcuts and murals were rescued by the German expedition from rubble of temple ruins. The paintings have a tremendous significance for the history of art for Eastern Asia as they undoubtedly represent the missing link between ancient Chinese art and the Grecco-Buddhist art of Gandhara region. Murals were painted in tempera colours on clay-coated walls. Iconography is derived from Gandhara sculptures and the style is Chinese.

Votive stūpas in red sand stone can be compared with the ones found in the caves of Northern Wei in China, dated AD 420-430. Kocho offered manuscripts in many languages and scripts: Sanskrit, Uigurian, Mongolian, Ancient Turkish, Chinese and Tibetan. A number of bronzes are also discovered from Kocho.

Kocho was one of the most important halting places for the travellers belonging to various races and countries. They required books in different languages and scripts and even bilinguals as aids to communicate. So in order to serve them, manuscripts were written in twenty-four scripts and seventeen languages. For example there is a manuscript written in Turkish with Sanskrit glosses in Vertula script. Discovery of pages from illustrated manuscripts has raised a number of questions related to Buddhist art and philosophy. Bilingual manuscripts are an important source to study the history of transmission of Buddhism. According to the German explorers in around 1897, five truckloads of manuscripts illustrated with pictures in coloured ink and gold paint were thrown into river. The story of destruction is painful for the scholarly world.

Toyok

Extensive complexes of Toyok stood on the southeast of Kocho, carved on the bare side of a mountain range. One of its caves was filled with hundreds of manuscripts. Once somebody tried to destroy the library by fire but was not successful.

Sengin

About three miles north of Kocho where the Karakhoja river issues from a narrow gorge lies the temple complex of Sengin. In spite of forbidding character of the landscape, the left or the western side of the ravine is studded with a line of temples, whilst the height on the right is occupied by many Indian relic memorials, stūpas. Some of them rise on the very edge of the stream.

Khotan

The history of cultural symbiosis between India and the kingdom of Khotan goes back to over two millennia. The oasis kingdom of Khotan situated to the south of Taklamakan desert and the massif of Kuen-lun, at the southern end of the Tarim basin, bathed by Yürüng-kash (white jade) and Kara-kash (black jade) rivers. it was an important agriculture and manufacturing centre, famous for its silk industry, dance, music, literary pursuits and commercial activities, for gold and jade exports.

According to the available accounts in Chinese by Hsüan Tsang himself and by his pupils Hui-li and Yen-tsung, the kingdom was founded by Emperor Aśoka's son Sa-nu and his ministers in the 3rd century BC. Hsüan Tsang's account is contemporary to Gośṛṅga-vyākaraṇa and his pupils' to the Prophecy of the Li Country. Hsüan Tsang in his memoirs names it as K'iu-sa-tan-na (breast of earth), formal name used in the region. The Iranians called it Ho-tan and the Indians as Kiu-tan, while it is known as Gostana or Gaustana in poetic and literary works in the T'ang period. Tibetans have transcribed the name as Hu-ten, Hiung-nu and Yu-tun etc. but translated as Li-yul.

Dandan Uilik

About seventy-five miles northeast of the city of Khotan, was one of the most important temple cities lying on the southern Silk Route. In the ruins of the Buddhist monasteries, crumbling away and buried in the desert sand, manuscripts and coins from 7th-8th century were found, and also sculptures in wood and clay. Paintings found from there are significant both for their subject matter and for iconographic relevance.

Niya and Loulan

Sir Aurel Stein, the great explorer of the sites of southern Silk Route, found wooden boards with inscriptions in Kharoṣṭhī, dated 263-330, from the temples of Loulan. Wooden sculptures include Buddhas and Bodhisattvas, *devetas*, monks, groups of musicians, and various animals. The local artists have left personal stamps in them. Wooden relics could survive in Central Asia because they were desert sand for centuries. Central Asia must have been rich in commercial timber during the middle of first millennium AD.

Miran

Miran was the capital of ancient city Shan-shan where laity and Śramaṇas practiced Indian religion; they used Indian books and Indian languages according to Fa-hien. A large number of wall paintings in the stūpa temples witness the account given by the Chinese traveller. The principal structure at Miran is a stūpa in a circular room. The story of Vessantara Jātaka covers the upper part. Paintings at Miran are known for their optical illusion, intelligently created by means of line, colour combinations and light and shade effect.

Although no monasteries stand today on the Silk Route, whatever has been discovered, is fragmentary and spread over in various collections but historically the material is invaluable because of the light that it throws on the vital role played by the Silk Route in the eastward transmission of Buddhism.

17

MONASTERIES OF KHOTAN IN TIBETAN LITERARY SOURCES

The history of cultural symbiosis between India and the kingdom of Khotan goes back to over two millennia. Khotan was given the name—Ratnajanapada or Ratnadvīpa because of the abundant availability of precious stone, jade. China began to import jade from Khotan in 800 BC. Though China never produced it but it always played an important role in their state as the most desirable stone. The Chinese believed in its heavenly origin, used it for manufacturing insignia for kings and ritual objects, and believed it to be an object of conferring immortality, a symbol of nobility, purity and beauty. Cultivation of virtues and expulsion of evil thoughts was also attributed to it.

Khotan flourished uninterruptedly from 3rd century BC, the reign of Sa-nu to AD 1010 under the kings of Vijaya dynasty. Tibetan books related to the history of Khotan, Gośṛṅga-vyākaraṇa and Prophecy of the Li country give an account of the reign of fifty-seven kings who ruled this prośperous kingdom, built a large number of monasteries for the consolidation of the state, housed images of divine beings, of Buddhas and Bodhisattvas, protectors, benefactors, guardians, eight classes and śrāvakas etc.

The history of Indo-Khotanese relationship is witnessed by a continuous flow of teachers and monks from India to Khotan and pilgrims from Khotan to India, who came in search of knowledge and also those who were destined to go to China but had a stopover there. Khotan situated on the Silk Route was crossed by the Chinese going to the west from their capital city Ch'ang-an; the northern route passed through Turfan and Kucha and the southern branched off at Dun-huang through Yang-Guan via Miran, Khotan and Yarkand and finally meets at the other end of Kāśgarh.

A large number of coins from the first century AD, have been discovered from Khotan bearing Chinese on the obverse and Prākṛt in Kharoṣṭhi script on the reverse. A number of Sanskrit manuscripts, translations and transcriptions of Sanskrit Buddhist texts are discovered from the sand buried monasteries. A Sanskrit-Khotanese book of conversation presents a dialogue between an Indian monk with a Khotanese. A *bhikṣu* is going to China to pay a visit to a temple of Mañjuśrī, on his way he takes a stopover at Khotan. They greet each other, *"śobhana svasti kuśalaśarīri,... tava prāsādāt kuśalaḥ,"* the monk says "*Kaśamira sthāne āgataḥ*", the Khotanese asks, *"hindūka deśe kim kāle āgatah"*, the Indian monk replies, "*samvatsara dvaya babhūva*", he further tells, "*Chīna deśe gacchami... Mañjuśrī bodhisattva paśyāmi*". He says that he is carrying books on Vinaya, Abhidharma, Vyākaraṇa and Vajrayāna (Bailey, BSOS 1937:9.521-43).

Tibetans had close connections with Khotan during AD 665-AD 1000, troops from various parts of Tibet visited Chinese Turkistan frequently. Some of its districts were under their rule (Thomas 1935:ix-x). References to these connections are scattered and fragmentary. Most of the texts discovered from Khotan consist of Buddhist texts, twenty-six with known titles and eleven without them.

The recognized Tibetan dynastic history *Rgyal-rabs-gsal-bahi-me-lon* briefly refers to it. Bus-ton's History of Buddhism is also uninformative. A few geographic references are given casually in the literature of the Bon sect. The Tibetan documents excavated by Sir Aurel Stein from the library of Ch'ien-fo-tung are Tibetan versions of Sanskrit Buddhist texts. There is a possibility of some light thrown by the books acquired by Paul Pelliot from the same library and kept at Bibliotheque Nationale at Paris. A History of the Kingdom of Khotan *Li-yul-gyi-lo-rgyus*, was published by Teishiya Shoten, Kyoto, Japan, in 1921, under the title *Yu-t'ien-kuo-shi*. It was translated into Japanese by Enga Teramoto. A chronological list of the dynasty can be reconstructed through the T'ang records and can be cross-checked with the references to the names preserved in the Khotanese texts.

Advent of Buddhism in Khotan

The kingdom was famous for its effluence, the monk Sanghavardhana while replying to the queries of a monk in Lihi-yul-lun-bstan says that the kings will dare each other and fight for Khotan and the Ārya king, whoever wins will act as the patron and through blessings of Indians, stūpas will be built and practice of *saddharma* will flourish. Āryasthāna is described as a site at the Gośīrṣa mountain, the first settlement where Indian Buddhists used to live.

Khotan received Buddhism in the 1st century AD according to the Prophecy. Bhagavān Śākyamuni, preaching the Chandragharbha-sūtra on Gṛdhrakūṭa mountain in Rājagṛha prophesied that Khotan would be the twenty first mansion of Tathagāta and would be protected by twenty myriad including Bodhisattvas, Śrāvakas, Eight Classes of Devas, Nāgas Kings etc. According to the Tibetan tradition and Hsüan Tsang, Vairocana, a monk from Kashmir introduced Buddhism during the reign of Vijaya-sambhava. Vairocana is a symbol of an all-powerful being, ruler of a boundless world according to the Avataṁsaka-sūtra. Primacy of Vairocana is based on another sūtra that is Brahma-jāla-sūtra. He is the transcendental aspect of Buddhahood. This symbolism was valuable for the kingdoms being newly unified. Worshipping colossal images of Vairocana became popular.

The Prophecy of the Li country refers to the following areas and the number of monasteries built in Khotan:

Huthen: There were 68 monasteries inside the fortress and behind it were 95 medium size monasteries, 148 small monasteries, 3688 household shrines, and 10,000 monks.

Mdo-lo and Me-sker area: There were 4 great monasteries, 100 private shrines, and 20 monks

Kam-sen, Pho-na and Be-rga-hdra, 'O-rgu : It had 23 great monasteries, 21 medium *vihāras*, 23 small and 839 private shrines with 438 monks living there.

Gyil-kyan to Kon-sen and Du-rya: Inside the fortress and behind it, there were 15 great *vihāras* and 963 monks lived there.

According to Stein, the oldest dated Buddhist monument is from AD 269 (Stein 1902:405). Fourth century records of the religious life of Khotan were brought to light by Fahien when he described Khotan in AD 399. He has given description of a large number of monasteries that had been built and a Buddhist festival that was held while he was there (Wild 1992, internet).

According to the Pophecy, Bhagavān Śākyamuni appointed the following to guard the kingdom:

1. Eight Bodhisattvas: Mañjuśrī, Samantabhadra, Avalokiteśvara, Mahāsthāma, Kṣitigarbha, Ākāśagarbha, Maitreya and Bhaiṣajya-rāja
2. Eightfold classes (*aṣṭayoni*): Deva, Asura, Gandharva, Kinnara, Nāga, Yakṣa, Mahoraga, and Garuḍa
   a. I. Devas: Kapila, Aparājita, Ākāśacakṣus, Sujaya,
      II. Devaputra: Suvarṇamālā, Susthiramati,
      III. Devis: Sthānavatī, Harīti, Aśokā, Devī,
   b. Asura: Śaṅkhinī
   e. Nāgas: Gṛhāvatapta, Hu-lor, Da-ci, Da-ra, Takṣaka,
   f. Yakṣa generals: Vaiśravaṇa, Sañjnāya,
   h. Garuḍa: Suvarṇākṣa,
3. Royal Personoges: Princess (*Kuladuhitā*) Vimalaprabhā and her brother, Prince Kumāra-vajrasena,
4. Local protectors: Ratnabala and Ratnaśūra (Khotanese creations, local deities)
5. Four Guardian Kings

Chandragarbha- and Sūryagarbha-sūtras are included in Mahāsannipāta. According to Sylain Lévi they were composed there. These sūtras contain geographical catalogues with lists of deities residing at each place. Such catalogues of guardians represent a means of bringing the religion up to date and up to place. Chandragarbhasūtra lists eight protectors of Khotan: Aparājita (son of gods), Sañjnāya, Gaganasvara (great yakṣas), Suvarṇamāla (yakṣa), Gṛhāvatapta (nāgarāja), Aṅkuśavatī and Sthānavatī (goddesses), Vaiśravaṇa (king) (East and West 23.1-2, March 1973 : 114). Most of them stand in pairs to guard the monasteries like Nio in Japanese temples and Yakṣas in the temples in Thailand. Local gods are incorporated into the Buddhist pantheon to bring the religion up to date and up to place.

Hsüan Tsang writes about a large number of monasteries and adherents to Mahāyāna. According to the Tibetan Prophecy of the Li Country Buddhism was introduced there in about 84 BC, 165 years after the origin of Khotan. When Fahien visited Khotan, on his way to India, in about AD 399/400 it was a major centre of Mahāyāna Buddhism. The distance from Gośṛṅga mountain from Khotan given by Hsüan Tsang is about four miles in the south-westerly direction (Thomas 1935:8).

Monasteries described in the Prophecy of the Li Country

1. Car-ma Monastery

The 3rd king of the Prophecy, Vijaya-sambhava, son of King Yehu-la built the Car-ma monastery. Two divinities Ākāśacakṣu and Maṇibhadra promised to guard it. Prior to this no monasteries existed in Khotan. The king acted as *dānapati*, donated for the construction on the advise of his Kalyāṇamitra, Ārya Vairocana, who propagated Buddhism in Khotan. The ministers and subjects also advised him to construct stūpas and monasteries. A number of buildings arose. King's retinue and masses also built small *vihāras* and kept relics of Tathāgatas, Bodhisttvas, Śrāvakas and Pratyekabuddhas, therein. He made a vow and prayed for a gong to the Tathāgata, the monk Vairocana appeared in the sky, an apparition of Mañjuśrī manifested, put a gong in the hands of the king and the sixteen Śrāvakas and expounded the teachings of the Buddha. The king struck the gong, its sound went on uninterruptedly for a week. An imprint of footsteps of the Tathāgata on a stone existed there. The monasteries were full of power and splendour.

The Śrāvakas were presented jewels so that they could be used when there will be no *dānapati*. The story continues further and says that a stūpa was summoned from Kashmir, containing the relics of seven Tathāgatas to honour Ārya Vairocana, the stūpa was there inside Gandhakuṭī.

Maṇibhadra is closely associated to Vaiśravaṇa as one of the Yakṣādhipatis in the maṇḍala of Dharma-dhātu-vagīśvara and he is also represented as one of the eight Aśvapatis who accompany Vaiśravaṇa. He has an angry face and rides a horse. In Tibetan pantheon he is of yellow colour and holds a flaming jewel in the right hand and a mongoose in the left hand. According to the commentary by Ichigyō on the Mahā-vairocana-sūtra (T1796), Manibhadra is one of the eight guardians - Maṇibhdra, Pūrṇabhadra, Pāñcika, Śatagiri, Haimavata, Viśākha, Āṭavaka and Pāñcāla.

After King Vijaya-sambhava, seven kings did not build any monasteries.

2. Go-ma-tir or Hgum-tir Monastery

The 11th king of the Prophecy, Vijaya-vīrya, built the monastery guarded by Vaiśṛavaṇa, Sañjnāya and Gṛhāvatapta. The Go-ma-tir or the Gomatī monastery founded in the 1st-2nd century, takes its name from a district name or from the river Gomā. It was a widely known monastery possibly situated below the Gośṛṅga hill on the bank of river Gomā. But the same name can be attributed possibly to other monasteries constructed in the same district.

According to the story related to its construction, Bodhisattva Maitreya transformed himself as Vijaya-vīrya, a king of Khotan. Once he saw a golden and silver colour light, outside the city, from the top of his castle. He followed it, reached Hgum-tir and saw a stag there. Immediately the stag turned into a Yakṣa generalissimo, Sañjanin. He told the king that he should build a monastery there for Ārya Buddhadūta and others- Khagadata, Khagaroyan, Khagadrod, who had come as Kalyāṇamitras. Buddhadūta himself came to expound the teachings of Buddha, the king remembered the vow made in his previous existence, fixed a peg on the sight and constructed Hgum-tir monastery.

3. Go-ma-sa-la-gan-dḥa Stūpa

King Vijaya-vīrya was busy worshipping at the Hgum-tir monastery, his Kalyāṇamitra told him about the stūpa that was built when Buddha Kaśyapa attained *nirvāṇa*, his relics were kept at the stūpa, which was protected by a mountain when Khotan became a lake. The lake dried up when Maitreya arrived there; the stūpa reappeared. Buddhas in past, present and future visited there; it became a *Buddhakṣetra* of Tathāgatas (Thomas 1935:8).

Buddha Kaśyapa was born in Benaras in the Deer Park at Asipatana, of Brahmin parents, Brahmadatta and Dharmavatī of the Kaśyapa *gotra* (for details see Malalasekera 1998:1.544-45).

Once a child got lost when the king had gone to the monastery of Hgum-tir to worship. After a search the child was found in the valley of Gautosana near the stūpa. The child was declared as a Morgubdesi (way shower), the first Arhat of Khotan and was set free. The king was told by his Kalyāṇamitra that the stūpa was protected by a mountain when Khotan became a lake. Later, the lake dried up and the stūpa reappeared when Maitreya came there. The sacred place became a *Buddhakṣetra* of Tathāgatas, all the Buddhas of past, present and future are supposed to be present there for prophecy and *sattvārtha*, welfare of human beings. The stūpa was guarded by Vaiśravaṇa and Sañjnāya, the Yakṣa *senāpati* and Grhāvatapta (Emmerick 1967:31).

Vaiśravaṇa was associated with the north as a guardian of riches according to the Mahayana texts. According to Candragarbhasūtra Vaiśravaṇa had become a special protector of the great Central Asian Mahayana centre. His iconography preserves a Central Asian character in Tibet. In a thangka painting he sits on a lion, wears an armour, holds a flag in his right hand and a mongoose in the left, from whose mouth, jewels and precious stones issue like a cascade. The acolytes surrounding him are eight *aśvapatis*, lords of horses, sitting on horsebacks. Another thangka painting representing Vaiśravaṇa's heaven, contains eight images in eight directions recognized as *aśvapatis* described in Mahāmāyūrī, Mahāsahasrapramardinī and Āṭānāīyasūtta of Dīghanīkāya (Tucci 1980:575).

Two different orders of ideas probably have melted one into the other, on one side Viśravaṇa is a lokapāla and on the other a king of horses. He was spacially appointed by Buddha to protect Khotan. He is a Yakṣa general and also a guardian king, one of the four guardians of the directions. According to Hsüan Tsang the Khotanese ruler claimed to be a descendant of the god. When Khotan became a desert, he made his home there. After founding the kingdom the king was afraid of remaining childless, he worshipped Vaiśravaṇa. He was blessed with a child, built a temple plentifully adorned with rare treasures (Soper 1959:240).

The kings of Khotan claimed their descent from Vaiśravaṇa asserting their close connections. Even one of the names of Khotan is Bishabu. Vaiśravaṇa presides over the north over Yakṣas, riches and war etc. He is one of the four *lokapālas* and eight *dikpālas*, a regent of the north. It is he who protects the continent situated to the north of Sumeru. He received the mission to protect Buddhism from Śakas, Yavanas and Pahlavas. In the countries of north, Hsüan-tsang also encountered the cult of Vaiṣravaṇa. According to him the monastery of Balkh was protected by his image. Vaiṣ ravaṇa is often identified with Kubera, the Hindu god of wealth, who presides over the riches.

Sañjnāya: Sañjnāya is one of the major guardians of Khotan. A complete chapter is devoted to him in the Suvarṇaprabhāsottamsūtra, emphasizing on the function of the four *lokapālas* especially on the divine protection given by them (East and West, 23.1-2, 1973:114). Fragments of the sūtra are found from Khadalik.

Gṛhāvatapta: He is a *nāga-rāja*, a dragon king. *Nāga-rāja* is a representation of a monarch of the world of the deified serpents. These serpents are imagined as snake-like demigods. They are also associated with great deposits of hidden treasures. Most of the stories cluster around the creature as being very powerful but pious and amiable and anxious to do its best to save the Three Treasures (Soper 1959:236).

4. Hgehu-to-śan or Gau-to-śan Monastery

The monastery was built by the 11th king of the Prophecy, Vijaya-vīrya, with a strong faith in Buddhism, in the 1st-2nd century AD, on the Gośṛṅga hill where Buddha delivered the prophecy, enshrining a splendid and shining image of Buddha Śākyamuni. Vaiṣravaṇa, Sañjnāya and the Nāga-king Gṛhāvatapta promised to guard the monastery. A perennial stūpa of Kāśyapa Buddha Go-sa-la-gan-da, was there on the plateau between the two dune like hills of sand.

The date of the Prophecy of Gośṛṅga should not be earlier than the second half of the 7th century AD when Tibetans became active in Khotan. The monastery is not described in the prophecy of Gośṛṅga which had been composed several centuries after its erection (Thomos 1935:7). It opens with a homage to Mañjuśrī. An arhat living at the Śaṅkāprahāṇa monastery predicted a bright future for the Gośṛṅga monastery, he says that the monasteries and stūpas at Khotan are protected by 500 Bodhisattvas. Out of them 250 have renounced the world and the other 250 have taken birth as householders. Further he adds that the mansion will be continuously enduring, as 1005 Buddhas of Good Aeon have been treading the Gośṛṅga monastery.

5. Monasteries of Eight Bodhisattvas

According to the Gośṛṅga-vyākaraṇa all the eight Bodhisattvas pledged to be present on the site of the Prophecy. They form the subject matter of special texts and play a fundamental role in the development of Tantric maṇḍalas. In the Mahākaruṇāgarbha-maṇḍala they are the major acolytes of Abhisambodhi Vairocana (Lokesh Chandra 1991:56). Following are the names of seven out of the eight Bodhisattvas. The eighth should have been Mahasthāma-prāpta, as he makes a pair with Avalokiteśvara:

	Monastery	Bodhisattva
1.	Par-spon-bye	Mañjuśrī
2.	Saṁghapāla	Samantabhadra
3.	Hjigs-tshogs-spon-byed Śaṅkā-prahāṇa	Ākāśagarbha
4.	Ye-ses-ri	Kṣitigarbha
5.	Bi-si-mo-na	Maitreya/Bishamon/Vaiṣravaṇa
6.	Ba-no-cho	Bhaiṣajyarāja
7.	Hod-can	Avalokiteśvara
8.	?	Mahāsthāma*

These are four pairs of Bodhisattvas:

Avalokiteśvara and Mahāsthāma-prāpta*, (flank Maitreya)

Mañjuśrī and Samantabhadra, (flank Śākyamuni)

Ākāśagarbha and Kṣitigarbha

Maitreya and Bhaiṣajyarāja

6. Śaṅkā-prahāṇa Monastery

The monastery was constructed by Vijaya-kīrti, seventh generation of the Khotanese kings, possibly in the 1st century AD, on the Śākya-giri hill, dedicated to Bodhisattva Ākāśagarbha. An arhat, Saṅgha-vardhana, a teacher of Vinaya, lived near the monastery. Originally he was from the Phru-ño monastery and was merely passing his summer months at the Śaṇkā-prahāṇa monastery (Thomas 1935:77).

No monasteries were built by two kings, no. 12, 13 of the Prophecy, after Vijaya-vīrya.

7. Stūpa and Monasteries of Po-ta-rya and Mazo

A stūpa and a monastery were built by the 14th King of the Prophecy, Vijaya-jaya to get absolved of the sin of killing silk worms. He had married a Chinese Princess Puṇyeśvarā, who had secretly brought silk worms and reared them in the Ma-za district. The king's ministers were ignorant of the value of silk worms, they complained to the king about rearing, the king ordered to set the rearing house of silk worms on fire. The queen extracted some worms and again secretly reared them, she produced Kashmir silk, showed it to the king and explained. The king repented on what he had done.

Ārya Saṇghaghoṣa was a monk who had gone from India to Khotan. The king invited him to be his Kalyāṇamitra and confessed his sin, built the monastery, gave away riches to the Tathāgatas, installed an image of Śākyamuni. The king, his ministers and subjects began to worship at the beginning of the first month of each year, at the powerful and splendrous monastery, guarded by Ratnabala and Ratnaśūra (Emmerick 1967:34)

8. Monastery of Hdro-tir

The monastery was built by King 15th of the Prophecy, Vijaya-dharma to absolve his sins of past, present and future as a centre of Mahāsāṅghika sect. Arya Dharmānanda acted as his Kalyāṇamitra. Vijaya-dharma was the youngest son of Vijaya-jaya but he became a king because his elder brother had gone to India in search of virtues and merits, the second brother became a monk and received the name Dharmānanda and came to India to study Buddhism and became an Arhat. When he came to know that his younger brother was committing sins through hunting, he decided to be his Kalyāṇamitra, went back to Khotan, made a hut at the foot of Non-bgyir mountain and began meditation. One day he disguised as a golden deer, when the king Vijaya-dharma saw him. He shot an arrow that struck the thigh of the deer, the deer fled to his hut, Vijaya-dharma chased him and got amazed to see his own brother in place of the deer. The king lamented and wished to confess to be absolved.

Dharmānanda told him that Śākyamuni along with his retinue of Bodhisattvas had gone to Khotan from Gṛdhrakūṭa, the two Bodhisattvas Kṣitigarbha and Rikṣata Aśoka remained there. Deva Jinarṣabha, Devī Aśokā and the Nāga king Takṣaka took a vow to guard the place. So the king was advised to build a monastery there.

Aśokā : She was a nun of Ñātikā. When Ānanda announces her death to Buddha at Ñātikā in the Giñjakāvasatha and inquires if she has been reborn the Buddha says that she has been reborn spontaneously in the Suddhāvāsa, destined never to return. Aśokā was also one of the two chief disciples of Maṅgala Buddha (third of the 24 Buddhas) (Malalasekera 1998:I.221)

Jinarṣabha: Jinarṣabha comes in the Vaiśravaṇa-maṇḍala in the third enclosure among thirty-two mahābalas, called Dharma-bhrātṛ by Mahāmāyūrī, they are brothers of Vaiśravaṇa according to Āṭavaka-sūtra (Tuci 1980:577).

Āṭavaka: He is one of the sixteen Yakṣa generals, a cannible Yakṣa and demon of jungal. Several texts are specially consecrated to him in the esoteric tradition (for details see Lokesh Chandra 1991:2.411-418).

The King Vijaya-dharma built another stūpa and a monastery inside the castle, within a little door in the south gate at the place of the Nāga-rāja Varuṇa, near the stūpa called Pa-ri-tha. He placed relics of the seven Tathāgatas in the stūpa. The king also procured relics of Prabhūta-ratna and kept them at the monastery Hdro-tir (Emmerick 1967:35).

9. Monastery of San-tir

Built by Prince Hdon-hdros, the eldest son of Vijaya-jaya and elder brother of Vijaya-dharma. The prince decided to build a monastery at San-tir, he came to India and then invited Ārya Samantasiddhi to be an abbot. Then he went to China in search of wealth. One of the king's ministers was condemned to death there in a dispute. Hdon-hdros requested the king to allow him to die at his place, but there was a miracle – milk flowed out of his body when he was struck with a sword. Hdon-hdros was greatly honoured and presented many gifts. He went back to Khotan but his younger brother Vijaya-dharma was not willing to welcome him. He ordered his brother to go to the site of San-tir. Hdon-hdros summoned his Kalyāṇamitra Samantasidhi who assisted him in constructing the monastery. He besought the gods of Trayastriṁśa heaven and the four guardians of the four directions came there. Hdon-hdros requested the divinities to perform dramatic shows; they played excellent music. People and the king's retinue went to listen to the music that was never-before heard. The king was unable to resist, he himself went to the vicinity of San-tir. The two brothers met, the younger brother requested to be pardoned. They joined hands and entered the monastery to worship. The gods and the Nāgas performed plays (Emmerick 1967:41-43).

10. Mjal-mo-kaka-ra-ṅa Monastery

The monastery was built by Vijaya-dharma, son of Vijaya-jaya, at the spot where the two brothers met. This was the first monastery of Hinayanist sect of Sarvāstivāda in Khotan. It was guarded by Deva Kapila. Dramatic plays and shows regarding Tathāgata's accomplishment of difficult tasks were performed at the midday on the seventh and eighth days of the first autumn months. The monastery is said to have a great splendour and power (Emmerick 1967:45).

Kapil: The first reference to Deva Kapila is found as a special protector of a Kashmiri missionary Dharmamitra. Images of Kapila are celebrated for their miracles. In a Nanking temple built in AD 474, Kapila was paired with Vaiśravaṇa as a *lokapāla*, painted at the rear wall of the Great Wall to guard the entrance on the dangerous northern quarter. A drawing of Kapila with Nārāyaṇa is incised on a northern Ch'i stele of AD 567. He is portrayed as a powerfully built warrior with a long beard, wearing a winged helmet that recalls a style of Sassanian crowns and armour of a conventionalized Chinese type. He holds a sword in his right hand and a trident in his left and stands on a diminutive ass (Soper 1959:229-30).

11. Sam-ña Monastery and Stūpa

The monastery and stūpa were built by the 16th king of the Prophecy, Vijaya-siṁha, son of Vijaya-dharma and guarded by Vaiśravaṇa and Deva Kapila. Vijaya-siṁha, the king of Ga-hjag led an army into Khotan and was defeated. The Khotanese king caught the King of Ga-hjag and to kill him. But Vijaya-siṁha pleaded for his release, promised to be his Kalyāṇamitra, got the name Ānandasena, went to Su-lig and subsequently became an arhat (Emmerick 1967:46-47).

12. Sru-ño Monastery

The monastery was built by the 17th king of the Prophecy, Vijay-kīrti, son of Vijaya-siṁha. Ārya Mañjuśrī was propagating the dharma in Kan-sen and acting as Kalyāṇamitra of king Vijaya-kīrti. Vijaya-kīrti, the ruler of Khotan, along with king Kanika and Gu-zan invaded and captured a city called So-ked in India. King Vijaya-kīrti obtained relics and kept them in the stūpa at Sru-ño. Mañjuśrī asked the king to wipe his hands five times downward and upward. When the king did so on the juniper site fixing peg, immediately there arose five juniper branches.

When the monks used to recite the dharma over there, voices expounding the law used to come from juniper. The monastery was guarded by Deva Sujaya and his two attendants, Siṁhamukha and Sum-pon (Emmerick 1967:47).

13. Monastery and Stūpa of Dharmakīrti

The monastery and stūpa were built by the 18th king of the Prophecy, Vijaya-saṅgrāma, son of Vijaya-kīrti. Vijaya-saṅgrāma was a brave man; he killed several beings. Once a man fighting lion came there; the king overcame it single handedly and killed. One day the king camped for a night on the bank of a small river, he saw light at a distance, in the morning he realized that the light was coming from an arhat Jñānayaśas, who was staying there. The king worshipped and asked him as what was he doing there. Jñānayaśas explained that the spot was an *adhiṣṭhāna* of former Tathāgatas, so the king was advised by him to construct a temple over there. The king was inspired by his instructions and confessed his sins. He took a golden bowl and made a vow (*praṇidhāna*). Numerous relics entered into the bowl, faith in the mind of the king increased and he built the monastery of Dharmakīrti and a stūpa. The relics that he received were placed there (Emmerick 1967:49-51). The monastery seems to be named after the king's father, Dharma-kīrti.

The 19th king of the Prophecy was, Vijaya-dharma, son of Vijaya-saṅgrāma.

No monasteries were built by 14 kings after Vijaya-dharma, (nos. in the Prophecy 20-33). During the reign of these fourteen kings Khotan was invaded by foreign enemies and monasteries were damaged. Khotanese kings also went abroad and led armies. After that Dru-gu 'A-no-sod led an army into Khotan and burnt monasteries on a large scale as far as Gautosana, the country was ruined, people became sad and dejected; they were not able to build new monasteries. The 34th king of the Prophecy was Vijaya-kīrti.

14. Hgu-zan Monastery

The monastery was built by the 35th king of the Prophecy, Vijaya-saṅgrāma, son of Vijaya-kīrti, guarded by Jinarṣabha and Maṇibhadra. Vijaya-saṅgrāma became a king at the age of seven, but when he reached manhood he called elders of the *saṅgha* and his ministers and made enquiries about destruction of monasteries. He collected his army and invaded those countries who had ruined them. On his return he came to the bank a river and saw seven monks practicing improper customs. At the first instance he disliked it but when he saw miracles performed by them, he was moved and realized that he had already committed sins by killing a large number of people. He paid homage to Ārya Arhat Po-na-na-re-ta and others. Then he built a monastery for them, called Hgu-zan (Emmerick 1967:51-52).

15. Bzah-ser-ma Monastery

The 36th king of the Prophecy, Vijaya-siṁha, son of Vijaya-saṅgrāma, built the monastery, guarded by Devas Haimavata and Āṭavaka. Vijaya-siṁha invited Ārya Arhat Dharmabala to perform *ṛddhi*, he took the king to the abode of Maitreya, Tuṣita. On coming back the king built the temple Bzah-ser-ma monastery and enshrined an image of maitreya and his retinue. He also constructed shrines for the Protectors (Nāthas), Devas, and Nāgas and housed their images (Emmerick 1967:53).

Vijaya-bala was the 37th king of the Prophecy.

No monasteries were built by the 38th - 43rd kings of the Prophecy.

The 44th king of the Prophecy was Vijaya-bala.

16. Gandhakuṭī Moanstery

Vijaya-saṅgrāma, 45th king of the Prophecy, son of Vijaya-bala built Gandhakuṭi and enshrined an image of Buddha. The king was impressed by an image of Chehupana that soared through air from Cugupan and came to Khotan, the king saw it and turned faithful to the Law (Emmerick 1967:55).

17. Bzah-saṅ-gre-re-ma Monastery

The monastery was built by the 45th king of the Prophecy, Vijaya-saṅgrāma, son of Vijaya-bala, guarded by Vaiśravaṇa and Sañjnāya. One day the kin in the gate house of the northern gate, high above the fortress of Hu-then, saw that a monk was doing obeisance to a householder and conversing with him. The king commissioned his minister and sent him to know the details. The minister told that the householder was an apparition of Ārya Mañjuśrī and the monk, of Ārya Kṣ itigarbha. The king went to them, worshipped and enquired as from where had they come. They disclosed that they had come from Buddhakṣetra from the east, the land of Tathāgata Akṣobhya. The king besought them and prayed to show through his miraculous powers the land of Tathāgata Akṣobhya. They did so, the king saw many Buddhas coming through air in their cars and emit rays that touched the king's head. The king was so impressed, he made images of all those Buddhas, led them in cars along the north street and worshipped (Emmerick 1967:55). Later it became a tradition that the great images were led along the north street during the first half of the first spring month. The king invited the twofold *saṅghas*, provided entertainment in the grove of Byan-chub Hbyun-gnas Bkra-sis Bsil-ba and performed the great adoration of Mo-hyo-ra for his Kalyāṇamitra Ārya Arhat Morgubdeśi.

The 46th king of the Prophecy was Vijaya-śāstra.

Four kings after Vijaya-śāstra, (47th-50th kings) of the Prophecy did not build any monasteries.

18. Bha-ba-ña Monastery

Vijaya-kīrti, the 51st king of the Prophecy built Bha-ba-ña monastery. According to the story, one day the king went to Hgum-tir. There a Nāga-king appeared and said that the spot where the king was standing was under his *adhiṣṭhāna*, so the king should construct a monastery there. The king made a vow that if the Āryas in Jambūdvīpa would be pleased to come there and take control, he would build a monastery. Seventeen Ārya Arhats came from the sky. Out of faith, the king and his consort built the monastery and a place of meditation called Bha-ba-ña. The monastery was guarded by Deva Aparājita and Maṇibhadra. When the monastery was being built, Khotan was attached to Tibetan dominions and was governed by the Mgar minister, Bcan-nen-Gun-ston (Emmerick 1967:57-58).

19. Ma-na-hdi Monastery

The monastery and stūpa were built by Vijaya-saṅgrāma, the younger, son of Vijaya-saṅgrāma. Once the king Vjaya-saṅgrāma and his son went to China, on their way back to Khotan their route was restricted by Dru-yu army. The father died in China and the son being too small was unable to return to Khotan. For twelve years the minister called Amacha Khemeg acted as regent. But on assuming the throne Vijaya-saṅgrāma, younger, built the stūpa and monastery of Ma-na-hdi for his Kalyāṇamitra, the monk Ārya Ba-ruñ-ca. He enshrined relics of Tathāgatas. The monastery is guarded by Deva Ākāśacakṣus and Yakṣa general Sañjnāya (Emmerick 1967:59-60).

20. Byi-za-gre-rma monastery

The 53rd king of the Prophecy, Vijaya-vikrama, son of Vijaya-saṅgrāma built the monastery when he returned to Khotan, for his Kalyāṇamitra Ārya Arhat Devendra, the Great. The monastery is guarded by Deva Aparājita and Maṇibhadra (Emmerick 1967:59).

Aparajita: A Yakṣa standing like Himālaya mountain, wears white dress, has a fierce face with three eyes, holds a goad in the right hand and a vase of treasure in the left (for detail see Lokesh Chandra, DBI 1.369-72). Aparājita was one of the Prtyeka-Buddhas (*Pacceka*) mentioned in the Isigili sutta.

21. Byams-pa-maitri Monastery

The monastery was built by the 54th king of the Prophecy, King Vijaya-dharma and the Chinese minister Ser-the-si for their Kalyāṇamitra Par-mog Jinasena of Hgum-tir. The monastery was guarded by Vaiśravaṇa (Emmerick 1967:61).

22. Khe-gan-peak Monastery

The monastery was built by King Vijaya-sambhava, the 55th king of the Prophecy and his minister Ka-the-si for their two Kalyāṇamitras, Udrendra Rod-ci and Dharmānanda and guarded by Vaiśravaṇa.

23. Su-stoṅ-ña Monastery and Stūpa

The 55th king of the Prophecy, Vijaya-sambhava built the monastery and the stūpa of Su-stoṅ-ña. Once Ārya Vairocana went to the grove of Car-ma monastery. On hearing of the wonderful personality, the King Vijaya-sambhava immediately went to the spot and worshipped with obeisance, Vairocana acted as his Kalyāṇamitra and expounded the essence of evil and virtuous deeds. The king became faithful, went back to the fortress and built a stūpa at the spot and named it as Su-stoṅ-ña. Later when the stūpa was in ruins, the king Vijaya-vāhana and the monk Hbah-la-si, who had come from China invited the Saṅgha of Car-ma to be their Kalyāṇamitra, built a monastery there, that was guarded by Vaiśravaṇa (Emmerick 1967:61).

Nunneries Built by Various Kings

24. Nu-ho-ña Nunnery

Nuho-ña at pa-rogzah of the upper river of hu-then was built by king Vijaya-siṁha. Vijaya-siṁha gained sovereignty when he was a child, but when the king grew up he killed seventy-five of his ministers because he remembered their contemptuous and disdainful behavior to the queen, the palace retinue and the female inmates. The king bore grudge against them. The king also built a monastery at the spot where he had killed the ministers. The monastery was guarded by Kīlahasta.

On returning to the fortress he cut off access from the palace where the king was, from the dwelling of the queen and her retinue and the female inmates. The queen Mokṣakoṣā and Sa-lu-ca along with her retinue worshiped, walked around the shrine and read dharma. Ārya Arhantī Yaśaprajñā and Sthya-su-ta and San-handa went from India to expound the law to those queens. 112 out of the retinue of the queen renounced the world (*pravrajyā*) went to get alms (*piṇḍapāta*) and attained arhatship. He was so amazed and pleased to see that, that he decided to build a monastery at that spot. He donated land, cattles, servants etc. (Emmerick 1967:63).

25. Yo-zo-hjo Nunnery

It was built by the queen So-rgya and guarded by Nāga kings Da-ci and Da-ra. The elder sister of So-rgya attained arhatship, came from China to Hu-then to act as Kalyāṇamitra of her younger sister (Emmerick 1967:65).

26. Zer-ro-hjo Nunnery

It was built by king Vijaya-śata and guarded by Deva Nandīśvara. Su-ha-cho-ha died in the abode of the younger brother of king Vijaya-śata. The king requested to meet his wife but she requested to be allowed to mourn for her husband for a week. She renounced the world, concentrated, meditated upon Buddhānusmṛti-samādhi, attained arhatship, took the name Buddhānandā. When the king went there, he was so surprised to look at Buddhānandā Ārya Arhantī and her miraculous power that he decided to build the monastery of Zer-ro-hjo (Emmerick 1967:67).

27. Po-yen-do Nunnery

It was built by king Vijaya-nanda and guarded by Vaiśravaṇa and Nāga-king Hu-lor. The daughter of he king Āryā-dharmabalā renounced the world, attained arhatship; she realized that she was the daughter of the Khotanese king Vijaya-mati. Āryā-dharmabalā went to Khotan with twenty nuns and related her previous history to her father, the king and displayed her miraculous powers. Thus the king built a monastery called Po-yen-do (Emmerick 1967:67).

28. Dro-mo-mjah Nunnery

It was built by king Vijaya-sambhava, the Lion and guarded by Deva Kapila. The king's mother renounced the world, became an arhat and meditated. She began to emit light in the evening; the king was unaware; he shot an arrow in the morning; he found his mother Āryā Arhantī Dharmā there. So he built a monastery called Dro-mo-mjah (Emmerick 1967:67).

29. Tra-ke-hjo Nunnery

It was built by the younger son of Vijaya-saṇgrāma and guarded by Sañjnāya, general of the Yakṣas. The queen Dru-gu-mo renounced the world, received the name 'A-su-ka-su-ma.

30. Ho-roṅ-hjo Nunnery

Queen Hu-ron, consort of Vijaya-saṅgrāma built for her daughters: Sita-ma-ta and Gau-sa-ra, who went from Kashmir to act as Kalyāṇamitras of their mother. The monastery was guarded by Nāga-kings: Hu-lor and Suvarṇākṣa (Emmerick 1967:69).

Appendix 1

Available dates:

Nirvāṇa of the Buddha	475BC
Aśoka's rule	273/292-236BC (55 years?)
Birth of Sa-nu	261 BC (30 years of Asoka's becoming a king?)
Foundation of Khotan	242/210 BC (19 years old Sa-nu)
	(234/265 years after the nirvāṇa of Buddha)
Vijaya-sambhava (3rd king)	215 BC
Vijaya-vikrama	
Vijaya-siṁha	AD 737-747
Vijaya-dharma	
Vijaya-vāhana	AD 763-785
Vijay-kīrti	AD 785-801
Vijaya-sambhava	912-966
Vijaya-śūra	967-977
Vijaya-dharma	978-982
Vijaya-saṅgrāma	AD 987-

A period of 1256 years from the 3rd king of the Prophecy to the 57th king.

Appendix 2

A list of guardians protecting various monasteries, stūpas and nunneries in alphabetical order:

1. 'A-ba-lha
2. Ākāśacakṣu
3. Aparājita
4. Aśokā
5. Āṭavaka
6. Caturmahārājika
7. Da-ci (Nāgaking)
8. Da-ra (Nāgaking)
9. Devī
10. Gṛhāvatapta (Ṅagaking)

11. Haimavat
12. Hjaṁ-bha-kehu-ta
13. Hu-lor
14. Jinarṣabha
15. Kapila
16. Kīlahasta
17. Maṇibhadra
18. Nandīśvara
19. Ratnabala
20. Ratnaśūra
21. Sañjnāya
22. Śaṅkhinī
23. Siṁhamukha
24. Sujaya and his attendants
25. Sum-pon
26. Suvarṇākṣa
27. Suvarṇa-puṣpa
28. Takṣaka
29. Vaiśravaṇa

LITERATURE CITED

Asia Major, vol. IV, part I, London.

Bailey 1982

H.W. Bailey, *The Culture of the Śakas in Ancient Iranian Khotan,* Caravan Books, New York, 1982.

Das 1973

Sarat Chandra Das, *Buddhist and Other Legends about Khotan, Journal of Asiatic Society of Bengal,* 1.V.

East and West, 23.1-2, March 1973.

Edgerton 1997

Edgerton, *Budhist Hybrid Sanskrit Dictionary,* Delhi, 1997.

Emmerick 1979

Ronald E. Emmerick, *A Guide to the Literature of Khotan,* Studia Philologica Buddhica, 1979.

Emmerick 1967

Emmerick, *Tibetan Texts Concerning Khotan,* Oxford Universtiy Press, 1967.

Encyclopaedia of Islam, Leiden, 1986.

Judy Bonavia 1990

Judy Bonavia, *An Illustrated Guide to the Silk Road,* Honk Kong, 1990.

Lokesh Chandra 1991

Lokesh Chandra, *Cultural Horizons of India,* vol. 2, New Delhi, 1992.

DBI - *Dictionary of Buddhist Iconography*, vol. 1,2, New Delhi, 1991.

Malalasekera 1998

G.P. Malalasekera, *Dictionary of Pali Proper Names,* Munshiram Manoharlal, New Delhi, 1998.

Nebesky 1956

Rene de, Wojkowitz, *Oracles and Demons of Tibet,* Hague, 1956.

Stien 1907/1902

Stien, Sir Aurel, *Ancient Khotan,* Oxford, 1907.

- *Sand Buried Ruins of Khotan,* 1902.

Soper 1959

Alexander C. Soper, *Literary Evidence in Early Buddhist Art in China,* Switzerland, 1959.

Thomas 1935

F.W. Thomas, *Tibetan Literary Texts and Documents concerning Chinese Turkistan,* The Royal Asiatic Society, London, 1935.

Tucci 1980

G. Tucci, *Tibetan Painted Scrolls,* Tokyo, 1980.

Wild 1992

Oliver, Wild, *The Silk Road*, 1992, internet.

18

APOTHEOSIS OF AN INDONESIAN KING OF THE SINGASARI DYNASTY

Devarāja concept links the function of divinity and sovereignty. A king and a god are guardians of each other, united in beneficence. This led to divinity of royalty and thence to royalty of icons. Deification of kings was a solemn act of legislation in Greece. For Persians Alexander was a king endowed by the supreme light god Ahurmazda. Kings and their consorts were lifted above ordinary mortals. In 290 BC Athenians hailed Demetrius as a true god. The Practice of offering honors to Augustus began in the East and penetrated to all parts of the empire. Iranians also practiced king worship. But when they embraced Buddhism, their kings were apotheosized as the Buddha. Distinctive, portrait like personalized features in Gāndhāra statues present evidence that kings were immortalized as divine statues. Buddha worship was blended with emperor worship.

Kings resorted to derive sanctity and power to sustain and rule as sovereigns. Divinization of the state is equal to legitimization in contemporary terms. Consecration of kings involved a complicated and long ritual called '*aindrābhiṣeka*' in Southeast Asia because Indra is the lord of Gods, 'Devarāja Indra'. The ceremony owes a great value for maintenance of social integrity and national unity.

Grand temples of Indonesia and images housed therein represent the dual principal of religion and politics, a symbiosis of royalty and religion, humanity and divinity. At the time of political instability the ambitious rulers of various dynasties sought transmission of divine grace unto them through evocation of transcendental powers. They resorted to religious activities to consolidate their political power, to earn vitality of the spiritual forces. For centuries dedication of religious monuments remained a testimony to the faith of the royal patrons and the transcendental source of power and legitimating. Such temples in Indonesia served the purpose of ancestor worship also.

Ancestor worship was a special task laid upon the kings, to establish ritual contact with their ancestors, to strengthen their political position through magical powers, acquired from them. Thus worship of posthumous images of kings in the form of Viṣṇu, Śiva or Buddha became a fashion. Use of divine images for announcing political hegemony was an important step taken by Kṛtanagara, a King of east Java, in the 13th century. He sent an image of his father Viṣṇuvardhana to Chandi Jago in order to ensure contact with the kingdom as his vessel state and his dynasty through the cult of ancestor worship. Moreover the kings themselves claimed to rule as incarnations of various divinities; Airlangga himself claimed to be an incarnation of Viṣṇu. His portrait image in the form of Viṣṇu riding a garuḍa was housed at his mausoleum at Belahan. Kṛtanagara erected his own image as an incarnation of Akṣobhya, which now adorns the Krusenpark at Surabaya. He was also deified as Harihara-ardhanārīśvara represented with his wife Vajradevī at Chandi Jawi. A posthumous image of King Anūśapati was enshrined as an incarnation of Śiva and of Ken Dedes as Prajñāpāramitā. Differences in facial features and heights of such images also hint at their being portraits of various rulers made and consecrated during their lives or posthumously.

Nāgarakṛtāgama an important Indonesian historical treatise mentions installation ceremonies of such images at the time of rites performed for final liberation of soul and importance of deified dynastic ancestors to the ruling kings[1] . The poet Prapañca refers to a number of religious domains visited by him and the king during an extensive journey through the land.

Śaivism flourished as the state religion under the rulers of the Mataram dynasty in Central Java and the dynasties of East Java. Balitungga (AD 898-910) a Śaiva king of the Mataram dynasty was succeeded by Dakṣa (AD 910 - 919) who is believed to have built Chandi Prambanan, one of the most glorious monuments in the history of Indonesian art and architecture. The temples of Prambanan, Penanggungan, Banon, Bedulu, Kidul and Singasari etc. housed a great variety of images of outstanding spiritual and political significance.

The centre of major political activities shifted from Central to East Java around first half of the tenth century. The shift was made by Sindok (AD 929-47). Art and literature flourished under the rule of Kediri (1045-1222), Singasari (AD 1222-1292) and Majapahit (AD 1292- AD 1520), the three great dynasties of East Java. Kṛtanagara was the last king of Singasari, suffering from tension in the inner circles, especially during the first decade of its existence. Kṛtanagara was initiated into secret Tāntric knowledge, required to combat the demonic forces that were rampant and for the welfare of his realm when he succeeded in AD 1268.

Following are the five images from the Singasari period, which have been selected for research on their historicity, patronage and symbolism:

1. Bhairava from the neighborhood of Singasari, kept at the Leiden Museum
2. Mahiṣāsuramardinī from Chandi Singasari, kept at the Leiden Museum
3. Gaṇapati from Chandi Singasari, kept at the Leiden Museum. (The search began with this of Gaṇapati sitting on a seat of skulls, an unusual characteristic feature).
4. Gaṇapati from Blitar, AD 1239
5. Guardians at Singasari

Most of the Singasari temples are in a miserable condition today. Temples are ruined and images are scattered. A number of statues have been taken to various collections in Indonesia, Holland and other parts of the world. Melting down of gold, silver and bronze images has left niches empty in the temples and a number of questions unanswered in the history of art. Broken inscriptions inscribed on the images or standing independently, supply inadequate information posing problems for the art historians. The above-mentioned images from Singasari, once stood in the partly restored temple or are found from the ruins, are masterworks of the period. Three of the images: Mahiṣāsuramardinī, Gaṇapati and the guardian were found from the Singasari temple which does not have any decorations at its lower part. This means that the temple was left unfinished, possibly due to political reasons.

A.J.Bernet Kempers in 'Ancient Indonesian Art' dealing with the iconographic details and styles makes a suggestion that the image of Bhairava possibly can be identified with Kṛtanagara or the Sumatran King Ādityavarman. The statement lacks symbolism behind their characteristic features and attributes.

Kṛtanagara is described as an empire builder in the classical Indonesian text, Nāgarakṛtāgama composed by Prapañca in AD 1365 and as a drunkard indulged in lust in the other text, Pararaton. He resorted to alchohol and sexual excesses, because an ecstasy was to be cultivated through them according to the Tāntric philosophy. As a great empire builder he was engaged in building up an anti Mongol defense front as the danger was assuming threatening proportions when Kublai Khan (1260-93) was sending envoys to the countries of South-east-Asia to demand tokens of submission. Repercussions of invasions in Eastern Asia demanded Kṛtanagara to unify Indonesia against the possible threat and consolidate his position. Once Kṛtanagara arrested the Mongol deputation and sent it back with disfigured faces; obviously he was aware of the danger.

Kings strived for gaining political victory through spiritual powers derived from dedication ceremonies. The Tibetan Buddhist preceptor, the Śākyapa Lama Phagspa had created a new inner Asian Buddhist concept of statecraft. Kublai Khan, the first emperor of the Yüan dynasty turned to Buddhism, initiated into Tibetan Tantric rites, worshipped Mahākāla to conquer south China and performed Hevajra ceremony before invading South-east Asia in AD 1264 and 1269 which was urged on him by his wife Chabi[2]. His initiation into the Hevajra maṇḍala was considered to be of great importance. He identified himself with the main figure of the maṇḍala while participating in the ceremony. Where this figure had a multiple form this could be realized by breaking it up into its component parts of simple one headed two armed figures. A number of fine and roughly life sized bronzes are discovered from the neighborhood of Peking. The group was used to build up a maṇḍala at Kublai Khan's Hevajra ceremony. The general appearance of Hevajra is of a sixteen year old youth of wrathful appearance clad in a tiger's skin, eight drinking vessels made of skulls with various divinities like Vāyu, Agni, Candra, Sūrya, Yama, Vasudhārā and Vāstupati sitting on them, are held in his left hands and animals are placed on the cups held in his right hands, while goddesses of aṣṭaśmaśānas sit around him[3]. Instead of eight faced and sixteen armed Hevajra embracing his prajñā and holding skull cups, a group of eight separate figures may have been chosen. The emperor with his consort sat at the centre of this group identifying themselves with Hevajra. The eight surrounding figures were placed as partial aspects of Hevajra.

When Kublai Khan embarked on a disastrous expansionist policy, vibrations were felt in Cambodia also. As a defensive ritual Hevajra ceremony was performed there at that occasion. In Indonesia, in consequence to Kublai Khan's accomplishment of magical powers, his cast as a *cakravartī* ruler, as an embodiment of Mahākāla, the fierce, intelligent protector deity, Kṛtanagara performed Bhairava ceremony in AD 1275 in the hope of developing the same magical powers. He had committed himself to unite Indonesia, to build up a sacred confederacy, to mobilize strength against the possible threat from China. Two principal advisors of the king were entrusted the responsibility to undertake necessary measures for his assumption of the divinity Bhairava, to support his policy. The image is identified as Buddha Bhairava by D G E Hall[4] and *Cakracakra* by A.J.Bernet Kempers[5] on the basis of the inscription on the statue. But as the inscription is partly damaged it is difficult to identify the deity as *Cakracakra* because the following letters are missing.

Bhairava Dedication by Kāpālikas

Kāpālikas are known for worshipping terrifying divinities like Bhairava and Cāmuṇḍā and indulging in horrid practices. They believed in eating meat and drinking wine in skull as a part of their rituals. It is a Tāntric or Pāśupat sect ritual of extreme antiquity devoted to śavavāda or necrophilia; Śiva is their deity aspected as Kapāleśvara. Kāpālikas smear their bodies with ashes of a corpse, go about naked, keep long matted hair. The Kāpālikas believe in obtaining frightful occult powers through drinking and sexuality. Kāpālikas literally mean "skull bearers". Such practices prevailed in north as well as in south India. They had a centre at Śrīśailam in Andhra Pradesh. A Buddhist nun is described to be practicing *kāpālikasādhanā* on Śrīśailam mountain. Hsüan Tsang has also referred to them (Encyclopedia of Indian Culture). Indonesian literature testifies existence of Kāpālika cult there. Kāpālikavrata, an observance of the Kāpālikas is mentioned in the classical text Udyogaparva (45.4): *san brāhmaṇa Kāpālikabrata nasi pinakopahāra nira*[6]. Kāpālika-vrata means the greatest vow that consists of eating food placed in human skull and smearing body with ash of human carcass. Kāpālikavrata is mentioned in the Sanskrit drama: Mālatimādhava. In India, Kāpālikas had established a strong centre at Ujjain. Fresh human ashes are brought to the temple of Mahākāleśhvara, daily for smearing the Śivaliṅgga. Similar cult rituals, dedicated to Śiva in his monstrous and macabre emanation as Bhairava have been found not only in East Java in Singasari but also in Bali and Sumatra in Indonesia. Descendants of the Majapahit dynasty still perform the Bhairava ceremony in Bali.

Bhairava (Singasari, Leiden Museum, 167 cms.)

An image of Bhairava from Singasari is carved as a naked figure, who has fangs and wears a skull crown. He sits on a dog or jackal. The cult held great fascination for the ruling and the priestly circles of the time in Indonesia. Skulls and cut off human heads constituting his ornaments and crown are a prominent feature. He carries a *triśūla*, (trident) and a *khaḍga* (sword) in his right hands and a *ḍamaru* (a kind of drum) and a skull bowl in the left hands; a string of bells is tied around his abdomen. The appearance is fierce because his eyes are round and rolling, nostrils are wide, he is laughing frightfully and dancing in *tāṇḍava* style. Bhairava is a terrifying form of Śiva-ghora or ugra. In Purāṇas and Āgamas he is also described as Brahmā-śiraścchedaka. According to Śrītattvanidhi (Rao, op. cit., p. 176) he should wear tiger's skin, carry a vajra and a *paraśu* (axe) in his right hands and a skull and a *śūla* (lance) in the left, he should wear a *jaṭāmukuṭa* (crown made of twisted locks of hair) and wear *kuṇḍalas* (earrings). According to Viṣṇudharmottara-purāṇa (III.59) he should have a flabby belly, round yellow eyes, side tusks and wide nostrils, wear a garland of skulls. Bhairava is described in three different forms: Baṭuka Bhairava, Svarṇākarṣaṇa Bhairava and a class of 64 Bhairavas. Baṭuka Bhairava is portrayed as nude, terrifying in appearance with protruding fangs, rolling and round eyes, his hands hold a sword, a *khaṭvāṅga*, a staff with a skull on the top, a *śūla* (lance) or a *kapāla* (skull). He is often accompanied by a dog. According to Baṭuka-bhairava-kalpa he has *jaṭā*s (locks of hair) of red colour, three eyes and red body. He is eulogized in Baṭuka-Bhairava-prātaḥ-smaraṇam as follows:

Prātaḥ namāmi baṭukaṁ taruṇaṁ trinetram
Kāmāspadaṁ vara-kapāla-triśūla-daṇḍam |
Bhaktārtināśakaraṇe dadhataṁ kareṣu |
Taṁ kaustubhābharaṇa-bhuṣitadivya deham ||2|| (Tripāṭhī p.48)

Baṭuka Bhairava is evoked in the morning, he is young, has three eyes, holds a skull, trident, a staff, performs *varada mudrā*, his body is decked with *kaustubha* gems.

Prātaḥkāle sadāhaṁ bhagaṇapatidharaṁ bhāladeśe maheṣam |
Nāgaṁ pāśaṁ kapālaṁ ḍamarūmatha sṛṇīṁ khaḍgaghaṇṭābhayāni ||3||
(Tripāṭhī p.48)

He is Maheśa with Gaṇapati on his forehead, carries a snake, a noose, a skull, a *ḍamaru*, a goad, a sword, a bell and performs *abhaya mudra*.

Digvastraṁ piṅgakeśaṁ trinayanasahitaṁ muṇḍamālaṁ kareṣu |
Yo dhatte bhīmadanṣṭraṁ mamavijayakaraṁ bhairavaṁ tan namāmi ||3||
(Tripāṭhī p.48)

I bow to Bhairava who gives victory, who dose not wear any clothes, whose hair is reddish brown, has three eyes, wears a garland of skulls, his teeth are dreadful.

Devadeva kṛpāsindho sarvanāśin mahāvyaya |
Sansārāsakta-cittaṁ māṁ mokṣamārge niveṣaya ||4|| (Tripāṭhī p.48)

O lord of lords, an ocean of compassion, the destroyer, the immutable, please put mind that is indulged in this world on the way to mokṣa.[7]

According to Śāradātilakatantra (20:59) Baṭuka Bhairava is of three types: *sātvika*, *rājasika* and *tāmasika*. In its *tāmasika* form he is worshipped to subdue enemies and scare away supernatural beings. He is portrayed naked, wearing a garland of skulls and has terrific fangs:

Vande nīlādrikāntaṁ śaśikalādharaṁ muṇḍamālaṁ maheśam
Digvastraṁ piṅgakeśaṁ ḍamarūm atha sṛṇiṁ khaḍgapāśābhayāni |
Nāgaṁ ghaṇṭāṁ kapālaṁ karaśarasiruhair bibhrataṁ bhīmadaṁṣṭram
Divākalpaṁ trinetraṁ maṇimaya-vilasat-kiṅkiṇī-nūpurāḍhyam ||[8]
Mastiṣkāntravasābhir dharita-mahāmāṁsāhutirjuhvatam |
Vahnau brahmakapālakalpitasurāpānena naḥ parṇa ||
Sadyaḥ-kṛtta-kaṭhora-kaṇṭha-vigalita-kīlāladharojjvalair |
Arcyo naḥ puruṣopahārabalibhir devo mahābhairavaḥ ||[9]

Thus most of the characteristic features of the image of Bhairava correspond to the details given in Sanskrit texts. Thus a hypothesis can be presented that the image of Bhairava represents King Kṛtanagara as his incarnation who was a devotee of the Kāpālika sect and its philosophy, who sought victory, aspired for instilling terror and attain *mokṣa*. The importance of instilling terror is described in Kaṭhopaniṣad (2.3.3) as:

Bhayādāsyāgnistapati bhayāt tapati sūryaḥ |
Bhayādindraśca vāyuśca mṛtyurdhāvati pañcama ||

The Demonic Guardian as Aghoraghaṇṭa (Singasari, ht. 3.70 mts)

Two gigantic squatting guardians sit in the square grassy field to the east of Chandi Singasari. These figures looking very strong, among such images, found from Indonesia, are half sunken into earth at a place where perhaps a gate once existed (Kempers 1959:pl.239). His terrifying character is visualized through curved eyebrows, bulging out round eyes, fangs with curled up lips and broad nose. His earrings are made of skulls, *kapālakuṇḍala*, the necklace that he is wearing is of an unusual design, sacred thread, *yajñopavīta* is made of a huge snake, he is kneeling with one leg folded up. His left hand rests on a heavy club, ending in vajra points, while the right hand is raised in a threatening posture with index and middle fingers straight and the other two folded. This should be the *ṣaṇ-mudrā* or *pañca-mudrā*. Another important feature is skulls in his crown, the space in between is filled with the same design as seen in his necklace.

Demonic figures are the protectors of the Doctrine as well as of the empire, from the enemies. Such peculiar character of demonic figures existed in Śaivite sects such as Śaivasiddhānta. The guardian figure sitting outside the temple of Singasari can be Aghoraghaṇṭa. Aghoraghaṇṭa is a Tantric priest in the Sanskrit drama, 'Mālatimādhava' by Bhavabhūti and Kapālakuṇḍalā is his disciple. Aghoraghaṇṭa is said to be *tantra-siddha-bhayaṅkara-kriyānuṣṭhāyī kaścid-vīrācārī*, a powerful being, indulged in horrible tantric acts, and Kapālakuṇḍalā, his disciple as *tantra-yoga-siddha-śālinī*, a woman who has accomplished *tantric-yoga-siddhi*. When the king resolves on mating of Mālatī and Mādhava, Mādhava despairing of success through Kāmandaka's aid alone, decides to win the favour of ghouls of the cemetery by an offering of fresh flesh. He hears cries from a nearby temple and rushes to save Mālatī from the priest Aghoraghaṇṭa and his acolyte Kapālakuṇḍalā who were about to offer sacrifice to the Goddess Cāmuṇḍā. He slays Aghoraghaṇṭ a. Aghora is a euphemistic title of Śiva. The character of Aghoraghaṇṭa seems to be close to *gurughaṇṭāla* in Hindustani. He is a *guru* with tinkling bells hung round his neck, a thorough knave[10].

The necklace worn by the guardian from Singasari shows similarity to the bone apron found in Tibetan art. A bone apron can be of bones only or made up of bone beads interspersed with beads made of materials in different colours, usually red and green, normally like the aprons worn by ḍākinīs as *śakti*s, female counterparts of demonic gods. A similar design is found in the neck ornaments also. According to Shambhala-lam-yig (The Road to Shambhala) such aprons were found in India in Ratnāgiri in Bengal (Pott 1951:118). It is described as one of the six articles used in Tantric ritual. Skull bowl, skull drum, trumpets made of femur, sacrificial knives, crowns and magic daggers are the other articles. Pieces of bones in the bone apron are said to be made of bones of enemies of the doctrine who had been defeated and destroyed. According to Hevajra-tantra (1.3.14, vol.1, p.58, 1.6.11-12, vol.1, p.64) the five symbolic ornaments worn by such deities are:

Deity	Ornament
Akṣobhya	Cakrī (diadem)
Amitābha	Kuṇḍala (earring)
Ratneśa	Kaṇṭhī (necklace)
Vairocana	Rucaka (bracelet)
Vairocana	Mekhalā (girdl)

Bone apron is the sixth ornament as mentioned in the commentary by Kanha on the Hevajra tantra. These articles should be compared with the ornaments and attributes of the demonic figures to support that the adherent identifies himself with the demonic figures[11]. Kāpālikas believed that if one would wear six signs: a necklace, an ornament, an ear ornament, crest jewel, ashes and sacred thread (*kuṇḍala, cūḍāmaṇi, bhasma, yajñopavīta* etc.), he would be exempted from transmigration. All the bliss is possible to be achieved through consumption of food in a skull, daubing one's limbs with the ashes of a corpse, consuming those ashes, holding a club, having a pot of liquor, and worshipping the divine beings as dwelling in it. They also adorned themselves with *rudrākṣa* beads. Their hair used to be matted and their skulls filled with ashes. It was believed that one could attain sainthood by undertaking these vows[12].

Gaṇapati as the General (Singasari)

Gaṇapati from Singasari is one of the finest examples of Javanese art. He carries his usual attributes: a tusk, a fly-whisk, a hatchet and a skull bowl but the use of skulls as decoration of his pedestal is a matter of scholarly attention.

Gaṇapati occupies a prominent position among devas, associated to Śiva in India and Indonesia. He is a physical aspect of Śiva who removes obstacles in the devotee's path, thus called Vighneśvara. Śiva appointed him as chief of the army of *gaṇa*s, a general, so he is called Gaṇapati. Gaṇapati has the power to do anything without any obstructions. Gaṇapati as a general is described in one of the famous kakavins 'Smaradahana' written in the first half of Kediri period. It is a story of Śiva performing severe penance. Heaven is threatened by the demon Nīlarudraka, but Śiva remains indifferent to what was happening around him. Bṛhaspati proposes Kāma, the god of love, to inflame Śiva's heart with love for Umā. Kāma approaches Śiva, launches flower weapons on Śiva, the weapons penetrate Siva's heart. He assumes a terrifying form. All the *deva*s worship him; he is relinquished and reminded of Nīlarudraka's powers granted by Śiva himself. Bṛhaspati and the other devas told that nobody but Śiva's son would have been able to defeat the demons. Feelings of love are aroused in Śiva's heart, he abandons yoga and approaches Umā. Their union was to bear fruit, gods bring Indra's elephant, Umā gets frightened at the sight of an elephant. Then a son is born with the head of an elephant. Śiva declares that his name shall be Gaṇa. He will be, by nature, remover of all obstacles and will destroy enemies[13]

Looking at the political scenario it may be concluded that defeating the enemies was the motive behind consecrating the image of Gaṇapati, found at the Singasari temple. The figure is bulky, benign and childlike, sits with his legs drawn up under his belly. His trunk is dipping into a skull bowl held by him. An axe and a rosary in his backhands are placed against a so-called Majapahit aureole made of stars radiating beams (Kempers 1959:pl.235). Skulls inserted in the seat and ornaments are an important feature of this image. They adorn his conical crown cap and are studded in his earrings and bracelets. Even his loincloth bears a design made of skulls. These features point to the general Bhairavist orientation of the Singasari court (Claire Holt 1967:80). The image is surpassed in size and dynamic quality only by a 14th century gigantic image of Gaṇeśa found at the garden at village Bara, situated to the south of Blitar. It was brought there from Jambi on the other side of Brantas River. According to the chronogram in words on its pedestal it is dated 1161 = AD 1239. So we can safely place the image in the early Singasari period (Kempers 1959:pl.212). Thus this image of Gaṇapati can be taken as representing the general who was thought to be an incarnation of Gaṇapati, the divine general.

Mahiṣāsuramardinī as the Queen (Singasari, Lieden Museum, ht. 157)

The worship of Śakti without Bhairava or of Bhairava without Śakti is incomplete as both of them are inseparable from each other in ritual. For *aniṣṭa nivṛtti* to desist from the undesirable or *abhīṣṭa pravṛtti,* to gain the desirable, both of them are to be worshipped together as mentioned in Yatidaṇḍaiśvaryavidhāna:

> *Śaktayaḥ sarvadā sevyaḥ sādhakair bhairavārcitaḥ* |
> *Atonyathā na siddhiḥ syāt kalpakoṭiśatairapi* ||[14]

Kṛtanagara resorted to the dedication of Mahiṣāsuramardinī as she is the mightiest of all the divine beings. Possibly it is a portrait image of the queen. According to Hindu philosophy she is a conglomeration of powers and glories of all the devas, especially created by them to kill the demonic force, Mahiṣāsura who had captured the *devaloka*, abode of the divine. Powers of Brahmā, Viṣṇu, Śiva, Indra, Kubera, Varuṇa and all the other gods merged into a single being, a woman with celestial beauty. She took her stand at the entrance of *devaloka* and challenged Mahiṣāsura and firmly killed him in a battle.

She is a frequently repeated theme in the religious art of the Śaiva world. Hundreds of such images are found from Indonesian temples. She was worshipped in Indonesia to gain a complete victory. The inscription on the back of Cāmuṇḍā image announces that a military action was about to take place against a territory named Sadeng, victory over *sakaladvīpāntara,* entire Indonesia, which was identified as Bali (Hall 1970:76). The inscription on this image from Ardimuljo near Singasari discovered in 1927 describes the revolt of Sadeng as a dangerous episode[15]. The Mahiṣ āsuramardinī from Chandi Singasari kept at the Leiden Museum once occupied the northern cella. She stands on a wounded bull with a demon emerging out of its head that was to leave the body of the bull. Apart from a shield none of the attributes of the goddess survives in her hands. She holds hair of the demon by her lower left hand. Her standing posture is powerful and dominant with legs wide apart. She is more expressive than the one standing outside the central shrine at Prambanan. She is forceful yet restraint in movement. Femininity is combined with power. The goddess is calm and impeccable with her glance lowered[16].

Thus it may be concluded that the defense cults flourished during the 13th century in Singasari. Images of Kāpālika cult, their invocation, intricate rituals and ceremonies were performed for prostration (*śaktipāta*), inspiration and attainment of the divine power, for the kings, to elevate them from humanity to divinity to be victorious.

Appendix

Important dates:

1264 Kublai Khan's consecration as Jina Buddha
1268 Kṛtanagara's accession to the throne
1269 Kublai Khan's consecration as Jina Buddha
1275 Kṛtanagara's assumption as divinity Bhairava
1281 Kublai Khan's expedition against Japan, failed
1285 Kublai Khan's failure in Tonkin and Champa
1286 Amoghapāśa image presented to Sumatra
1289 Insult of Mongol deputation by Kṛtanagara
1293 Jayakatwang of Kediri established Majapahit
1294 Mongol armada to Java

Reference

1. Clair Holt, *Art in Indonesia,* New York, 1967:80
2. Petricia Berger and Teresa Tse Bartholomew, Mongolia, *The Legacy Of Chinggis Khan,* Thame and Hudson, 1996:50
3. Peter H. Pott, *The Maṇḍala of Heruka,* CIBA Journal, No. 50, 1969:30-31
4. D G E Hall, *A History of South-east-Asia,* Macmillan, New York, 1970:74
5. Bernet Kempers, *Ancient Indonesian Art,* Cambridge, 1959:79
6. P.J.Zoutmulder, *Old Javanese-English Dictionary,* Leiden, 1982:I.797
7. *Śrī Baṭuka Prātaḥ smaraṇam,* Rudradevatripathi, p.48
8. *Tāmasam dhyānam,* Rudradeva Tripathi p. 69
9. *Bharatiya Sanskriti Koṣa* 2.241-43
10. *New Hindustani-English Dictionary,* S.W.Fallon, London, 1879:997
11. P.H.Pott, *Introduction to the Tibetan Collection of the National Museum of Ethnology,* Leiden, 1951:115-18
12. Benjamin Walker, *An Encyclopedic Survey of Hinduism,* Hindu World, London, 1968:526-27
13. P.J.Zoetmulder, *Kalangwan,* Hague, 1974:291-95
14. Rudradeva Tripathi, *Śrī-Baṭuka-Bhairavasādhana,* 1982:20
15. DGE Hall, *Historians of South-east-Asia,* London, 1961:160 fn. 224
16. Claire Holt, *Art in Indonesia,* New York, 1967:78

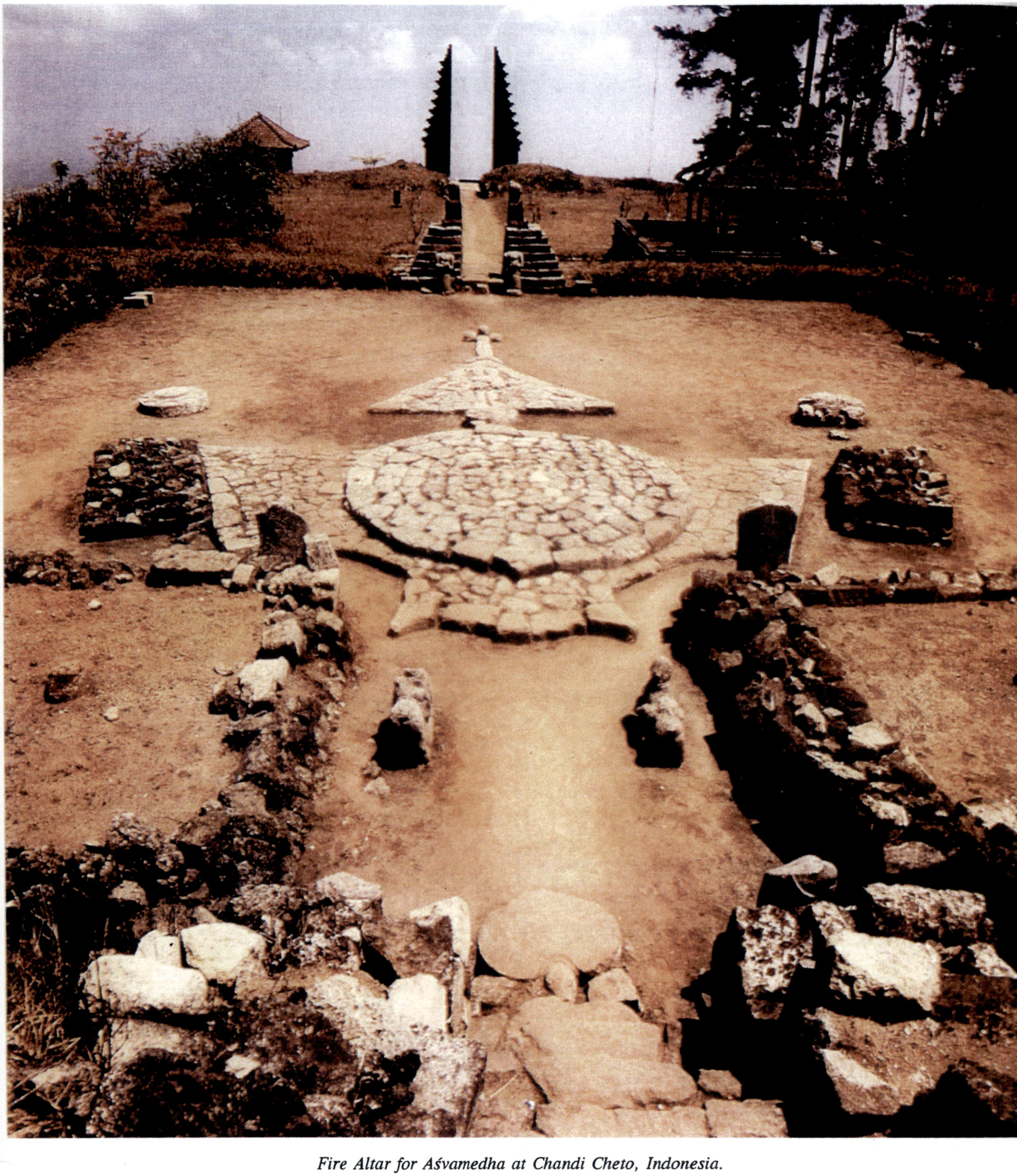

Fire Altar for Aśvamedha at Chandi Cheto, Indonesia.

19

FIRE ALTAR FOR AŚVAMEDHA CEREMONY IN INDONESIA

Chandi Cheto in the island of Java in Indonesia, built on fourteen terraces on mount Lawu, is a fifteenth century structure. The focal point for this chapter is its eighth terrace where an enormous figure of a bird is built. Along with the bird there are three circles, a triangle with animal figures engraved on it, six platform-like seats, a liṅgga, some divine images, guardians and animals. The date of the construction of the temple, suggested by the animal figures carved on the triangle is AD 1451 and those given in the inscriptions are: AD 1468, 1472 and 1475. The flat figure of the bird is identified as an enormous bat by Bernett Kempers (pl. 335).

Possibly the temple was built for royal consecration of the lingga and performance of Aśvamedha sacrifice. Kempers writes that there is a circle containing a seven-pointed star in front of the bat's head and two are on the sides with nine-pointed stars. Above the middle circle there is a triangle with nine animal figures engraved on it. These are: three frogs, a crab, a mini crab with a long spine, three iguanos and an eel with an ascetic's coiffure. Guardians stand on either side of the gateway on the 8th terrace. There are six platforms: four square and two rectangular. The highest terrace (no. fourteen) has pointed stones.

Chandi Sukuh and Cheto stand on the western slope of mount Lawu, at a height of 910 and 1470 mts. above sea level. They are the last temples constructed by the Hindu-Javanese kings of East Java, as a clarion call to defend the Hindu-Javanese civilization, suffering from political instability, inter dynastic rivalries and internal as well as external threats. Moreover growing Islamic community posed a danger to their classical culture and rule of Hindu-Javanese kings. Eventually fifteenth century turned into a period of decline for the Majapahit Empire.

Hypothesis

The temple was built for a royal consecration of the liṅgga and an Aśvamedha sacrifice. The enormous flat figure of the bird, falcon or śyena was the Vedic altar meant for the performance.

Fire Alter for Aśvamedha

A Vedic altar for Aśvamedha fire may be piled in different forms, such as that of a trough (*droṇa*), a chariot wheel (*ratha-cakra*), a falcon (*śyena*), heron (*kaṅka*), eagle (*suparṇa*): *śyenacitam cinvīta suvargakāmaḥ/* ....(Taittirīya-saṁhitā 5.4.11). In Mahābhārata a falcon shaped altar for *agnicayana* was constructed by Yudhiṣṭhira for Aśvamedha ceremony.

The flat figure on the 8th terrace of Chandi Cheto can be identified as *śyena*, a symbol of power. *Śyena* means a hawk, falcon and violence. *Śyena-karaṇam* means burning on a separate funeral pile, a hawk like, i.e. rash and desperate. It is the name of a strong bird of prey in Ṛgveda (1.32.14, 118.11,163.1, 165.2). Later in Post-Vedic Sanskrit (AV. 3.3.4, vii.41.2, 11.9.9) it means a falcon or a hawk. It is the swiftest bird (Taittirīya-saṁhitā 2.4.7.1, 5.4.11.1; Saḍviṁśa-brāhmaṇa 3.8) and a source of terror for smaller birds (Ṛgveda 2.42.2; Av. 5.21.6). It is the strongest of birds (Kāṭhaka-saṁhitā 37.14). It attacks herds (Ṛgveda. 4.38.5). This corresponds well enough with the eagle's known habit of carrying off young lambs. It watches over men, *nṛ-cakṣas* (AV. 7.41.2), refers, no doubt to its lofty flight in air (Macdonell & Keith 1982:2.26). It brings the Soma from heaven (see Bloomfield, Journal of the American Oriental Society 16.1-24).

Aśvamedha Performed on mountains

Performance of Aśvamedha on mountains was a common phenomena in ancient India. Āśvamedhika-parva (25) of Mahābhārata says that Aśvamedha-yajña was performed in the northern Himālayas near mount Meru by Yudhiṣṭhira:

Meruṁ parvatamāsādya himavatpārśva uttare |
Kāñcanaḥ sumahān pādastatra karma cakāra saḥ ||

Chandi Ceto stands on mount Lawu. Mount Lawu stood in the middle of the triangle formed by the three states: Salatiga in the north, Surakarta in the south and Kediri in the east. It was transformed into mount Meru by Bhre Daha to construct temples and perform rituals for gaining political power.

The temples were built to triumph over adverse forces threatening the core values and to ward off destabilization of the Javanese state by external aggression. Rites were performed on the slopes of volcanic mountains at the sanctuaries on terraces. The three temples built to ward off the impending auguries, formed a sacred cosmic triangle, that bathed the surrounding area of Central and East Java with the beneficial radiation. The triangle intended to be renaissance of dharma, called *dharmodaya* in Sanskrit, the resurgence of *dharma* and thereby national stability and integrity.

Empowerment of the Javanese Kings

Javanese always turned to their ancestral faiths, guardians and protectors and performed rituals and ceremonies to invoke the protective powers to seek help when their empires ran into difficult times. They performed sacred rituals to renew their divine mandate to rule. Such ceremonies were performed periodically or in time of crisis and threats to their lands. Kings were empowered through sacred rituals by the kraton *purohits* to become *cakravartins*. It was thought to be a sacred duty of a king to fight to extend boundaries of his kingdom. According to Āśvamedhika-parva (7) of Mahābhārata, it is a duty of a *kṣatriya* to conquer the earth. Special temples were constructed for such activities by kings and members of royal families.

East Javanese kings sought resurgence of their political power at the time of crisis, through religious measures, during the fifteenth century. They invoked protective powers for divine empowerment, performed rituals and ceremonies, constructed temples, enshrined images, worshipped and consecrated liṅggas.

Liṅgga Worship

Śaivism was the official religion of the Majapahit state. Royal patronage was always available for the ambitious enterprise for temple building for national defense and empowerment of kings. The liṅgga found from Chandi Cheto, should have been from the main sanctuary and consecrated by the then ruling king. Such liṅggas were worshipped for sovereignty. The Svāyambhuva liṅgga was superior and its safety was the sacred duty of the state. If removed from its setting or thrown out it would cause destruction of the king and his kingdom. It is described in the Uttarakāṇḍa of Rāmāyaṇa, that Rāvaṇa worshipped the golden liṅgga. He always used to carry it with him wherever he used to go. He worshipped it constantly for sovereignty.

Decline of the Majapahit Empire

Kṛtanagara, a powerful King of the Singasari dynasty, achieved supremacy over other kingdoms of Central Java, several states of Sumatra and some overseas territories of the archipelago. He laid the foundations of the Majapahit Empire (AD 1293-1520). The religious and political hegemony of Majapahit Empire began to decline by the end of the 14th century. There was a loose system of external dependencies and tributary states stretching from Java to Sumatra, Malaya and the Eastern islands with the Imperial capital at Majapahit.

Suhita's brother Bhre Tumapēl/Kṛtavijaya ruled in AD 1447-1451. King Bhre Pamotan ascended the Majapahit throne in AD 1451 after a turmoil. In AD 1451-1453 Bhre Pamotan/Rājasa-vardhana held his court at Kahuripan. His reign was followed by a kingless period from AD 1453 to 1456. Then Hyang Pūrvaviśeṣa ruled from AD 1456-1466. In AD 1460 an ambassador of Hyang Pūrvaviśeṣa caused a scandal in China by killing six priests of another mission in a drunken brawl. Bhre Panden Salas/Singha-vikrama-vardhana reigned in AD 1466-68/78. In AD 1478 the capital city of Majapahit, the machinery of Imperial Govt. and the surrounding territories were brought under Islamic rule. A Hindu king Raṇavijaya was ruling in AD 1486.

1. Internal factors leading to the decline of Majapahit:

a. Weak agricultural economy of Majapahit was not in a position to compete with the economic powers of the coastal Islamic community.

b. Regional rebellions against the central authority, were a threat for political stability.

c. Dynastic conflicts and protracted civil wars between the rulers of the Majapahit and the powerful house of Daha with its kraton at Kediri led to disintegration of the Empire.

d. The rulers of Daha had a perpetual quest to wrest the supremacy over Java. Their quest was insatiable. It culminated in Bhre Daha's uprising against Queen Suhita in AD 1437.

Bhre Daha and other nobles believed that the policies of Daha-Kediri were detrimental to the preservation of core values and institutions of Hindu-Javanese civilization and Queen Suhita should be replaced and the throne to be assumed by effective protectors of the social, cultural and the religious heritage. So Bhre Daha rebelled against Suhita in AD 1437. He sought divine empowerment to become a *cakravarti* king.

2. External factors leading to the decline of Majapahit:

a. Expansionist policy of Chinese Imperial Court under the Mongols was a threat to them because China was interested in setting up a system of tributaries in South-east Asia by encouraging the Majapahit dependencies to secede and join the Peking's vigorously promoted hegemony in that part. The sovereignty of Majapahit with its overseas dependencies on the Malaya peninsula and Sumatra, was eroded.

b. Direct and indirect pressure was exerted upon Majapahit from Peking. Suhita was unable to counter them by military force, so she sought to accommodate by compromise and concessions. Chinese were appointed by her to administer the port cities of Java. Such appointments facilitated the access of the Chinese to the highest places at Suhita's court. The privilege attached to their status became a source of serious resentment and disloyalty among nobility and some native aristocratic Javanese families.

3. Danger from Islamic settlements:

Emergence of the Islamic commercial communities in the port cities of the coastal regions of Sumatra and Central Java, on the periphery of the empire posed a danger for Majapahit. The two factors: expansionist policy of China and growth of Islamic community, were inter linked. Chinese admiral Cheng Ho in the Chinese Imperial navy was a Hanafi Muslim. Chinese had built a mosque in Java that was visited by him in AD 1413. He promoted the strategic interests of the Chinese Court and also of the Chinese Muslims in the coastal cities. It was a time for Majapahit to meet the challenges, but Queen Suhita was not in a position to face them and adopted a policy of compromise.

Bhre Daha was keen to become a c*akravarti* king, the ruler of the world, ruling the entire Java including the territories of Majapahit. He sought empowerment.

Kūrma, Tortoise: A Symbol of Brahmā

At the centre of the falcon on the 8th terrace of Chandi Cheto is a tortoise. A series of small tortoises is seen in front of the stairs. On the other terraces also, there is a tortoise in front of the steps. It is a symbol of creation. A legend suggests that Prajāpati having assumed the form of a tortoise, created living beings. *Kūrma* and *Kaśyapa* mean the same object. All the creatures are said to be descended from *Kaśyapa* (Śatapatha-brāhmaṇa 7.5.1.5): *sa yat kūrmo nāma/ etadvai rūpam kṛtvā prajāpatiḥ prajā asrjata yadasṛjatakarot tadakarot tasmāt kūrmaḥ kaśyapo vai kūrmas tasmādāhuḥ sarvāḥ prajāḥ kaśyapa iti*Ç (Kane 1941:2.2.715). In Aśvamedha a paste of buttermilk, honey and yogurt was applied on the body of a tortoise to be kept for the ceremony.

Animals Sacrificed for Aśvamedha

There are five kinds of animals carved on the triangle above the head of the falcon at Chandi Ceto. This symbolizes that the ritual includes all classes of animals. In the chapter on Aśvamedha in Mādhyandinīya Śatapatha-brāhmaṇa (13.2.4) there is a section that describes sacrifice of village and forest animals. (Kane 1941:2.2.1247). Before piling up the fire altar five animals were sacrificed. Their heads were placed into the altar and their trunks were thrown in water, which was used to make bricks from clay. *Kātyāyana-śrauta-sūtra* (16.1.32) permits putting up clay heads in place of sacrificing animals. It also prescribes to place golden images of the animals.

Six Platforms on the Terrace

Four square and two rectangular platforms are built along the terrace on the eighth level. Possibly four of them were meant for the four queens who accompanied the king for the ceremony, the fifth for the king and the sixth for the *purohita*. According to the *Dharma-śāstras* four queens represent the four directions. The first queen, *Mahīṣi*, is accompanied by princesses, the second queen Vāvātā, the most beloved of the king is accompanied by girls from the *kṣatrīya* families, the third queen, Parivṛkti comes with the girls of village chiefs and the fourth queen, Pālāgalī comes with the girls of lower class (Kane Hindi version, I.566). Thus all the four classes of society are represented. The guardians of the four directions are invoked: Āpyas, Sādhyas, Anvādhyas and Maruts (Kak 2002:49). Another possibility is that the four seats were for Hotā, Udgātā, Adhvaryu and Brahmā, the four Brahmins and the fifth for the king and the sixth for the queen.

The theme of the four-fold division of royal power runs throughout the rite. The four divisions symbolize four cardinal directions. They are also the base, the body, the activity and the division of the king and their embodiments. The reference to the four divisions is to emphasize gathering together of the universe that is broken into so many in ordinary appearances. The power of the king rises to the heaven as the sun ascends the heaven after its rejuvenation (Kak 2002:56).

Aśvamedha-yajña

It may be concluded on the basis of the above mentioned remains found from Chandi Cheto, that the temple was built for an Aśvamedha ceremony, wherein religious and political elements were deftly inter-woven. Kings performed it to establish their supreme sovereignty and thereby to become *cakravatīs*. When Indra's energies or vital powers departed from him, the gods restored them by means of this sacrifice: *Indrasya vai yatra/ indriyāṇi vvīryāṇi vvyudakkrāmāns tāni devā 'etenaiva yajñena punaḥ samādadhur yyattpayoggrāhaśca surāggrāhaúcca gṛhyanta* '.......(Śatapatha-brāhmaṇa 12.8.1.1).

Aśvamedha, one of the most significant rituals is a celebration of social harmony achieved by transcendence of fundamental conflicts between various sources of power. It allows a king to renew his power. He may rule a smaller or a bigger kingdom.

Aśvamedha has been described as a celebrated sacrifice since Vedic age. Aśvamedha is also the name of a prince mentioned in a hymn of Ṛgveda (5.27.4-6, cf. Ludwig, Translation of Ṛgveda 3.275) which contains a *dānastuti* of Tryāruṇa, and to which three verses have been added in praise of Aśvāmedha. It is the patronymic of an unnamed prince, who is mentioned in a *dānastuti* in the Ṛgveda (8.68.15,16) (Macdonell & Keith 1982:1.69). In Mahābhārata there is a chapter on the ceremony performed by Yudhiṣṭhira, entitled Āśvamedhika-parva. Several monarchs are enumerated in Śatapatha-brāhmaṇa (13.1-5) and Taittirīya-brāhmaṇa (3.8-9) who performed the sacrifice. A paramount sovereign or a crowned king who is not *sārvabhauma* may perform this sacrifice (Āpastamba-śrauta-sūtra 20.1.1, Lāṭyāyana-śrauta-sūtra 9.10.17). A king, who performed the ceremony a hundred times, would be able to acquire the throne of Indra himself.

A particular type of horse was selected, consecrated and was let loose after certain ceremonies. A victory card was fixed on horse's head. It was accompanied by soldiers and representatives of the king to wander from one kingdom to another. Those who opposed the sovereignty of the king could stop the horse and tie it. Then the king had to defeat him before conducting the *yajña* (Mani 1975:67).

Its performance was considered to be a feat and an achievement in the case of a monarch like Samudragupta, whose coins bore the legend of *Aśvamedha parākramaḥ* (Salitore 1981:140). In the eighteenth century Savai Jayasingh, King of Amber, performed an Aśvamedha (Kane 1941:2.2.1239). Śatapatha-brāhmaṇa (13.1.6.3) states: *rāṣṭram vā aśvamedhaḥ*, Aśvamedha is the national or royal sway. It sums up the various aspects of the sacrifice that associates all classes of people in its year-long ritual. The power of a king mirrors in the power of a brāhmaṇa.

Śatapatha-brāhmaṇa 13.3.7 details the importance of performing Aśvamedha. The sacrifice is called strengthful, plenteous, obtainment, distinction food, excelling in hitting and so on. So it provides all to the one who performs this ceremony: *yatraitena yajñena yajante sarvvameva pprabhūta bhavati* (1) ... ...

In Āśvamedhika-parva of Mahābhārata (8-10) Yudhiṣṭhira is advised to perform four types of *yajñas*: *Rājasūya, Aśvamedha, Sārvamedha* and *Naramedha* and donates bountifully at the time of *Aśvamedha* like Lord Rama, the son of Daśaratha and his forefathers.

Conclusion - The fire altar built to the shape of a bird *Śyena,* a series of small tortoises, animal figures carved on the triangle, six platforms built on the terrace and the mountain, were supposed to be a sacred place on which the temple Chandi Cheto was constructed, for performance of Aśvamedha-yajñā ceremony by a Javanese king to overcome the dangers posed by internal as well as external factors leading to instability, rivalries and finally to the decline of the Majapahit empire.

Appendix 1

Chronology of events

1. 1222 Ken Angrok/*Rajasa.*
2. 1227 Anūṣapati, (stepson of no.1, Ken Angrok).
3. 1248 Tohjaya (son of no.1, Ken Angrok).
4. 1248 Viṣṇu-vardhana (son of no.2, Anusapati).

   1268 Kṛtanagara (son of no.4, Viṣṇu-vardhana).
5. 1289 Kṛtanagara expelled the Chinese ambassador of Kublai Khan.

6. 1292 Jayakatwang of Kediri (ususrper), assassinated Kṛtanagara.

7. 1293 Vijaya/Kṛtarājasa Jaya-vardhana (nephew and son-in-law of Kṛtanagara defeated Jayakatwang with the help of Chinese. He moved to a new capital named Majapahit and laid the foundations of the new empire Majapahit that consisted of Singasari and Daha-Kediri.

Chinese troops failed in their invasion

8. 1309 Jayanagara (son of no.7, Kṛtarājasa Jaya-vardhana and his Sumatran Queen Dara Petak).

9. 1329 Tribhuvana (daughter of no.7, Kṛtarājasa Jaya-vardhana).

10. 1350 Hayam Wuruk/Rājasanagara (son of no. 9, Tribhuvana). A period of peace and prosperity. His empire consisted of 14 depedencies. He indulged in all pleasures: beautiful maidens from Janggala and Kediri were selected for him and the prettiest girls of those captured were brought to his harem (Hall 1970:91).

1373 Chinese established suzerainty over Dharmāśraya.

1374 Chinese suzerainty over Palembang.

1375 Chinese suzerainty over Malayupura.

1376 Chinese recognized Suvarṇabhūmi as an independent state.

11. 1389 Vikrama-vardhana (nephew and son-in-law of no. 10, Rājasanagara) His reign was a period of rapid decline. Vīrabhūmi refused to recognize the authority of Majapahit, which fatally weakened Majapahit control over subject states (Hall 1970:92).

1401 Civil war broke out.

1405 Chinese court dispatched Admiral Cheng Ho to Sumatra. He landed with his fleet on the shores of Java three times: for the first time he came in 1405 and for the third in 1413. In his last journey he visited the mosque of the Chinese community.

1406 Vīrabhūmi was assassinated, and his head was brought to Majapahit as a token of the restoration of the unity of the kingdom.

1408 King Vikrama-vardhana accorded a permanent status to a Chinese representative. Copper coins minted in China circulated throughout Majapahit. A mosque was built by Chinese Muslims.

1429 Vikrama-vardhana dies.

12. 1429 Suhita (daughter of no. 11, Vikrama-vardhana).

1437 Bhre Daha rebelled against Suhita and occupied the throne of Majapahit for a short time.

Suhita led a counter attack and Bhre Daha retreated into NE of Surakarta. Established an independent state.

Bhre Daha consecrated a Royal liṅgga to claim a mandate of a *cakravartin* to rule the whole of Java.

Suhita's forces set the royal palace on fire, Suhita resumed the throne.

Bhre Daha retreated into Old Mendang, Gribigan and Kemoelan region, located northeast of Surakarta, established a new state and declared it independent of Majapahit.

Western gate of Sukuh was built.

1440 Daha consecrated the liṅgga at Sukuh to reclaim the lost throne by a brahmin of the Giridhra-vardhana family, Majapahit's old rival.

1443 A statue of Bhīma was consecrated at Chandi Sukuh.

13. 1447-51 Bhre Tumapel/Kṛtavijaya (son of No.11, Vikrama-vardhana).

1449 Bas relief at Sukuh: Bhīma kills Bakāsura.

1451-53 Bhre Pamotan/Rājasa-vardhana held court at Keling Kahuripan.

1451 Date of Ceto through animal figures.

1453-56 Interregnum (Hall 1970:93).

1456-66 Bhre Venker/Hyang Purvaviśeṣa.

Ambassador of Hyang Purvaviśeṣa caused a scandal in China by killing six priests of another mission in a drunken brawl (Hall 93).

1466 Bhre Venker died.

1466-68 Bhre Panden Salas/Siṁhavikrama-vardhana.

A copper plate of 1473 refers to Siṁhavikrama-vardhana as the sole king of Yavabhūmi, comprising of two kingdoms Janggala and Kediri.

1468 Abandoned kraton at Majapahit.

1468-78 Bhre Kṛtabhūmi.

1475 Dates given in the inscriptions at Ceto.

Youngest of the four sons of Sinagara.

Majapahit had lost its supremacy in Java.

Unification

1478-86 Raṇavijaya, reigning. Resisted Islamization.

1486-1527 Girīndra-vardhana Dyah Raṇavijaya ascended the throne of Majapahit with the consent of its nobles without a fight. The long cherished ambition of his predecessors was fulfilled. The spirit of the chandis triumphed.

1516 Pati Udara, reigning.

1527 Fall of Hindu kingdom.

LITERATURE CITED

Aśvalayana-śrauta-sūtra, Nārāyana-krta-vrtti-sameta, Śrī-Lāl-Bahādur-śastrī Kendrīya-sanskrit-vidyāpītham, Nūtana-dillī, 1994-5

Hall 1970
Hall, D.G.E., *A History of South-east Asia,* Macmillan, New York 1970

Kak 2002
Subhash Kak, *The Aśvamedha,* Motilal Banarsidas, Delhi 2002

Kane 1941
Pandurang Vaman Kane, *History of Dharmasastras,* II.II, Bhandarakar Oriental Research Institute, Poona 1941

Kempers 1959
Kempers, Bernet, A.J., *Ancient Indonesian Art,* N.V. Boekhandel Antiquariaat en Uitgeverij C.P.J. van der Peet, Amsterdam, 1959

Macdonell and Keith, 1982
Macdonell and Keith, *Vedic Index,* Motilal Banarsidas, Delhi, 1982

Mahabharata
Dr. Pt. Śrīpāda Dāmodara Sātvalekara ed., *Mahābhārata,* Svādhyāya Mandala, Balasara, 1977

Majumdar 1986
Majumdar, R.C., *Suvarnadvipa,* Vol. 1, Gian Publishing House, Delhi, 1986

Mani 1975
Vettam Mani, *Puranic Encyclopedia,* Motilal Banarasidas, Delhi, 1975

Maxmüller 1900
Maxmüller, F. Max, *Sacred Books of the East,* XLI, Oxford, Clarendon Press, 1900

Salitore 1981
Salitore, R.N., *Encyclopaedia of Indian Culture,* Vol. 1, Sterling Publishers, New Delhi, 1981

20

THE EARLIEST SANSKRIT DOCUMENTS FROM INDONESIA

Languages advance with the advancement of civilizations, new inventions require new terminology. The source for the new terminology enriching a language must be rich. Sanskrit stood as the richest language in the early years of Christian era for most of the countries of the Asian sub-continent. It became a language of the intellectual elite and a major uniting force among them. Nothing could replace Sanskrit, a language par excellence, a language so divine and rich. Indian religions: Śaivism, Vaiṣṇavism and Buddhism, were the main carriers of Sanskrit abroad. It went as a vehicle of the knowledge of things Indian. As an international language for the people of the Southeast Asian countries, it played an important role in their cultural lives also.

Sanskrit served as the language of learning, it contributed towards intellectual advancement, gave greatest amount of freedom of thought and action enriching the languages and literatures, raising aspirations of life, ideals and tendencies, modes of living and thinking, social, political, economic and spiritual life. It forms the substratum in the simple life of the people. An alphabetical culture was introduced with Sanskrit; non-writing people became writing people. They began to give the highest honour to the poets Maharṣi Vyāsa and Vālmīki, in the countries of Southeast Asia.

The earliest lithic records from most of the countries in SEA are in Sanskrit. The first inscription from South Vietnam formerly known as Champā is from Vo Canh a place on the sea coast is inscribed in Sanskrit language and in Kuṣāṇa script of Kaniṣka's period. The date ascribed to the record is 2nd-4th century. Thirty inscriptions discovered from Telaga Batu to the east of the city of Palembang in Sumatra bear the inscription that reads *Jayasiddha yātrā*. Some of them have an additional word *sarvatattva*, evidently they were laid by pilgrims as Telaga Batu was a place of pilgrimage. There are other inscriptions also which record *śrīvijaya jayasidha yātrā* in order to celebrate a victory over Śrīvijaya. Three or four lines in Sanskrit in late Pallava script are sometimes written on bricks of hardened clay.

A high erudition in Sanskrit marked the culture of Cambodia for many centuries. This is amply proved by the Sanskrit inscriptions found in large numbers all over Cambodia from 5th to14th century AD. The first collection of these inscriptions was published as early as 1885. The first dated inscription belongs to the reign of Jayavarman II (AD 475 - 512). The Angkor Borei inscription of AD 533 probably represents the ruins of the ancient city of Vyādhapura surrounded by a rampart, (Majumdar 1953:8). In Laos lithic records begin to appear from AD 1283. Their script is known as Dhamma (=*dharma*); this is the script that is used in inscriptions, poetry, romance, administrative records and correspondence etc.

In Indonesia Sanskrit influenced all the spheres of social and cultural life. It changed their ways of thinking, feeling and living. Their day begins with greeting in Sanskrit: *om svastyastu;* while in Thailand it is *udaya svasti*. The earliest Sanskrit inscriptions discovered in Indonesia are from the fourth century A.D.

1-4 Four inscriptions by Pūrṇavarman from Borneo, c Śaka 322, c 400 AD

Four inscriptions inscribed on octagonal pillars finely hewn, were discovered from Kutei, east of Borneo in 1880, written in Sanskrit. The script used in them is fourth century Pallava Indian script. Kutei was a centre of Indian art and culture. The kingdom seems to have been prosperous. Brāhmaṇas were men of learning, *aśvamedha yajña* was seen as the highest ceremony for over lordship. A golden image of Viṣṇu, images of Gaṇeśa, Nandī, śivaliṅggas and other several images are discovered from there. The inscriptions give details of the first king Aśvavarmā who was ceremonially initiated according to Hindu rites. *Varman* means 'an armous'. It was a popular title taken by the kings in SEA. In Cambodia there were many kings who used it as a suffix to their names: Jayavarman, Guṇavarman, Rudravarman and Bhadravarman etc.

The first inscription among this group of four, says that King Aśvavarmā was the son of the great King Kuṇḍuṅga who established a dynasty. He had three great sons, who were brilliant like the three fires. One of them, who was the eldest, most powerful and self restraint, Mūlavarmā performed a *yajña* ceremony and the pillar was erected by the Brāhmaṇas:

Śrīmataḥ śrīnarendrasya kuṇḍaṅgasya mahātmanaḥ|
Putrośvavarmā vikhyātaḥ vaṁśakartā yathāṁśsumān||
Tasya putraḥ mahātmanaḥ trayastraya ivagnayaḥ|
Teṣāmtrayāṇām pravaraḥ tapobaladamānvitaḥ||
Śrīmūlavarmā rājendro yaṣṭvā bahusuvarṇakam|
Tasya yajñasya yūpoyam dvijendraiḥ samprakalpitah||

According to the second inscription the glorious King of the kings Mūlavarma donated twenty thousand cows to the Brāhmaṇas who were brilliant like fire and they in turn erected this pillar of glory at a place called Vaprakeśvara:

Śrīmato nṛpamukhyasya rājñaḥ śrī mūlavarmaṇaḥ |
Dānam puṇyatame kṣetre yaddattam vaprakeśvare ||
Dvijatibhyognikalpebhyaḥ viṁśatirgosāhasrikam |
Tasya puṇyasya yūpoyaṁ kṛto viprairihāgataiḥ ||

All the prominent Brahmaṇas, sages and people are requested to listen to the meritorious deeds of the king who donated bountifully, cows and all that the Brāhmaṇas required in the third inscription:

Śrīmadvirājakīrtteḥ rājñaḥ śrīmūlavarmaṇaḥ puṇyam |
Sriṇvantu vipramukhyāḥ ye cānye sādhavaḥ puruṣāḥ ||

Bahudāna jīvadānam sakalpavṛkṣam sabhūmidānaṁca |
Teṣām puṇya gaṇānām yūpoyam sthāpito vipraiḥ ||

In the fourth inscription the king is compared to Bhagīratha, the son of King Sagara:

Sagarasya yathā rājñaḥ samutpanno bhagīrathaḥ |
..............*Mūlavarmmā*.................. || (Raghu Vira 1978:29-34)

These are the earliest written record of Indo-Indonesian contacts but the exact date is unknown. The term Yavadvīpa for Java comes for the first time in the Rāmāyaṇa by Vālmīki. Literally it means an island shaped like a barley corn, a very apt graphic name parallel to Āmradvīpa, a mango island, a synonym for Śrīlanka and Katāh *dvīpa* for Kedah in Malaysia.

5-8 Four inscriptions from Jakarta by Pūrṇavarman, c Śaka 372, c 450 AD

In the second half of the 5th century the kingdom of Taruma was situated in west Java near the northern coastal area. It can be guessed on the basis of inscriptions in Pallava script that the art and technique of writing came from south India. By that time Indonesians had mastered Sanskrit language, the concept of *nagara*/town was known to them. These inscriptions are from Ci Aruton, Jambu, Kebon kapi and Tugu. The King Pūrṇavarman is referred to in three of these inscriptions. Java was divided into three kingdoms, Pūrṇavarman's kingdom Trauma was in the extreme west, Kalinga or Holing was in the centre. (Sarkar 1971: 6-9).

a. Tugu inscription

In the Tugu inscription *rājādhirāja* the overlord of the kings, who was strong armed and *guru* and had reached the famous town, is mentioned to have the honour of digging Chandrabhāgā river:

Purā rājādhirājena guruṇā pīnabāhunā |
khātā khyātam purīm prāpya chandrabhāgārṇavam yayau ||

Another river Gomatī was dug through the camping ground of pitāmaha rājarṣi:

Āyatā śaṭsahasreṇa dhanuṣāṁ sa śatena ca |
Dvāviṅśena nadī ramyā gomatī nirmalodakā ||
Pitāmahasya rājrṣervvidāryya śibarāvanim |
Brāhmaṇairgosahasreṇa prayāti kṛtadakṣiṇā ||

[Pūrṇavarmā] dug the charming river Gōmatī, of pure water, in length six thousand one hundred and twenty-one dhanus, [That river] by digging through the camping ground of the grandfather and royal sage, floweth forth after having been endowed by the Brāhmaṇas with the gift of a thousand cows.

Digging of rivers gave him both fame and merits. Gomatī and Chandrabhāgā are the examples of geographical names found in Java. Endless lists can be made of Sanskrit names, names of divine or mythological powers and super human figures. It has left an unmistakable impact on the vocabulary of the Javanese; traces are found in legends and traditions, and genealogies of kings.

Some of the names of divine beings have become common nouns; Surabhi is a cow in general; Takṣaka can be any serpent and a Brāhmaṇa is a priest, etc.

b. The Ci-aruton Rock Inscription

Augmenting reign of the King Pūrṇavarman, the illustrious ruler of Taruma is described in the inscription, comparing his footprints to Lord Viṣṇu. He ruled for a fairly long period when Indo-Aryan culture had become popular there:

Vikrāntasyāvanipateḥ Śrīmataḥ Pūrṇavarmaṇaḥ |
Tārumanagarendrasya Viṣṇoriva pādadvayaṁ ||

Of the mighty ruler of the world the illusrious Purnavarman (who is) lord of the town of Taruma (his) pair of footprints are comparable to Visnu's.

The script of the inscription is Pallava Grantha character of archaic variety.

c. Kebon Kopi inscription

The inscription is small and damaged. Two huge footprints of an elephant are carved on both the sides of the inscription. Again the King is mentioned as a ruler of Taruma, possibly he is Pūrṇavarman. The inscription speaks about Airāvata like footprints of the Lord of Taruma who is great in conquering ..:

..........*Jayaviśālasya tārumendrasya hastinaḥ* |
..........*airāvatābhasya vibhātīdampādadvayaṁ* ||

Here shineth the pair of footprints of the .... Airavata-like elephant of the lord of Taruma (who is) great in conquering.....

d. Jambu inscription

The inscription was found from Jambu from the top of a hillock, to the west of Bogor. A pair of footprints is carved over the inscription, representing him as ever dexterous in demolishing towns of enemies. The inscription in two lines is in *sragdharā* meter, incised after the death of the king; a military hero Pūrṇavarman of Taruma. His armor is said to be impenetrable to the arrows of the multitude of enemies:

Śrīmāndātā kṛtajño narapatirasamo yaḥ purā tārumāyām |
Nāmnā śrī pūrṇavarmmā pracuraripuśarābhedya vikhyātavarmmo ||
Tasyedaṁ pādavimbadvayam arinagarotsadane nityadakṣam |
Bhaktānām yandripānām bhavati sukhakaram śalyabhūtam ripūṇām ||

(Sarkar 1971:1.1-10)

Illustrious, magnificent, true to his duty was the unequalled lord of men, the illustrious Pūrṇavarmman by name, who once (ruled) at Tārumā and whose famous armour was impenetrable to the arrows of a multitude of enemies. Of him, this is the representation of the pair of footprints which, ever dextrous in demolishing towns of enemies, is salutary to devoted princes (but) like darts to his enemies.

9. Tuk Mas inscription, c Śaka 422, c AD 500

The inscription on a large boulder was found from the spring called Tuk Mas at the foot of the volcano Merabu in Central Java. Water shoots up at a number of places while Tuk Mas is said to be the biggest of all those fountains. Tuk Mas literally means Golden Spring. Presence of Śaivism and Vaiṣṇavism is witnessed by the space above the inscription filled by sixteen symbols connected to the worship of Śiva and Viṣṇu: two water pots, a trident, an axe, a club, four lotus rosettes, a knife, a wheel, a conch, a shell and a mace. The spring is compared to the river Gaṅgā gushing out, originating from pure lotuses:

Iyantuśucyamburuhanujata kvacicchīlvālukānirgateyam |
Kvacitprakīrṇṇa subhāṣitatoya samprasrata medhyakarīva gaṅgā ||

Originating from pure (or bright) lotuses, (here from), gushes out this (spring or streamlet), which is as purifying as the Ganges, coming out in some places from stone and sand, in others, spreading out its auspicious and cool water.

Devotion to Viṣṇu and Śiva has played an important role in the religious, philosophic and art history of SEA. They have inspired mighty monuments in brick and stone, images in stone and bronze and panels on temple walls.

10. Canggal Inscription by Sañjaya Śaka 654, 6th Oct. AD 732

There is a gap between the Sanskrit inscriptions by Pūrṇavarman of the 5th century and the 8th century inscription incised at the auspicious occasion of the construction of a Śaivite temple at Canggal, SE of Borobudur. The Canggal inscription is the earliest dated record discovered from the ruins on Gunung Wukir incised beautifully and legibly in middle Grantha script of Southern India. It records erection of a Śiva liṅgga by King Sañjaya of the Mataram dynasty in Kuñjarakuñja in the island of Java:

Śakendre vigate śrutīndriyarasairangīkṛte vatsare |
Vārendau dhavala trayodaśītithau bhadtrottare kārttike ||
Lagnekumbhamaye sthirāṅśavidite prātiṣṭhipat parvate |
Liṅggaṁ lakṣaṇalakṣitannarapatiśśrīsañjaya śāntaye ||1||

When the year of Śaka king that is brought to numbers with four, five and six (654) was passed, on Monday, the thirteenth day of bright half of the month which follows Bhadrā in (the month) of Kārtikka, while the *lagna* stood under Kumbha in the part called "fixed", the king, the illustrious Sañgaya for obtaining tranquility established on the hill a lingga with auspicious marks.

According to Stutterheim Kunjarakunja was the name of the district where Sañjaya erected this sanctuary. Sañjaya as a king of the Mataram dynasty, is also mentioned in an inscription discovered from Kedu in Central Java, dated 907. It gives a list of the predecessors of the reigning king Mahārāja Balitungga, Sañjaya is the founder of the dynasty, all the remaining eight kings bear the title "Śrī Mahārāja". King Sañjaya is accredited with sensational conquests in Bali, Sumatra and even in Cambodia upto the borders of China (Hall 1970:46). The chandi was built by Sañjaya as an outward sign and manifestation of his claim to over-lordship and to demonstrate his greatness.

Lord Śiva is eulogized in 2nd-4th ślokas giving a detail iconography to protect and grant perfect bliss to his kingdom:

Gaṅgottuṅgga taraṅgga rañjita jaṭāmaulīndu chūḍāmaṇir|
Bhāsvatbhūti vibhūtidehavikasannāgendrahāradyutiḥ||
Śrīmatsvāñjali koṣakomalakarairdevaistu ya stūyate|
Sa śreyo bhavatām bhavo bhavatamassūryo dadātvadbhutam||2||

He who is a Sun in the darkness of the world; who has for his crest-jewel the moon on his matted locks which are beautified by the surging waves of the Ganges; on whose body dazzling with brilliance of ashes, scatters its brilliance the necklace of snakes; who is praised by the gods with graceful and soft palms (of their hands) folded in the form of a vessel; he, Śiva, may bestow on you the most perfect bliss!

Bhaktiprahvair munīndrairabhinutamasakṛt svarganirvāṇahetor|
Devairlekharṣabhādyairavanatamakutaiścumvitaṁ ṣaṭpadābhaiḥ||
Aṅgulyātamtrapatram nakhakiraṇalasat kesarārañjitāntam|
Deyāt śam śāśvataṁ vas trinayanacaraṇāninditāmbhojayugmam||3||

May that irreproachably beautiful pair of feet lotuses of the three eyed one (Śiva) which are constantly praised by the greatest sages by bending low in homage for their salvator in heaven, which are kissed by the greatest of gods and demons and others with their bent crowns which are (comparable to) the bees (that kiss the lotus); whereof the end is decorated by bright filaments of rays (issuing) from nails; may (that pair of feet) grant you perpetual bliss!

Aiśvaryātiśayodbhavatsumāhatamapyadbhutānāṁ nidhis|
Tyāgaikakantaratastanoti satatam yo viśvamayaṁ yoginām ||
Yostabhistanubhirjagatkarunaya pusnati na svarthato|
Bhuteṣaśśaśikhaṇḍabhūṣita jaṭasya tryamabakaḥ pātu naḥ||4||

May the three-eyed one (Śiva) whose matted locks are adorned with the crescent moon; who, by reason of excess of his divine attributes is a receptacle of great and even wonderful things; who, given to solitude, by his renunciation (of all things) always creates the wonder of yogins; who by his eight-fold bodies and through compassion, but not selfishness, sustains the universe, may be the lord of all beings, protect you!

These are followed by a prayer to Brahmā for gaining complete success. He is described as the self created, one who is revered by the gods, who has fixed the regulations of the world to the post of the *Vedas*, who is the source of religion, worldly prosperity and desire; whose body dazzles like gold and whose matted locks are comparable to the flames of the fire of his own body, may be the lord of yogins the venerable one, reward you with success:

Vibhraddhemavapussvadeha dahanajvālā ivodyajjaṭā |
Vedastambhasubaddhalokasamayo dharmmārthakāmodbhavaḥ ||

Devairvvanditapādapaṅkajayugo yogīśvaro yoginām |
Mānyo loka gururaddadātu bhavatāṁ siddhiṁ svayambhūr vibhuḥ ||5||

Viṣṇu is third in Trimūrti, he is the lord of Śrī, so he is prayed for prosperity. The form of Viṣṇu described here is in his Śeṣaśāyī form. He lies on the surface of the watery bed, petals of his eye lotuses are red through meditation, he is behymned by the gods for protection, he is always frowningly viewed by the goddess Śrī on seeing the beauty of her own image reflected on the side levels of the jewels on the upturned crown of the king of serpents.

In the following *ślokas* the island of Java is said to be abundantly supplied by rice grains and other seeds and rich in gold mines. And there is a place dedicated to Śambhu surrounded by the Ganges. The beautiful woodlands are inhabited by elephants. There ruled a king of noble lineage called Sannah, like a father who had subdued his enemies and protected the world for a long time doing justice like Manu. When he had gone to heaven due to the result of his accumulated merits then his son Sañjaya ruled the island. He is compared to mount meru possessing manifold qualities, looked bright like molten gold, he had most of the auspicious signs of a great man. He was honoured by the learned, excelled in bravery and other virtues like Raghu, overthrew many circles of feudal lords, his splendour spread in all the directions like Sun:

Yasmincāsti sāgarormiraśanāṃ śailasstanīmmedinīm |
Śete rājapathe jano na cakiścorairna cānyairbhayaih ||
Kīrttyāḍhyairalamarjjitāśca satatandharmmārthakāmā naraiḥ |
Nūnaṃ roditi roditīti sa kalirnnāsyaṅga cihnyānya bhuḥ ||

(Sarkar 1972:1.15-24)

He is ruling the earth which has for her girdle the waves of the sea and for her breasts the mountains, people can sleep on roadside without being startled by the thieves or by other fears. And men, rich in fame, always earned in plenty (the three aims of life, viz.) religion, wordly prosperity and the objects of desire. Certainly Kali is crying much in despair as no sign of his limbs is shining (i.e. is in existence).

The kings in SEA countries erected images of the divine in accordance with their own forms and features or they were apotheosized by their descendants after death. In this context also the king seems to have identified himself with Lord Śiva and ruled the kingdom.

11. The Inscription of Kañjuruha (Dinaya) Śaka 682, 28th Nov. 760 AD

Two stone fragments were found from Merjosari, NW of Malang kept at the then Batavia Museum dated Śaka 682, the earliest written record in Old Javanese script. It has some similarities with the Canggal inscription. The inscription opens with an account of the royal dynasty, Devasiṁha is followed by his son Limva known as Gajayāna. Gajayāna founded a temple dedicated to Agastya and enshrined an image made of black marble with the help of the officiating priests. Yatis and Veda knowing priests are particularly mentioned, a guesthouse was also constructed for the pilgrims. The cult of Agastya is closely associated to Śiva worship transmitted from south India. In most of the Śaiva temples images of Guru Agastya are enshrined along with images of Śiva,

Gaṇapati and Mahiṣāsuramardinī. The inscription is a witness to the popularity of Śaivism in Java which culminated in the tenth century. Writing of Śaiva philosophical texts began with the coming of Śaiva philosophy, over a hundred manuscripts on Śaivism are discovered from various parts of Indonesia. Bhuvanakoṣa is the earliest and the largest containing 525 *ślokas* in Sanskrit with commentary on them in Old Javanese. Sculptors and architects were given instructions in Sanskrit, e.g. the texts followed by the architects and sculptors who worked at Borobudur or Prambanan temples, were all written in Sanskrit.

12. Inscription of Kalasan, Śaka 700, 778 AD

The inscription was found at Kalasan in the plains of Prambanan to the east of Jogyakarta. Kalasan is a Buddhsit sanctuary dedicated to the worship of Tārā. The main image no longer exists there, possibly it was made of bronze and must have been taken away, posing problems for further research. The script of the inscription is Pre-Nāgarī similar to the 8th-11th century North Indian characters and differs from the earlier inscriptions.

The inscription witnesses close cultural contacts between India and Indonesia during the rule of Śailendras. It describes the foundation of a splendid temple dedicated to Tārā and opens with a laudatory verse to her. Foundation was laid down by the *guru* of the Śailendra king and an image was sculpted, a dwelling place was built for the monks who knew the vehicle of the discipline. All this was done by *ādeśaśāstrins* viz. Pangur, Tavan and Tirip in the prosperous reign of the king who was an ornament of the Śailendra dynasty. On this occasion a village was granted to the congregation of the Kalasan monks. Reference has been made to Kariyana Panankarana Śrīmān. The name is also found in the list of Mataram kings, given in Kedu inscription.

13. Kelurak Inscription, Śaka 704, 782 AD

The inscription was discovered from Kelurak to the north of Chandi Lara Jongrang incised in Old Nagari script. It opens with a salutaion to the three jewels: *namo ratnatrāyaya* and pays homage to Lokeśvara, Bhadreśvara, Viśveśvara, Vāgīśvara etc. An image of Mañjuśrī is enshrined for the welfare of the world: *rakṣārtham sarvasatvānām Mañjuśrī pratimākṛtiḥ*. *Vairīvaravīramardana,* a great king who torments and crushes his enemies is said to be the ornament of the Śailendra dynasty: *śailendravaṁśatilakena mahodayena yasyakrambujarājaḥ śirasā praṇamya.* The priests are said to be well versed in Vaipulya, the king is recommended by Tathāgata for the welfare of the world. The head of the king is purified by the dust of the feet of his *guru*, *caraṇaraja*. Mañjughoṣa, Mañjuvāk and Mañjuśrī are venerated for the protection of the kingdom, Mañjuśrī holds a blue lotus, his major attribute. The image of Mañjughoṣa was ordered by Kumāraghoṣa. Mañjuvara is the scarer of all fears and protector in darkness. Stability and protection of the kingdom again seems to be the aim of the king.

14. Ratu Baka inscription, Śaka 714, 792 AD

Ratu inscription, discovered in five fragments is incised in Pre-Nāgarī script. Paleographically it can be connected to Eastern India. Śailendra king Dharmottuṅgadeva possibly is the genetive of the king's name. The inscription opens with a salutation to the cave which is illuminated by the pious words and is a place for meditation and learning: *dhīgambhīraguhayaṁ smṛtiśīlaḥ sadvākyadhātūjvalo*, it is said to have friendship with knowledge: *maitrī prasravaṇena niyataṁ svaccham suramyam,* the place is not ruffled by strong winds of popular cults: *sānurvāridhilokadharmapavanairugrairna saṅkampitah,* the Sumeru like cave preserves the accumulated merits of highly learned people: *taṁ saṁvaddhasumerumurjjitaguṇam jñānograsa.....,* disciples are said to have learnt from there and return home. The cave temple is compared to the Abhayagiri monastery of Srilanka meant for the learned scholars. The monastery was founded by the king Dharmottuṅgadeva. The king wishes the monastery to flourish. Avalokiteśvara Bodhisattva is praised to do away with the sufferings of all the human beings and save them from attachments: *kṣapaya padmapāṇe prāṇinām kleśajālam* and *abhaya jinasūnoḥ padmapāṇeḥ kṛpāloḥ*. The disciples studying there are said to be well versed in the code of Manu: *manusasanajña bhavanti*.

15. Kayumvungan Inscription, Śaka 746, 824 AD

This is another inscription found from Kareng Tengah in the Temanggung division of the residency of Kedu broken into five pieces. 15 *ślokas* in Sanskrit are followed by description in Kavi. The king again is said to be an ornament of the Śailendra dynasty. According to the 11th śloka it was inscribed on the occasion of installing an image of the Śailendra king apotheosized as Śrī Ghananātha, that is Indra with others, worthy of worship. Most probably the Śailendra king had died in 812 AD and the occasion was the ceremony of his deification.

The king is described as a hero of immortal might, a lion among men, equal to Yama, a source of supreme knowledge and merit, worthy to be venerated: *amitabala, siṁha, daṇḍadharātulamahājñānapuṇyaprasūti*. Many kings were tormented by his furious powers: *caṇḍapratāpaparitāpita bhūribhūpaḥ*. He is the exalted king Samarottuṅgga, his most beloved daughter constructed the everlasting temple of Jina and she is said to be Pramodavardhanī in *śloka* no 10. In the last *śloka* it is prayed that the monastery, the assemblage of the virtues of Sugata may last for so long as the underground fire breathing hot remains, as the wise see, unsurpassed through the openings which are in its control, so long as the Earth remains, and Meru inhabitated by gods remains, so long as the Vṛtra of the sky scatters his own rays (Sarkar 1971:64). The description reminds of one of the popular *ślokas*:

Yāvat sthāsyanti girayaḥ saritaśca mahītale |
Tāvad rāmāyaṇī kathā lokeṣu pracharisyati ||

16. Plaosan Inscription

The inscription with a broken corner was found from the ruins of Chandi Plaosan. The name of the king is not mentioned but he seems to be from the Śailendra dynasty. The date of the inscription is not certain but most probably it is prior to 9th century. The king is compared to Mahādeva who showers boons: *smaraharavarṣadbhujayottuṅgadevasaṅgaṁ,* his body shines devoid of any old age infirmities: *vijarākāya vibhāti guṇavibhāmala putrajananam.* His wife is compared to Tārā: *bhārya tāreva virajati*. The king is consecrated on that day, who represents an image which is an embodiment of all the forms of religion:

Naranāthābhisaṁskārabharo vibhāti bhāsvaraḥ |
Dhammasaṁsāra samitapratimāprati .... ||

The king left the place for religious exercise and wore monk's clothes. A temple of Jina had been built by constant flow of Gurjara people, who bowed down to Sugata with devotion:

Satatagurjaradeśasamāgataissugatabhāktibhārapraṇataiḥ .....|
.... *krīyate jinamandiram* ||

The use of Śaka era in all the inscriptions is eloquent in its silence that Indian calendar was adopted by the Javanese using names of months, era, days, other chronological terms; even numerals are taken from Sanskrit.

Sanskrit meters used in the inscriptions

It is evident from the large number of meters used in inscriptions Sragdhara, Upendravajra, Indravajrā, Upajāti, Pṛthivī, Śārdūlavikrīḍita, Vasantatilakā etc. that the Javanese had mastered the art of writing poetry. Two important texts Amaramālā and Chandaḥkiraṇa/Chandakaraṇa were the major source for the writers. Amaramālā is the Sanskrit lexicon, it is not based on Amarakoṣa. Chandaḥkaraṇa means composing of meters, if the other reading is accepted then it means rays of meters. It is a comprehensive manual comprising several elements including alliteration, prosody, rhetoric, synonyms, homonyms and the like. It served as a practical compendium for aspiring poets of which Amaramālā was a part that begins with listing of words with the same letter in the sequence of Sanskrit alphabets, such words are required by poets for stylistic effects.

Aim of the Kings: Peace and Stability

Through most of the inscriptions it is evident that peace and stability was the aim of the rulers. They not only gave patronage to religious but also to literary activities for the cause. Literary works gave fame to the kings and social and cultural stability to the country. Dharmavansa Teguh was a great patron of literary works. Most of the Kakavins could be possible because of his blessings. Composing Kakavins based on the story of Mahābhārata was also supposed to be auspicious. In the commentary of the first *śloka* of Virāṭaparva the writer says: *kunaṅ mātaṅ yaṅ cinarita katattvan ira, mangalya namitta prakṛti nikan virāṭaparva saṅkathā apan prasiddha gumavay.* (Phalgunadi 1992:22).

Sanskrit became the soul of Javanese literature, the Javanese wrote valuable poetry and prose literature in a language steeped in Sanskrit; a steady and rapid progress was made. Rāmāyāṇa and Mahābhārata became the major source for the literary tradition. According to the commentary to the second *śloka* of Bhīṣmaparva the king Dharmavaṁśa Teguh Sanskritized Javanese: *śrī dharmavaṁśa teguh anantavikrama, saphala maṅgalya nin maniket prakṛta ning bhiṣmaparva. Nihan ta samaropa nikan carita, swasti !* (Gonda 1936:8). In Virāṭaparva the writer says: *sira ta dharmavaṁśa teguh anantavikrama ngaran ira, umilva maṅggala niṅ maṅgjavakna byasamata* (Juynboll 1912). Various concepts related to birth, death and life after life in the Old Javanese and Balinese literature are derived from the post epic Sanskrit literature. Infernal regions are called *narakaloka;* Yamālaya is the residence of the tormented; a special infernal region is called *asipatravana*, sword leaf forest. A considerable number of Sanskrit words in religious texts, in the domain of mysticism, religious practices, rites ceremonies and laws, *karaśodhana, tālabhedana, gaṇitri, nabaśakti, mṛtyuñjaya, saptavriddhi, dwijottama* etc.

The eldest son is called *santāna*. The Indonesians still practice a system of medicine linked with religion and magic. *Śleṣman* is mucus, *tunna* is cut, *muṛccha* is fainting. Sanskrit was a strong source of nomenclature for most of the SEA countries. Thus an all round enrichment of Indonesian language through Sanskrit opened immense dimensions of development and enrichment of man in his totality.

LITERATURE CITED

Sarkar 1971.

Himansu Bhusan Sarkar, *Corpus of Inscriptions of Java,* Firma K.L. Mukhopadhyay, Calcutta, 1972.

Gonda 1936.

Gonda J., *Bhismaparwa,* Bandoeng, 1936.

Hall 1970.

Hall, D.G.E., *A History of South-east Asia,* New York, 1970.

Juynboll 1912.

Juynboll J.J., *Virataparva,* the Hague, 1912.

Majumdar 1953.

Majumdar R.C., *Inscriptions of Cambodia,* The Asiatic Society, Monography series, Vol. 8. 1953.

Phalgunadi 1995.

Phalgunadi I Gusti Putu, *Bhiṣmaparwa,* New Delhi, 1995.

Phalgunadi 1992

Virāṭaparva, New Delhi, 1992.

Raghu Vira 1978

Raghu Vira, *India and Asia,* International Academy of Indian Culture, New Delhi, 1978.

21

SANSKRIT TEXTS IN CHINESE AND TIBETAN TRANSLATIONS

Sanskrit texts found their way across the boundaries of India when Buddhism was transmitted to the countries in East, Far-East and Southeast Asia. They were translated into the languages of the people whoever accepted them as a medium of higher civilization. It was an order of Śākyamuni himself that his teachings should reach the people in their own languages. The Chinese translated thousands of Sanskrit books into their language for an in-depth understanding of the knowledge, coming from the West (India). The majority of such scriptures reached China via the Silk Route, spanning through the vast deserts of Central Asia. Explorations and excavations in the past two centuries have brought to light a large number of Sanskrit texts translated into Chinese, Tibetan, Uigur, Turkic, Sogdian, Khotanese, Tokharian and Kuchean. But there are some that were taken to China via Sri Lanka by sea route.

Chinese Translations

According to the widely accepted view, the extent Chinese translations of the scriptures imported overland, belonging to the second century AD, are the oldest and those that arrived via sea route, are from the beginning of the 3rd century AD. However, a tradition holds that the first translation of Indian scriptures occurred during 246-219 BC, during the reign of the Chin dynasty, when eighteen wise men carried the scriptures from India to China. Although there was a negligible interchange between the two countries at that point of time, but still it cannot be refused that one of the missions sent by Aśoka was received by the Chinese emperor.

The exact date of the official transmission of Buddhism into China given on the basis of inscriptional evidence, is AD 67, when two Indian scholars—Kāśyapa Mātaṅga and Dharmarakṣa reached China on an invitation of the King Ming Ti of the Late Han dynasty who had dispatched a mission in AD 64, that returned in AD 67. The king ordered to build a monastery to honour and facilitate them to translate the Buddhist scriptures. It was named as White Horse Monastery, because the two scholars had carried sūtras on white horses. They settled in Loyang and first translated the Sūtra of Forty-two Chapters. It is a collection of moral and religious sayings of the Buddha. It also throws light on the development of Buddhism in India from the time of Mahāparinirvāṇa of the Buddha to the time of the two translators and gives ample information about the most essential doctrines of the faith among the Chinese people. Possibly it was a collection of the extracts from various canonical texts. The work became so popular that it underwent many translations, editions and revisions in China.

From then onwards, there was an unbroken tradition of translating Sanskrit books into Chinese. Thousands of these translations are available today. The best-known are contained in the Tripiṭaka. The earliest manuscript containing the first four *ślokas* of the four *Mahākāvyas* by the great poet Kālidāsa, is discovered from the Dun-huang caves in China. A large number of translations are lost over the past centuries, but still China preserves a large number of Sanskrit books, now lost in India forever.

Chinese historical records supply names of a large number of scholars from India, China and the kingdoms in Central Asia. They translated thousands of books beginning from the first century. After the two above-mentioned Indian scholars, comes Dharmarakṣa who translated four or five other Sanskrit books into Chinese but they are lost. Possibly one of them was Lalitavistara or Aśvaghoṣa's Buddhacarita while the others were—Daśa-bhūmika-kleśa-chedikā, Dharma-samudra-koṣa-sūtra, Jātakas and a collection of 260 *śīlas* or precepts.

Loyang was one of the vibrant centers of Buddhist learning. 359 books were translated by twelve translators who were active at a monastery, during the Han supremacy, in the first to third century AD Chinese scholars, well versed in Sanskrit were engaged in translation in collaboration with Indian scholars. 176 Sanskrit texts were translated by the most celebrated translator—An-Shih-Kao, a Prince from Parthia. He reached China in AD 148 and carried on translation work till AD 170. Today only 55 out of 176 of his works are available in the Ming Chinese Tripiṭaka.

In AD 200 the later Han dynasty was followed by a period of Three Kingdoms. During that period popularity of the devotion to Amitābha gave way to translation of both the versions of Sukhavātī-vyūha-sūtra, longer and shorter. Moreover its popularity can be judged by twelve translations of the Amitāyus-sūtra. In AD 224 Dharmapada was translated into Chinese by an Indian Śramaṇa, Vighna. 189 Sanskrit works were translated during the 48 years of power wielded by the rulers of the Wu dynasty. Today only 56 are available.

During the rule of the Western Tsin dynasty, Indian intellectuals were active in the then-capital, Loyang. A large number of Sanskrit books on Mahayana were translated by the Indian and the Chinese monks working in collaboration. Twelve of those scholars translated 447 works, of which just 153 are extent. Another great translator produced 210 translations, but only 91 exist today. Saddharma-puṇḍarīka-, Lalita-vistara- and Pañca-viṁśati-prajñā-pāramitā are the prominent sūtras among them.

Mahayana sūtras in Sanskrit are the best-known examples of Sanskrit texts found in China. The term Mahayana is first used in Prajña-pāramaitā-sūtras—Aṣṭasāhasrikā-prajñā-pāramitā and Pañca-viṁśati-prajñā-pāramitā. The sūtras equate perfection of wisdom with the unconditioned Dharmakāya itself. As one of the most popular sūtras Pañca-viṁśati-prajñā-pāramitā-sūtra was first translated by Dharmarakṣa in 286 and later by Kumārajīva. Aṣṭa-sāhasrikā-prajñā-pāramitā-sūtra was translated twice by Kumārajīva in 408 and Lokakṣema in 179, in 10 fascicles each.

During the rule of the Eastern Tsin dynasty (317-420), 233 Sanskrit books were translated into Chinese. Fa-hsien is one of the better-known scholar pilgrims of the time, who came to India in search of knowledge, in AD 399. Mahā-parinirvāṇa-sūtra and Mahāsānghika-bhikṣuṇī-vinaya are the best known among his translations.

Kūmarajīva, a descendent of a royal Indian family, was so famous for his wisdom that he was taken as a prisoner by the Chinese to propagate Buddhism. The king appointed more than 800 monks to assist him to translate. He retranslated a large number of sūtras more accurately and completely. More than 300 volumes were produced. To this date his translations are taken as the best. A few of them are—Daśa-sāhasrikā-prajñā-paramitā, Vajracchedikā, Saddharma-puṇḍarīka, Sarvāstivāda-prātimokṣa, Sutrālaṅkāra and Dvādaśa-nikāya-śāstra and Mādhyamaka-śāstra. Brahma-jāla-sūtra introduced by Kumārajīva has always been considered in China as the chief code of law of the Mahayana school. He translated Satyasiddhi-śāstra written by Harihara that does not survive in Sanskrit.

Bodhidharma, the Indian monk from Kāñcīpuram, transmitted the philosophy of *dhyāna*, that became popular in China as Ch'an and in Japan as Zen. In Mahayana Buddhism the most systematic treatment of the ten stages, leading to enlightenment are offered in the Daśa-bhūmika-sūtra translated by Bodhiruci in AD 508-35. Several sūtras on *yoga* were translated later.

Abhidharma-koṣa translated into Chinese by Paramārtha in AD 563-67, offered the most tangible detailed psychological approach to the analysis of the factors of existence (*dharmas*). Buddhāvataṁsaka-nāma-mahā-vaipulya-sūtra was translated by Buddha-bhadra in AD 418-21 and by Śikśānanda in AD 695-99. Bodhisattva-bhūmi, the sūtra of Bodhisattva's spiritual states, a partial translation of the Yogācāra-bhūmi-śāstra was done by Dharmakṣema between AD 414 and AD 426.

Nāgārjuna's Mūla-mādhyamaka-kārikā was one of the most important treatises in the Sino-Japanese Buddhism. Its principle philosophy was the refutation of the views believed to impede the attainment of enlightenment and the revelation of the true meaning of Buddhism by means of middle way of the two levels of truth. Saddharma-puṇḍarīka-sūtra, translated by Kumārajīva during the Late fourth or early fifth century, served as the most important text for the T'ien T'ai school of Chinese Buddhism. But when the sect was transmitted to Japan, the sūtra got eclipsed by Mahāvairocana-sūtra, translated and abbreviated by Śubhākarasiṁha in AD 716-35. The original title of the text is Mahā-vairocanābhisambodhi-vikurvītādhiṣṭhāna-vaipulya-sūtrendra-rāja-dharma-paryāya.

The third division of the Tripiṭaka is devoted to Vinaya or moral regulations. Dharma-guptaka-vinaya, a treatise on Four Category Vinaya, was translated by Buddhayaśas in AD 410-412. Avadāna, a collection of stories was translated by I-ching in AD 710. He was followed by many scholars like Upaśūnya, son of the king of Udyāna, Sanghapāla, Guṇabhadra, Bodhiruci, Gautama Prajñāruci, a Brāhmaṇa from Benaras, Narendrayaśas, and many others. Emperor Harṣavardhana sent an envoy to China in AD 641 and two Chinese missions were dispatched to India. It was the time when pilgrim scholar Hsüan-tsang set out for a mission to India in AD 629. He carried 124 books with him, which were later translated by him with the help of scholars appointed to assist him.

The Chinese Tripiṭaka is the most important source to survey Sanskrit texts in Chinese translations. It contains three piṭakas—Sūtra, Vinaya and Abhidharma by high-ranking Indian scholars and by non-Buddhist teachers of Vaiśeṣika and Sāṅkhya schools of philosophy. Moreover other famous works, commentaries, histories and catalogues of Buddhist scriptures composed in China were included in the Tripiṭaka. But when the Tripiṭaka is compared with Kañjur and Tañjur only 444 of the 1114 Kañjur books are found in the Chinese. Of the missing books, 115 belong to the exoteric or revealed teaching and 555 to the esoteric or secret teaching. In the case of Tañjur, only 107 of a total of 3559 books have been translated or transcribed into Chinese, leaving out 3452. Thus, Chinese Buddhist literature, which spans almost one thousand years of translation, from the first to the tenth century AD, of translation activity is much smaller than the Tibetan. Thus Tibetan literature is the biggest mine.

Tibetan Translations

Tibetans have preserved a rich heritage of Sanskrit texts in translations. They are sacred to them, and receive divine honour because they embody the word of the Buddha and contain the knowledge coming from his land. These Sanskrit texts reached Tibet, the Land of Snow, by virtue of the efforts and tenacity of the scholar missionaries both from India and Tibet. The task was accomplished by ignoring the dangers and discomforts lying on their way. Tibetan scholars translated, in collaboration with Indian masters, books on various fields of knowledge from Sanskrit, for a perfect understanding of the Indian theories. Temples and hermitages were no disturbance zones and the most suitable places for them to undertake the momentous task. Indian and Tibetan scholars were assisted by Nepalese Pandits also, e.g. Śīlamañju and Śāntibhadra.

Some of the Indian scholars went to Tibet on invitations by the court, others left India to escape the raging Islamic storm. A large number of Buddhist scholars migrated to western Tibet from Kashmir where Buddhism was a flourishing religion. Tantric system in Tibet was designated as Kashmiri system. There are three important periods of Tibetan literature. The first, the classical period is from the mid 7th century to the end of the 14th century. It began with Thonmi Sambhota. It was a period of major translations from Sanskrit. It came to a halt after the invasions by Chingis Khan and Bakhtyar Khilji when the great Buddhist monasteries of Nālandā, Odantapurī and Vikramaśilā were destroyed. The second phase began in the early 11th century and ended by the 17th, an era of fresh impulse. The third period beginning in the first quarter of the 18th century saw Tibetan language as the sacred language of Higher Asia.

In AD 629 King Naradeva, 32nd descendent of an Indian royal family, became the initiator of Buddhism and Buddhist literature. He commissioned Thonmi Sambhota, one of his ministers, to go to the Āryadeśa and study in Magadha, both under Brāhmaṇa and Buddhist scholars. Before that there was no alphabet in Tibet. Thonmi Sambhota came to India accompanied by sixteen scholars. He modelled alphabets for Tibet on the basis of the Nāgarī letters. On going back he composed eight works on grammar and writing. The king himself studied his grammar in aphorisms (*sūtrāṇi*). He undertook one of the greatest literary ventures, which continued for a thousand years.

Tibet became one of the most powerful nations in the 8th century. Translation of Sanskrit texts came to be undertaken in real earnest and on a larger scale than before. It reached its peak in the reign of King Ral-pa-cen, in the first half of the 9th century. During his period the existing translations were revised and those, which had not been rendered into Tibetan, were at once accurately translated. More than half of the books contained in the present Tripiṭaka were translated during that period, with meticulous care both in the use of terms and in modes of expression.

The next King Lang-dar-ma was a rabid anti Buddhist, so the translation activities came to a standstill. But it was again revived when Rin-chen-bzang-po came to the throne in the second half of the 10th century and the head of the Vikaramaśilā University of India, Atīsā went to Tibet. He was given the super royal reception for his deep learning, purity and demeanor. Tibetans discovered the path of exalted excellence under his guidance. He worked there for thirteen years and finally died there in AD 1053. But wherever Tibetan Buddhism prevails, he is remembered as the highest of all the venerables.

Translation of Sanskrit works went on steadily for centuries till the end of the seventeenth century. Definite rules for translation were laid down. Translations were exactly word-to-word, accurate, faithful and literal, and it was possible for everyone to study them. Each translation was a joint production of an Indian *Paṇḍit* and a Tibetan *Lotsava* or translator. Together they were called Lo-pan. According to the supplement attached to the Derge edition the number of Indian scholars engaged in translation was 107 and of those from Tibet was 222.

In AD 1340 available texts were collected, carefully coordinated and properly classified by the great historian and redactor Bu-ston, into two collections—Kañjur and Tañjur. The Tibetan classification is into Sūtras and Śāstras. Sūtras are utterances of the Buddha and Śāstras are those written by the subsequent teachers through interpretations. The sūtras are collected in Kañjur, in 108 volumes while the Śāstras are collected in Tañjur, consisting of 225 volumes. In all there are 1108 works in Kañjur and 3458 in Tañjur. Some of these texts are translated from Chinese and some from Apabhraṁśa. Kañjur and Tañjur are xylographs printed from wooden blocks. There have been several editions of Kañjur and Tañjur. Their complete sets in India are kept at Vishvabharati in Shantiniketan, The University of Calcutta, Vangiya Sahitya Parisad, the Royal Asiatic Society of Bengal, the Bihar and Orissa Research Society and the Theosophical Society, Adyar.

There are a large number of Sanskrit texts translated into Tibetan including Kāvyādarśa by Daṇḍin, translated by Śrīlakśmīkara, Meghadūta by Kālidāsa, translated by Sumanaśrī. In metrics are the books like Chandoratnākara by Ratnākara and Vṛttimālā-stuti by Jñanaśrīmitra.

Similarly there are Sanskrit grammars like Pāṇini-sūtra, Prakriyākaumudi by Ramacandra, Cāndra-vyākaraṇa by Candragomin, Kalāpa-vyākaraṇa by Sarvavarman and Sārasvata by Anubhūtisvarūpācārya. Besides them there are many other texts on Sanskrit grammar. Some of them are unknown in the history of Sanskrit Grammar written by Pt. Yudhiṣṭhira Mimāṁsaka. A few examples of works incorporated in Tañjur, on grammar are: Cāndra-vyākaraṇa-sūtra, Viṁsatyupasarga-vṛtti-nāma and Varṇa-sūtra, Uṇādi-vṛtti by Chandragomin, Varṇa-sūtra-vṛtti, Adhikāra-saṅgraha-nāma, Vibhakti-kārikā, Tiṅanta, Sambandhoddeśa, Dhātu-kāya, Aṣṭa-sāhasrikāmañjuśrī-sábda-vyākaraṇa-vṛtti, Kalāpa-sūtra, Kalāpa-sūtra-vṛtti-nāma, Kalāpa-sūtra-vṛtti-siṣyahitā-nāma, Dhātu-kāya, Syādyanta-prakriyā, Tyādyanta-prakriyā-vicarita-nāma, Sarasvatī-vyākaraṇa-sūtra. Vyutpatti, Nighaṇṭu, Vyākaraṇa-mūla-triṁśaka-nāma, Śabda-śāstra, Aṣṭamahāpada-mūla, Samyak-vāk-pramāṇoddhṛta-sūtra, Dṛṣṭi-krama-nirdeśa, Artha-viniścaya-ṭīkā, etc.

Other fields of knowledge were not unknown to the Tibetans. In the field of lexicography there are Amarakośa, its commentary, Kamadhenu by Subhūti Chandra and Muktāvalī or Viśva-locana Abhidhāna-śāstra by Śrīdharasena. Among the books on Nīti, one finds Āryakoṣa by Ravigupta, Subhāṣita-ratnāka-daṇḍa by Āryaśūra.

In the field of medicine, there are a large number of works. A few of them are Aṣṭāṅga-hṛdaya of Vāgbhaṭṭa, its commentary Brahmaveda Śāraṅga-dhara-caraka by Sarvahita-mitradatta and Aśvāyurveda-saṁhitā of Śālihotra. Yogaśataka, Jīva-sūtra, Ācārya-nāgārjuna-bhāṣita-avabheṣaja-kalpa, Vaidyāṣṭāṅga-hṛdaya-vṛtti, Aṣṭāṅga-hṛdaya-saṁhitā-nāma, Aṣṭāṅga-hṛdaya-nāma-vaidūryaka-bhāṣya and Padārtha-candrikā-prabhāsa-nāma-aṣṭāṅga-hṛdaya-vṛtti. Others are—Rasa-siddhi-śāstra-nāma, Rasāyanaśāstroddhṛti, Sambuddha-bhāṣita-pratibimba-lakṣaṇa-vivaraṇa-nāma, Pratibimba-māna-lakṣaṇa-nāma, Caturaśīti-siddhābhisamaya, Aṣṭapadī-kṛta-dhūpa-yoga, Aṣṭapadī-kṛta-dhūpa-yoga-vidhāna-bhāṣya, Yuddha-jaya-nāma-tantra-rāja-svarodaya-nāma, Āyur-gaṇita-phala-prakāśa-nāma, Svarodayārtha-samgraha and Svarodaya-lagna-phalopadeśa.

Nagnajita's Citra-lakṣaṇa and Ātreya's Pratimāna-lakṣaṇa are the outstanding Śilpaśāstra works. Tibetan translations included texts on chemistry also, for example there is Sarveśvara-rasayāna of Īśvara. There are translations of works on subjects related to ocean, *sāmudrika*, such as Sāmudrika-vyañjana-varṇana. Some of the books on narrative literature are : Lokānanda-nāṭaka-nāma by Candragomin, Nāgānanda-nāma-nāṭaka by Harṣadeva, Subhāṣita-ratna-kāraṇḍaka-kathā by Śūra, Śīla-parikathā, Kaliyuga-pari-kathā, Vivekakathā, Udāna-kathā, Anityārtha-pari-kathā, Jātakamālā, Jātakamālā-ṭīkā, Haribhaṭṭa-Jātakamālā-nāma etc.

A number of texts on logic are included in Tañjur, for example Pramāṇa-samuccaya-nāma-prakaraṇa, Pramāṇa-samuccaya-vṛtti, Pramāṇa-vṛtti-kārikā, Pramāṇa-viniścaya, Ālambana-parīkṣā, Trikāla-parīkṣā-nāma, Hetu-cakra-ḍamāru, Nyāya-bindu-nāma-prakaraṇa, Hetubindu-nāma-prakaraṇa, Sambandha-parīkṣā-prakaraṇa, Vādanyāya-nāma-prakaraṇa, Pramāṇa-vārtikālaṁkāra etc. Prajña-śataka-nāma-prakaraṇa, Nītiśāstra-prajñā-daṇḍa-nāma, Nitiśastra-jantu-poṣaṇa-bindu-nāma, Gāthā-koṣa-nāma, Śata-gāthā, Vimala-praśnottararatna-mālā-nāma, Cāṇakya-nīti-śāstra, Nīti-śāstra, Sāmudrika-vyañjana-varṇana, Tanu-vicāraṇa-śāstra-saṁkṣepa, Vārdhakī-siddhilābhākhyāna, Nārīsidhi-lābhākhyāna, Sukhadeva-siddhi-lābhākhyana, Śālihotrīyasvāyurveda-saṁhitā-nāma, etc. are some the other known works.

Among the famous Tibetan scholars, a frequent collaborator was, Rin-chen-bzaṅ-po (Ratnavajra), the disciple of Gaṅgādhara. According to the available literary documents Rin-chen-bzaṅ-po translated Sanskrit texts into Tibetan with the help of Indian masters, collaborators and disciples. His translations can be divided into three sections : (a) 17 Sanskrit texts on Śāstras and Tantras included in Kañjur (b) 32 commentaries on sūtras (c) 108 commentaries on the tantras. Some of the collaborators were Śraddhākaravarman, Padmākaravarman, Subhaṣita, Kamalagupta, Dharmaśrībhadra,

Subhutiśrībhadra, Gaṅgādhara, Buddhabhadra, Vijayaśrīdhara, Tathāgatarakṣita, Devākara and Atīśa.

Among them Śraddhākaravarman is outstanding, who collaborated in the translation of the following sūtras and commentaries: Homavidhi, Sarva-śuddhi-saṁskāra-sūtra-piṇḍita-vidhi, Yogānuttratantrārthāvatārasaṅgraha, Sarva-tathāgata-tattva-saṅgraha, Sarva-tathāgata-kāya-vāk-citta-rahasya-guhya-samāja and Śrī-paramādi-mahāyāna-kalpa-rāja, two commentaries on Prajñāparamitā-nava-śloka-piṅḍārtha and Hasta-bala-prakaraṇa Kāya-traya-stotra-vivaraṇa, Śrībhagavadābhisamaya, Heruka-viśuddhi, Sarva-buddha-samayoga-tantra-pañjikā, Sarva-buddha-samayoga, Pradīpoddyotana, Ṣaḍaṅga-yoga-ṭīkā, Vajra-jāpa-ṭīkā, Jñānavajra-samuccaya-tantrodbhava-saptālaṅkāra-vimocana, Piṇḍīkrta-sādhana, Pañcakarma, Svādhiṣṭhāna-krama-prabheda, Abhisambodhi-kramopadeśa, Amṛta-kuṇḍalī-sādhanā, Guhya-samāja-maṇḍala-deva-kāya-stotra, Guhya-samāja-vivaraṇa, Samantabhadra-sādhana, samantabhadra-sādhana-vṛtti, Guhya-samājābhisamaya, Saṅkśipta-maṇḍala-sūtra-vṛtti, Paramādiṭīka, Māyājāla-pañjikā, Pratiṣthā-vidhi, Karuṇodaya, Nāma-saṅgīti-vṛtti, Mañjuśrī-nāma-saṅgīti-ṭīkā, Vajravidāraṇi-dhāraṇī-ṭīkā, Vajra-vidāraṇī-dhāraṇī-vyākhyāna-bṛhaṭṭīkā, Vṛtti-pradīpa, Ārya-mañju-ghoṣa-stotra, Madhyama-bhāga-traya-vidhi and Piṇḍīkrama-sādhana and Karmākara-stotra.

Sanskrit texts contained in the Tañjur and Kañjur have a historical and academic importance because most of the originals are lost. Thus a study of the Tibetan Buddhist literature stands as Buddhist literature valuable source for a better understanding of a comprehensive history of Sanskrit literature.

22

SANSKRIT IN JAPAN

Sanskrit manuscripts crossed the boundaries of India along with transmission of Buddhist philosophy, art and thought, and reached Japan via Central Asia and China. Thousands of Sanskrit texts were translated into Khotanese, Tokharian, Uigur and Sogdian in Central Asia, on their way to China and Japan. They traveled with scholars and pilgrims, adventurers and the politically ambitious, and prospered there, often by virtue of state patronage. Sanskrit was carried not merely as a medium of communication but as a divine language in which were written sacred words of the Buddha, the words that could lead them towards enlightenment. But with destruction of monastic libraries in Central Asia most of the Sanskrit literature perished leaving behind a large number of fragments which are discovered by the great explorers from Germany, Russia, British India, Sweden and Japan. Only those manuscripts and texts are discovered as complete which were taken to Nepal and Tibet or other parts of Asia. Their translations into Tibetan, Chinese and Mongolian etc. are another important source for a study of lost Sanskrit literature.

Among ancient Sanskrit manuscripts, strewn in the monasteries nestling on high mountains and waterless deserts, the earliest known ones going back to the first century AD, found from Afghanistan, are in a sad condition. Following them are the fragments of a Sanskrit manuscript of a drama: Śāriputraprakaraṇa, from the Kushana period, that is second century AD, discovered from Qyzil in the Turfan area of Central Asia.

Two Indian scripts that were used to write Buddhist scriptures and edicts of Ashoka are Brāhmī and Kharoṣṭhi. Kharoṣṭhi was used in Northwestern India and in the neighboring area of Central Asia roughly between fifth century BC to third century AD. Ashokan edicts discovered from two places in the NW, in modern Pakistan are written in Kharoṣṭhi. But Brāhmī came into common use in the NW after the third or fourth century AD, displacing Kharoṣṭhi.

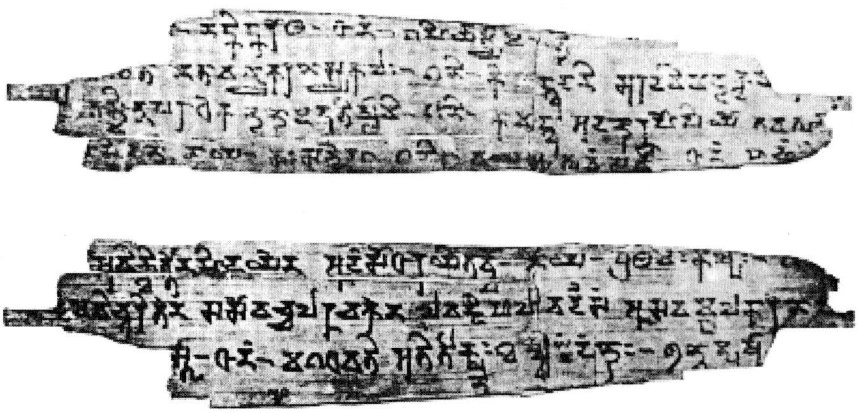

The earliest known Sanskrit manuscript in the world, going back to the Kushan period, that is, the second century A.D. It was discovered from Qyzil in the Turfan area of Central Asia. They are fragments of a Sanskrit drama.

In Japan, the emperors in search of transcendental values embraced the tradition of sūtras written in Sanskrit as a core for national unity and integrity. Today a rich literary treasure of Sanskrit literature consisting of *dhāraṇīs, tantras, sūtras* and other texts has been kept for nearly 1400 years. Entry of Sanskrit Buddhist scriptures into Japan became their identification with the central axis of human advance when Buddhism opened up unfathomed spheres of thought as soon as it reached officially in AD 552.

Philosophical speculations opened up new avenues and horizons. The idea of *bahujanahitāya bahujanasukhāya* overwhelmed the minds of the Japanese to such an extent that the great Prince Shōtoku Taishi decided to carve out the first constitution, known as 'Seventeen Article Constitution' based on the Buddhist ideology. He himself wrote commentaries and lectured on Saddharmapuṇḍarīka-sūtra, Śrīmālā-devī-siṁhanāda-sūtra and Vimala-kīrtti-nirdeśa-sūtra. These sūtras can be heard in the daily recitation of the Japanese up to the day. With the coming of a new philosophical political system the country began to emerge out of a clan system to a state system and the constitution was promulgated. This was the first time when Sanskrit manuscripts entered Japan.

The second milestone in the history of Japan as a state stands during the reign of Emperor Shomu who used Sanskrit sutras as a core to create a unified country and himself became a supreme monarch. During mid eighth century he dispatched Sanskrit sūtras to all the provinces and ordered for their recitation on fixed days and time. And thus the whole of Japan began to unite. The system of education saw a phase of democratization in the ninth century with creation of Sanskrit based alphabets, invented by the monk scholar Kōbō Daishi.

The language of Mahayana sūtras and the northern Hinayana Buddhist sūtras was Sanskrit and they were written in northern Brāhmī characters. Brāhmī gave the basis to a number of scripts in Asia to be devised. The scripts developed on the basis of North Indian style of Brāhmī are different from those developed from the South Indian style of Brāhmī. The scripts in Southeast Asian countries like Srilanka, Burma, Thailand, Cambodia etc. are derived from southern Indian scripts so they follow rounded form of Brāhmī. Brāhmī characters in North India different to a certain extent from those used in the south. But the difference became more marked with passing of time. The northern characters became very angular while those in the south became noticeably rounded.

The oldest printed item from China dated AD 757, is Sanskrit mantras written for Goddess Pratisarā, in ornamental Rañjanā script, concentrically around the figure. World's oldest printed book dated 11th May 868, is Vajracchedikā-sūtra on transcendental wisdom, written on paper, which is now kept at the British Museum.

Manuscripts in Gupta script

Uṣṇīśavijayā-dhāraṇī and Prajñāpāramitā-hṛdaya-sūtra

The Sanskrit manuscripts found in Japan are much older than those found in India. Uṣṇīśavijayā-dhāraṇī and Prajñāpāramitā-hṛdaya-sūtra, written on palm leaves were taken to Japan

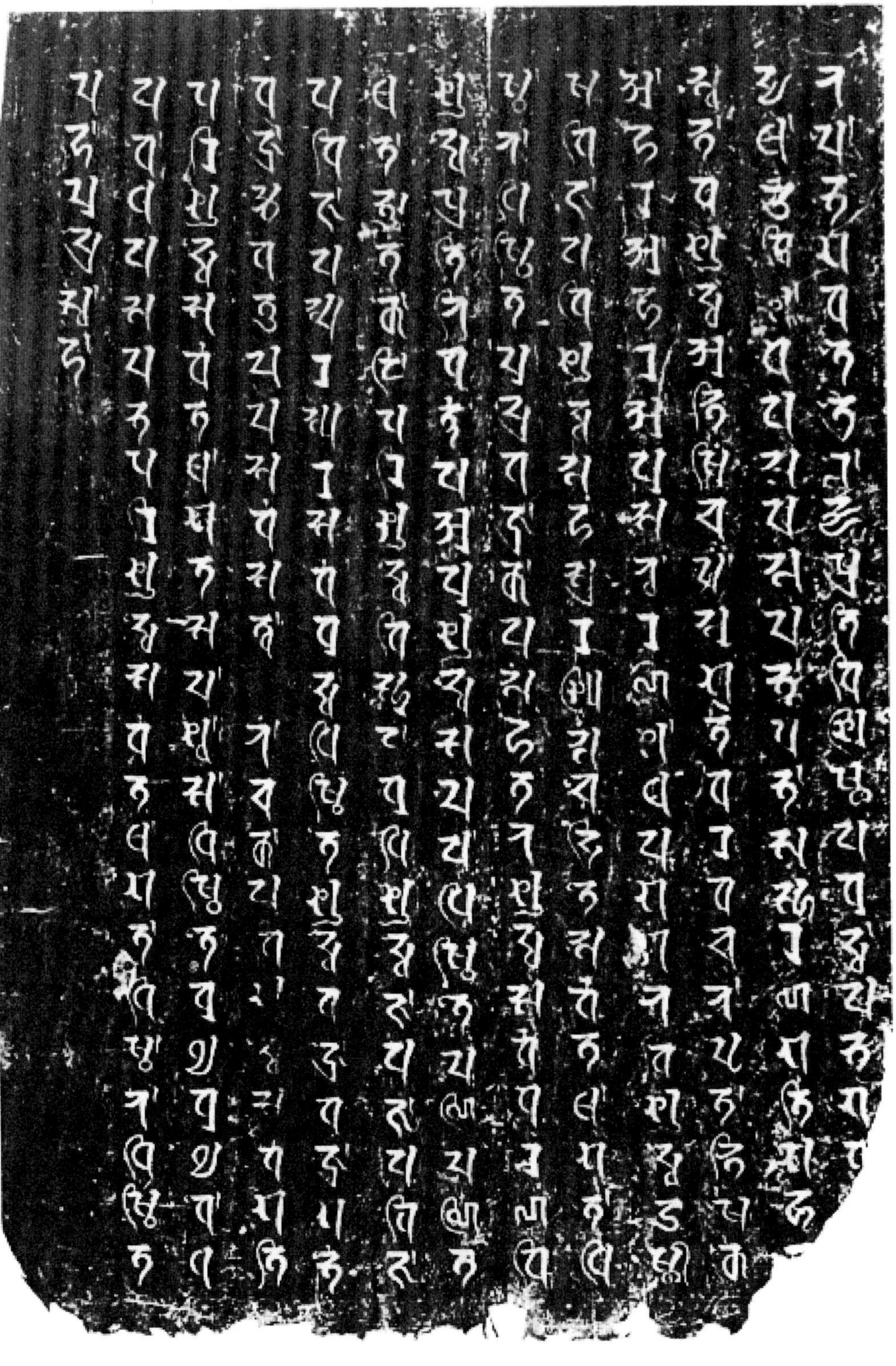

A Sanskrit inscription on an octagonal pillar, erected in A.D. 1104 in the Lo-yang district, China, discovered by Prof. Raghuvira. The last line reads: MAHĀMUDRE SVĀHĀ.

from China in 609 which most probably belonged to Monk Yashi and before him they were in the possession of Ācārya Bodhidharma who had gone from India to China in AD 520. Certainly the manuscripts cannot be dated later than the first half of the sixth century being evidently written by an Indian scribe. In spite of their transmission from India to China and from there to Japan and preserved there over the past fourteen centuries, they are legible although having suffered partly on the margins and partly due to fading of ink. They are primarily valuable for their paleographic antiquity. The material and the techniques used and the style of writing resemble those which were used in India later also.

Prince Shōtoku Taishi drew up the first Japanese constitution in Seventeen Articles where in the Triratna: Buddha, Dharma and Sangha were a fundamental factor. The new order was consecrated by the Usṇīśavijayā-dhāranī. Its Sanskrit manuscript in Gupta script is preserved at the Hōryūji monastery. Hōryūji means the temple for the flourishing of Dharma—*dharma-vardhana-vihāra.*

The manuscript of Prajñāpāramitā-hṛdaya was copied by Jiun Sonja in the eighteenth century, the last of the Sanskritists of Japan in the traditional style. He lived from AD 1718 to 1803. A saint of great learning and noble virtues, he stands unique in the history of Mantrayana as the doyen of traditional Sanskrit studies in Japan, and in recognition thereof he was given the honorific title 'Sonja' which means '*ārya*' or 'a*rhat*". Nobody else in Japan was given this honor.

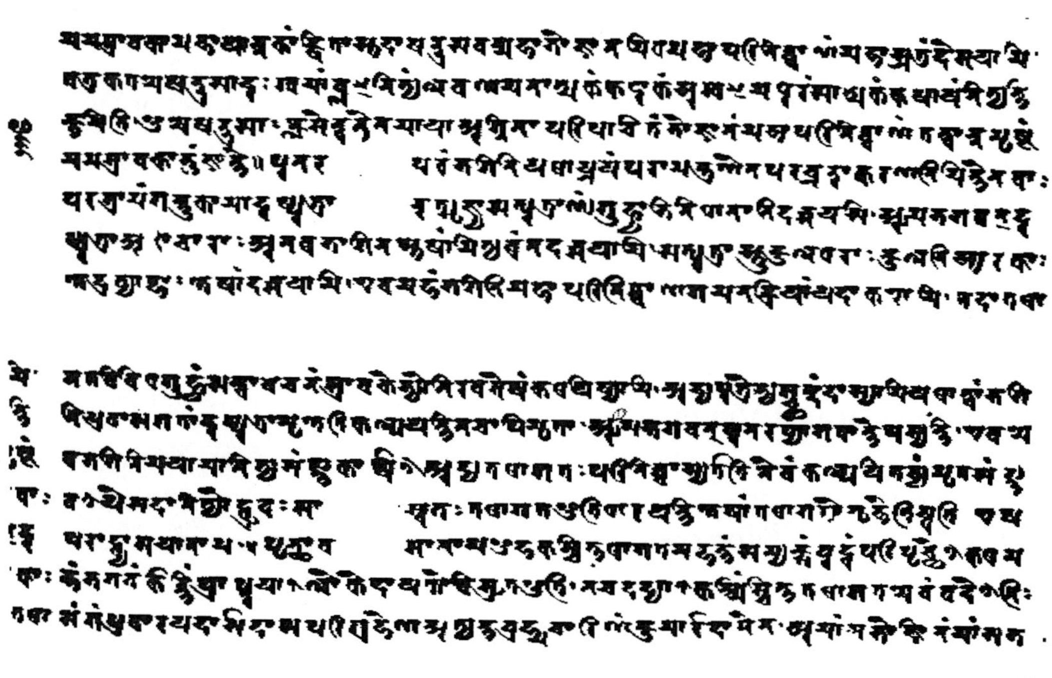

45

A page from a Sanskrit manuscript preserved at the Reihokan Museum , Koyasan, 8th century

Manuscripts in Sharada script

Seven palm leaf manuscripts in the Tōji, Kairyōji, Seiryōji, Kōkiji, Gyōkusenji, Shitennōji and Tennōji monasteries in the Kansai district are identified as a part of Abhidharmakoṣa of Sarvāstivāda by some of the Japanese scholars but Prof. Matsuda Kazunobu believes them to be folios of Lokaprajñapti, a part of Prajñapti-śāstra of Sadpāda of Sarvāstivada. Prajñapti-śāstra is found in Chinese and Tibetan versions also. Lokaprajñapti is a part of Prajñapti-śāstra of Maudgalyāyana, the other two parts are Karaṇaprajñapti and Karmaprajñapti. It is an important point to be noted that the Chinese translation dates back to 11th century while the Japanese manuscripts are dated 9th century.

1. The folio kept at the Tōji monastery speaks on five *skandhas*, aggregates.

2. The one that is in Kairyōji deals with the twenty-two *indriyas*.

3. The subject matter of the folio kept at Seiryōji is on *anuśaya*.

4. The manuscript from Kōkiji monastery talks about 'end of *kalpa* and *sapta sūryodaya*'.

5. The manuscript from the Gyōkusenji temple gives a description of mount Sumeru.

6,7. The manuscript kept at the Shitennōji monastery contains 170 folios and the one at the Chionji monastery has 172 folios. The subject matter of these manuscript is teaching the effects of one's deeds. If someone follows *paritāpa dharma,* evil actions then he goes to hell called *niraya* but those who follow *aparitapa dharma,* they are bound to go to heavenly abodes called *sugati*. The lesson is taught through stories.

The folios preserved at the Gyōkusenji temple are similar in content to Gilgit manuscript identified as Dharma—skandha.

Sanskrit manuscripts in the possession of the Faculty of Letters, University of Kyoto:

Aparimitāyur-dhāraṇī

Abhidharmakoṣa-vyākhyā

Abhidhanottrottara-tantra

Aṣṭasāhasrikā-prajñāparamitā-sūtra

Others

Hymn to Thousand-armed Mañjuśrī

A complete tantra devoted to Mañjuśrī was translated by Amoghavajra in AD 740 (Nj. 1044, T 1177a, K 1272, STP. 16.6378) on imperial orders. The Master explained the Sanskrit text and Hye-ch'o wrote it down. On 19th February 742, Vajra took the Sanskrit manuscript to an Indian teacher, gave it to Monk Mokṣānanda Bhaga[vān] for being returned to Ratnabodhi of India and Srilanka.

Along with the main tantra, there is a Sanskrit hymn of 108 epithets of Sahasrapātra Mañjuśrī called Sempatsu Monju in Japanese in Taisho Tripitaka (1177b, 20.776-777) (Lokesh Chandra Dictionary of Buddhist Iconography 2003:8.2240) in Siddham script. Its source goes back to the T'ang dynasty. There is another dhāraṇī written in Siddham in Nagatani Hoshi's collection of Sanskrit *mantras* brought from China by Kōbō Daishi which is based on some other source.

Mañjuśrī is related to the state when he is called as follows in the hymns:

Mahāmaṇḍala-śāsakaḥ, ruler of the vast state
Rājyadadaḥ, giver of the state
Cakravarti, monarch
Jitāntakaḥ, destroyer of the vanquisher

ॐ सहभाषितमात्रेण विद्या सर्वार्थ-साधनी। मञ्जुघोषेण सत्वानामतुज्जत्पज रक्षा या।।१
सर्वदुर्गतयः शान्ता कम्पिता मारवाहिनी। देवाः प्रमुमुदुः सर्वे त्रस्ता भुवः विनायकाः।।२
अस्यां जपितमात्रायां धारण्यां शापशमन्याम्। दशासंख्येयकोट्यो हि मुक्ता संसारपारकाः।।३
मञ्जुश्रिया कुमारेण मञ्जुघोषप्रमुक्ताभा। अभूद्वसुमती तदा सशैलवनकानना।।४

(Devanagari transcription of the following text)

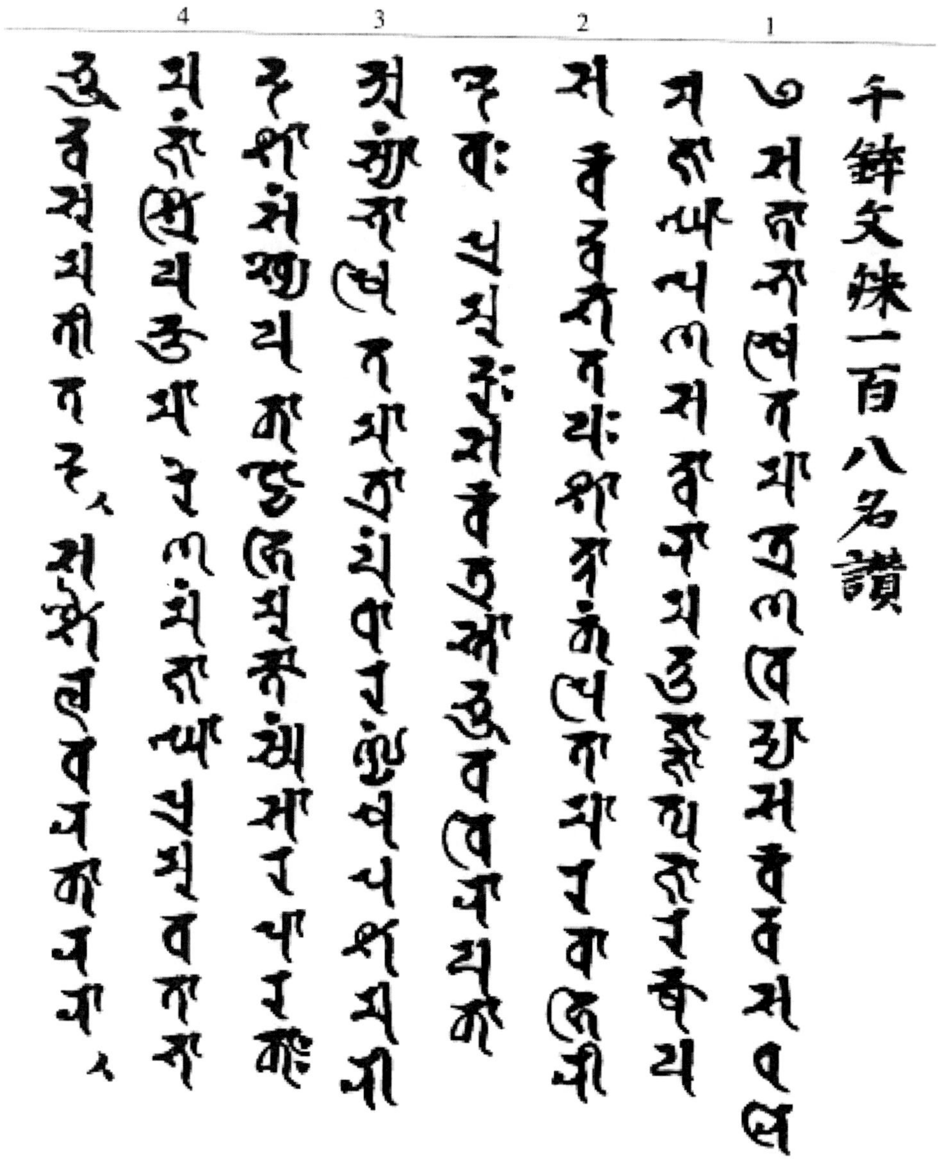

Mañjuśrī is a symbol of *śastra* and *śāstra,* weapons and scriptures. He looks lovely and pleasing and holds a double edged sword in his right hand and a manuscript of Prajñāpāramitā placed on a blue lotus in his left hand. The sword cuts across delusions and destroys all that stands against truth. Symbolically it represents righteousness, justice, equity, love and creativity. The book is a symbol of transcendental wisdom. His ride, a golden haired lion is a symbol of action and energy.

Samantabhadra-caryā-praṇidhāna-rāja

Samantabhadra-caryā-praṇidhāna-rāja is a prayer in melodious *ḍoḍhaka* stanzas, which ranks among the most beautiful expressions of Buddhist piety and has been used for worship in all the cointries of Mahayana Buddhism ever since 4th century AD. It is found at the end of Gaṇḍavyūha in Sanskrit manuscripts as well as in the Chinese and Tibetan translations. It is also found as an independent text and was translated into Chinese several times in the 4th and 8th centuries and into Tibetan in the 9th century. Its manuscripts are found in the collections of Sanskrit manuscripts at Paris and Cambridge. The Peking xylograph edition consists of 19 folios and gives the Sanskrit text in Lantsha and Tibetan characters. It was copied by Sage Jiun Sonja, a teacher of the Shingon sect, who was born in the 57the year of K'ang-his of Sheng-tsu of Ch'ing dynasty (AD 1718). He used to recite the text of Samantabhadra-caryā-praṇidhāna-rāja and other texts daily. He was well versed both in exoteric and esoteric doctrines, particularly in the Vinaya teachings.

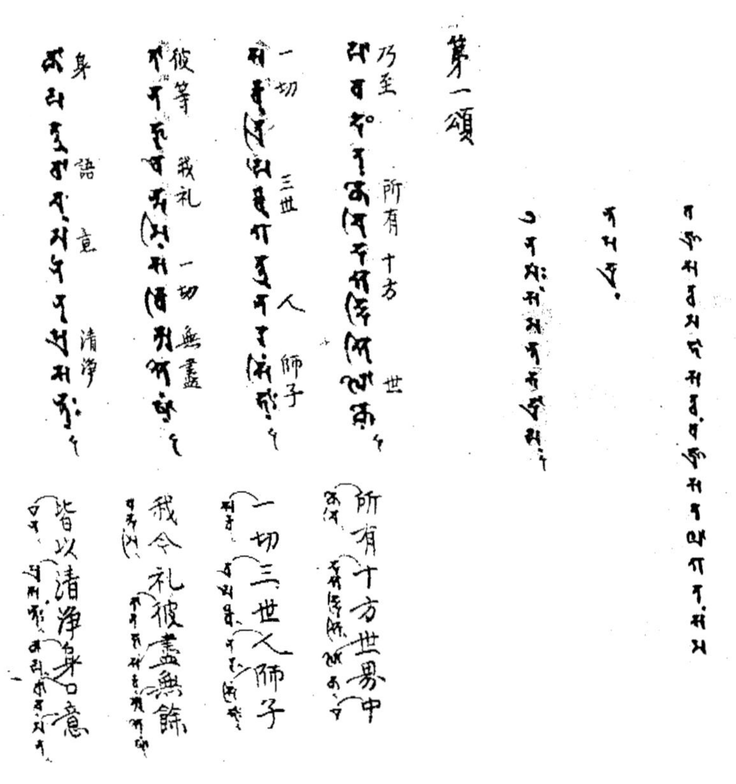

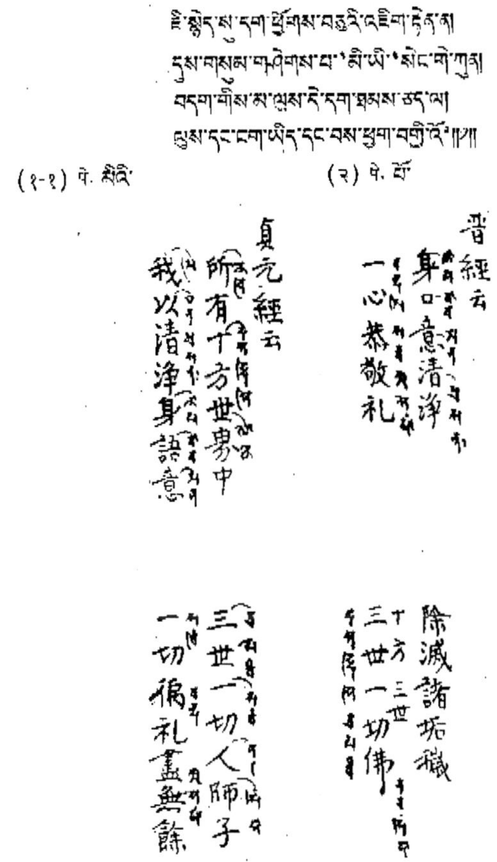

The above pages are taken from the xylograph reproduced by the International Academy of Indian Culture, presented to Prof. Dr. Raghu Vira by the Akademia Nauk of the USSR. The same xylographic edition is referred to in 'A Catalogue of Japanese and Chinese Books and Manuscripts' by Bunyiu Nanjio. Sanskrit text is given in Siddham characters with lateral Chinese word-meanings, followed by three translations in Chinese. The first is by Amoghavajra (AD 746-771) of the T'ang dynasty, the second is a translation by Buddhabhadra (AD 420) of the Eastern Tsin dynasty and the third is done by Prajñā (AD 796-798) of the T'ang dynasty. (Sushma Devi, Samantabhadracaryā-praṇidhāna-rāja, International Academy of Indian Culture, New Delhi, Śatapitaka vol. 4). Sanskrit books translated into Chinese are the lost heritage of India. The Taishō edition of the Tripiṭaka comprises over 3360 works translated from Sanskrit.

The great sage Jiun Sonja was a man of great virtue. At the age of 14 he became thoroughly familiar with Siddham. He was a talented calligrapher. His calligraphy was highly regarded. His writings comprise a thousand fascicules (*kwans*). Some of them were published by the 'Jiun Sonja One Hundred Fiftieth Death Anniversary Commemorative Society '. International Academy of Indian Culture, New Delhi, also published some of his works in two volumes.

A large number of hymns were taken to Japan from China for recitation on special occasions. Special musical notations were written to chant the mantras. This special genre of music is termed Bombai or Shōmyō. To this day there are special colleges of Buddhist music at Kyoto and Kōyasan.

Siddham

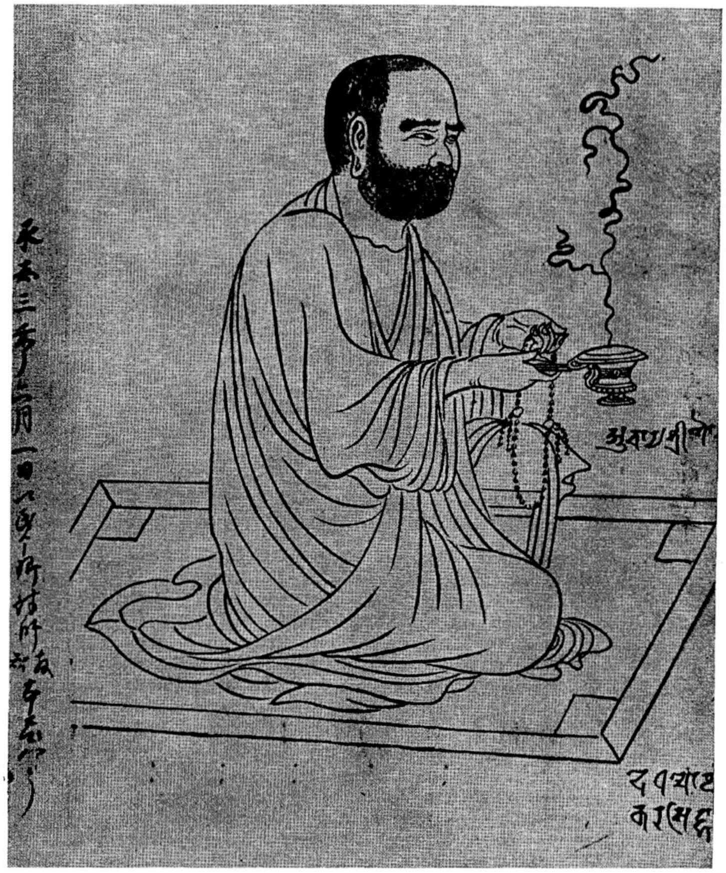

Portrait of the Indian scholar Śubhakarasiṁha from a ninth century scroll

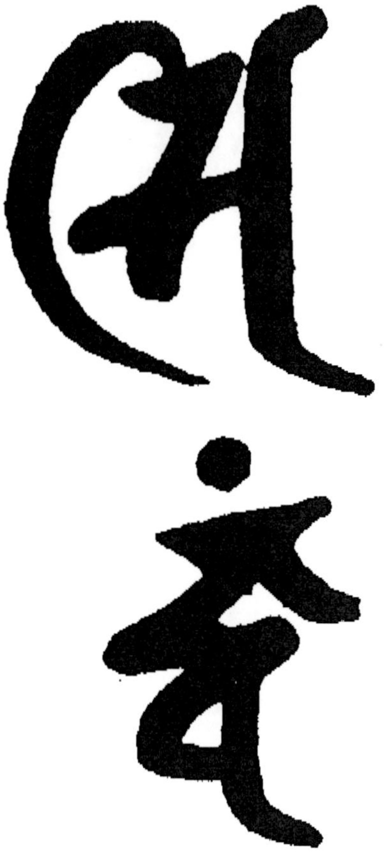

'Siddham' written by a Japanese calligrapher

Most of the Sanskrit manuscripts taken to China during the T'ang dynasty were written in Siddham. It is a variety of Brāhmī, and an elder sister of Nāgarī, which owed its popularity in China and Japan especially to the rise of Mantrayana Buddhism. It was used for writing *dhāraṇīs, mantras* and seed syllables, *bījakṣaras*. It became a living script of such intrinsic value as to deserve a place in the realm of fine arts and is indeed considered on a par with painting. It is used for calligraphic and decorative purposes. A number of Chinese and Japanese monks devoted themselves to study the script and for more than a thousand years they guarded the treasure of Indian culture. It is the Nāgarī scrip of eighth-ninth century which was introduced to Kōbō Daishi by the Kashmiri scholar Prajñā. It has been designated by the Japanese as Shittan, a corruption of Sanskrit term Siddham. This form of Nāgarī has a calligraphic charm of its own, in expressive curves and subtle nuances of brush and ink. It is also written in sturdy and dynamic strokes of a wooden stylus.

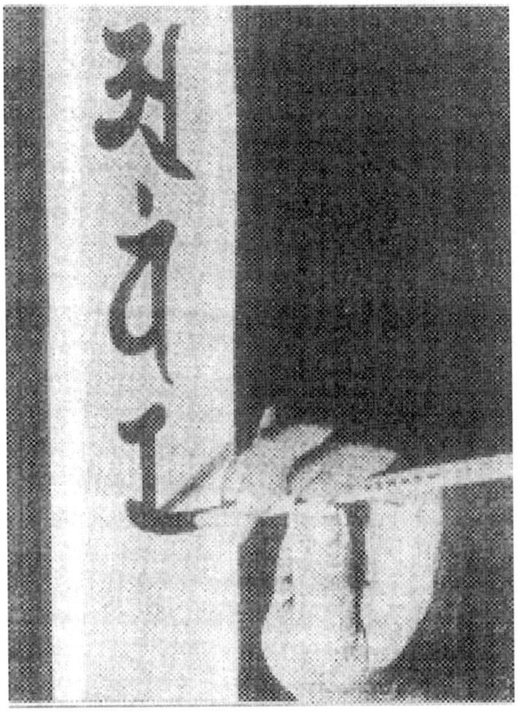

Writing in siddham script with a brush

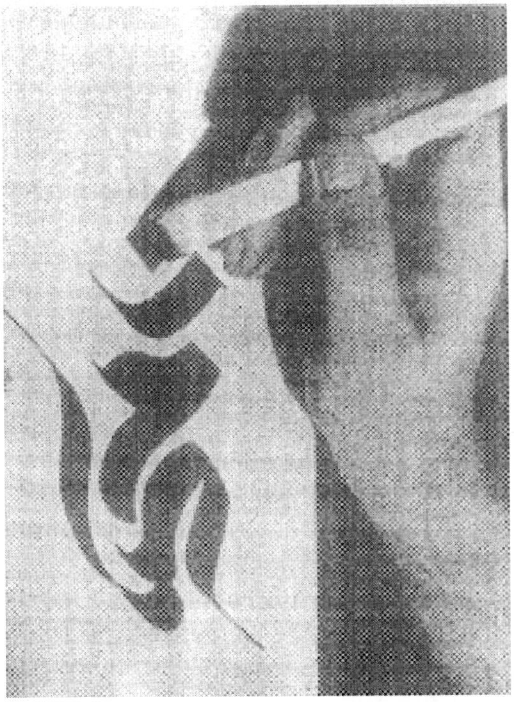

Writing with a stylus

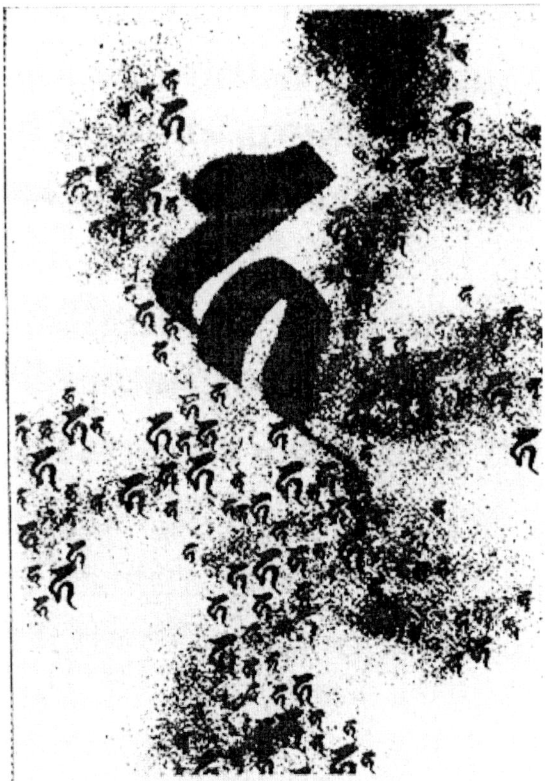

'ha' written in siddham artistically by a Japanese artist

Though Amoghavajra propagated the correct writing of the Indian script and evolved a unified system of transcribing Sanskrit sounds with Chinese characters yet the Tantric teachers stressed that a mantra transcribed as accurately as possible could never be as efficacious as those written in the original script. Subhakarasiṁha, Vajrabodhi, Amoghavajra and other masters used a variety of Brāhmī scripts that were widely used in India. Thus the script became the style of writing favored by the Chinese and the Japanese Buddhists for writing *mantras* and *dharanis* which has remained in fashion till the present day.

The script was used in India around 1000 AD as has been written by the Arab scholar Alberuni: *"The most generally known alphabet is called siddhamatrka which by some is considered as originating from Kashmir... ... . But it is also used in Varanasi .. .. The same writing is used in Madhyadeśa.. ... ... "*

The term Siddham is also mentioned by I-ching: *They (Indians) begin their (Sanskrit) study with the His-t'ang-chang or Siddham writing tables. This book is also called his-ti-ra-su-tu (siddhiarstu) ... ... .This means success and good luck. ... ... "* Every time the teacher used to write a new paradigma on the writing board, he would first write at the top *'siddham'* or *'siddhirastu'.* This is why the script was called 'siddham'.

The word 'siddham' became a common parlance, a designation for script, a colloquial equivalent of the literary word *lipi* and the Chinese pilgrims adopted this term 'siddham' for the form of the Indian script that they found in use there in the 7th-9th century. Since the boards used for teaching this script were called 'siddham writing boards' this term was later used as the title of books containing elementary writing lessons (R.H.Van Gulik, Siddham pp. 52-55)

In China and Japan the name Brāhmī actually refers to the siddham script. Another northern-Brāhmī derived script is Tibetan devised for writing translations of Indian texts around the seventh century AD. The Hangul writing system of Korea is said to have been created under the influence of the Tibetan script.

Siddham Letters as Objects of Worship

Bījaksaras, the symbolic syllables written in Shittan are objects of worship when they represent the essence of the divine beings, such as 'अ' is written for Agni, 'च' for Candra, 'इ' for Indra and so on. Sūrya in Japan represents the time aspect of human life, and alongwith Candra it denotes eternity in cosmic order. The seed syllables are placed on lotus flowers to indicate their divine origin.

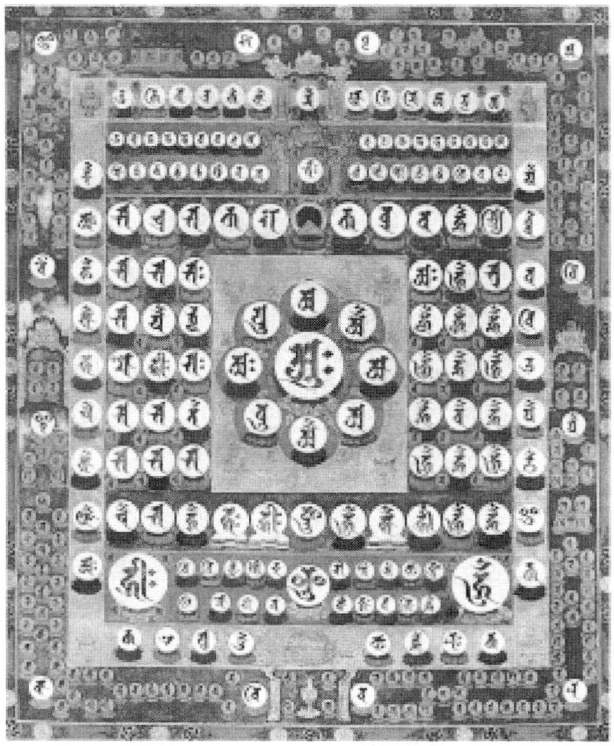

Siddham letters used as seed syllables representing various deities of Mahākaruṇāgarbha-maṇḍala

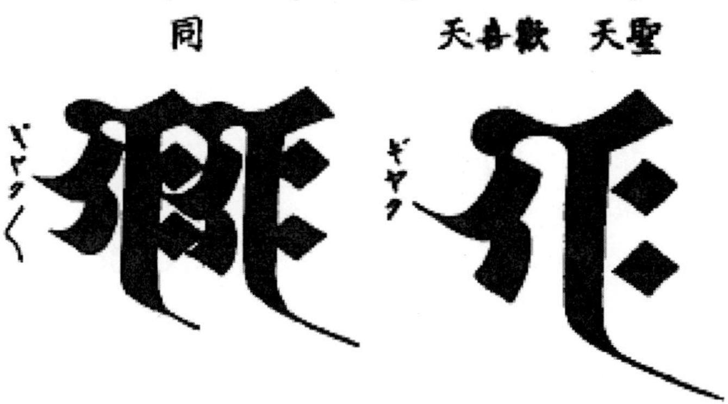

'gaḥ gaḥ' and 'gaḥ' written in siddham as seed syllables for dual Gaṇapati and Gaṇapati

Many Japanese who do not know Sanskrit are familiar with the Indian Siddham letters. Thus Buddhist sūtras inspired the finest calligraphy and printing styles in Japan. No book was printed outside a temple. The Japanese manuscript is a commentary on the Lotus Sutra, by Shōtoku Taishi (AD 573-621). He was a symbol of the special relationship between Buddhism and the state. The earliest surviving example of printed matter in Japan is Hyamanto darani, One Million Pagoda dhāraṇī which belongs to AD 764-770 produced by the order of Empress Shōtoku as thanksgiving for the defeat of a rebellion. Emperor Shōmu (701-56) strongly promoted copying the entire Buddhist Tripiṭaka. Thus sūtra copying became a major industry in Japan. Wooden tablets called *sotōbas* i.e. stupas, written in Siddham letters are often found in cemeteries.

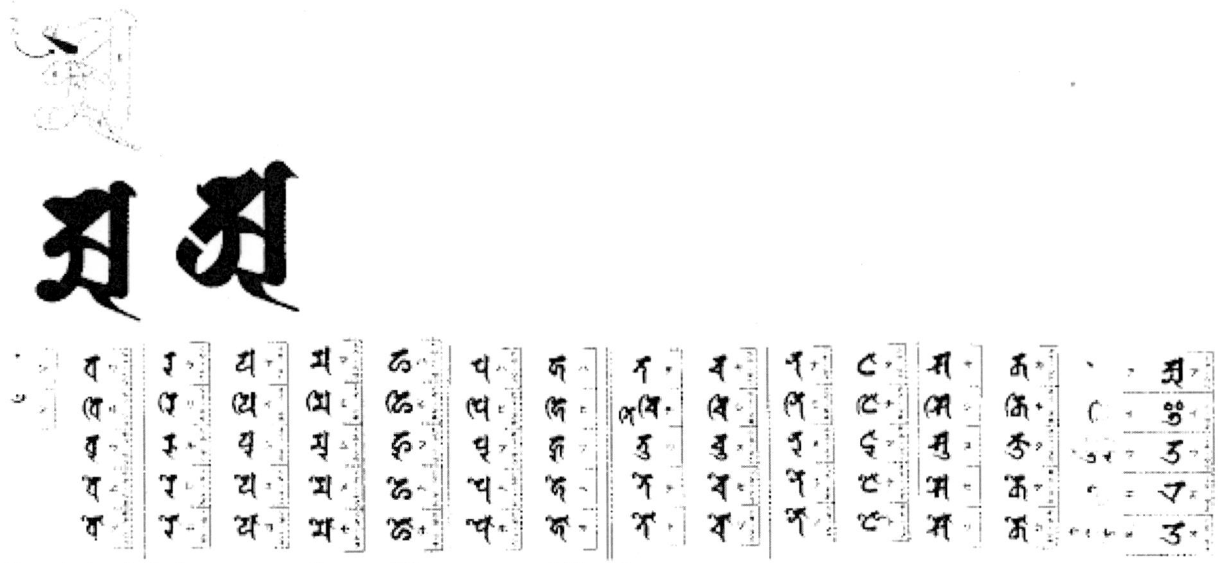

Sanskrit alphabets written in siddham script according to Hiragana and Katakana sound sequence

The Japanese alphabets Katakana and Hiragana are based on the Sanskrit sound sequence: a, i, u, e, o, ka, ki, ku, ke, ko, ……… . The alphabets were devised by the great monk Kōbō Daishi who began to democratize education by founding a school for the children of the common people. Hiragana alphabets are the cursive form which was woven into the Iroha poem. Iroha uta contains 47 letters, each letter occurring only once. It was a literary marvel. It is a free translation of a Buddhist poem composed in ancient India:

Sarve saṁskārāḥ anityāḥ utpadavyayadharmiṇaḥ |
Teṣām vyupaśamaḥ sukham avadat mahāśramaṇaḥ | |

The new syllabry was a revolutionary step in Japan's civilization. It is called '*dhvani pañcāśikā*'. To this day every Japanese begins his education with this eroha poem. Some times dictionaries are arranged in this sequence.

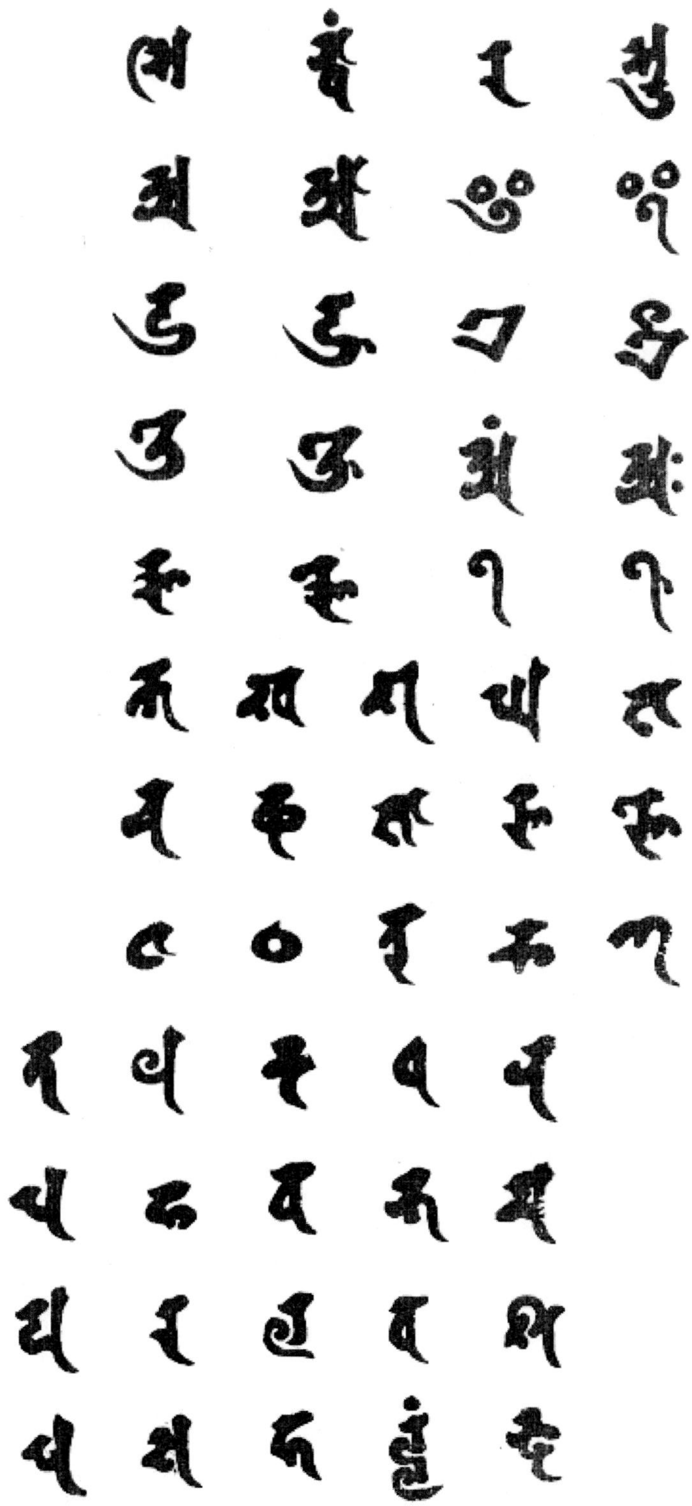

Siddham letters written by a modern Japanese calligrapher

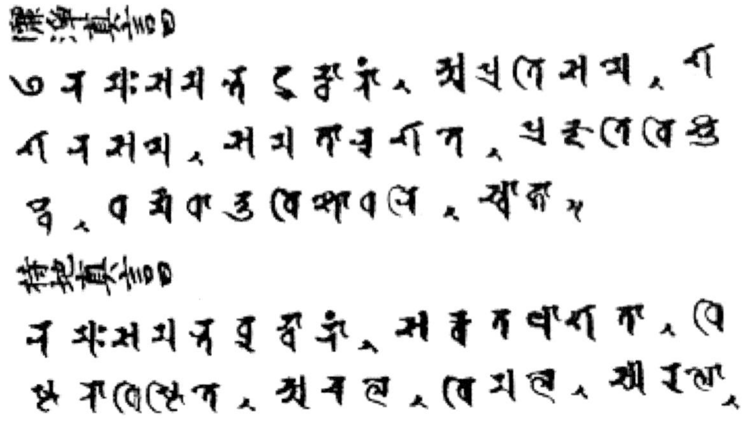

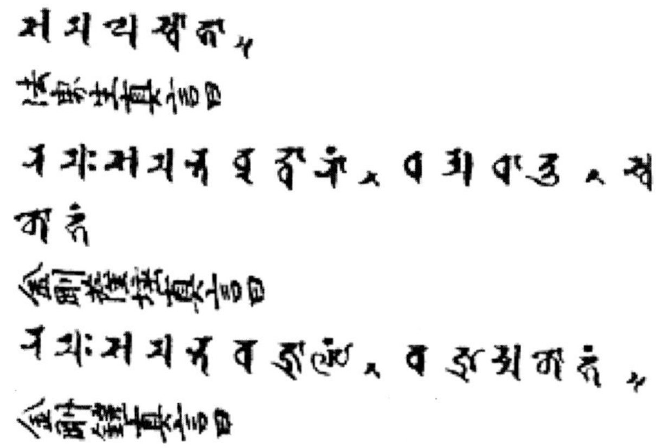

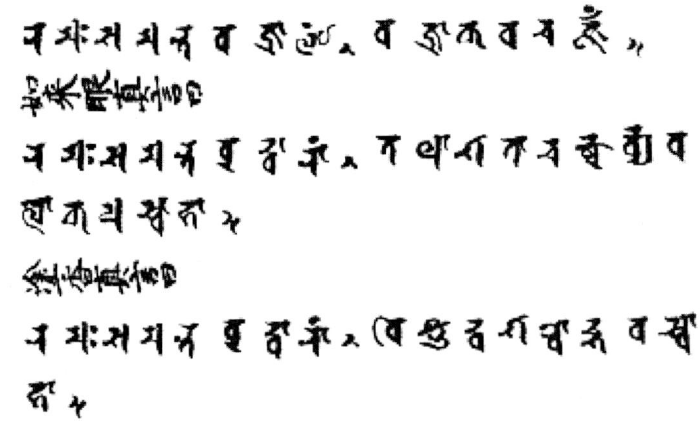

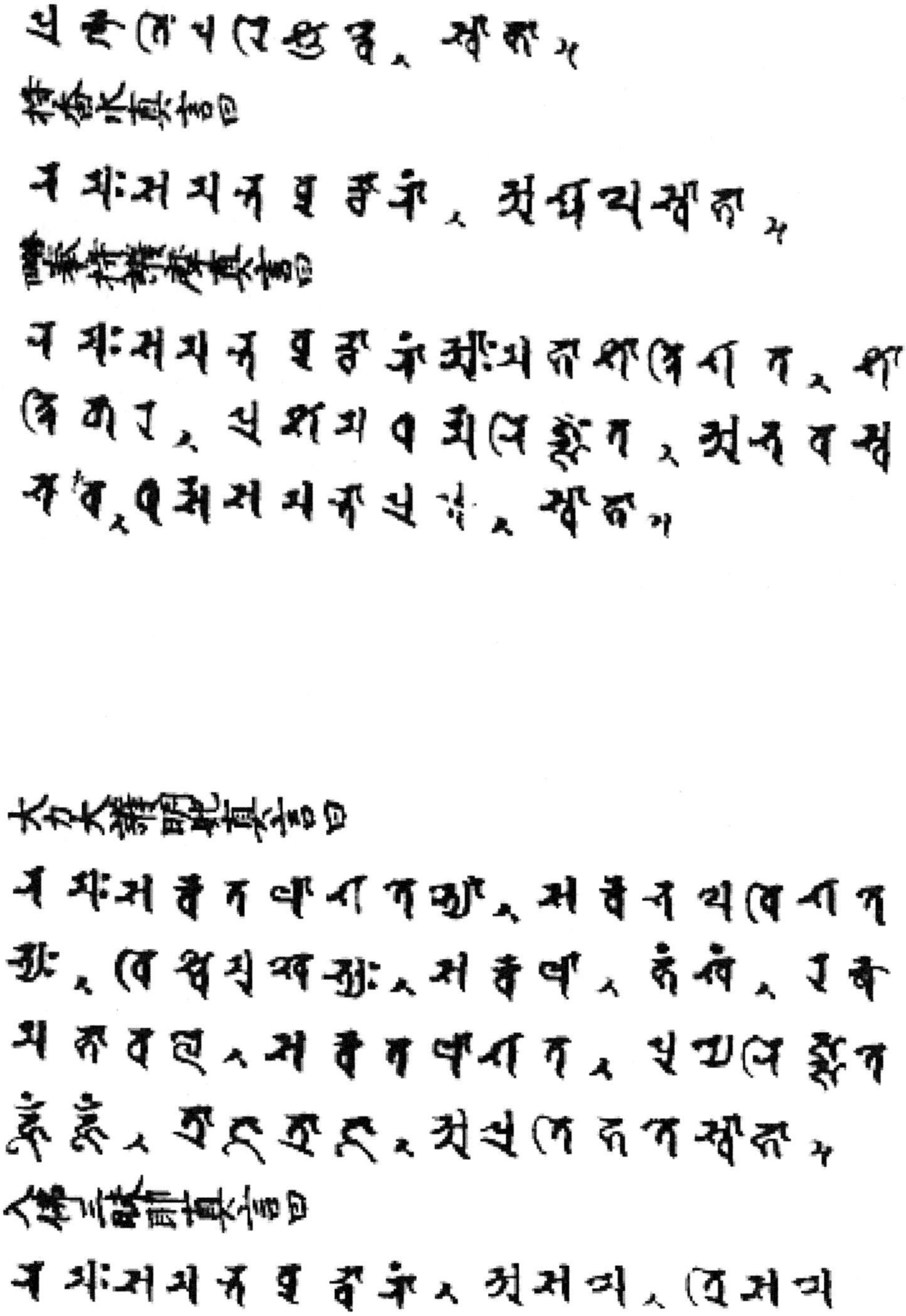

Mantras written by Monk Kōbō Daishi

Sanskrit is a common linguistic inheritance of India and Japan. In Japan '*bandai*' was used in place of yours truly at the end of a letter. It is Sanskrit '*vande*'. The Japanese word '*tsunumi*' for drum is Sanskrit '*dundubhī*'

Usage of Indian script as sacred has an uninterrupted history in Japan. Here is 'अ' calligraphed by Kakuban (AD 1095-1143). The initial letter 'अ' is emerging from a pristine white eight-petalled lotus, situated on the adamantine plane of the vajra. The sound symbol 'अ' is prime among all letters and the supreme immutable: *akṣarānām akāro 'smi* (Gītā 10.33). Sacred Calligraphy became creative compassion.

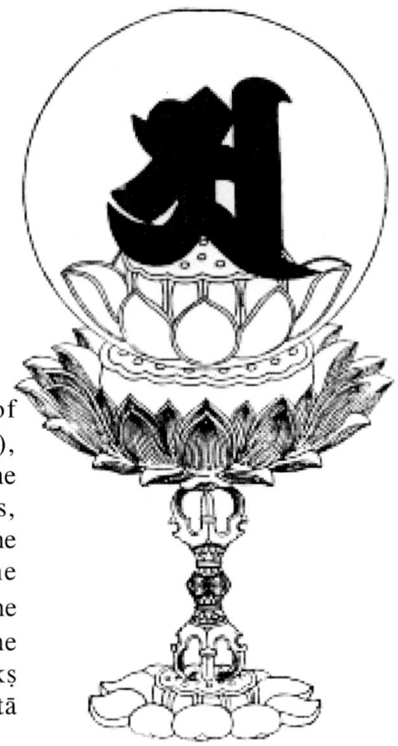

अ in the calligraphy of Kakuban (AD 1095-1143), emerging from a pristine white eight-petalled lotus, situated on the adamantine plane of the vajra. The sound symbol a अ is prime among all letters and the supreme immutable: akṣ arāṇām akāro 'smi (Gītā 10.33)

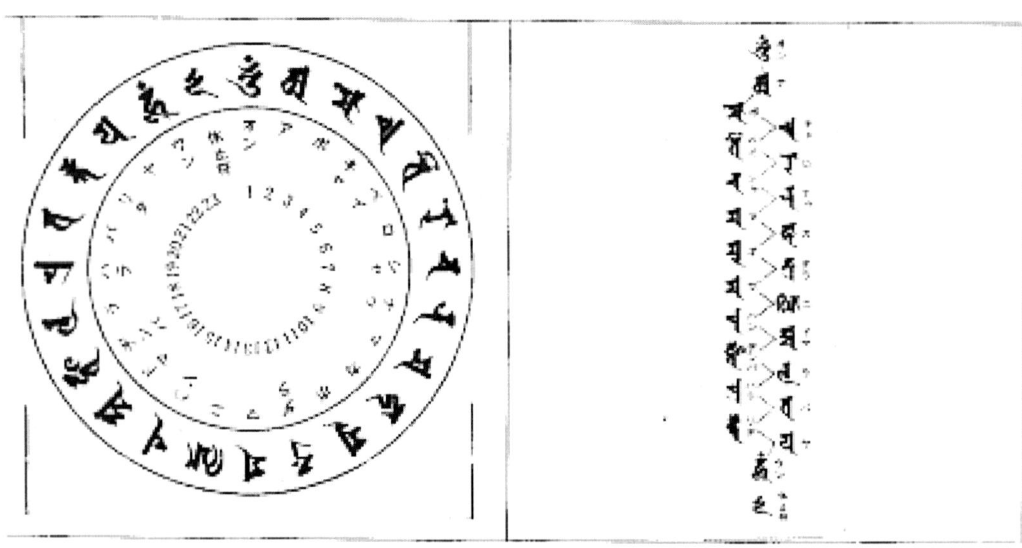

A Sanskrit dhāraṇī written artistically

Prof. Nagara is one of the most outstanding living masters of siddham calligraphy. His brush bruises against the canvas, shaping itself in the reflexion of dynamism. He tries to reach out to the Buddha in his calligraphy of force and strength. As a professor of design at an institute of technology his calligraphy is the sound mingling with the mind and merging with mists, drifting in mountain vales.

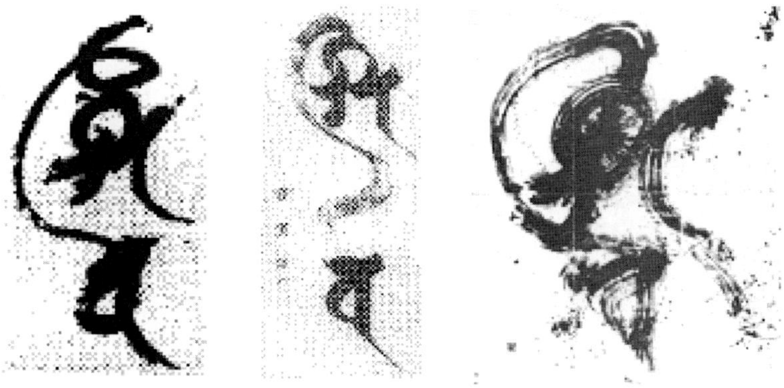

'Śiva' written in three different styles by Prof. Nagara

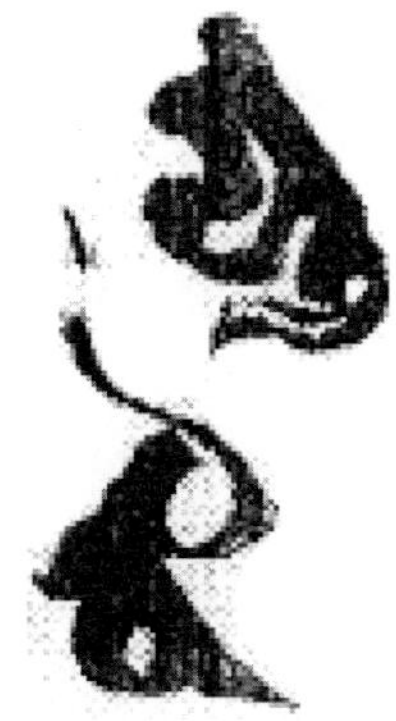

Vāyu

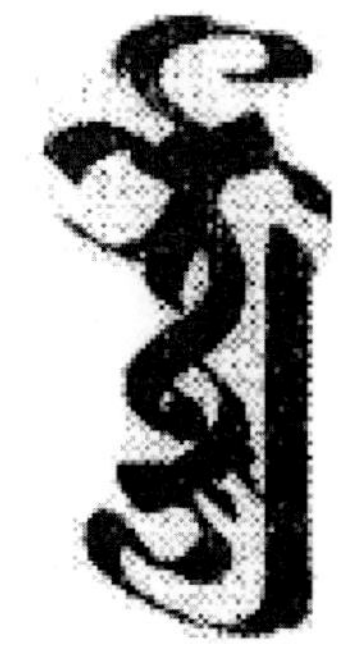

Bhaiṣajya

Through the storming calligraphy the artist expresses the tempestuous mind of Lord Shiva, delimited by free and vigorous strokes. The holy waters of the river Gaṅgā meander across the dark and majestic Himalayas in a running brush in its indomitable tāṇḍava.

Vāyu is written in simple pure lines, rustling in the mind as cosmic breath. As wind blows unobstructed in the sky, so do the supernatural power of the Buddha emancipate all beings. The energy of Vāyu in the space of Nothingness expresses the intensity to be free from all things.

Bhaiṣajya, the symbol of Bhaiṣajyaguru, the Buddha of healing, is written in monumental, absolutely final and sweeping in a downward movement. It has the boldness of a sword that defends the faith. It is the dance of hand on paper.

The rich black strokes against a pure white space are warm and moving, angered or meditative, expressing many levels and moods. Curves are expressive and linear nuances are subtle. Thus making calligraphy a path of illumination.

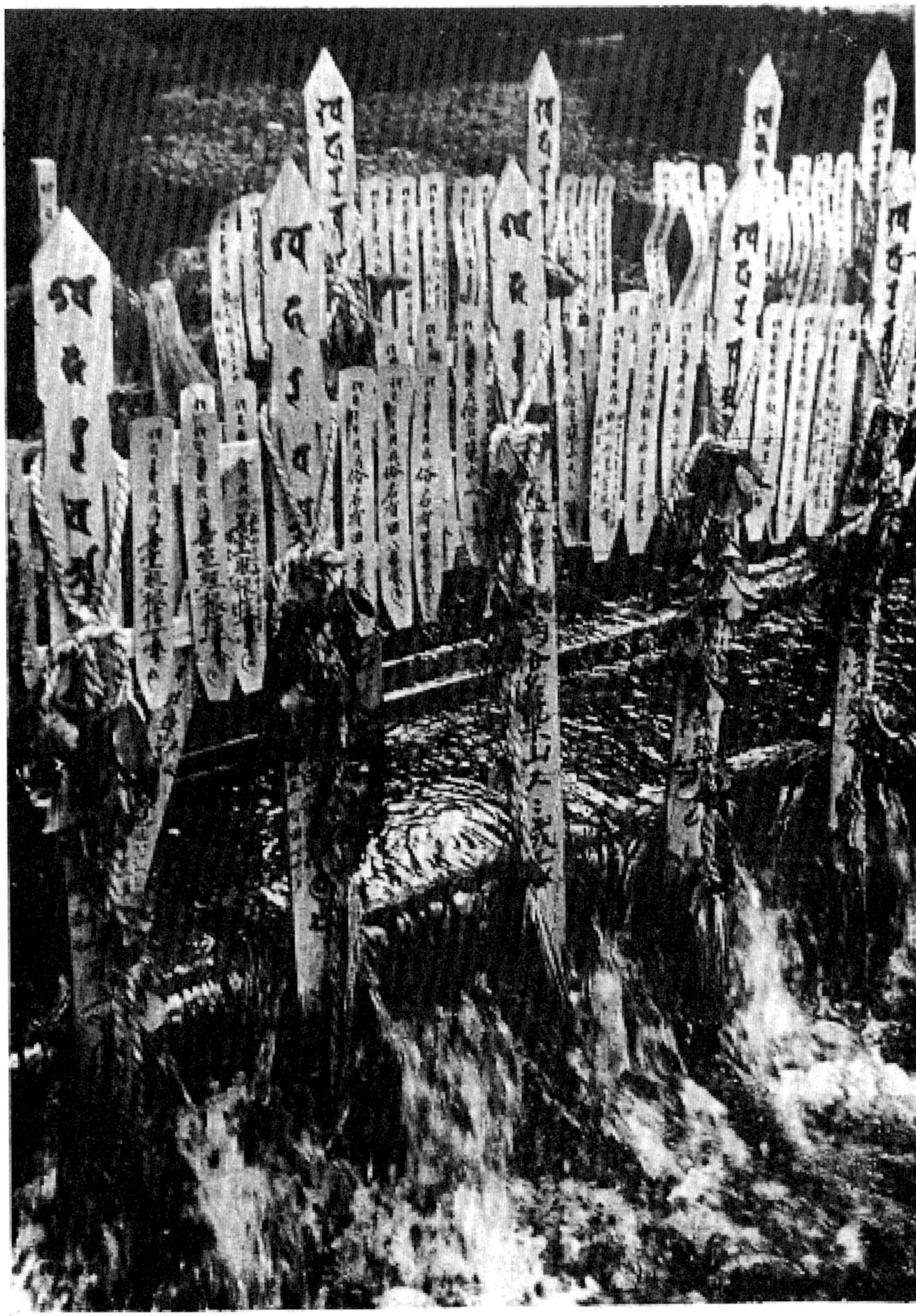

'a, vi, ra. hūm, kham' written in siddham on palm leafs and tied near a river in Kōyasan in Japan

यन्मङ्गलं क्षितितले दिवि नागलोके रत्नत्रयं सुगतरत्नसुताभिधानम्।
क्षेत्रं जनैश्च शुभसंचयबीजपुष्टैस् तन्मङ्गलं भवतु शान्तिकरं तवाद्य॥

yan maṅgalaṁ kṣiti-tale divi nāga-loke ratna-trayaṁ sugata-ratna-sutābhidhānam/
kṣetraṃ janaiś ca śubha-saṃcaya-bīja-puṣṭais tan maṅgalaṁ bhavatu śānti-karaṁ tavādya//

Devanāgarī transcription of the following maṅgala-gāthā written in Siddham script with Kana transcription, published in the Edo period

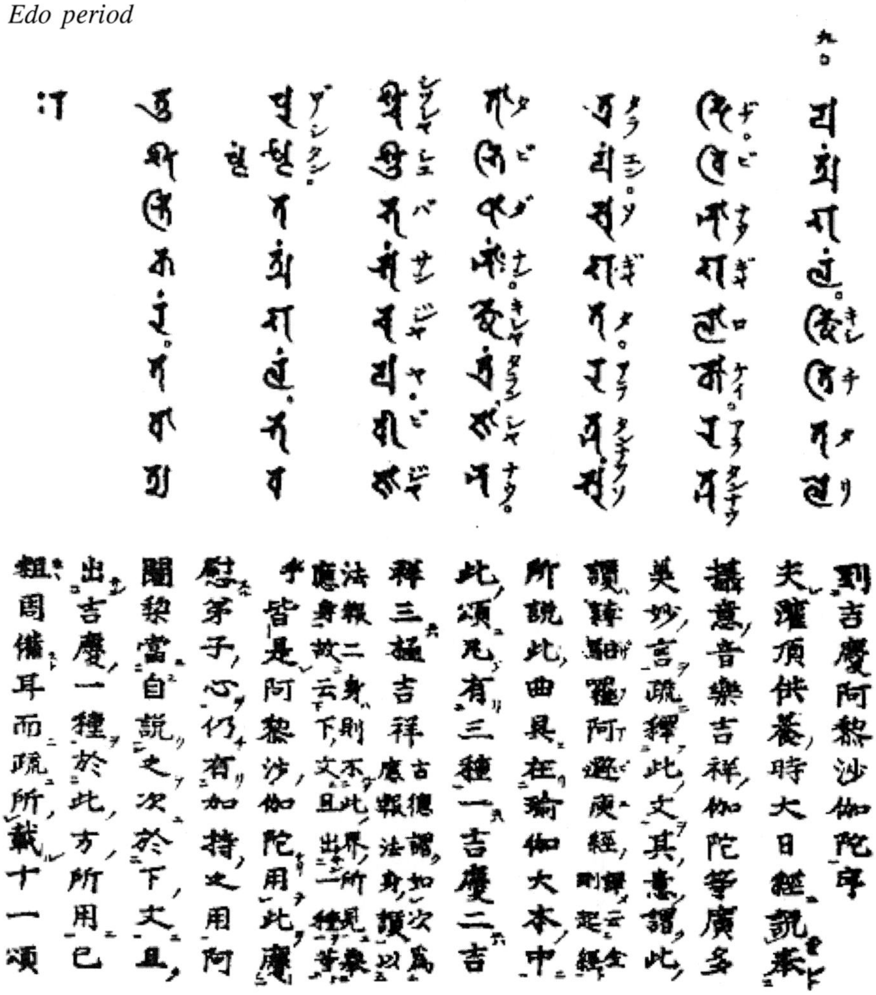

Thus it may be concluded that a language does not stand in isolation. There is an aura around it. Geographical features, ways of living and thinking of the people, their historical and cultural backgrounds, customs and beliefs influence the development of a language. Moreover it advances with advancement of civilization and higher levels of thought, because new discoveries and experiences constantly require coining of new terms which in turn enrich a language.

23

SANSKRIT IN SOUTHEAST ASIA

Sanskrit served as the language of learning, contributed towards intellectual advancement, gave greatest amount of freedom of thought and action. It forms the substratum in the simple life of the people. An alphabetical culture was introduced with Sanskrit, non-writing people became writing people who bestowed the highest honors to Maharṣi Vyāsa and Valmīki in the Countries of Southeast Asia.

Study of Sanskrit in Southeast Asia requires a wider angle in research incorporating not only the existing documents but also the traces and references, scattered in lithic and literary works including a comprehensive study of the civilizations and cultures, before it reached the island countries. Their political history, religious and philosophical systems, customs and traditions, even geographical conditions are not to be left aside because languages do not stand in isolation, they advance with advancement of civilizations and later serve as a mirror to reflect their characteristics. New inventions require new terminology. The source for the new terminology and enrichment of a language must be rich. In the early years of Christian era the purpose was served by Sanskrit in the countries of Southeast Asia which had become the language of the intellectual elite.

Sanskrit crossed the boundary of India in the early years of the Christian era along with the religious systems and thought. It had the prestige of being an international language in ancient times, playing an important role in the cultural lives of the people. It reached wherever Śaivism, Buddhism or Vaiṣṇavism were carried, wherever the epics like Rāmāyaṇa or Mahābhārata, Vedas and Vedāngas were received warmly. It carried new systems of administration, moral and social values and ideas embedded with deep philosophical thoughts.

The valuable works in Sanskrit: Rāmāyaṇa, Mahābhārata, Purāṇas, Āgamas, and books on philosophy, *nīti-śāstra* (science of ethics and morality), *kāvya* (poetics), *alaṅkāra* (rhetorics), *chanda* (prosody), grammar and lexicons were known in SEA.

The people inhabiting the island countries began to record their heroic deeds in Sanskrit. So the study of Sanskrit in Southeast Asia begins with the lithic record written in Sanskrit in the scripts derived from Indian scripts. All the known examples of scripts found in the inscriptions in SEA show different types of Brāhmī script, datable to the period from the 2nd century to the 5th century AD. The earliest specimens are written in a script that is strongly reminiscent of that of Kuṣāṇa inscriptions of probably the 2nd century AD, while apparently later inscriptions are in a kind of Gupta script. In Laos the beginning of script goes back to 1283 AD; lithic records begin to appear from that period onwards. Their script is know as Dhamma (=dharma), the script used in inscriptions, poetry, romance, administrative records and correspondence etc.

Vietnam

The earliest known examples of writing in SEA are a number of small inscriptions on seals discovered from Oc-eo, west coast of Ca-mao peninsula in Southern Vietnam. The earliest inscription found from Nha-trang district of Vietnam (formerly known as Champa), discussed as Vo-canh inscription is written in south Indian type of script which can be compared with that of Īkṣvāku inscriptions of Andhra Pradesh. It dates back to around third century AD (Casparis 1975:12-13). Inscriptions in Champa are often bilingual, written partly in Sanskrit and partly in Cham, in a script which is similar to the south Indian writing (Diringer 1949:403). The Tra-kieu inscription of the seventh century is in Sanskrit and celebrates Vālmīki. Champa was a renowned center of Sanskrit and Buddhist learning and a Chinese military mission was sent against king Shambhuvarman to bring to China, 1350 Sanskrit Buddhist works as war booty. In 752, the teacher Buddhasthira was invited to Japan by Emperor Shōmu to join the consecration ceremony of the image of the Great Buddha at Tōdaiji monastery. He introduced Sanskrit music and dance in Japan that is a part of Imperial repertoire to this day (Sharma pg. ix-xi).

Cambodia

A high erudition in Sanskrit marked the culture of Cambodia for many centuries, amply proved by the Sanskrit inscriptions which have been found in large numbers all over Cambodia extending from 5th-14th century AD. The first collection of these inscriptions was published as early as 1885. The first dated inscription belongs to the reign of Jayavarman II (475AD ṣ 512 AD). The Ankor Borei inscription of 533 AD probably represents the ruins of the ancient city of Vyadhapura surrounded by a rampart (Majumdar 1953:no.6).

Sanskrit literature

Sanskrit was used as the language of administration in Cambodia uptill the 14th century. As a language of the elite its literature was seen as the most valuable source for advancement. According to the available lithic records in Cambodia, study of Pāṇini's grammar was highly placed. In Phnom Sandak inscription King Jayavarman II has been extolled for his knowledge of Pāṇini's grammar. While describing the glory of the king in the most extravagant phrases, a verse is added which has a double sense applicable to both the King and the grammarian.

The verses in the inscriptions containing pun on the rules of Pāṇini indicate that the writers of those inscriptions were thoroughly conversant with the grammatical treatise. According to an inscription King Yashovarman himself composed a commentary on the Mahābhāṣya. The minister of the king was an expert in Horāśāstra. Manu is mentioned as a legislator. A verse from Manusmṛti is reproduced verbatim. A reference is made to Vātsyāyana as the author of Kāmasūtra and Viśālākṣa as having composed a treatise on *nīti*. The famous medical treatise of Suśruta is also mentioned in an inscription. The Pre Rup inscription contains four verses alluding to Kālidāsa's Raghuvaṁśa, repeating sometimes the very words used by the great poet himself. The records frequently refer to Trayī or Vedas, Vedānta, Smrti and the sacred canons of the Buddhists and the Jainas. While going through the inscriptions from Cambodia one can easily find allusion, alliteration, simile etc., commonly used in Sanskrit literature in India. Meters used in the inscriptions are Vasantatilakā, Upendravajrā, Upajāti, Mālini, Śārdūlavikrīḍita, Sragdharā, Āryā and Mandākrantā etc. (Majumdar 1953:p.233). Such inscriptions bear ample evidence of a highly flourishing state of Sanskrit literature in Cambodia.

Tracing Indian historical facts

An indepth study of Cambodian inscriptions from the Indian point of view is long awaited. They can be helpful in filling some of the gaps in Indian history. For example the date of Jagadguru Śankarācārya (AD 788-820) has been decided on the basis of the inscription from the Imperial temple Prasat Kandol Thom (Majumdar 1953:No.54), dated 878-887. The inscription is written by the teacher of King Indravarman who was a disciple of Bhagavān Śankarācārya. His name was Śivasoma and he was the grandson of King Jayendrādhipati Varman (verse 29,30). Śivasoma was well versed in all the disciplines. He had studied the *śastras* from Bhagavān Śaṅkara himself (verse 39). His teacher (Śaṅkara) is eulogized as another Rudra, unique receptacle of all disciplnes, learned in Vedas, and born in a Brāhmaṇa family (verse 40). The inscription is written in Sanskrit language and Pallava script.

Śāstrotsava

Literary achievements and celebrations was a fashion in ancient SEA, especially in Cambodia and Indonesia. For example King Sūryavarman had ascended the throne in 1034 Śaka, immediately after accession the young king performed the initiation (*dīkṣā*) of the royal priest, studied different religious subjects beginning with sacred mysteries, celebrated the grand literary ceremony, sastrotsava (Majumdar 1953:No.167). Reference has been made to the daily recitation of Purāṇas, Rāmāyaṇa and Mahābhārata in the inscriptions that reveal a thorough acquaintance of their authors with them. There were Brāhamaṇas proficient in Vedas and Vedāṅgas, ministers had a profound knowledge of Dharmaśāstras. Gifts of texts of Rāmāyaṇa, Mahābhārata and Purāṇas and their daily recitation, has been mentioned in the Veal Kantel inscription of Bhava Varman. (Majumdar 1953:19).

१. श्रीवीरवर्म्मदुहिता स्वसा श्रीभववर्म्मणः।
पतिव्रता धर्म्मरता द्वितीयारुन्धतीव या ॥
२. हिरण्यवर्म्मजननीं यस्तां पत्नीमुपावहत्।
द्विजेन्दुराकृतिस्वामी[१] सामवेदविदग्रणीः।
३. श्रीसोमशर्म्मार्कयुतं स श्रीत्रिभुवनेश्वरम्।
अतिष्ठिपन् महापूजामतिपुष्कलदक्षिणम्॥
४. रामायन[२]पुराणाभ्यामशेषं भारतन् ददत्।
अकृतान्त्रहमच्छेद्यां स च तद्वाचनास्थितिम्॥
५. यावत् त्रिभुवनेशस्य विभूतिरवतिष्ठते।
योय ए … … … ॥

६. धर्म्मां शस्तस्य स्यान् महासुकृतकारिणः।

... ... ॥

७. हतस्तु[३] हर्त्ता दुर्बुद्धिर्य एकमपि पुस्त(कम)॥

An inscription refers to the gift of a manuscript of Sambhava, a work of Vyāsa, which should be a section of Ādiparva of Mahābhārata called Sambhava Parva. Such references in the inscriptions testify the existence of Sanskrit imprecations are invoked against those who destroy the manuscripts deposited in the temples. The Prasat Prah That inscription (Majumdar 1953:no.41)-refers to the deposit of a manuscript of Sambhava adhyāya:

------ द्र (?) शरैश् शके दिने------चतुर्द्दशे ।
------ स्थितये दत्तं संभवपुस्तकम् ॥१॥
भवज्ञानेन निहितं व्याससत्रनिबन्धनम्।
यो नाशयति दुर्बुद्धिः निरये स चिरं वसेत् ॥२॥
सन्तानमेव वञ्चन्[२]यः व्याससत्रविनाशकृत्।
यावत् सूर्य्यश्च चन्द्रश्च स वसेत् नरकेषु वै ॥३॥

A short record *"Om Jaiminīye svāhā"* displays great reverence for Pūrva Mīmāṁsā and indicates that its author was regarded as a deity and was regularly worshipped (Majumdar 1944:63).

Indonesia

The oldest inscription in the Indonesian archipelago belongs to a large group of inscriptions including a considerable number of inscriptions of the mainland SEA, particularly Malaya peninsula, southern Thailand, Cambodia and southern Vietnam. The scripts of these inscriptions are identified as Vengi script used in Vengi or Vengipura, in the Godāvarī delta of present Andhra Pradesh and Pallava which was also used in some of the inscriptions in Srilanka. Local varieties of scripts were based on such Indian scripts, emphasizing the importance of local genius, needs and tastes. Three or four inscriptions are written in Tamil script also (Casparis 1975:12-13, 68).

Thirty inscriptions discovered from Telaga Batu to the east of the city of Palembang in Sumatra bear the inscription *Jayasiddha yātrā*, some of them have an additional word *sarvatattva*, evidently they were laid by pilgrims as Telaga Batu was a place of pilgrimage. There are other inscriptions also which record *śrīvijaya jayasidha yātrā* in order to celebrate a victory over śrīvijaya. Three or four lines in Sanskrit in late Pallava script are written on bricks of hardened clay.

Java as a center for Sanskrit studies

Java was a famous center for studying Sanskrit as has been written by Itsing, the Chinese pilgrim who stayed there for six months to study grammar before coming to ndia. After that he came to Nālandā, stayed for ten years and then again returned to Indonesia, stayed for four years and translated a number of Sanskrit texts into Chinese. He has written in his memoirs that a few decades before him another Chinese scholar Hui-ning had come to Indonesia and lived there for three years to study Sanskrit under the teacher Jñānabbhadra. Itsing also refes to the popularity of Buddhacharita by Aśvaghoṣa (Hall 1970:42).

Sanskrit brought a higher level of thought which changed ways of thinking and living, leaving a profound impact on all the spheres of life in Indonesia. A large number of Sanskrit manuscripts discovered from there witness a rich tradition of Sanskrit learning and writing. Most of them are written in Old Javanese or Old Balinese scripts which look close to each other and are derived from the Pallava script of South India. In the texts written in Sanskrit, verses are followed by commentaries in regional languages.

Indonesian literati had an access to all the branches of Sanskrit learning and they put these disciplines to the best of use in the emergence of their own creative literature like Rāmāyaṇa Kakavin, Parvas are written in Old Javanese, a large number of texts on Śaiva philosophy, books on *nīti* and hymns written in praise of the divine.

Parva-saṅgraha written in Old Javanese during the ninth century mentions the exact number of stanzas in Mahābhārata. It should be seen as an important reference to find out which version of Mahābhārata from India had traveled to Indonesia comprising the said number of stanzas.

Works for teaching Sanskrit written in Indonesia

Methods of Sanskrit teaching in ancient India are illustrated in the texts identified as 'saḥ vṛkṣaḥ'. They are meant to teach intricacies of Sanskrit grammar and poetry. Svarasamhitā is an eclectic collection of stray bits of grammar, *kāvya, bīja mantras,* synonyms and the like. It contains fragments of Jānakīharaṇa, a Sanskrit kāvya on Indonesian soil. The classical curriculum of a poet comprised grammar, metrics, dramaturgy, lexicography and poetics. The Chinese pilgrim attests the study of Sanskrit grammar called 'śabdavidyā' in Java. Early versions of Sanskrit texts like Bhartṛhari's Śatakatraya, are given a generic name 'Kṛtabhāṣā'. Kṛtabhāṣā means texts written to teach Sanskrit Bhāṣā.

Major systems of Sanskrit grammar like Pāṇini, Sārasvata, Vararuci, Kāśatṛtsna and Kātantra can be traced in Indonesia, specially their sections on *sandhi*, nominal compounds, and some declensions and conjugations. The Kārikās of Kātantra on the cases are known under the title of 'Karakasaṅgraha' and are to be found in an Indonesian lontar entitiled 'Laṅkṛta'. Its purpose is stated at the end to be the authoritative interpretation and appropriate comprehension of the metaphysical or spiritual precepts of the *guru*. Bali has preserved to this day two different commentaries on Kārakasaṅgraha, one from the grammatical and the other from the philosophical view point.

Colophons of such texts are interesting for the history of Sanskrit literature. For example the colophon of the grammatical text by Vararuchi says:

Kātantrem ca mahātantre dṛṣṭvā tena manīṣiṇā
Bālāvabodhanatvāya kṛtaḥ kārakasaṅgraha |

If we accept the reading of 'Kantrem' as 'Katantre' then it can be presumed that there was a Mahātantra which was abbreviated as Katantra and the present text is again an abbreviated text done by Vararuci. But if we accept the reading as 'Kātantram' then it means that the present text Kātantra is a brief version of a Mahātantra.

The grammatical text by Vararuci comprises of Sanskrit verses followed by a commentary in Kavi. Svaravyañjana does not follow the Māheśvara sūtras; the alphabets are taught in the sequence of *ku*, *cu*, *tu*, *tu*, *pu*. The manuscript is written paper.

Sasnkrit lexicography is richly represented by the Amaramālā, Daśanāmā, Ādisvara,, Ekalavya, Samuhavacana, lists of monosyllabic words and several other texts without titles. Amarakoṣa is not the source of Amaramālā. The synonyms given in Amaramālā are to be compared with other Sanskrit lexicons.

शिवं सर्वगतं शान्तं सर्वज्ञं सवादिगुरुम् ।
प्रणम्यामरमालेयं नामलिङ्गं निगद्यते ॥१॥
रोदसि सवितुर्दीप्तिः पाताले रत्नदीधितिः ।
अर्थप्रकाशनाय च [सर्वत्र] पृथिव्यामियम् ॥२॥
पुं-नारी-क्लीब-सामान्यं काण्डानि हि यथाक्रमम्।
तथा पर्याय-जात्यर्थं विशिष्टं लिङ्गमुच्यते ॥३॥
श्लोकपादान्त-मध्यस्थः सनिबन्धी पूर्वकैः पदैः।
पादादिस्थः परैर्यान्ति नर-स्त्री-क्लीब-वाचकाः॥४॥
अमरास्त्रिदशाः प्रोक्ता गीर्वाणा विबुधाः सुराः।
वृन्दारका अदितिजा निर्ज्जरा दानवद्विषः॥५॥
लेखाः स्ववर्सिनोऽस्वप्नास् त्रिदिवेशाः सुधाशिनः।
देवाः स्वर्ग्गसदाऽमर्त्या ऋभवोऽमृतपास्तथा॥६॥
आदितेयाः सुमनसः सुपर्व्वाणे दिवौकसः।
देवतास्ताः स्त्रियामुक्ताः षण्ढेऽथ दैवतानि च॥७॥
शिवः सर्व्वो विरूपाक्षो महादेवो महेश्वरः।
श्रीकण्ठः शंकरो भर्ग्गः सोमधृङ् नीललोहितः॥८॥

(A page from Amaramālā, CHI 6.145)

Alaṅkāra or literary embellishment is known so far from a solitary text which commences with the words: *saḥ vṛkṣaḥ*. This text records a faithful record of the oral teaching with the constant repitition of the phrases, as if it were a live tape recording of a classroom. It is an interesting document of ancient pedagogic. In India too a teacher sitting under a tree would commence his lessons in *alaṅkāra-śāstra* with the tree itself, for it was the immediate environment of the taught.

Chandaḥ-karaṇa

Chandaḥ-karaṇa is the earliest known chrestomathy, a comprehensive manual, comprising several elements including alliteration, prosody, rhetorics, giving metres, synonyms of Amaramālā and homonyms. It belongs to the genre of literary text books or reference works which were studied by aspiring writers as well as consulted by accomplished authors. Sang Hyang Kamahāyānikan speaks of *Vayākaraṇa,* grammar and *prakaraṇa,* logic as two important disciplines, so *chandakaraṇa* is the third dimension, the elegance of speech. It served as a practical compendium for aspiring poets of which Amaramālā was but a part. It begins by listing words with the same letter, in the sequence of Sanskrit alphabet. These words were required by poets for alliteration and other effects.

Learning of Sanskrit is a must till today for elegance of style and for the creation of new words for new ideas. It was an established practice not so long ago that Jānakīharaṇa was one of the texts studied by those in Srilanka who desired to obtain proficiency in Sanskrit language.

Several Rāmāyaṇa texts were prevalent in Indonesia: Jānakīkāvya, Caritra Rāmāyaṇa and Bhaṭṭikāvya. The Indonesian version of Rāmāyaṇa known as 'Rāmāyaṇa kakavin' and its relationship with the Bhaṭṭi-kāvya deserves a detailed analysis. The opening verse of the Rāmāyaṇa Kakavin can be compared to the Bhaṭṭikāvya:

Abhut nṛpatiḥ vibudha sakhaḥ
Hana sira ratu dibya renon
Parantapaḥ
Prasasta ring rat musihnira pranata
Śrutānvitaḥ
Jaya paṇḍita rin aji kabeh
Daśaratha ity udahṛtaḥ
San Dasharatha nāma ta moli

Indonesian lontars have conserved some early versions of Sanskrit texts, for instance there is a known version of Bhartṛhari's work with the captions: lokayātrā, saṁsāra-nindā, viṣaya heyatā.

Ślokāntara

Ślokāntara is an important text consisting of 83 *ślokas* in Sanskrit followed by commentary in Old Javanese written on palm leaves. In general it corresponds to the *nīti* texts of Sanskrit literature. It deals with ethical topics, without any systematic classification like truth, charitable gifts, *vidyādāna* or imparting knowledge, the law of *karma,* diseases of persons descending from hell as against the joys of those coming from heaven, the five *yamas* and so on.

नास्ति सत्यात् परो धर्मो नानृतात् पातकं परं।
त्रिलोके च हि धर्म स्यात् तस्मात् सत्यं न लोपयेत्:॥७॥

(Slokantara 7)

Kavi, or Bhāṣā Kavi, the language of poetry, and the Kavi script were introduced in the 8th century into Java by immigrants from Gujarat, but according to some scholars it was a local and a later development of a south Indian script during the 5th century AD, most probably from the Coromandal coast. A Javanese tradition quoted in 'Aji Saka', attributes the introduction of writing into Java to a Brāhmaṇa called Tritresta. Some scholars accept it to have originated from early Grantham. Prototypes of lithic Grantha character are found in the distant lands of Malay archipelago and the coats of Indo-China (Diringer 1949:423).

All the texts on Saivism found from Indonesia are written in Sanskrit with a commentary in Old Javanese following each stanza. None of them has been found going parallel to any text in

Sanskrit so far. But their in-depth study may lead to a better understanding of Sanskrit and Tamil texts on Śaivism.

Bhuvanakoṣa

Bhuvanakoṣa is the earliest and the largest Śaiva text discovered from Indonesia, written in Sanskrit followed by commentary in Old Javanese (Goris 1931:39). The text is divided into eleven chapters called *paṭala*s and opens with *om avighnamastu*. Muni Bhārgava requests Lord Śiva to teach him the principles of *mokṣa, śūnya pada*, which can be visualized by a *yogi*. Through meditation, mind becomes uncluttered and purified and enters the state of *acyuta śūnya* as man has the potential to experience qualitatively different levels of perceptions and awareness. He attains the knowledge of four stages of awareness: *jāgrat, svapna, suṣupta and tūrya* to establish immediate contact with the supreme lord, the reality which allows comprehension and experience of life's meaning, value and purpose. Then he apprehends the law of universal order—the truth, the beautiful and the good, *satyam śivam sundaram*.

The second half of Bhuvanakosa talks about *caryā* as a method to be one with Śiva. The first method among them is besmearing the body with ashes, *bhasmasnāna*, an act of a Pāśupat ascetic, for purification. One surrenders oneself in one's mind to the supreme lord until the goal is achieved. Then one does not return from the state of liberation. The Supreme lord is regarded both as *sakala* and as *niṣkala* in manifestation.

Bhuvanasaṅkṣepa is another important Śaiva text in which Lord Śiva, the first preceptor of the doctrine reveals the highest reality to Kumāra Ṣaṇmukha and Bhaṭārī Umā. There are 115 stanzas followed by commentary in Kavi. It deals with the body as the bearer of the gods (*deho devaśarīrabhṛt*), the correspondence of the macrocosm and the microcosm. Umā and Kumāra are keen to know about *yoga* by which one can attain emancipation. They already know scriptures revealing evolution of the world and they want to have an insight into the origin of the lord, the reason of his existence as he is the Creator of the world, universe, deities and men. Everything comes out of him and merges into him (Lokesh Chandra, vol.5, 1997:pp 02-156).

Bṛhaspati-tattwa is a work on philosophy. Parallel thoughts and phraseology to every significant statement in Bṛhaspati-tattwa are found in India right from Kashmir and Nepal upto Bengal, Orissa, Andhra, Tamil, Kerala and Gujarat. Stuti and Stava is a collection of 955 hymns in Sanskrit sung in praise of Buddhist, Śaiva and Vaiṣṇava deities like Āditya, Agni, Brahmā, Durgā, Maheśvara, Caturdeva, Pañcamahābhūta, Bhuvaneśvarī and so on. It includes a number of *dhyānas* and *kavacas*. The hymns are collected from various kinds of manuscripts such as Buddhist and Śaiva daily and death rituals. Sometimes these hymns are found in single manuscripts but some of them can be seen in a far greater number of manuscripts. Another Śaiva text 'Sivarātrikalpa' is based on a Telagu original. The Indonesian manuscripts are important for a study of the early phases of modern Indian languages.

Sanskrit became a source, an elixir of life for the Old Javanese poets and prose writers who assimilated Sanskrit terms for higher levels of thought to such an extent that in the Old-Javanese-Dutch dictionary there are 6790 Sanskrit words and 6925 words of Old Javanese.

Sanskrit, the lingua franca of ancient times was the language of sacred literature which affected and fashioned the language and literature of the indigenous population of South-east Asia. This contributed to the creation of art of writing through the scripts adapted from the Indian. Sanskrit language and literature made deep inroads into the vocabulary of large parts of Southeast Asia. Its dimension was astonishingly large people in SEA had a freedom to accept this literary culture differing from state to state but they never lost the basic identity as a whole.

LITERATURE CITED

Casparis

J.G.de Casparis, *Indonesian Palaeography*, Leiden/Koln, E.J.Brill, 1975

Coedes 1937

George Coedes Orient, *Inscriptions de Cambodge*, Ecole Francaise d'extreme, Tome VI, Planches CCXLIV, Paris, 1937

Diringer

David Diringer, *The Alphabet*, Hutchinson's Scientfic and Technical Publications, 1949

Goris

Roelof Goris, *Bijgrage tot de Kennis der Pud-Javaansche en Balineesche Theology*, Leiden, 1931

Finot 1915

Louis Finot, *l'Ecole Francaise, Notes de Epigraphie*, XIV-XX, Hanoi, 1915

Lokesh Chandra

Lokesh Chandra, *Culltural Horizons of India*, Vol. 3, International Academy of Indian Culture and Aditya Prakashan, New Delhi, 1993

Culltural Horizons of India, Vol. 5, International Academy of Indian Culture and Aditya Prakashan, New Delhi, 1997

Majumdar 1953

R.C.Majumdar, *Inscriptions of Kambuja*, The Asiatic Society Monograph Series Vol. VIII, Calcutta, 1953

Sharma

J.C.Sharma

24

SEARCH FOR SHAMBHALA AND KĀLACAKRA BY YURI AND NICHOLAS ROERICHS

George Nicholas Roerich, affcctionately called Yuri Roerich by the Russians, fostered the ties of Indo-Russian cultural friendship through academics. He undertook an arduous journey to explore the roots of our bonding and deepened it. He was born in 1902 in Novgorod region in Russia but he made India his home, almost throughout his academic life. His father, Nicholas Roerich was a great philosopher, painter, thinker, explorer, archaeologist and a cultural activist, whose paintings not merely scan the beauty and immensity of nature but are imbued with a vision. The Himalayas painted by him are the symbols of India's eternal culture; where present meets past, and future.

His mother Yelena Roerich is called the mother of Agni Yoga, the teachings of living ethics. Agni, proclaimed by the Rishis of the Himalayas is all ascending, omniscient and all pervading. Yelena preached that the hope for ease at all ages made people forget the greatest; no one can ever ascend through such a life. The Russians made a fiery angel as one of their most mystical ancient icons. For them flaming are the wings of ever striving Sophia, the Wisdom.

Yuri's brother, Svyatoslav was a renowned artist who spent most of his time in Bangalore. The family of scholars and artists lived an active social life in India. Since before independence they were close to Pt. Nehru, Mr. K.P.S. Menon, Dr. Radhakrishnan and several other outstanding public figures of the time. Svyatoslav and his wife Devika Rani saw the last of their lives in 1993 leaving a legacy behind.

Yuri Roerich was one of the Russians who dreamt about the abodes of light, sought knowledge by inner accumulation. For him the *tejas* of *manas*, the light bearing quality was as real as the radiant emanation created by the tension of thought. Fire and light burn ignorance. Agni Yoga says that darkness cannot withstand the daring of light. The radiance of divine beauty is inexpressible in words.

He carried in his heart the fire of life. At an early age in 1918 he joined his father to go abroad to study under the eminent Indologists and Sanskritists in Europe and America. Prof. C. Lanman, a renowned scholar of Sanskrit was his teacher at the Harward University. While he was doing his bachelor's degree he got deeply interested in the spiritual life of the Tibetans. To do the Master's degree he became a student of prominent orientalists Sylvain Levi and P. Pelliot at Paris University at the School of Oriental Languages.

As a child he was grown up in Petersberg. The family had close connections with the most renowned scholars who had a profound respect for the Oriental culture and its spiritual heritage. St. Petersberg was a famous centre for studies in Tibetology, Sinology and Indology. At a tender age Yuri developed a keen interest to study the Asian culture seriously. Indology in Russia became one of the most fascinating subjects for him. He tried to search the history of Indo-Russian cultural relations and wrote a research paper in 1945. The available information was exceedingly scanty. India was a favourite theme of fables and tales in Russian. They had discovered a few images of the Buddha from the burials in the south. First hand information about India had reached Russia only in the 15th century. Bari Javalamukhi was a place of pilgrimage in Baku while famous pilgrimage place Javalamukhi is in Kangra. Some Indians were living at Astrakhan. The Russians had translated the Bhagavadgita and published it in 1787. Yuri also wrote about the Russian musician, Gerasim Lebedev who played an important role in the renaissance of the Bengali theatre. The first Devanāgari types were cast in Russia in St. Petersberg. Foundations of Sanskrit studies were laid by the enlightened statesman Count S.S.Uvarov.

Yuri Roerich studied ancient Egyptian and Mongolian languages in Russia and then went to London to study Sanskrit at the Indo-Iranian department of Oriental Languages School. The Russians often used to go to Germany and England to study the Indian classical language, Sanskrit that was seen as closely linked to Buddhology, Tibetology, Sinology and Indology.

Yuri Roerich was on a test of courage when he went on an expedition with his father through the countries of Central Asia, through unapproachable lands of Tibet and Mongolia. By that time Yuri had become mature to carry out research independently in a number of areas: linguistics, history of culture, archaeology, ethnography and the religions of these areas. They travelled facing hardships and obstacles from Kashmir over the Karakoram mountain range in Zinjiang through the Gobi desert and the Tibetan plateau to Sikkim and Darjeeling. The expedition fulfilled the dream of many Russians.

While staying in Sikkim with his father Yuri Roerich was busy in studying Buddhist monuments, Tibetan culture and colloquial speech. At that time he collected material that formed basis for his famous book Buddhist Painting. His approach was serious and scientific. There he began to compile Tibetan-Sanskrit-Russian-English dictionary also.

Knowledge of Tibetan language helped Yuri Roerich to undertake the difficult task of deciphering and translating the biography of Chag Lotsava Chos-rje dpal (the translator Dharmavāsin), a Tibetan monk pilgrim. It is an important source for Indian history. Like Fa Hien, Hsüan-tsang and I-tsing, Dharmāvasin was a Buddhist. Hundreds of Indian monks had gone to Tibet and a large number of Tibetans came to study at the universities of Nālandā, Takṣaśilā etc. but Dhrmavāsin seems to be the only one to leave such extensive notes about India, her people, customs and institutions. The biography opens with a salutation to Mañjughoṣa.

Yuri Roerich was the director of the institute of Himalayan Studies in Kullu from 1929 to 1941, founded by Nicholas Roerich, his father. The centre at Kullu had become important for research on Central Asia studies. Among a number of his research works Paralokasiddhi is an important treatise on the continuity of the flow of consciousness and the existence of the world beyond. It was written by Acharya Dharmottara and translated into Tibetan by a Kashmiri Pandit Bhavyarāja and the well known Tibetan Lotasava Pa-tshab Ni-ma grags. It has always been a crucial problem which invoked heated debates between the Buddhist philosophical schools.

While staying in the valley of Lahul, the north-west of Himalayas, now in Himachal Pradesh, Yuri twice had a chance to attend the ceremony of "Stone Breaking" performed by the lama actors from Spiti. It was one of the religious plays that enjoys special veneration. Its performers are considered to possess supernatural powers. The purpose of the ceremony is to destroy an evil spirit that takes its abode in stone. The ceremony was first performed by the great Mahāsiddha Thanston rgyal-po, a famous builder of a bridge on Yaru tsang-po. When the ceremony was complete the chief lama actor recited the story to him that enabled him to record and research. Yuri at that time was sad to say, "a few decades more and the Land of Snows will see the last of its religious actors".

Yuri Roerich had an insight into the Tibeto-Mongol relations at all levels: philosophic, cultural, religious and linguistic. Dealing with the linguistic studies he has written about the Mongols who had connections with Central Asia and had obtained a large number of Sanskrit loan words in Sogdian and Uigur garb. The philosophic terminology was incorporated without an attempt to translate them. Tibetans had their first contacts with them in the 13th century. Phags-pa Lama was the author of the so called National square script which was introduced by the Imperial edict in 1269 AD. Then onwards the Tibetan translators began to translate into Mongolian.

Research on the Epic of King Kesar of Ling is another important work by Yuri Roerich. It is a heroic saga of Tibet and Mongolia, an important constituent of their folklore. The first information about the legend reached Europe in 1771-76 when P. S. Pallas, an explorer wrote "Gesser in Mongolia". Some of the chapters were translated and a brief account was given by scholars but the knowledge of its various versions, its genesis had not advanced very far. So Yuri took it to make a survey of all the then existing versions and solve the intricate questions related to the origin of the epic, its date and translation into Mongolian.

Mixed dialects of the Mongols spoken in the monasteries were a subject of Yuri's studies. Later in his life he produced a number of experts on Tibetan, Mongolian and Sanskrit.

All through his academic life Yuri Roerich worked for the enhancement of Indo-Russian cultural friendship. Outstanding Indian personalities, great scholars like Prof. Raghu Vira, Rabindranath Tagore, Rahul Sankrityayan, S.K.Chatterjee were impressed by his extraordinary abilities. He had close connections with all of them to exchange material and views. On going back to his country in 1957 he kept on participating actively for friendly ties. He worked as Head of the Department of History, Religion and Philosophy of India at the Institute of Oriental Studies at the Academy of Sciences of the USSR. He migrated to the heavenly abode in 1960 but will live for centuries in the great works of historical importance.

Predecessors of Yuri Roerich

Written records on Indo-Russian friendship go back to 12th-13th century, when "The Relations About India" or "The Story of India: the Rich" was written in Russian. It was a derivative via a Slavo-Serbian translation from Latin. The Russian version passed through numerous manuscript editions over several centuries and remained popular till the 19th century. Arrival of an Indian hero to Russia and the descriptions that he gave about India, was the central theme in the ballads of Dyuk Stepanovich. The standard epithet for India in Russia was 'rich' or 'bounteous', the land of plenty and splendour. A number of Russian scholars have researched the history of Indo-Russian relations (Kemp 1958:1)

Lebedev's contribution to impart knowledge about India and her language was almost the first and noteworthy attempt. He believed in the basic unity of human society and contemplated upon the affinity of the Russian customs with the Indian. He stressed on the importance of studying the correct pronunciation of words and separate sounds as the guide to understanding the structure of the spoken languages, as well as the traditional Indian pronunciation of Sanskrit, neglect of which resulted in the loss of the real meaning of the roots of the language (Kemp 1958:145).

Bayer was the first European scholar to note the similarities between Persian, Greek and Sanskrit. He used to spend all his spare time in studying Sanskrit. He referred to Kāśī as the '*Academia Indorum*' and presented general observations about the functions of Indians, Sanskrit literature and science (Kemp 1958:140). Ivan Pavlivich Minaev (1840-90), a Professor of comparative grammar at the University of St. Petersberg undertook journeys to India, Nepal, Burma and Srilanka, three times with the assistance of Russian Geographical Society. He published a number of papers and books on Buddhism and philology. He should be honoured as one of the outstanding scholars who interpreted India. His initiative on research on India was followed by other well known Russian orientalists like Baron von Stal Golstein who came to India in 1903-4 and Professor Shcherbatsky who came in 1909-10 (Kemp 1958:151).

Tolstoy Leo Nikolayevich (1828-1910), a great novelist and moral philosopher, eventually began to feel uneasy leading a prosperous life in 1876. He had a craving for a religious justification of his life. He began to advocate a religion that was purely anthropocentric. He preached that the aim of man is to achieve happiness, which is possible only through virtual actions and by loving all men and freeing himself from the appetites of greed, lust and anger. He believed that all forms of violence are equally wicked. He became interested in Indian philosophy. Through the theosophists and Leo's contacts with Mahatma Gandhi, Indians got the inkling of his interests. In his last years he adopted a new mode of life. He preferred to be dressed like a peasant and adopted a vegetarian diet. He preached austerity and finally gave away all his worldly belongings.

The Russians who visited India in the 19th century left facsinating observations. Prince A. D. Saltuikov, a talented painter toured India and between 1841-45 for his own pleasure and artistic experience. V. V. Vereshchagin (1842-1904) came to India twice in 1874 and 1882 (Kemp 1958:151).

Helena Petrovna Blavatsky (1831-1891), founded the Theosophical Society in 1875. She travelled to India and Indonesia and spent some time in Tibet in 1856. Again she set out for an extensive travel in Near East Asia and Egypt and visited Tibet again in 1868. The aim of the Theosophical Society was promotion of the studies of the comparative religion, philosophy and science and to investigate the unexplained laws of nature and powers latent in man. Blavatsky came to India in 1879 with Colonel Olcott and established the permanent headquarters of the Theosophical Society at Adyar. Her collected writings were published at Adyar in 7 volumes. Her works include 'The Secret Doctrine', 'The Key to Theosophy' and 'Voice of Silence' (ER 1987: vol. 14, p. 502).

Shambhala: The Utopia of Tibet

Shambhala is an appreciation and emulation of the ideal of an enlightened society that it represents. It does not matter, whether it is a fact or fiction. It is an ideal world that man has always tried to visualize on earth. Utopia is an ideal commonwealth, whose inhabitants exist in perfect conditions. Utopia is used to denote a visionary reform. The word first occurred in Sir Thomas More's work published in Latin. The idea of Utopia is far older in literature. The word was coined by Sir Thomas More, meaning 'nowhere'. His kingdom of Utopia existed in here and now. It could be realized if man would desire to make it so. It had a revolutionary appeal.

Utopia is full of happiness. The ancients wrote of a golden age in a distant land. Theocritus' writing in Alexandria, chose Sicily. Virgil who knew Sicily, shifted the terrain to Greece and thus became a literary progenitor of the rural paradise known as Arcadia. It is an ideal description of Sparta in Plutarch's life of Lycurgus. The similar idea occurs in Greek, Celtic and Arab legends, which describes an earthly paradise in the west or in Atlantic Ocean. In More's Utopia, the imaginary voyager arrives at the ideal state. Many Utopias are satires. Others are based on socialistic ideas (EB 1965: vol. 22, p. 913-14).

Pure Lands of the divine are abodes of light situated at the heights of the Himalayas, a symbol of purity and serenity, a place of beauty and magnificence, spiritualism and idealism. They are the sacred symbols of ascent and treasure of the world. Its snow covered mountain ranges are the place for Shambhala.

Shambhala, a place of peace and prosperity was governed by wise and compassionate rulers. Stories related to the legendry kingdom of Shambhala were a source of learning. Many Buddhist teachers believed that the Kingdom of Shambhala is not to be regarded as an external place but as the ground or root of wakefulness and sanity that exists as a potential within every human being (Chogyam 1988:25-26).

The Tibetans believe that the kingdom of Shambhala can still be found, hidden in remote valley somewhere in the Himalayas. Roerich, in search of sages painted Himalayas as abode of Shambhala, the place of highest knowledge, the most exalted. All the teachers journeyed to the mountains. The most inspired songs, the most superb sounds and colours are created on the mountains.

Tibetan visionaries travelled in trance to Buddhist purgatories and on awakening they gave detailed accounts of the punishments waiting for sinners. Others found treasures consisting of texts and sacred objects, hidden by Guru Padma-sambhava during the times of persecution. They are to be rediscovered with the assistance of supernatural beings for the benefit of the humanity. Ecstatics and visionaries point the way to earthly paradise such as the mythical kingdom of Shambhala (ER 1987:14.502).

Shambhala is a symbol of a future hope, a combination of power and virtue. Nicholas Roerich says that both Ladakhis and Mangols await fighters and builders of life. They endow them not only with a leonine courage but with serpentine cunning and the tirelessness of a stag. How wondrous it is to observe the growth of the consciousness and its forging of heroic symbols! (N. Roerich, Altai Himalaya, pg. 111). Shambhala was painted as a symbol of victory over the invaders. He was pictured amongst swords and spears and impenetrable armour. A three dimensional Shambhala was carved in Leningrad.

Shambhala is the place of origin of the Kālacakra-tantra, located in the Northeast of India. It plays an important role in Tibetan Buddhism as a source of auspiciousness. A key part of the myth is that the saviour of humanity will come out of Shambhala when the world would be dominated by war and destruction. Various speculations concerning its precise location, range from the areas of Central Asia to China and the North Pole. One must accept that the importance has less to do with the possibility of locating it than with the spiritual quality associated with it.

The twenty five teachers who proclaimed the Kālacakra teachings also play a role in the Shambhala myth. It is believed that when the twenty-fifth *guru* would come into being, a golden age will dawn and all negative forces will be overcome. Rigden-japo, Kulika-rāja, the ruler of Shambhala is indefatigable, ever vigilant in the cause of mankind. His magic mirror sees all events on earth. His powerful light can destroy all the darkness. His immeasurable riches are ready to aid all the needy ones who offer to serve the cause of righteousness. The third Panchen Lama composed a guide for finding this kingdom (Shambhala Dictionary of Buddhism and Zen, 1991).

Special schools of Shambhala had been established in the more learned monasteries. Monasteries in Tibet and Mongolia were seen as transformations of Shambhala and special Datsans, Shambhalin Datsans were added to the existing monasteries.

Nicholas Roerich: In Search of Shambhala

Nicholas Roerich looked at Shambhala as an imaginary kingdom, untouched by man, situated in the secret recesses of the Himalayas. Nicholas traversed the heights of the sacred Himālayas. In his memoirs of the expedition he writes about the 'Himālayas as Abode of Light'. For him it is the 'Sacred symbol of ascent'. He visualises Sikkim as 'Treasure of snows'. He is a sage among the sages when he writes about the 'Rishis' in the Himālayas, 'Ascending the heights and 'From Kailāśa'. He was fascinated by the legends and mysteries that he discovered during his expedition. Himalayan prophecies were a symbol of future hope for him.

Nicholas Roerich was fascinated by the stories and mysteries of Shambhala, the indestructible land, told by Lamas who had been there. A Buryat Lama revealed that he had gone through a narrow passage. From the deepest of his heart, he wished the Pure Land to be on this earth, to link the two worlds, to unite them.

Nicholas Roerich wrote that Tashi Lamas were closely linked to Shambhala because they were high protectors of Kālacakra. Its teachings were spread by Atīśa. Moruling monastery in Lhasa was one of the most learned monasteries practicing it. During his expedition, he tried to search Shambhala. He spoke to one of the Lamas-our scientists seek each spark concerning this remarkable realm. A similar kind of curiosity can be seen in other scholars also. Csoma de Körös had an inkling of what Shambhala was when he visited the Buddhist monasteries. Grüenwedel translated the book of the famous Tashi Lama, 'The way to Shambhala'. They were trying to discover as how a great truth is concealed under secret symbols. Truly the ardent scientists also desired to know about the Kālacakra.

Nicholas Roerich once told the Lama that he owned a manuscript of Kālacakra. He had studied most of the then-existing works on the history of Shambhala; he had read the book 'The red path to Shambhala' by T'aishan. He had a fascination for Mongolian songs on Shambhala. In Turfan and Turkestan he was shown the caves with long unexplored passages to reach the *āśrama* of Shambhala.

On hearing the story, the Lama was convinced of the sincerity of Nicholas Roerich and explained that Shambhala is far beyond the ocean. It is the mighty heavenly domain. It has nothing to do with our earth. Only at some places in the Far North, one can discern the resplendent rays of Shambhala.

Nicholas Roerich in his essay 'Abode of Light' writes that he spoke to a Lama to express his eagerness- Lama, if the great warriors are incarnated, will not the activities of Shambhala take place here on our earth. Lama replied- everyone, here and in heaven, all benevolent forces shall come together to destroy the darkness. Each one who will help in this great task shall be rewarded a hundred fold upon this very earth and in this incarnation. All sinners against Shambhala will perish in this very incarnation, because they have exhausted mercy. Nicholas further asked- how the simple people are helped by Shambhala and in what manner does the might of Shambhala manifest itself among the humble? In Turfan and Turkestan he was shown the caves with long, unexplored passages to reach the *āsrama* of Shambhala.

Yuri Roerich on the Kālacakra and Shambhala

The search for a road to Shambhala and spiritual communion with the kings of Shambhala has always been a favourite subject among the ascetics and holy men of Tibet. Legends and oral tradition accumulated around the problem of locating Shambhala invoked Yuri's interest in the history of spread of Kālacakra doctrine in the Realm of Shambhala and Tibet. A Westerner had mentioned the story of two Jesuite fathers who found Shambhala to be famous in Bhutan. They tried to search the way to Shambhala, but could not accomplish the objective.

George Roerich in his paper on "Studies in the Kālacakra-tantra" published in the Journal of Urusvati, vol. ii, by Urusvati Himalayan Research Institute of Roerich Museum in 1932, has written that the teachings of Kālacakra exercised a powerful influence on the religious life of the Tibetans. They produced a voluminous literature dedicated to the system. Most of the Mongolian and Tibetan monasteries gave instructions in the intricate system of mysticism in their special faculties like Tashi-lumpo at Shigatse.

Kālacakra belongs to the Anuttarayoga, the highest among the Tantric system. It is closely interwoven with the problems of the Realm of Shambhala, and the question as from where the Kālacakra system was brought to India in the second half of the 10th century. Besides several works included in the Kañjur and Tañjur, commentaries and abbreviated versions of the Kālacakra-mūla-tantra are attributed to the twenty-five kings of Shambhala. A text included in Kañjur is said to have been translated into Tibetan from a manuscript from Shambhala: Bhagavān-Vajrapāṇi-guhyābhideśa-tantra-rāja. Yuri studied the works on Kālacakra-tantra by the following authors:

Bu-ston Rin-chen-grub	1290-1364	Commentary
mKhas-grub dGe-legs dpal-bzaṅ	1385-1438	Grel-chen (comm.)
Gos-lotsava gSon-nu dpal	1392-1481	Blue Annals
Brug Padma-dkar-po	16th century	A chapter on Kala.
Tārānātha	1575-?	Guide books
Panchen bLo-bzaṅ chos-kyi rgyal-mtshan	1571-1663	Extensive comm..
Sans-rgyas rgyal-mtsho	17th century	Baidurya dkar-po
Sum-pa mkham-po	18th century	dPag-bsam Ijon-bzaṅ
kLoṅ-rdol bla-ma Nag-bdaṅ blo-bzaṅ	1719- ?	Sham. & spread of Kala.

(G. Roerich 1932:153-165)

Many of the religious histories have disappeared but still a fairly good number existed in Tibet. None of them were translated from Tibetan into any other language, Yuri felt that they were waiting for a laborious task of a scholar who could venture to penetrate into that Sancta Sanctorum of Northern Buddhism. He wrote about the great historians and commentators of the Tantra. One of them is mKhas-grub dge-legs dpal-bzaṅ (1385-1438), a great disciple of Tsoṅ-kha-pa. His commentary written in 1434, occupies several volumes of gsum-'bum (collection of works) of the Lhasa edition. It was the basis of the most of the later works.

'Deb-ther snon-po' or the 'Blue Annals' or cGos-lo'I Deb-ther, the annals of Gos-lotsava is another historical work, composed in 1478 by the scholar translator Gos-lotsava gson-nu dpal (1392-1481). It contains a whole chapter dedicated to the history of the spread of Kālacakra-tantra doctrine up to the 15th century. Yuri Roerich translated the voluminous work 'Blue Annals' into English from the Kum-bde-glin monastery edition. The old edition was destroyed during the Nepal-Tibet war of 1791 and the third edition existed in Amdo at the Zorge-gompa near the great monastic establishment of Labrang.

Blue Annals share the history of Buddhism by Bu-ston Rin-po-che, the distinction of having been the main source of information for all the later historical compilations in the land of snows. Alexander Csoma de Körös was the first to mention its name. Blue Annals (pg.769-70) says that Jam-sa Śes-rab, a native of upper Myan was learned in numerous *piṭakas*. He performed austerities for many years. In his dreams he visited many paradises such as Sukhāvatī and others (G. Roerich 1976, folio 8b).

Yuri studied the works of Tārānatha, Tashi Lama Panchen blo-bzaṅ chos-kyi rgyal-mtshan, Sum-pa mkham-po, Sans-rgya-mtsho and many others. While presenting the "Studies in the Kālacakra-tantra" his object was to translate certain Tibetan historical texts on the Kālacakra doctrine and the Realm of Shambhala and thus prepare the way for a translation and an exhaustive commentary.

A description of the road to Shambhala given in a special class of literature, known as road descriptions fascinated Yuri. One of them, found in Tañjur is entitled Kalāpāvatāra, translated into Tibetan from Nepalese. Prof. Grüenwedel had published its German translation. An anonymous work on the description of the sphere of Shambhala was brought to the Himalayan Research Institute. Yuri Roerich was willing to edit the text and tried hard to trace more sources for Shambhala.

Yuri discovered that Shambhala lam-yig has been composed by Lama sTag-tshan ras-chen of the 17th century. He went through the translation of its passage by Dr. B. Laufer (G. Roerich 1932:153-165).

Date of *Kālacakra-tantra*

Several versions of the first preaching of the Kālacakra-tantra were present in different traditions in India and Tibet. They represent different traditions but all of them agree that the doctrine was preached by the Buddha at the stūpa of Śrī-Dhānyakaṭaka. The abridged commentary composed by Acalagarbha says that the doctrine originated from Shambhala and the king Sucandra heard it at Śrī-Dhānyakaṭaka. According to the writings of Rva-Lotsava and Bro-Lotsava Buddha preached it in the year of his passing away while others believe that it was preached at the time of his enlightenment. According to some authorities the Kāla was preached by the Buddha in his 80th year at Śrī-Dhānyakaṭaka (Amarāvatī) upon the request of Sucandra (Zla-bzaṅ). According to Bu-ston Rin-po-che the Buddha preached the Kāla system in the year of his enlightenment. According to him the statement that the Buddha had preached it in the year of his passing into *nirvāṇa* at Śrī-Dhānyakaṭaka should be rejected.

On the basis of Tibetan tradition, the date ascribed to Kālacakra-tantra should be AD 804. The tradition says that The law of Kla klo (Moslems) was established in Mecca and the Hijri era began in AD 622. Vimala-prabhā-ṭīkā says that a terrible war took place among the Devas, Dānavas and Mlecchas in the city of Baghdad. It was an age of destruction and pillage of Buddhist centres. At that time Kālacakra was seen as the source of spiritual message to be saved and relieved. The performance of *abhiṣeka* was meant for joy of the mundane and the transcendent worlds.

The Tibetan tradition assigns victory over the Kla klo with the aid of gods to Rudracakrin, who restored the Buddhist law. They believe that 182 years after the power of Kla klo had begun, eGyal dko' began to calculate the cycle of Kāla (J. Upadhyāya 1986: xxii-iii).

The Mūla-vimala-prabhā-ṭīkā describes the early Islamic history, as found in any competent work. It says that illustrious Mañjuśrī would be born in the north of Sītā river in Shambhala. 800

years after the birth of Mañjuśrī, in the land of Makha (Mecca) a community of Mlecchas would grow. At that time the principles of *jyotish* would vanish and those hostile to Buddhism will perish. But the Buddhists would be saved on the term of practicing Kālacakra-tantra. The given dates are as follows:

Date of Kālacakra	AD 804
Beginning of Hijri era	AD 622
Birth of Mañjuśrī	BC 178
Birth of Śākyamuni	BC 778

The fundamental tantra was revealed by the Buddha to Zla ba bzaṅ po, who made a summery of it, composed an explicative commentary in 60,000 verses and wrote in a book, revealing its meaning to the people of Shambhala. He dedicated the maṇḍala of Kālacakra, made from various precious stones, displayed many miracles and entered nirvāṇa. It was further preached by others for hundreds of years and Ni mai sin rta, at the full moon in the month of Caitra initiated the *ṛṣi* with the maṇḍala dedicated by Zla ba bzaṅ and wrote three thousand verses, a summary of the fundamental tantra.

In transmission of Kālacakra-tantra, Buddhas and Bodhisattvas stand as *guru* and *siṣya*. Vajrapāṇi Sucandra prayed to the Buddha to receive the illuminating tantra from Him. He preached to the people of Shmabhala, dwellers of a village Ṣaṇvatī to the north of Sītā. To synthesise (Ekakalka) the people of diverse casts, Sucandra Yaśa became known as Kalki. Thus there has been a lineage of Kalki of Vajrakula. Some of them are: Candra, Sureśvara, Teji, Somadatta, Viśvamūrtī, Suresan, Yaah, Puṇḍarīka, Sūryaprabha, Sucandra, Kṣitigarbha, Yamāntaka, Jambhaka, Māmaka, Khagarbha, Lokanātha, Yamādi and Daśakrodha.

According to the Tibetan tradition Rudracakrin corresponds to the figure of Kalkin to whom Klon rdol bla-ma compares the king with an innumerable army of soldiers set out and to the south of Sītā river he fought a great battle in the country of Rum-pa C'a rgyal of the Kla klo and their master was vanished (Tucci 1980:599).

Kalki is the 10th incarnation of lord Viṣṇu. He protects the world from the animals and destroys the evil doers. Jayadeva in Gītagovinda has described him as:

Mleccha-nivaha-nidhane kalayasi karavālam
Dhūma-ketumiva kimati karavālam, Keśavadhṛta-
Kalki-śarīra jaya jagadīśa hare. (Gitagovinda 1.10)

According to him this vast literature is of utmost importance for a study of Central Asian Buddhism. The knowledge of the Tantric terminology of the Indian system of astronomy and astrology is also essential. These colleges attached to the monasteries taught astronomy, astrology and Sanskrit.

Yuri penetrated the tenets of the system, its abstruct character and symbolism. He tried to compare the doctrine with other ancient systems. Teachings preserved as the Kālacakra-tantra are considered to be among the most profound wisdom of Tibetan Buddhism.

According to the great commentary on the Kālacakra-tantra by the 19th century Buddhist teacher, Mipham, the land of Shambhala is in the north of river Sītā, and country is divided into eight mountain ranges. The palace of Rigdens, or the rulers of Shambhala is built on a top of a circular mountain at the centre of the country. The mountain is said to be Kailāśa. The palace, which is called the palace of Kalpa, comprises of many square miles. In front of it to the south is a beautiful park known as Malaya, and in the middle of the park is a temple devoted to Kālacarka that was built by Dawa Sangpo.

Path to Shambhala

The abbot of the monastery Wu-t'ai Shan in the book, 'The Red Path to Shambhala' describes the way into this forbidden place. At the end of it, there is a characteristic detail to the effect that the traveller saw on the very edge of the safeguarded place, a caravan of Mangols with salt, although they did not suspect the nearness of the dwelling.

'The Road to Shambhala', a Tibetan manuscript by the third Tashi Lama, one of the most esteemed priests of Tibet, was translated by Prof. Grüenwedel.

A Buryat Lama gave the details of his journey to Shambhala when he was led through an underground passage. The passage sometimes became so narrow that one could hardly push through the thorough bed ram, which was being led into the forbidden place. Mongolian lamas also speak about several safeguarded places within the boundaries of Khangai and Gobi.

Going to Shambhala through vision

It is believed that Ācārya Kālacakra-pāda was taught the system of Kālacakra-tantra by Padma-dkar-po, a manifestation of Bodhisattva Avalokiteśvara. He was a Kṣatriya from India and born when his royal parents performed the rite ensuring the birth of a noble son (*kulaputra*). He was known as a manifestation of Mañjuśrī (G. Roerich 1976:756). Venerable Tārā had blessed the *ācārya* and had once told him that in the northern Shambhala there exist many tantras and commentaries, taught and prophesied by the Buddha. He was advised to go in search of them and listen to them. In the opinion of some scholars he had joined a caravan of merchants and proceeded towards Shambhala. According to others he was guided by a phantom monk. Others believed that Tārā herself guided him but still there are scholars who say that he visited Shambhala in his vision and obtained the doctrine from Avalokiteśvara himself. This last statement should be preferably accepted.

Tibetans and Mangols proclaim the path of folk consciousness, the national dignity and the dream about the hero of freedom. At the time of wars, destruction of monasteries and pillage by indignant invaders the prophecies of Shambhala and Maitreya became popular. It was predicted that Maitreya would be incarnated after the wars. But the final war shall be fought for the true teachings. Anyone, rising up, against Shambhala shall be destroyed. Each warrior of Shambhala shall be invincible. The Lord will hasten himself. His banner is already above the mountains. It will encircle the central lands of the blessed ones. Those who accept him shall rejoice. The treasure is returning from the west and fires of jubilation are kindled on mountains. Teachings issued from Bodhagayā shall return, when the procession carrying the image of Shambhala shall pass through the lands of the Buddha and return to the source (N. Roerich 1947:64-67).

Nicholas in his article on Shambhala writes that Shambhala sounds as the most real symbol of the great future in the endless deserts of Mongolia. In the narratives, songs and folklores, Shambhala is contained as the most revered message of the east. He who knows nothing of Shambhala, has nothing to state that he has studied the east and knows the contemporary.

The depth of faith created more than one Shambhalas in India and abroad. There is a Shambhala in Uttar Pradesh, one in Haryana, another in Orissa? As there are more than one Ayodhyas, there is one in Uttar Pradesh, another is Ayutthiya in Thailand; the River Ganga flows in India but the longest river in Cambodia is called Mekong (Māṅ Gaṅgā). There are a number of Rāmanagars and Kṛṣṇānagars or cities named after Gandhi and Nehru in various parts India.

Maṇḍala of Shambhala

During their expedition Roerichs watched a dance performance, meant to pay homage to the mountain Kañchanjuṅgā. The dance was performed at the specific time in all the monasteries. People from various parts of the Himalayan region were dressed up differently. Sikkimis were in red short garments, wearing conical and feathered hats, Bhutanese looked sober, people from Kham were red turbaned , Nepalese wore small round caps, people from Lhasa were in Chinese like garments, the Lepchas and Sherpas were looking timid and quiet. All of them had gathered to pay homage to the five treasures of Kañchanjuṅgā.

Trumpets were roaring and drums were beaten. The protector of Sikkim entered in red and golden mask carrying a short spear in his hand. He danced and completed the magical circles. Then the protectress emerged as Kalki or Ḍākinī with skulls adorning her head, wearing dark colour garments, to perform the sacred dance. She performed her invocation and sat down.

One by one, the protectors of the Five Treasures of Kañchanjuṅgā emerged, they were ready to fight for the holy mountain because in its caves, all the treasures were supposed to be guarded for centuries. They were to guard the hermits who sent their blessings from the depths of the mountains. They were dancing and brandishing swords and protecting with shields (N. Roerich 1947).

In the thangka painting of Shambhala from Mongolia visualizing the Kingdom of Shambhala, kept at Musee Guimet, Paris, the painting is divided into two sections, the mythical kingdom on the right surrounded by a double range of snow covered mountains, Rudracakrin, the last king of Shambhala holds the court in the palace of Kalāpa. Ninety three palaces of the vassals are represented all around. Nine kings of Shambhala fill the top section of the maṇḍala. The left side of the painting represents a war scene at the end of the dark age of the world. It is believed that Rudracakrin will appear on his white horse followed by his general Hanumanda. He will crush the barbarians in the west and will allow the Buddhist teachings to spread around the world.

The mighty ruler of Shambhala, Rigden Japo sits at the centre of the glorious and majestic abode. Ferocious battles are fought below to destroy the enemies. The artist lamas worked with great honour and veneration. They believed that the time of the great advent was nearing and the apoch of Shambhala had already set in (Rhie & Thurman 1991:157-8). G. Tucci in his Tibetan Painted Scrolls has described another thangka. The smaller circle represents Kalāpa, Kulika's (rigs ldan) royal palace built in the country of Shambhala. Tradition places it vaguely in the north, an itinerary given in the Tanjur, cxxx,12, Ka la pai ajug pa shows the way to his place of Central Asia but not yet clearly defined.

Shambhala is round like an eight petalled lotus, a heaven consecrated to Kālacakra's glory. Like Uḍḍiyāna, the centre of Ḍākinī, Shambhala is a place of devout, who try to reach there in order to be redeemed from sins. It was later transfigured into a distant heaven. The houses filling the second tier represent the ninety-six minor kingdoms surrounding Kalāpa. Houses and temples are multiplied and on the interior side small figures of the deities are placed inside the palaces. A warrior on a horseback stands out. Rudracakrin (Drag po ak'or lo) piercing with his lance, an enemy, fallen on ground. The inscription declares him to be Byas pai blo. Above Rudracakrin a warrior on a horse back is shooting an arrow to the opposite side, his name is Hanumanda. The thangka is identified by Prof. Tucci as Kālacakra's story and the victory of king Rudracakrin over Kla klo, i.e. the Moslems (G. Tucci 1980:pl. 211-213). Rudracakrin was the last king of Shambhala. He who knows Shambhala, knows the future. Shambhala is a symbol of aspirations for a bright future almost like Kalki - 'The Future of Civilization'.

LITERATURE CITED

Chogyam 1988

Chogyam Truhgpa, *Shambhala: The Sacred Path of the Warrior,* Boston & London, 1988.

EB

Encyclopaedia Britannica, London, 1965

ER 1987

Encyclopaedia of Religion, Macmillan Publishing company, New York 1987.

G. Roerich, 1932

George Roerich, *Studies in the Kālacakra-tantra,* Journal of Urusvāti, Himalayan Research Institute of Roerich Museum, vol. ii, published by Urusvāti Himalayan Research Institute of Roerich Museum 1932.

G. Roerich 1976

George Roerich, *Blue Annals,* Motilal Banarasidas, Delhi 1976.

J. Upadhyaya 1986

Jagannatha Upadhyaya, ed., *Vimalaprabhā-ṭīkā of Śrī-laghu-kālacakra-tantra-rāja* by Kalki Śrī Puṇḍarīka, Kendrīya Uccha Tibbati Shiksha Sansthāna, Sarnath, Varanasi 1986.

Kemp 1958

P. M. Kemp, *Bharat-Rus,* ISCUS, Delhi 1958.

N. Roerich 1947

Nicholas Roerich, *Himālayas: The Abode of Light,* Nālandā Publications, Bombay 1947.

- *Altai Himālayas,* A Travel Diary, Jarrold Publishers, London.

Rhie & Thurman 1991

Marylin M. Rhie, Robert A. F. Thurman, *The Sacred Art of Tibet,* Thames and Hudson 1991

Shambhala Dictionary of Buddhism and Zen, 1991

Shambhala Dictionary of Buddhism and Zen, translated by Michael H. Kohn, Shambhala, Boston 1991.

Tucci 1980

Tucci, Guiseppe, *Tibetan Painted Scrolls,* Rinsen Book Co. Ltd., Kyoto 1980.

25

HEVAJRA IN BUDDHIST LITERATURE, IMPERIAL CEREMONIES AND ART

Tantric art follows the principles of demonisation and feminisation. The Tantric deities look demonic, but are not demons; they look awe inspiring, but are compassionate at heart; they look religious, but perform secular functions; they hold objects of destruction, but are worshipped for protection and victory. The feminine forms are embodiments of *prajñā,* powers of the respective divine beings. The clasping postures indicate oneness of the *prakṛti* and *puruṣa.*

Such Tantric deities of the Buddhist pantheon, looking wrathful, mysterious, awe-inspiring and esoteric, represent the outrageous and exuberant quality of energy, which cannot be challenged. They hold attributes of war—skull cups full of blood, *khaṭvāṅga* topped by human head or other weapons of vigorous destruction of enemy such as vajra, sword, bow and arrow etc. Garlands made of human heads falling down up to knees, the ferocious way of dancing on corpses, trampling down human bodies and an effect of a terrible sound produced by a *ḍamaru* or a bell, held by them add to their ferociousness.

The protective Tantric deities, fall into the following categories:

1. Deities of *rakṣācakra*
2. Vidyārājas
3. Dharmapālas
4. Deities of state: Cakra-samvara and Heruka
5. Protective deities of maṇḍalas
6. Deities of territorial significance

Heruka, as one of the Tantric deities of state, is of five types as classified by Anuttara-yoga-tantras:

1. Samvara 2. Hevajra 3. Buddha-kapāla 4. Mahāmāyā 5. Ārali (Wayman 1973:234-5)

Thus Heruka has been used as a generic term for Samvara, Cakrasamvara, Trailokyākṣepa Hevajra, Kapālī Hevajra, Buddhakapāla of Niṣpannayogāvalī, Mahāmāyā and Ārali (Lokesh Chandra 2002:5.1393). This gave rise to some confusion as written by Rob Linroth in 'Ruthless Compassion' (1999:pp 268-70)—The images of Hevajra could equally be considered images of Heruka,... ... ... Hevajra is a form of Heruka and at an ultimate level, they cannot be distinguished. He writes about the regional variations restricted to posture, presence of consort and four different forms of Hevajra described in Hevajra-tantra... ... ...

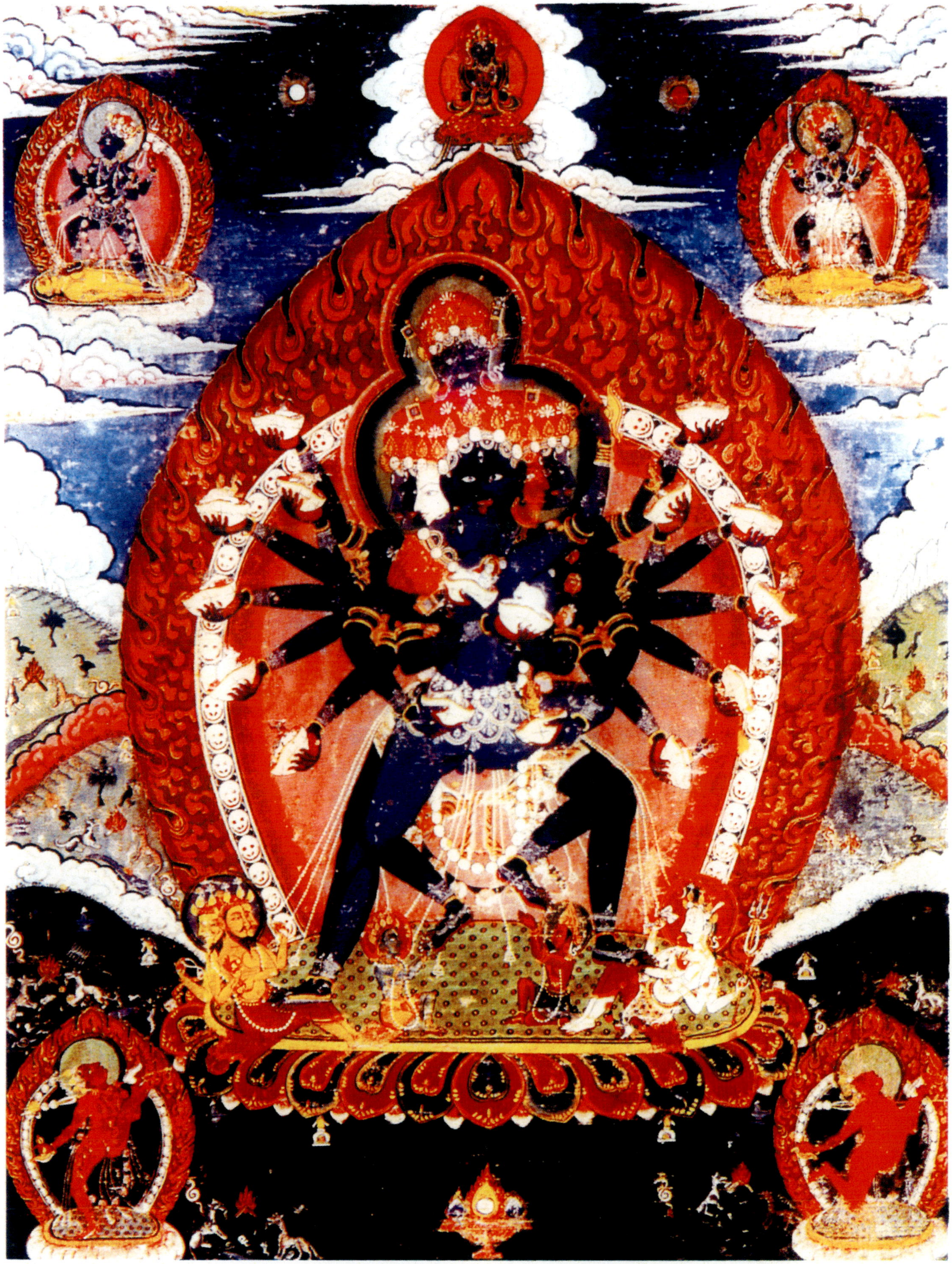

Sixteen armed Hevajra, Tibetan thangka painting

Especial Tantric works are devoted to the worship of Hevajra as one of the most popular deities of the Buddhist pantheon. Hevajra is the central deity of Sampuṭa tantras (Toh. 381) and Hevajra-tantra (Toh. 417). He holds weapons in the Sampuṭa-tantra, and is called Śastradhara and holds crania in the Hevajra-tantra, and is called Kapāladhara. The drawings of eight forms of Hevajra in Darba (1938:191, 192, 193, 194, 195, 196, 197,198, 199, 201, 202, 203 ,204, 205) follow the text in Niṣpannayogāvalī, word by word and helps to understand the minute variations in the Sampuṭa- and Hevajra-tantras. Thus Tibetan sources are the most reliable for a comprehensive analysis of various forms of Hevajra.

Transmission of the Hevajra-tantra:

Hevajra-Tantra is one of the special Tantric works devoted to the worship of Hevajra. It belongs to the late Mantrayana tradition and was composed in NE India during the 8th century. It was written after the Sarvatathāgata-tattva-saṅgraha (Snellgrove 1959:18). Vajragarbha, who wrote a commentary on Hevajra-tantra states that the tantra that consists of two parts (*kalpa*) and 750 *ślokas*, is but a shorter version of the original work that had thirty-two parts and 500,000 *ślokas* (Snellgrove 1959:16). Hevajra-tantra is work of ritual that circles around Hevajra and Nairātmyā.

As an Anuttarayoga-tantra text of profound import, it was brought to light by Kampala and Saroruha, which had developed certain powerful means of mental and physical control. These masters are known collectively in both Indian and Tibetan traditions as Siddhas. Saroruha, who is credited with bringing the tantra to light, and whose interest in it is proved by his commentary and several short works (*sādhana, vidhi and stotra*) concerned with the Hevajra cycle, is also known as Padmavajra. Both he and Kampala appear as contemporaries of King Indrabhūti II, who had received instructions by both of them. Hevajra-tantra existed in its present form towards the end of the eighth century. A commentary on Hevajra-tantra, Yogaratna-mālā was authored by Kṛṣṇa or Kānhā who had succeeded from Indrabhūti II, through Jālandharī (Snellgrove 1959:13).

It was first introduced into Tibet during the late 10th century as one of the most renowned works. It was adopted in Tibet by Ka-gyu-pas (bKah-rgyud-pa) and the Sa-kya-pas (Sa-skya-pa) for whom it became a fundamental treatise to which they devoted much work of exegesis (Snellgrove 1959:10). Hevajra-pañjikā, also known as Yoga-ratna-mālā was written in the 9th century by Mahā-siddha and Paṇḍit Kṛṣṇācārya (Farrow & Menon 1992:vii). Sakya ye-shes (993-1050), known as Brg-mi, one of the earliest Tibetan master studied in Nepal with Shāntibhadra, a disciple of Ratnākara-śānti of Vikramaśilā, became a disciple of Prajñā Indraruci while travelling through Eastern India. After a gap of thirteen years, he met the Kashmiri Paṇḍit Gayādhara, became his disciple and translated the Hevajra-tantra, Cakra-samvara, Mahābala and Vajra-ḍāka in collaboration with the master (Crystal Mirror, vol. vi, A Journal of Tibetan Nyingma Meditation Center, Dharma Publishing, Berkley, USA 1984, pp. 420). In 1057 AD Pao-tchang carried it from India to China and it was translated into Chinese. (Tohoku 417, T 892, Nj. 1060, Peking 10 Tr. Gayādhara, Sakya-ye-shes 993-1050, Rv. Gihon-nu-dpal; Crystal Mirror 6.326).

Ritual of legitimation

The history of tradition of legitimation of kings goes back to the 5th century BC in the Hellenistic tradition. As the figures to be honoured became more important, a switch was made from heroic to divine honours. The greatest honour given to the greatest people led to divine symbolism. The first known case of divine cult of a living human falls at the end of the 5th century BC in the Hellenistic world. The cults of Hellenistic kings were modelled on divine cult. A temple of a god and a sanctuary of a hero, marks of divine cult were raised over the tomb of Sellucus of Syria by his successors (Price 1987).

Hevajra ceremony by Kubali Khan as an act of legitimation

In the Hindu-Buddhist world divine empowerment was sought to enhance one's own power and prestige through rituals and dedication ceremonies. It was believed that by practicing a set of exercises, the energy flows from the divine to the devotee. Tantric rituals were seen as a path for gaining political victory through spiritual powers. Through Hevajra ritual a devotee acquires the same supernatural powers as are possessed by Hevajra. Hevajrasekaprakriyā describes the ritual as how a disciple of Tantra identifies himself with the five Tathāgatas through the agency of various rites of consecration performed on him by his teacher.

Kublai Khan, the first emperor of the Yüan dynasty was the grandson of Chingis-khan. He turned to Buddhism and initiated into Tibetan Tantric rites, worshipped Mahākāla to conquer South China and performed Hevajra ceremony for Southeast Asia in AD 1264 and AD 1269 which was urged on him by his wife Chabi (Berger and Bartholomew 1996:50). He and his Tibetan preceptor Sakyapa Lama Phagsapa had created a new inner Asian Buddhist concept of state craft—the dual principal—compelling enough to challenge China's Confucian system of heavenly mandate, ancestral homage and moral rectitude. A manuscript of Hevajra Tantra was given to Kublai Khan by an image of Mahākāla disguised as a *brāhmaṇa,* who told him to perform the Hevajra rites for success. The image was used in a ritual to aid the Mongols in their struggle against the Southern Sung. The Emperor slept with the Hevajra Tantra and Phagspa gave him the consecration of Hevajra Tanta to further his imperial designs.

Kublai Khan was initiated into the maṇḍala of Hevajra. When participating in the consecration ceremony the adept had to identify himself with the main figure of the maṇḍala. Where this figure had a multiple form this could be realised by breaking it up into its component parts of simple one headed and two armed figures. The suggestion has been made because around 1920, in the near neighbourhood of Peking, a number of fine and roughly life-sized bronzes of an unmistakable Tantric character were discovered and photographed by E.E. Schlieper (Pott 1969).

The group of bronzes was used in building up a maṇḍala at Kublai Khan's Hevajravasita. Instead of eight faced and sixteen-armed Hevajra embracing his prajñā *śakti,* holding skull cups with the various deities and animals and surrounded by the eight mothers of cemeteries, a group may have been chosen of eight separate figures, each consisting of a deity embracing his prajñā. At the centre of this group the emperor and his consort were identified with the total figure, of which the eight surrounding figures were but partial aspects (Pott 1969:31).

By 12th century the ideas and images quickly flowed in eastern, southern and northern directions. Islam alone proved an impenetrable barrier.

Other images of Hevajra

Bengal was an important centre for the teachings of Hevajra in the 12th century, from where the tradition travelled to Nepal and Tibet, and from there to Mongolia and China. Hevajra cult thrived in Southeast Asia also. It went to Thailand from Bengal via Burma. It had a considerable influence on the highest levels of society. Hevajra was an important deity of the royal cults, utilised to improve relations with Tibet and as a part of an attempt to local political legitimation.

Images of Hevajra found from various Buddhist sites of Cambodia and Thailand can be associated with royal cults. The concept of Devarāja, the central fact on Khmer life was an object of vast program of temple building. As spiritual power, it served as the core to hold the kingdom together. The compelling power of Hevajra images seems to have contributed to the cult, which sponsored commemorative monuments more so than monasteries.

One complete and one partial metalwork maṇḍala of Hevajra is known to exist and a large number of stone and metal images are found in Thailand and Cambodia. One estimate suggests their number to be forty. At the early 12th century site of Phimai, both Hevajra and his attendant *yoginī* are well represented on reliefs and a number of Hevajra and *yoginī* metal-works have been recovered from the environs. A large stone bust found at Angkor Thom and acquired by Metropolitan Museum of Art, New York is Hevajra (Linroth 1999:274).

The greatest and the most important among the monuments of Padang Lawas in Sumatra, is Bahl I, dated as 11th-12th century work by A.J.Bernett Kempers in 'Ancient Indeneisan Art' (1959:76). An image from Bahl II, identified as Heruka is from the central chamber. It was smashed into pieces, particularly its face is damaged. The divinity dances on the dead body of a man. His attributes are a vajra in the right and a skull cup in the left hand. The shaft of *khaṭvāṅga* is pressed against his breast. It fits entirely in the sphere of Tantric ritual that is aptly expressed in the terrific laughter expressed in one of the inscriptions at Padang Lawas: *haha hāhā hūm huhū hehai hohau hāhā om aḥ hūm!* (Linroth 1999:268-70).

(Chronological list of some of the available images of Hevajra:

12th century	Bengal
12th century	East India
12th century	Bengal
12th-13th cen.	Khmer and Thai
14th century	Dun-huang
14th century	Tibet
14th century	Zangskar
14th century	Ladakh

Warlike characteristics of Hevajra

a. The two-armed Hevajra in the Hevajra maṇḍala of the Sampuṭa Tantra, is called Trailokyākṣ epaḥ, one who conquers the three worlds. According to Monier Monier Williams (Sans. Eng. Dic.) *ākṣepaḥ* means: one who throws down (Mahābhārata), to strike with a bolt (Rāmāyaṇa (vi-78.5), to convulse, to cause to tremble (Suśruta), to chase, to drive out of the place (Mahābhārata iii.539:bh.P.)(1899:128,co.3)

b. Hevajra in three of his forms stands on corpses which indicates his inherent power of defeating enemies. It has been described in one of the classical works of Indonesia, Sutasoma (125.10) that Heruka was worshipped on the battlefield: *sumadhya ri turuna bhatara heruka* (Zoetmulder 1982:621).

c. Five crania decorating his head and a garland of wet human heads worn by Hevajra and the attributes like vajra, sword, skulls, bow and arrow, wheel etc. that he holds, symbolise his warlike characteristics.

d. Hrdaya mantra in the maṇḍala of Sampuṭa Tantra is—*hṛdaya mantraḥ om deva pichuvajra hūm hūm hūm phaṭ svāhā*. His mantra in the Hevajra-tantra is—*om deva pichuvajra hūm hūm hūm phat svāhā hṛdaya ṣoḍaśa-bhujasya*. He holds a vajra that has a quality to subdue because '*pich*' means to press flat, to squeeze (Turner 1966:460). Thus Hevajra is a divinity who holds a vajra that can squeeze (the enemy).

e. The mantra for the Vāg-Hevajra of the Sampuṭa Tantra: *om jvala jvalabhyo hūm hūm hūm phaṭ svāhā,* refers to his qualities of destroying by burning.

f. Hevajra wears different types of ornaments: According to Hevajra Tantra (1.3.14, vol.1, p.58, 1.6.11-12, vol.1, p.64) the five symbolic ornaments are:

Cakrī	(diadem)	Akṣobhya
Kuṇḍala	(earring)	Amitābha
Kaṇṭhī	(necklace)	Ratneśa
Rucaka	(bracelet)	Vairocana
Mekhalā	(girdle)	Amoghasiddhi

Bone apron is the sixth mentioned in the commentary by Kanha on the Hevajratantra. Skull bowl, skull drum, trumpets made of femur, sacrificial knives, crowns and magic daggers are the other articles. Pieces of bones in bone apron are said to be made of bones of enemies of the doctrine who had been defeated, destroyed and so forth. These articles should be compared with the ornaments and attributes of the demonic figures to support that the adherent identifies himself with the demonic figures (Pott 1951:115-118). Kāpālikas believed that if one would wear six signs: a necklace, an ornament, an ear ornament, crest jewel, ashes and sacred thread (*kuṇḍala*, *cūḍāmaṇi*, *bhasma*, *yajṃopavīta* etc.) he would be exempted from transmigration. All the bliss is possible to be achieved through consumption of food in a skull, daubing one's limbs with the ashes of a corpse, consuming those ashes, holding a club, having a pot of liquor, and worshipping god as dwelling in it. They also adorned themselves with *rudrākṣa* beads, their hair was matted and their skulls filled with ashes. It was believed that one could attain sainthood by undertaking these vow (Walker 1968:526-27).

Thus Hevajra is an embodiment of power kratos-theos (*kratuh*).

Fearful am I to fear itself, with my necklace made of a string of heads, and dancing ferociously on a solar disc. Black am I and terrible with a crossed vajra on my head, and my body is smeared with ashes ... ...

Eight forms of Hevajra:

Eight forms of Hevajra fall into two categories because on the basis of the Tibetan tradition and Niṣpannayogāvalī, various forms of Hevajra can be classified as follows:

Sampuṭa-tantra, (Śastra-dhara) :

a. 2 armed	sKu (Kāya-H)	Nairātmā	NSP 5(1)	Darba 199
b. 4 armed	gSun (Vāk-H)	Vajra-vārāhī	NSP 5 (2)	Darba 201
c. 6 armed	Thugs (Citta-H)	Vajraśrṅkhalā	NSP 5 (3)	Darba 203
d. 16 armed	sNin-po (Hṛdaya-H)	Nairātmā	NSP 5 (4)	Darba 205

Hevajra-tantra, (Kapala-dhara):

e. 2 armed	sKu (Kāya-H)	Nairātmā	NSP 8 (1)	Darba 193
f. 4 armed	gSun (Vāk-H)	Vajra-vārāhī	NSP 8 (2)	Darba 195
g. 6 armed	Thugs (Citta-H)	Vajra-śrṅkhalā	NSP 8 (3)	Darba 197
h. 16 armed	sNin-po (Hṛdaya-H)	Nairātmā	NSP 8 (4)	Darba 191

a. Kāya-Hevajra (sKu Kyai-rdo-rje) (Sampuṭa-tantra)

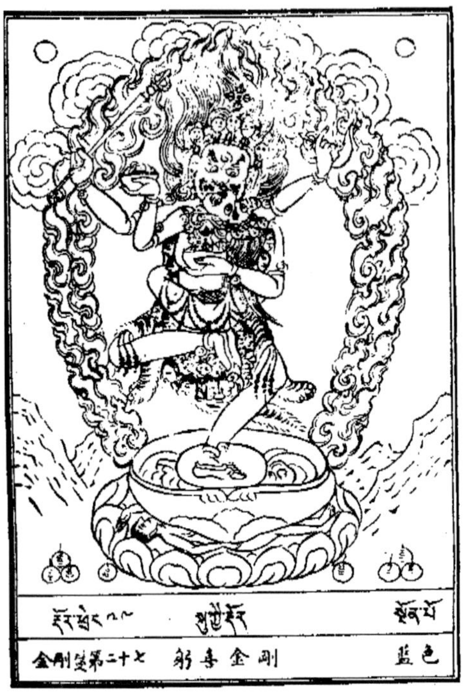

On a polylotus, corpse, blood-filled skull and sun. stands Hevajra, convulser of the Three Worlds (Trailokyākṣepa, 'Jig-rten gsum kun-tu bskyod-pa), black in color, with one face and two arms, the right holding up a five-pointed-vajra club in the act of striking, the left bearing a blood-filled skull marked with a vajra and embracing the consort Vajra-nairātmā (rDo-rje bDag-med-ma), who is blue, with one face and two arms, holding knife and skull. He has three round, red eyes. His lord of the family is Akṣobhya, seed syllable is hūm; general heart mantra is *om aḥ hūm hrīm svāhā,* individual mantra is *om Trailokyākṣepa hūm hūm hūm phaṭ svāhā.*

b. Vāk-Hevajra (Sampuṭa-tantra)

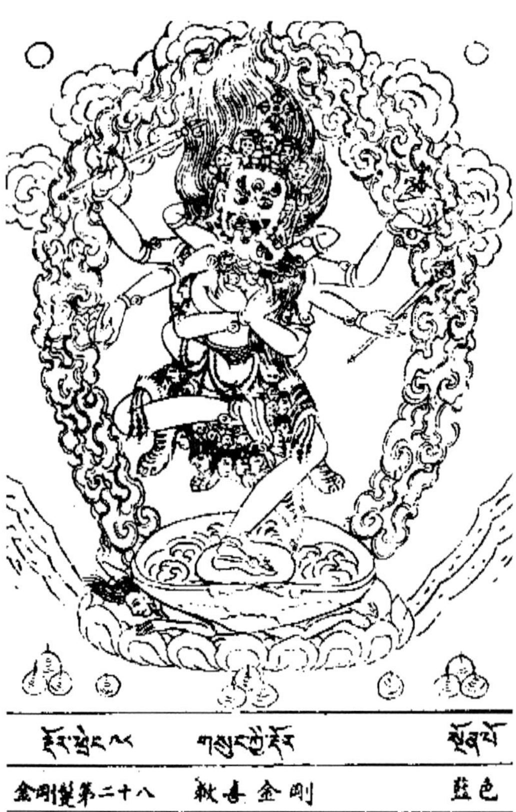

On a polylotus, corpse, blood-filled skull and sun stands Vāk-Hevajra, black, with one face and four arms, the first right hand is brandishing a club, marked with a five-pointed vajra, the first left is holding a blood-filled skull marked with a vajra, and the other pair of arms are embracing Vajra-vārāhī (rDo-rje phag-mo), who is similar to him. He has three round, red eyes.

The lord of the family is Akṣobhya, seed is *hūm*, general heart mantra is *om aḥ hūm hrīm svāhā*; individual mantra is o*m jvala jvalabhyo hūm hūm hūm phaṭ svāhā*.

c. Citta-Hevajra (Sampuṭa-tantra)

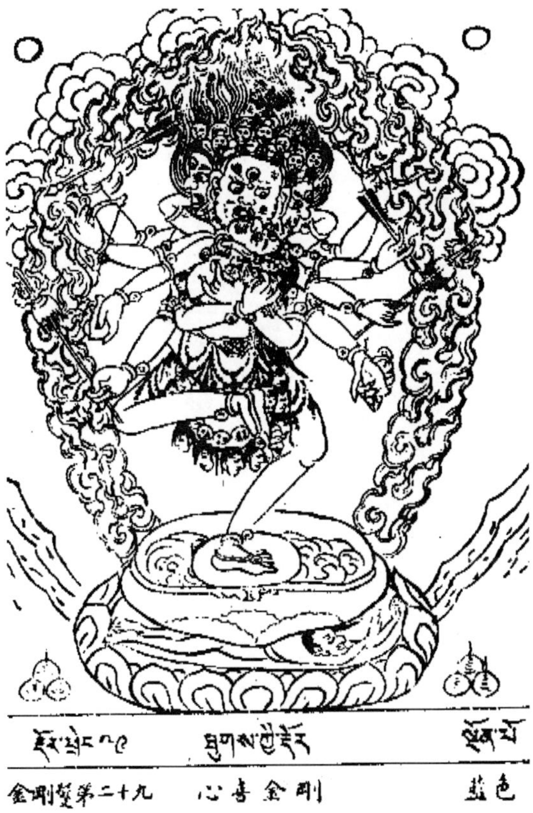

At the centre of an eight-petaled polylotus is a corpse, on whose heart rests a blood-filled skull, and upon this, a sun. On this stands Lord Citta-Hevajra, black, with three faces—black, white and red, and six arms. The first pair of arms is, holding vajra and vajra bell while embracing Vajra-śṛṅkhalā (rDo-rje lu.gtl-rgyud-ma), who is similar to him. The other right hands hold an arrow and a trident, the left a bow and a skull. Each face has three round, red eyes. His pale yellow hair streams upward and is marked with a crossed vajra? He is crowned with five dry skulls and has a necklace of fifty fresh human heads. He is adorned with the six symbolic ornaments and wears a tiger-skin loincloth, tied at the back. He stands in ardha-paryaṅka dancing posture with the right toenails pressed against the left thigh. Both Father and Mother are crowned with the Lord of the Family, Akṣobhya. The seed at Hevajra's heart is *hūm;* the heart mantra for the three Herukas or Kāya, Vāk and Citta Hevajras is: *om aḥ hūm hrīm svāhā*. The individual mantra of Citta-Hevajra is: *om kṛti kiṭi vajra hūm hūm hūm phaṭ*. The mantra of the consort is *om aḥ lam hūm phaṭ*. The attendants of this maṇḍala are a subset of those of the 39-deity Sampuṭa Vajradhātu maṇḍala, (Ngor 111), whose principal deity is, however called Akṣobhya.

d. Ḥrdaya-Hevajra (Sampuṭa-tantra)

At the centre of the eight-petaled polylotus are the four Māras: Skandha-māra in the form of yellow Brahmā, Kleśa-māra, as black Viṣṇu, Mṛtyu-māra as white Maheśvara, Devaputra-māra as pale yellow Śakra. On the top of them is a blood filled skull, and upon this, a sun. On this stands Lord Hevajra, black, with eight faces, sixteen arms and four legs. The principal face is black and he is loudly laughing, the right side face is white and the left is red, and the upper face is black in color and baring fangs; the remaining are black. Each face has three eyes, making twenty-four in all. His pale yellow hair streams upward and is marked with a crossed vajra. His first pair of hands, holding a vajra and bell, embrace blue Nairātmā, who holds a knife and a skull. The remaining right hands hold, in order: sword, arrow, wheel, skull, club, trident and hook; the left—lotus, bow, raised khaṭvāṅga, skull, jewel, threatening forefinger and noose. He is crowned with five dry human heads and his necklace is made of fifty fresh ones. He is adorned with the six

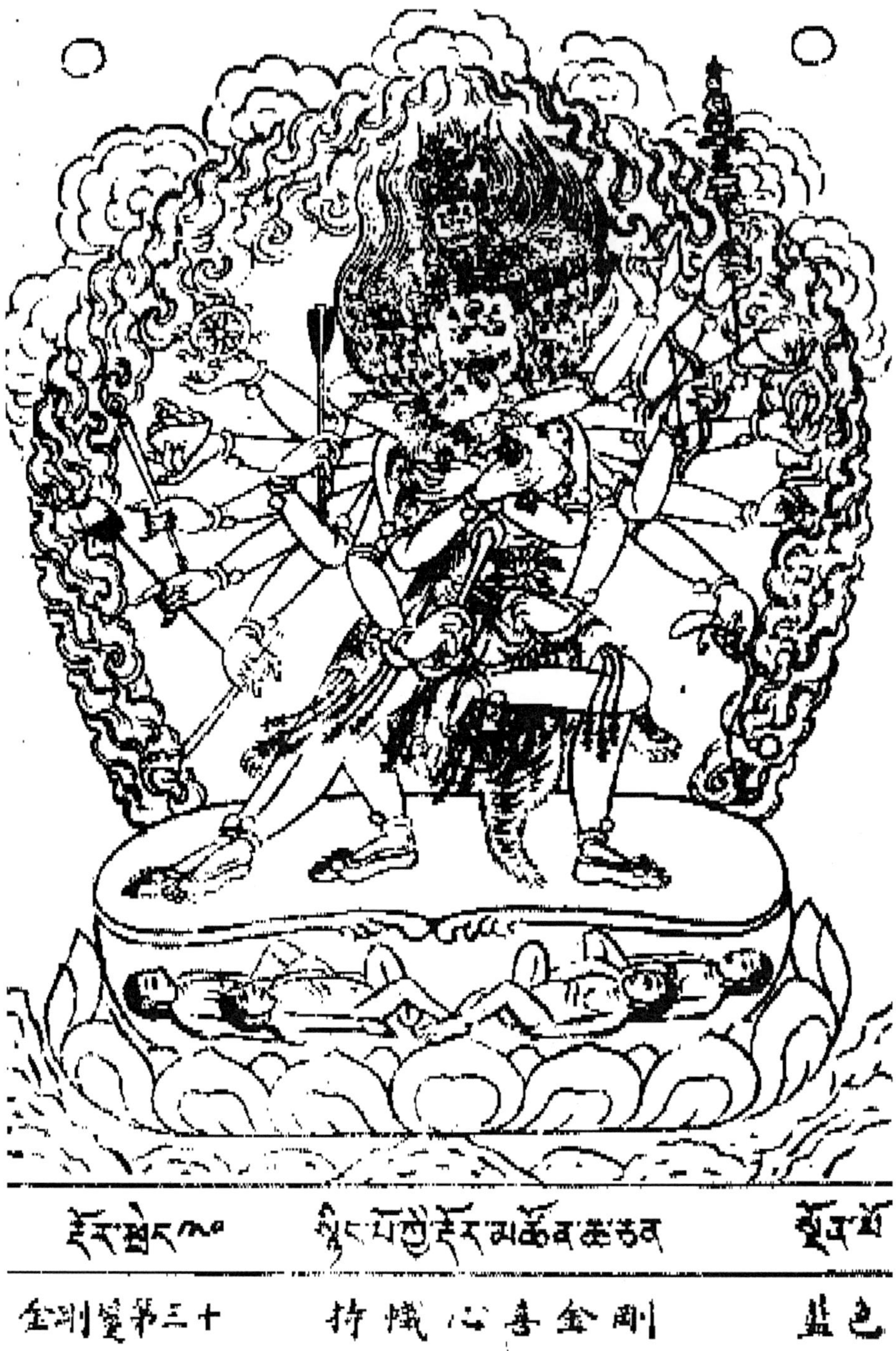

symbolic ornaments and wears a tiger-skin loincloth tied at the back. He stands with two legs in *ardha-paryaṅka* and two in *ālīḍha* posture (right leg extended).

Seal (both Father and Mother): Akṣobhya; the seed at the Lord's heart is *hūm*. His heart mantra is *om deve picu vajra hūm hūm hūm phaṭ svāhā*; heart-mantra of the consort is *om a nam vajra nairātmaye hūm phaṭ svāhā* and All-purpose mantra is Ghasmari *om om svāhā*.

e. Kāya-Hevajra (Hevajra-Tantra)

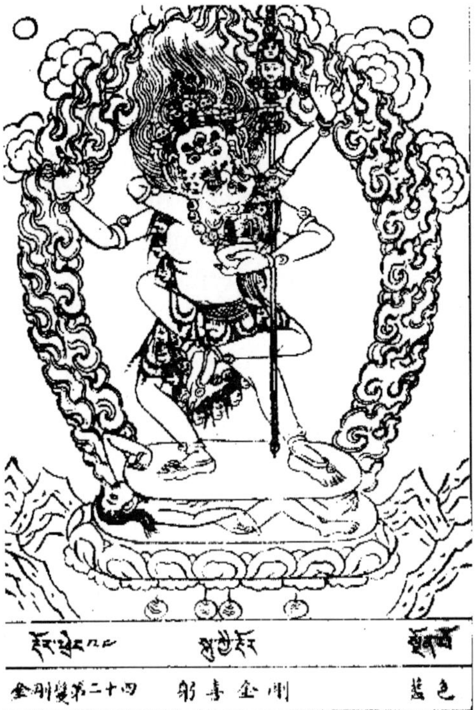

According to Niṣpannayogāvālī he is Hevajra but Hevajra-Tantra (1.3.13-16) identifies him as the main deity (*cakreśa*) of the nine deity maṇḍala in vajrāvalī (no. 24). He embraces his consort Nairātmā, holds a vajra in his right hand and a vajra-kapāla and a khaṭvāṅga in the left hand. Darba (1938:193-194) states that he is the Kāya-Hevajra of the Heruka family in the Hevajra-tantra. In Sādhanamālā 244 he is single, *ekavīra,* and without consort.

According to Hevajra-Tantra, on a polylotus, corpse and sun disk stands Body-Hevajra, blue, with one face and two arms, the right holding a vajra, the left holding a vajra-marked skull and embracing Vajra-Nairātmā (rDo-rje bDag-med-ma). A khaṭvāṅga leans on his left shoulder. He is dancing in *ardha-paryaṅka*, and wears six symbolic ornaments as Citta-Hevajra. His seal is Akṣobhya, seed is *hūm,* heart mantra is *om Trilokyākṣepa hūm hūm hūm phaṭ svāhā* (*om* Convulser of the Three Worlds, *hūm*).

f. Vāk-Hevajra (Hevajra-Tantra)

On a polylotus, corpse and sun disk stands Vāk-Hevajra, blue, with one face and four arms, one of his right hands is holding a vajra and one left a skull full of blood, the other pair of arms is embracing Vajra-vārāhī (rDo-rje phag-mo), who is similar to him. He is dancing in *ardha-paryaṅka*, and wears six symbolic ornaments, as Citta-Hevajra. Seal of both deities is Akṣobhya, seed is *hūm,* heart mantra is (Hevajra): *om jvalaj jvalebhyo hūm hūm hūm phaṭ svāhā*.

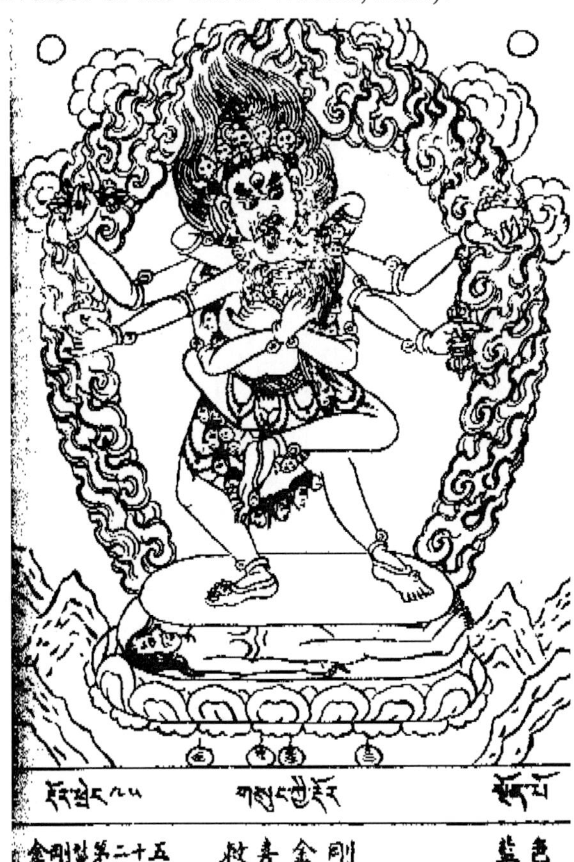

g. Citta-Hevajra (Hevajra-Tantra)

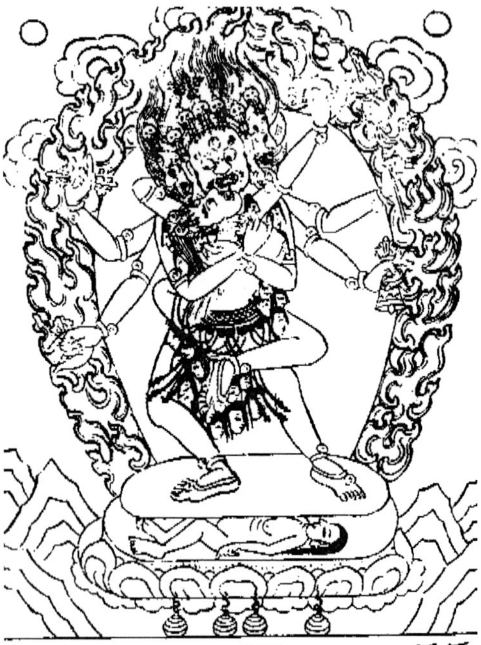

金刚鬘第二十六 心喜金刚 蓝色

On the stamens of an eight-petaled polylotus lies a corpse, and on its heart a sun disk. On this is Citta-Hevajra, blue in color, with three faces—principal blue, right white and left red and six arms. Two right hands hold a vajra and a knife, two left a trident and a bell; the remaining pair of arms embrace Vajra-Śṛṅkhalā. He is dancing in ardha-paryaṅka with right leg extended and left bent, and is imbued with the nine dramatic sentiments. Each face has three eyes and four bared fangs, and frowns with knitted brows. His tawny, upward-streaming hair is marked on top with a crossed vajra. He is crowned with five dry human heads, has a necklace of fifty fresh ones and is 'sealed' with the six symbolic ornaments. His seal is Akṣobhya, seed is *hūṃ*; heart mantra (Hevajra) is: *oṃ kiṭi kiṭi vajra hūṃ hūṃ hūṃ phaṭ svāhā.*

h. Hṛdaya-Hevajra (Hevajra-Tantra)

At the center of an eight-petaled polylotus are the four Māras—Kleśa-māra and others lying on their backs, in the forms of yellow Brahmā, black Viṣṇu, white Maheśvara and yellow Indra. On their hearts rests a sun, on which is Lord Hevajra, black in colour, naked, with eight faces, sixteen arms and four legs. He is dancing, imbued with the nine dramatic sentiments, with two legs in *ardha-paryaṅka* and the other two in *ālīḍha* posture (left bent, right extended). The principal face is black, the first right is white, the first left is red, the upper face is smoke-coloured and ugly, and the other two on either side are black. All of them have three round, red eyes, four huge, bared fangs and a vibrating tongue, and are frowning with knitted brows. His gleaming, tawny hair streams upward and is marked on top with a crossed vajra. He is adorned on the forehead with five dry, skinless human heads and has a crown of the Five Buddhas. The sixteen hands hold sixteen skulls. With the

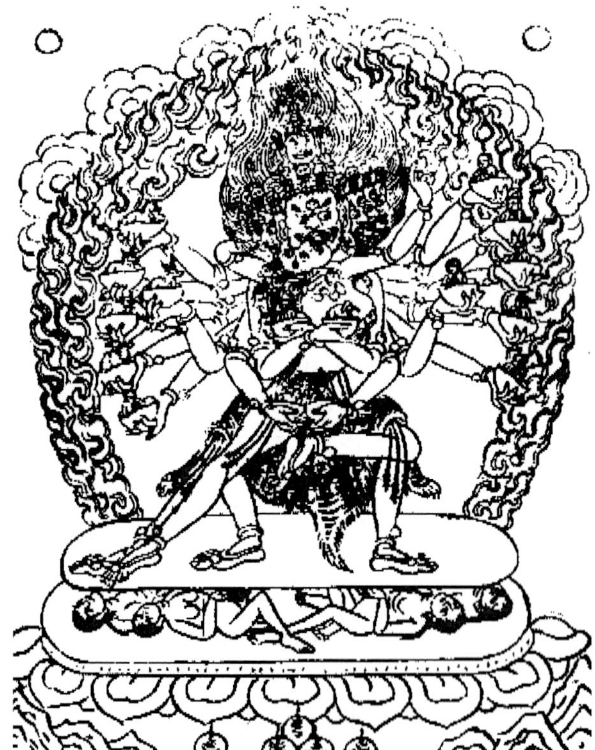

金刚鬘第二十三 持颅心喜金刚 蓝色

first pair of arms, whose skulls contain a white elephant and the yellow earth-goddess Pṛthivī, he embraces his consort. In the other seven right skulls are: a horse, an ass, an ox, a camel, a human being, a *sarabha*, and an owl or a cat. In the other seven left hands are Varuṇa, Vāyu, Tejas, Candra, Aditya, Yama and Dhanada (=Kubera). He is adorned with the six symbolic ornaments—circlet, earrings, necklace, bracelets, girdle and ashes, a string of fifty fresh (blood-dripping) human heads, armlets and anklets. Lord of the family of both deities is Akṣobhya, seed-syllable (Hevajra) is *hūm*, heart mantra of the principal deity is *om deva picu-vajra hūm hūm hūm phaṭ svāhā,* near-heart mantra is *om vajra kartare Hevajra ye hūm hūm hūm.*

Trailokyākṣepa-Hevajra (Kyehi.rdo.rje) is illustrated in Darba (1938:199) as Kāya-Hevajra (Sku Kyahi-rdor) as the central deity of his seventeen deity maṇḍala. (Willson & Brauen 2000: no. 462-473, p. 403-404)

Śastradhara-Hevajra		**Kapāladhara-Hevajra**	
right hands	left hands	right hands	left hands
vajra	bell	elephant	Varuṇa
sword	lotus	horse	Agni
arrow	bow	ass	Candra
wheel	khaṭvāṅga	bull	Sūrya
skull	skull	camel	Yama
club	jewel	mongoose	Vasudhārā
trident	threatening forefinger	monk	Vāstupati
hook	noose.		

Kapāla-dhara with 16 arms

(Bronze, National Museum of Ethnology, Leyden)

Hevajra is depicted as a sixteen year old youth of wrathful appearance, clad in tiger-skin. He has eight pairs of arms and in Yabyum posture with Vajra-Vārāhī, his prajñā or female partner. In his eight left hands he holds drinking vessels made of skulls in which various deities are seated and in the right hands are similar skull cups containing animal figures. These animals are said to be rides of the respective deities but they are not the respective rides according to the Purāṇic or the Buddhist tradition.

Prajñā of Hevajra

P.H.Pott in 'The Maṇḍala of Heruka' (CIBA Journal No. 50, 1969) writes that Hevajra is usually depicted as a sixteen year old youth of wrathful appearance, clad in tiger skin. He has eight pairs of arms and is always represented in the yab-yum of Vajravārāhī, his prajñā, or female counterpart. Evidently, according to NSP 5 and 8 his prajñās are: Nairātmā, Vajra-vārāhī and Vajra-śṛṅkhalā, embraced by him in different forms as follows:

Śastradhara

2 armed	Nairātmā	NSP 5(1)
4 armed	Vajra-vārāhī	NSP 5 (2)
6 armed	Vajraśrṅkhalā	NSP 5 (3)
16 armed	Nairātmā	NSP 5 (4)

Kapāla-dhara

2 armed	Nairātmā	NSP 8 (1)
4 armed	Vajra-vārāhī	NSP 8 (2)
6 armed	Vajra-śrṅkhalā	NSP 8 (3)
16 armed	Nairātmā	NSP 8 (4)

Nairātmya (absence of the notion of selfhood):

There are a large number of *sādhanas* of this goddess in the Sādhanamālā where she is associated with the rite of *vaśya,* subduing, in which she is specially proficient (Snellgrove 1959:16).

Vajra-vārāhī

Vajravārāhī, the consort of Hevajra is portrayed as a vanquisher of enemy. She holds attributes of war while in embrace. Vajravārāhī mantra *(aṣṭapada arcanā mantraḥ)* has *ajite aparājite*, 'unconquered', *vijaye* 'victorious', *sarvabhūta-bhavāyahe* 'a terror to all beings', *trāsanī māraṇī prabhedanī parājaye* 'you who terrify, kill, tear to peaces and triumph. Perfection of wisdom is symbolised in a feminine divinity, the goddess Prajñāpāramitā. She is the supreme truth of the void. In Hevajra-tantra she is Nairātmyā, absence of the notion of selfhood, and it is in her that the *yogi,* as means, is substantiated. Hevajra comprehends the whole truth as much as does the Goddess Prajṃāpāramitā. In order to emphasize the essential identity of the idea the female form is made to transmute into the male, and the two which are thus identified are *nirvāṇa* and *saṁsāra*. (Snellgrove 1959:24).

The whole maṇḍala is an idealized representation of the identity of *nirvāṇa* and *saṁsāra* (Snellgrove 1959:29). Vajra and lotus derive their whole significance from their masculine and feminine connotations (Snellgrove 959:24). Vajra-Vārāhī was a protectress of Khotan (for details see Lokesh Chandra, Vajra-Vārāhī as the protectress of Khotan). She looks demonic like Hevajra but is not a demoness, she is compassionate and is worshipped for protection and victory.

LITERATURE CITED

Berger and Bartholomew 1996

Petricia Berger and Theresa Tse Bartholomew, Mongolia, *The Legacy of Chinggis Khan*, Thames and Hudson, 1996

Darba 1938

Dar-ba Ho-thog-thu Blo-bzaṅ-bstan-ḥdzin-hjigs-med-bdaṅ-phyug of the Sṅag-pa Grwa-tshaṅ of Bkra-śislhun-po monastery, Mitra daṅ rdor-phreṅ-gi lha-tshogs-kyi gtso-boḥi sku-brñan Mthoṅ-ba-don-ldan, reproduced Delhi 1985 (K.Tsewang Taru)

Farrow & Menon 1992
G.W. Farrow & I Menon, *The Concealed Essence of the Hevajra-tantra*, Motilal Banarasidas, Delhi, 1992

Kempers 1959
A.J.Bernett Kempers, *Ancient Indeneisan Art* Harward University Press, Cambridge, 1959

Linroth 1999
Rob Linroth, *Ruthless compassion*, Serindia Publiacations, London, 1999

Lokesh Chandra 2002
Lokesh Chandra, *Dictionary of Buddhist Iconography*, Aditya Prakashan, Delhi, 2002

Monier Williams 1899
Monier Monier Williams, *Sanskrit-English Dictionary*, Clarendon Press, Oxford, 1899

Pott 1951
P.H.Pott, *Introduction to the Tibetan Collection of the National Museum of Ethnology*, Leiden, 1951

Pott 1969
P.H.Pott, *The Maṇḍala of Heruka*, CIBA Journal No. 50, 1969

Price 1987
S.R.F. Price, *Ritual and Power*, Cambridge University Press, Cambridge 1987

Snellgrove 1959
D.L. Snellgrove, *The Hevajra Tantra: A Critical Study*, Oxford University Press, London Oriental Series, vol. 6, London 1959

Turner 1966
R.L.Turner, *A Comparative Dictionalry of the Indo-Aryan Languages*, Oxford University Press, London 1966

Toh.
Hakuji Ui et al., *A Complete Catalogue of the Tibetan Buddhist Canons* (Bkahgyur and Bstan-hgyur), Sendai (Tohoku Imperial Universoty), 1934

Walker 1968
Benjamin Walker, *An Encyclopedic Survey of Hinduism*, Hindu World, London, 1968

Wayman 1973
Alex Wayman, The Buddhist Tantras, Samuel Weiser, New York, 1973

Willson & Brauen 2000
Willson & Brauen, *Deities of Tibetan Buddhism*, Wisdom Publications, Boston, 2000

Zoetmulder 1982
P.J.Zoetmulder, Old Javanese-English Dictionary, Leiden 1982

Crystal Mirror, vol. vi A, Journal of Tibetan Nyingma Meditation Center, Dharma Publishing, Berkley USA 1984

26

BANNER OF PEACE

Peace : The Ultimate Goal

Presentation of Banner of Peace and the Pact to protect cultural, spiritual, artistic, historical and scientific monuments from the hands of ruinous wars, is a historically valuable achievement for humanity for its past, present and the future generations. The concept of world peace initiated by Prof. Nicholas Roerich goes back to the times of Indo Europeans, when the great Slavs shared a common language. The Vedas implore peace in the heavens and peace in the atmosphere, peace on the earth and peace on the flowing waters, peace for the herbal and plant life and peace for the past, present and future: *om dyauḥ śāntirantarikṣadhvam śāntiḥ prithivī śāntirāpaḥ śāntiroṣadhayaḥ śāntiḥ vanaspatayaḥ śāntih viśvedevāḥ śāntir brahma śāntiḥ sarvamchāntiḥ śāntireva śāntiḥ sa mā śāntiredhi*. Peace is the greatest aim toward which man should strive in fulfillment of his natural ends.

Peace within and peace without is the ultimate goal, an imperative for humanity on the path of an all round development. Peace was the target at which all shafts were sped because a hope for progress and transcendence becomes dim in its absence. It is the perfection of joy, which implies not the mere negative, the absence of disturbing passions and desires but chiefly their right direction. It is not just negation of war and unrest, it can mean well being and fulfillment of goals of religious and social life. In ancient Hebrew thought *shalon,* meaning peace, refers to well being, to material and spiritual conditions that were joined together. As a social concept peace was visible and produced a harmonious relationship in the family, in society and between nations. In the history of Church peace has been seen on one hand as calm for the soul and on the other as social and political reconciliation and establishment of just order. Positive social efforts for peace were illustrated in the words and actions of the famous Indian ruler Emperor Ashoka who had renounced war for the well being of the people.

War and Peace

Political developments can never be permitted to threaten cultural heritage. So the nature of war was a question in the mind of Prof. Nicholas Roerich who wished to protect humanity from ruining. The Spanish Jesuit theologian Francisco Suarez held that the cause of making war must be just. A similar view was taken by Hugo Grotius who argued that war should be waged only within the bounds of law and good faith. This conception survives in the assumption behind such 20th century international organizations as the League of Nations and the United Nations that only wars fought on behalf of international interests, such as maintenance of world peace are just.

Roerichs for Peace

Prof. Nicholas Roerich agreed that "man is born not for destruction but for love, friendship and service to his fellow men" as has been argued by the great humanist Desiderius Erasmus in his 'Anti-polemus, or the Plea of Reason, Religion and Humanity Against War' in 1510.

Roerichs were determined for maintenance of peace in the world. Prof. Nicholas Roerich was more of a prophet and a preacher, a guru so notable. As a patriotic nationalist his first scholarly work involved archaeological search for Russia's beginning. He wrote long poems and books on history and archaeology. The great personality of Nicholas Roerich encompasses the loftiest concepts, the highest aspirations of mankind, and tremendous efforts for peace throughout the world. He had directed his quest towards the unconquerable heights of the Himalayas to the greater and the deeper significance of spiritual life, purity of thought and aspirations for transcendence. As a humanist Nicholas Roerich thought about the fate of the whole humanity, always trying to rise above what a man can be. The oriental garments worn in another portrait reveal his personality as a seeker of the spiritual essence. Through the life and works of Nicholas Roerich humanity gets brilliant ideas and loftiest philosophy as the conscious and awakened mind desired to see the world on the path of the quest for harmony and peace.

Banner of Peace

Banner of Peace is a gift to the humanity. In a portrait painted by Svetoslav Roerich, Nicholas Roerich holds in his hands an ancient carved casket, a symbol of his gift to the humanity. The works of the great masters survive their deaths and so does the Banner of Peace that has protected the cultural heritage preserved in the sacred places like monasteries of Kyoto and Nara, a fruit of the untiring toil of a thousand years, years of devotion and dedication. The Roerichs were closely involved in Peace Pact, functioning in a historical context involving several cross cutting traditions. The message presented by the Banner of Peace was infinitely deep, forming the core of his thoughts, meant for the benefit of the people: *bahujanahitāya bahaujanasukhāya*. It contains three jewels enclosed by a circle. The three jewels are the Buddhist symbol of the holy triad in which every professing Buddhist takes his daily refuge reciting: *buddham saranam gacchāmi dhammama saranam gacchāmi sanghama saranam gacchāmi*. The Buddha is the propagator of new path, the pioneering spirit behind the new ideology, the *Dharma* signifies the Words of the Buddhas, a new philosophy, and the *Sangha*, which originally signifies the Buddha's order of monks, is generally interpreted as congregation of the monks. *Sangha* means becoming one with others; becoming one means harmony, and that means strength. In the Banner of Peace, Prof. Roerich is the pioneering spirit, his ideas are the dharma which gives protection and the *sangha* is the parties joining him in the great endeavor.

The three dots on the Banner signifying protection of arts, science and spirituality remind me of the three steps taken by Lord Viṣṇu in his incarnation as Vāmana. Vāmana measured the whole of the earth in the first stride and the heavens in the second and asked for space for the third. The king who boasted, was taken aback because Lord Viṣṇu had asked him for space for spiritual development, so crucial for humanity. The first stride represented the military might, the second scientific advancement and the third, spirituality.

Prof. Nicholas Roerich presented the Banner as a symbol of fulfillment of his dream of saving the historical monuments. The three dots are like the three jewels, a full expression of cintāmaṇi, the wish-granting jewel in Buddhism. Cintāmaṇi has the power to produce whatever one desires, it symbolizes the virtue and the power of the Buddha and the scriptures; the Buddha who had discovered the mysteries of life beyond the ravages of strife.

Inspiration for Peace Pact

Prof. Nicholas Roerich was sad at the destructive and restrictive powers that dissolve the religious cement that unites people to people. His eyes are full of a feeling of gloom that looms large for the languages and communication links that were lost, and pain for the blows of destruction, disputes and separations. He wrote an account of the city of Urga and its monasteries and monuments as they existed. He had witnessed a politically sensitive situation during his stay (Sep. 1926-April 27) there, where there was a threat wiping out culture, putting the countries in isolation. He aspired for a new era, an era of Shambhala, when he saw disappearance of symbolic and the occult objects of veneration and monks becoming soldiers. His experience during the expedition, and an in depth study of Lamaist Buddhism, embedded deep in his mind, strengthened his feelings for establishing peace.

Henry Wallace and Nicholas Roerich

The Roerichs as Russians, living abroad, serving as guardians of the native tradition of Russian scholarship were also pursuing Buddhism, Sanskrit and Tibetan studies opening up new horizons for the Mongols and the Tibetans to study and value their own traditions. Nicholas Reorich shared with Henry Wallace his love for the occult and the mystical attributes of Buddhism and an appeal of arcane and mysterious symbols containing the hidden meaning of life. Both of them had a passion for world peace and global unity. Symbols providing clues to the future Utopian Shambhala and the Second Coming can be found in the cultural traditions which if once destroyed are ruined for ever, never to be reconstructed again.

Henry Wallace, the then Secretary of Agriculture was inspired by Nicholas Roerich and advocated for Peace Pact because he had a strong interest in the Second Coming of the Christ. And so he was enthusiastic for Roerich's plans for protection of cultural treasures and the monuments, preserving them in times of war. Because such centers of spirituality serve as resorts for the spiritually hungry werein the great monks had erected images of the symbols of aspirations leading towards the radiant future.

Wallace in April 1935 volunteered fulsome praise of Nicholas Roerich in recommending him for the Nobel Peace Prize for his peace banner project protecting the valuable monuments from destruction that preserve religious traditions; the deep rhythmic droning of the chants, the muffled rumbling of the drums, loud clangs and blaring of cymbals and trumpets, and above all the somber people touching their inherent spirit.

Buddhism and World Peace

Roerich said that the true teachings meant activism and hard work not passivity and withdrawal and fatalistic acceptance. Abodes of the sacred enshrine the true inner spirit of the people, the people coming from deserts and mountains visit them to draw the hidden source of power. He claimed that Buddhist teachings actually forecast modern science, that they were eminently modern and they were certainly not indefensible, superstitious, or illogical or anti-scientific. Buddhism embodies substantive and eternal values that we abandon at our peril. The spiritual teachings are aught to be pursued by everyone everywhere, they embody universal truths and no one is a complete person who does not study them and follow them in the ways he lives.

Roerich found Lamaism a complex and multifaceted culture, providing social customs, esthetics, satisfactions, and variety, and relief from an often dull and difficult existence. He found a great deal of modern science in traditional Buddhism: The foundations of Buddhist philosophical teachings … … … Reveal an extraordinary affinity with … … … the latest, the newest achievements, in the domain of our scientific world concept.

NR noted in Sinkiang: places like Khotan have exhausted their old sap and can be rejuvenated only by a radical reconstruction … … Life has become dusty and brains have become rusty. A flash of vigorous lightening is needed (Altai Himalayas pp. 194-5). As a seeker of Shambhala Nicholas Roerich presented a painting to the Mongols in 1926 and recorded .. .. when the image will reach Urga, then will flash the first light of the New Era — the truth.

Conclusion

Humanity owes a great debt in present and will continue to do so in the coming centuries, to Prof. Nicholas Roerich for pioneering the idea that came to be a turning point in the history of culture, preserving the monuments from the destructive hands of atomic war and vandalism that could have reduced the centres of spirituality to ashes or heaps of stones or could have buried them under sand, for ever. His long cherished desire was fulfilled when monasteries in Kyoto and Nara in Japan were saved from bombing during the second world war. Abodes of spirituality nurturing the idea of Shambhala, a promised land, a coming paradise where goodness would rule and virtue would triumph. And this is true power, which is the foundation of peace: *sakti hi to śānti ka ādhāra hai*.

27

ROLE OF SUVARṆAPRABHĀSA-SŪTRA IN THE POLITY OF EAST ASIA

The Japanese emperors functioned both as religious and political leaders. There are a number of references when they used religious means for political gains. For them recitation of Suvarṇaprabhāsa-sūtra and the ceremonies based on it were meant for peace and prosperity of the country, for its protection from enemies, for the wellbeing of the public and the rulers, and to save the masses from calamities because in the forth chapter (I'tsing's translation) it promises four kinds of blessings to the countries in which it is read: the kings of those countries shall be free of diseases and other calamities, their life will be long and obstacle free, they will have no enemies, their warriors will be brave and strong, and there shall be peace, abundance and joy, and *saddharma* will prevail everywhere. The Four Divine Kings and the retinue of Yakṣas will protect those kings (Visser 1935:439). In the fifth chapter Brahmā and his followers, Indra, the Four Divine Kings and all the Yakṣas utter a solemn vow to protect and propagate the sūtra and to protect the priests who explain it as well as the people of the countries (Visser 1935:440). Those who hear this sūtra will be provided protection by day and by night by the world protectors with their ministers and chief servants by millions of Yakṣas, Sarasvatī, Hārīti, Dṛḍhā Prithivī, and the thirty-three kings etc. (Emmerick 1979:2). The goddesses ensure defense, intellectual and economic power to the readers of the sūtra (Visser 1935:440). Moreover Goddess Śrī was considered to be the mightiest protectress of faithful believers (Visser 1935:434).

Suvarṇaprabhāsa-sūtra (Jap. Konkwômyôkyô, Ch. Chin-kuang-ming tsui-sheng-wang-ching, abbreviated as Tsui-sheng-wang-ching, Mizuno 1982:202) was one of the Buddhist sūtras that reached Japan in the seventh century others being Śrīmālā-devī-siṁhanāda in AD 605 (Jap. Shōmangyō), Saddharmapuṇḍarīka-sūtra (Jap. Hokkekyô) in AD 606 and Vimala-kīrtti-nirdeśa-sūtra (Jap.Yuima-kyô) in 656, (Visser 1935:3-5) when Shotoku Taishi, as the first statesman, took important steps for establishing a centralized system of Govt in Japan. He composed a 'Seventeen-article Constitution' which is based on the Buddhist philosophy of welfare and well being of the people '*bahujanahitāya*' and '*bahujanasukhāya*'. The constitution represents a set of moral injunctions rather than being a body of law.

Protection of the Nation

Chapter six of Suv. is devoted to the worship of the Four Divine Guardian Kings (Jap. Shitennō). They promise with all their numberless followers to protect the kings together with their families and countries, who attentively listen to this sūtra and respectfully make offerings, reading receiving and keeping this sacred text. Shōtoku Taishi and the Soga family built the Shitennōji monastery to worship Four Divine Kings, who are guardians of the four directions and protectors of Buddhism, as a fulfillment of a vow to them, for the Soga victory over Mononobe in A.D 587. The temple was complete in 596 in Osaka.

In 660 the ceremony of 'lecture on the Suv.' began in the court because it reads that when a foreign threat appears, if a king makes hundred images of Buddha and invites hundred priests to lecture on the sūtra, then hundred demons or gods will protect the king. At that time T'ang and Silla had defeated Paikche and were threatening Japan, so the ceremony was held in the court to pray for protection of the state.

When Emperor Shōmu established the provincial monasteries called 'kokubunjis' he called them 'monasteries for the protection of the country by the Four Divine Kings (to be obtained by means of) the Suv.' The provincial monasteries were always situated near the central seat of the provincial government.

A special festival Gosaie, one of the 'Three Festivals of Nara', celebrated during the New Year at the Daigokuden in the Palace was intended to fulfill the Imperial vow to protect the stat. Priests of great learning were invited for a vegetarian entertainment and were requested to expound the Saishōōkyō (I'tsing's translation). They were also offered Imperial robes. The Emperor used to come in person on the first and the last day of the celebration to listen to the sūtra. On other days he used to send an official of the Supreme Council of State to take the official leadership. It remained an annual event from AD 802 to 1467, instituted by Emperor Kwammu (Visser 1935:471).

The first translation of Suv. by Dharmarakṣa II is mentioned for the first time in Japan in AD 676, together with Ninnokyō. In AD 680 expounding of the Suv. was begun in the palace and various Buddhist monasteries (Visser 1935:14). Later it was translated by I-tsing (Konkwōmyō Saishōō-kyō) in AD 700-712 which was far more extensive than that of Dharmarakṣa. It contains many magic formulae (entirely lacking in the latter), which must have been the reason why in Japan the sūtra was soon superceded by the Saishōōkyō (after AD 734). Because I'tsing's translation was complete, Kobo-daishi wrote two commentaries on it. It was one of the three sūtras of protecting the country in the ninth century when it was explained by the Shingon priests such as Shinen in 813 and Sancho in 860 for the welfare of the state.

Protection of the country being paramount, a meeting was devoted to Kāruṇika-rāja-prajñā-pāramitā-sūtra by Empress Saimei in AD 660 (Visser 1935:12). In this sūtra the Buddha explained to King Prasenajit and others as how they could protect their countries against all kinds of calamities by means of divine power of the great Bodhisattvas of the Five Quarters. Under the Ritsuryō system of Govt. the emperor's political and religious roles were of prime importance, as titular head of the state. Ritsuryō policy towards Buddhism was consistent throughout the Nara period. The established leaders were concerned about the temporal power of the Buddhist institutions. In the Govt.'s view priests were appointed to work for prosperity and protection of the nation (Matsunaga 1978:116).

Chanting sūtras associated with Tantric rites, for protection of the nation became a practice during the Nara period. The major sutras closely associated with these rites were—Saddharmpuṇḍarīka, Kāruṇika-rāja-prajñā-pāramitā and Suvarṇaprabhāsa-sūtras. It had captured the interest of the aristocracy becoming the main current of the next era (Matsunaga 112).

On account of the vow of the Four Divine Kings that they would protect the country against calamities, sorrows and pestilence where the Saishōōkyō would be explained, read and propagated, Emperor Shōmu in AD 741 commanded the foundation of a temple and a seven storey pagoda in each province. Copies of sūtras were distributed to those temples. Monasteries for twenty monks and nunneries for ten nuns formed a part of these temples. The duties of the incumbents were to read publicly on fixed dates the Saishōōkyō sūtra. On those days hunting and fishing were forbidden for the laity. He himself intended to make copies in golden characters to be sent to be deposited in the pagodas of the provincial monasteries called 'monasteries for the protection of the country by the Four Divine Kings'.

In AD 804 the Emperor Kwammu speaks of 'The Vegetarian Festival of the First Month' which was also called Saishō-e or Konkwomyō-e, celebrated in the Daigokuden of the Palace, the great Palace festival for protection of the state. Suv. was one of the three sūtras chosen by Emperor Shōmu for protection of the state, others being: Saddharma-puṇḍarīka-sūtra and Ninnokyō. All those who wished to become monks or nuns had to learn them by heart. Shōmu had ordered the monks and nuns to purify themselves by ritual baths and to read the Saishōōkyō two or three times a month.

Emperor Nimmyo a faithful believer in the protecting power of Saishōōkyō, ordered that all the temples who had sustenance fiefs, rice fields and gardens should present gifts to the monks who performed the rites of Saishōōkyō (Visser 1935:475).

Legitimation of the State

In classical antiquity legitimation of the ruler and the kingdom was through religion by way of construction of monasteries, recitation of sūtras, Imperial ceremonies and other religious activities. Emperor Ashoka interpreted his imperial calling as a humanitarian mission. Political unification of under his empire came through his royal patronage for Buddhism. His faith in Buddhism led him to power.

Rulers followed the way of transformation of the regal self to divine status; the sovereigns called themselves 'Lords of the world'. Deification of a king was possible during his life time also. Among the deified royal personages the most dramatic expression for regal symbolism is the Hierothesion built in the first century BC by King Antochus I of Kommagene (69-34 BC), a small state in the highlands of what is now Turkey. At an altitude of some 7000 feet, upon the tallest peak of his dominion, now called Nimrud Dagh, this king erected a complex of statues and ritual structures to demonstrate his divine status among the gods, to extol his royal lineage and to create focus for the worship (Sengupta 147).

References to legitimation of state through religious activities are abundant in history. To give an example from the medieval history one can talk about the Asokan pillar transported from Topra by Firoz Shah down the Yamuna, to Delhi seeking legitimation for the empire. It was installed in Ferozshah Kotla where it stands to this day.(Gopalakrishnan 2006:20-21)

Technical legitimation comes from constitution. In Japan Shōtoku Taishi made the Seventeen article constitution to seek unity and welfare of is people. The second article of the constitution reads: revere the Three TreasuresţThe Buddha, the Law and the Community for these are ... ... the supreme objects of faith in all countries. Shōtoku Taishi was fully aware of the political significance of Buddhism as stabilizing and unifying force for the nation. In 603 he set up hierarchic ranks at the court which bore the names of virtues.

In 684 provincial governors had been ordered to install Buddhist shrines in their official houses. In 710 Empress Gemmyo decreed to establish a permanent capital in Heijokyo/Nara. Like the Chinese capital of Ch'ang-an, it was laid out with careful attention to the requirements of geomancy or divination. Great avenues ran from south to north and east to west. The principal thoroughfares were lined with great monasteries and temples.

Shōmu's reign saw a close connection between government and religion. Buddhist festivals were regularly celebrated in the palace and rituals formed an important part of court ceremonial. In 784 when the capital was shifted from Nara to Kyoto, Enryakuji was founded on mount Hiei which could offer protection to the country.

Legitimation of the Rulers

Buddhism was a useful instrument in the unification of the country in China. The period when Empress Wu Chao was to ascend the throne was characterized by a strong desire for political and religious reforms. She sought consent from the two titles that she took: Cakravarti and Bodhisattva. A massive support was given by official Buddhism headed by the court monks. Religious outlook played a significant role in urging a decisive change in the political leadership in China. Empress Wu Chao wrote in the preface to the translation of Avataṁsaka-sūtra in 699 claiming that she had in the preceding kalpas planted the Causes. She was allowed to receive Buddha's prophecies. She says that in Mahāmegha-sūtra and Ratnamegha-sūtra there are prophecies of the Buddha that concern her. She commanded I-tsing to translate Suv. as has been written in the colophon of the translation discovered from Duh-hunag caves: Newly translated, bound and corrected at the Hsi-ming monastery in Ch'ang-an in obedience to the Imperial order by the Tripitaka Master of the Law I-tsing on the 14th day of the 10th month Ṁ Ṁ the third year of Ch'ang-an of the Great Chou (17th Nov. 703) (Forte 87).

At the end of the opening gāthā of the Suv. it is said that those who hear this sūtra and repent and lay hold of it and keep it within their hearts, shall obtain a superior root of virtue, praised by the Buddhas (Visser 1935:263).

Unfication of the State

Before the coming of Buddhism Japan saw a period of great clans. The Imperial clan head had a large degree of primacy over his fellow clan heads but it was probably based more upon his religious than political importance. There was no clear theory of government hierarchy or bureaucracy. Shōtoku Taishi and his Soga sponsors set themselves to control the territorial magnates and clan heads and increase the national strength and unification. Shōtoku Taishi was fully aware of the political significance of Buddhism as a stabilizing, reforming, civilizing and unifying force for the nation. With active support from the government Buddhist temples served as religious, educational and philanthropic institutions (E B 1966, vol. 12 pg. 883).

In AD 645 Taika reform movement was initiated. The plan for new cenralized govt. was inaugurated under the guidance of Prince Naka no ōe and the Nakatomi clan leader Fujiwara Kamatari, modeled after the style of T'ang China. Private landholdings were abolished, provincial governments and bureaucratic offices were established and a system of equal land distribution and taxation was put into practice. The movement offered a solution to create a strong centralized government. Empress Suiko created a governing board of the priests. In AD 645 an Imperial envoy was sent to announce a policy of Govt. control of the clergy to display the power of the new govt. Just as the conscious policy existed to adopt Chinese political system, the implementation of Chinese Buddhism seemed desirable. The Emperor was made the supreme leader of the Buddhist faith. It was a reconciliation of the new religion with Imperial role. Buddhist festivals came to hold importance equal to state functions. Buddhism was placed under Imperial control and monks and nuns under supervision. Emperor Temmu (AD 673-686) was the most devout sovereigns, increased Buddhist ceremonies and rituals in the palace and decreed that sutras such as Suv. be recited for the nation. In 685 he set forth an edict that Buddhist shrines be built in every house in the province. Using Buddhism as a unifying force he sent messengers to all the provinces to expound the Suv. along with Prajñāpāramitā-sūtra in 676 (Visser 1935:13).

As a means of extending its provincial control, the Ritsuryo government decided to imitate the Chinese system of national temples. This had been inspired by Empress Wu Chao in honor of the Mahāmegha-sūtra (Ch. Ta-yýn-ching) at the end of the seventh century in the capitals and prefectures of China in an attempt to legitimate her succession to the throne. They soon became the most prestigious bureaucratic temples

As a step towards unification of the country Empress Jito sent hundred copies of Suv. to various provinces in AD 694, so that the sūtra could be read without fail when the moon of the first month was in her first quarter. The fee to the priests was to be given from the public revenues of the province. Again in AD 696 an Imperial order was given by her to expound the sutra and that every year on the last day of the twelfth month ten persons of pure life should be made to enter the religion apparently to cause felicity of the New Year (Visser 1935:15).

Just as Empress Wu in China initiated Ta-yün system as a justification for a female usurpation of the throne, Emperor Shōmu visualized the kokubunji system as a means of strengthening Imperial hegemony. The Emperor primarily visualized the project as a means of reuniting the nation that had become exceedingly restless under the harsh Ritsuryo system. The temple for Great Buddha at Nara was built as the symbolic centre of the kokubunji system. The site of the temple was known as Konshoji but its name was changed to Konkomyōji and finally to the Tōdaiji which assumed the position of the foremost of the official temples. This led to Buddhism finally achieving the status of a national religion. The effort was an antecedent of the National Temple system that was to come into being in 741 under Emperor Shōmu (Matsunaga 21-23). There was precedence for the establishment of provincial temples in practice of the Sui and T'ang emperors who had similarly ordered to set up in each provincial capital a Buddhist temple and a shrine for Taoist rites.

The sūtra promises in the first chapter that those who hear the sūtra or cause others to hear it and those who honor it will be honoured throughout numerous millions of aeons. They will obtain wonderful and immeasurable felicity, and be protected by the Buddhas and Bodhisattvas of ten directions. The emperors in Japan saw recitation of Suv. on various occasions and ceremonies based on the sutra in the country as well as palaces as a meritorious act.

Wellbeing of the Rulers

Reading of sūtras began to mark special ceremonies or were recited for recovery of emperors from illness or other reasons, for example when Emperor Kōtoku was to move to a new palace 2100 priests and nuns were invited to read the canon and 2700 lights were lit in the courtyard for the consecration ceremony (Visser 1935:8-9). One hundred priests were invited to read the Suv. in the palace in AD 686 to save Emperor Temmu's life (Visser 1935:14).

Bhaiṣajyaguru-sūtra was expounded for recovery of Emperor Temmu from illness. In 702 when Emperor Mommu was ill, a great amnesty was granted throughout the empire, a hundred men were caused to become monks, and order was given to expound the Suv. in the four home provinces (Visser 1935:437). It was also used against calamities like too abundant rain. Sūtras were read to cause rain also.

Wellbeing of the People, Proseperity and Happiness

Those who hear the sūtra with pure minds and good intentions … … most severe misfortunes are extinguished for ever … … Chapter 7 is devoted to the worship of Devī Śrī (Jap. Kudoku-ten i.e. Kichijoten). The goddess of felicity was worshipped by means of Kichijo-kekwa or rites of repentance based upon I-tsing's translation of the sūtra. Although the first translation of the Suv. was done in AD 414-423 by Dharmarakṣa II (Nanjio 127) but the translation by I-tsing (Konkwōmyōkyō-saishōōkyō, Nanjio 126) was the most popular version of the sutra in China done in AD 700-712 (Visser 1935:431) because it was far more extensive than that of Dharmaraksa's translation.

The ceremony Kichijo-ten kekwa-ho meaning 'Rite of Repentence in Worship of Devī Śrī is based upon the Konkwōmyō Saishōōkyō. In chapter eight of the Suv. Devī Śrī, the goddess of blessing virtue, worships the Buddha and promises to bestow all kinds of wealth and felicity upon the readers of the sūtra. At the end of chapter nine, section twenty-two, she is the head of the devas who promised to devote their whole heart to the protection of the sūtra and of those who received and kept it, and to cause them to be free from sorrow and to obtain perpetual felicity. The Buddha pronounces that all the sins will be obliterated, evil deeds will be purified and will be done away by Kichijo-sen of the Wonderful Law. It will always give immeasurable joy, all roots of wisdom and all ornaments of beneficence virtue.

In order to promote prosperity of the temples, the happiness of the Imperial house and the people, and purity of the country forty nine eminent monks were invited in AD 743 to the Tōdaiji monastery also known as Konkwōmyōji to read the Suv. sūtra's translation by I-tsing, seven times for seven days. All the monks of the country were ordered to read the same sūtra in their monasteries simultaneously. Killing of any living beings was prohibited during those days (Visser 1935:454). Again in AD 745 the Emperor ordered for recitation of Saishōōkyō in all the temples of the capital when there was an earthquake. It was followed by a proclamation to the provincial monasteries and nunneries because in his opinion severe earthquakes were due to the fact that the local authorities had been neglectful in fulfilling the ordinance (Visser 1935:455).

In AD 822 Emperor Saga ordered to celebrate Kichijo-kekwa to worship the two goddesses Śrīdevī and Sarasvatī, for seven days and nights in the provincial monasteries and nunneries, on account of the bad condition of the crops caused by drought (Visser 1935:453).

To Save the Nation from Calamities

An Imperial order was given by Empress Jito in AD 692 to expound the Suv. in the capital and in the four home provinces to save the country from floods (Visser 1935:14). Suv. was read by an Imperial order in AD 703 in the four great temples of Nara: Yakushiji, Gangōji, Kōfukuji and Daianji and then four days later messengers were sent to Shintō gods of the famous mountains and great rivers to pray for rain. In AD 705, in the fourth month, when heavy draught prevailed, the emperor Mommu had the same sūtra read in the five great temples of Nara: four of the above mentioned and Hōryuji being the fifth, in order to save the people from suffering.

When smallpox epidemic threatened Japan in 723, an edict was issued that every province should make an image of Śākyamuni and copy Daihannyakyō. But the epidemic did not terminate and the Emperor Shōmu decreed that each province was to build a seven storey pagoda and make ten copies of Konkwōmyō-kyō-saishōōkyō and Hokkekyō to be enshrined in the pagodas. Also each province was to establish one official temple to be entitled 'Temple for Protection of the Nation by the Four Divine Kings of the Konkwōmyō-kyō' and a 'Temple for Eliminaton of Sins by the Lotus sūtra'.

Peace in the Country

The paths of evil do not lead to peace. The mighty voice of the Golden Drum sings a hymn saying: The Drum of Golden Light gives a wonderful sound which reaches innumerable worlds and extinguishes the direst sins of the three evil paths of fire, blood and swords and all kinds of torment and danger of mankind (Visser 1935:268)

I'tsing's translation of the sūtra called Saishōōkyō has been mentioned for the first time in Japan in AD 734. The monks and nuns who were to propagate Buddhism were asked to learn by heart the whole text of the sūtra along with Hokkekyō and lead a pure life. Thenceforth I'tsing's translation was used in Japan which became popular as Konkwōmyō-kyō-Saishōō-kyō. The Kokubunjis established in 741 were called Konkwōmyō-Shitennō-gokokuji, although they were also destined to promote peace in the state by reading the Saishōōkyō (Visser 1935:437-8).

In AD 728, 640 copies of the sūtra in sixty four covers were distributed, ten copies to each province, which already possessed eight or four chapters of it. The day on which those copies arrived there, they were ordered to have them read for the sake of peace in the state. In 737 Emperor Shōmu invited seven hundred monks to read the Daihannyakyō and Saishōōkyō in fifteen apartments of the palace in order to promote peace in the state. He had invited the Vinaya Master Dōji who had returned from China after expounding Prajñā-pāramitā-hṛdaya-sūtra in the Chinese palace in Ch'ang-an and appointed him as expounding master for the Konkwōmyōkyō Saishōōkyō meeting in the principal buildings of the Imperial palace. Again in 738 he proclaimed that Saishōōkyō should be read throughout the country to promote peace.

In AD 776, Empress Kōken taking over the reigns after Shomu, aspiring for peace in the country, seasonable weather, good crops and happiness of the people, proclaimed that the high ranking priests in all the great temples must explain Saishōōkyō (Visser 1935:456).

Imperial Festivals and Ceremonies

I'tsing's translation of the sūtra was recited to celebrate New Year's festival in AD 749 when Emperor Shōmu ordered to celebrate Kichijo-kekwa, or the rites of repentance in all the temples of the country (Visser 1935:455). It was stopped as an annual celebration by Emperor Kōnin in 771 but in the same year he reestablished it as he wished to save the country from constant famine caused by the storms and rains which had spoiled the crops (Visser 1935:463).

Emperors used to participate in the Kichijo-kekwa rite and Saishōōkyō recitations in the Daigokuden to ascend to the throne and to receive New Year greetings (Visser 1935:475). After the death of Emperor Kōnin, his eldest son and successor Kwammu Tennō ordered that on the 49th day of his father's death and on his first anniversary all the monks and nuns must read the Saishōōkyō in order to promote happiness for the deceased Emperor after his death (Visser 1935:465).

A festival called Gosaie or Misaie or Saishōe or Konkwōmyōe, meaning vegetarian entertainment of priests or meeting devoted to the Suv. was celebrated as an annual Imperial festival from AD 802-1467. Another festival devoted to the translation of the sūtra by I'tsing was also an annual festival from AD 830-1445 celebrated in Yakushiji monastery (Visser 1935:444). They were led by priests of the highest rank.

Harmony with Shintoism

In AD 741 a copy of Saishōōkyō along with Hokkekyō written in golden characters were presented to the Hachiman Jingu shrine. To mark the occasion eighteen persons were admitted into the religious order, five horses were given to the temple and the building of the three storey pagoda was commanded, to present prayers and thank offerings to Hachiman with regard to former lives.

LITERATURE CITED

EB 1966

Encyclopedia Britannica, 1966

Emmerick 1979

Emmerick, R E, *The Sūtra of Golden Light*, Pali Text Society, London, 1979

Forte

Forte, Antonino, *Political Propaganda and Ideology in China at the End of the Seventh Century*, Napoli

Gopalakrishnan 2006

Gopalakrishnan, Sudha, *Tattvabodha, Essays from the Lecture Series of the National Mission for Manuscripts*, vol. 1, National Mission for Manuscripts and Munshiram Manoharlal Publishers Pvt. Ltd., 2006

Ienaga

Ienaga, Saburo, *History of Japan*, Japan Travel Bureau, Inc., Tokyo,

Matsunaga 1978

Matsunaga, Daigan and Alicia, *Foundation of Japanese Buddhism*, Buddhist Books International, Tokyo, 1978

Mizuno 1982

Mizumo, Kogern, *Buddhist Sūtras*, Kosei Publishing Company, Tokyo, 1982

Nanjio 1883

Nanjio, Bunyiu, *A Cataelogue of Chinese Translation of the Buddhist Tripitaka*, Oxford, 1883

Nitobe 1931

Nitobe, Inazo, Japan, *Some Phases of Her Problems and Development*, Ernest Benn Limited, London, 1931

Sansom 1997

Sansom, GB, Japan, *A Short Cultural History*, Charles E. Tuttle Company, Tokyo, 1997

Sengupta 2005

Sengupta, Arputha Rani, ed. *God and King*, Regency Publications, New Delhi, 2005

Suvarṇaprabhāsa-sūtra

Suvarṇaprabhāsasūtra, ed Śriśītānsuśekharavāgaci Sharma, Mithila Vidyāpītha, 1967

Visser 1935

Visser, Dr. MW de, *Ancient Buddhism in Japan*, E J Brill, Leiden, 1935

INDEX